The Family Novel in Russia and England, 1800–1880

The Family Novel in Russia and England, 1800–1880

ANNA A. BERMAN

OXFORD
UNIVERSITY PRESS

OXFORD
UNIVERSITY PRESS

Great Clarendon Street, Oxford, OX2 6DP,
United Kingdom

Oxford University Press is a department of the University of Oxford.
It furthers the University's objective of excellence in research, scholarship,
and education by publishing worldwide. Oxford is a registered trade mark of
Oxford University Press in the UK and in certain other countries

Impression: 1

Published in the United States of America by Oxford University Press
198 Madison Avenue, New York, NY 10016, United States of America

British Library Cataloguing in Publication Data

Data available

Library of Congress Control Number: 2022937047

ISBN 978–0–19–286662–2

DOI: 10.1093/oso/9780192866622.001.0001

Printed and bound by
CPI Group (UK) Ltd, Croydon, CR0 4YY

*Part I is for my Aries/Berman clan of all generations
and with all its lateral spread.*

Part II is for Erik, who gave me my marriage plot (English style).

*And Part III is for Caryl, who has been intentional family
since long before I knew a name for it.*

Acknowledgments

If it takes a village to raise a child, this book has taken two villages: English and Russian. I am deeply grateful to all the scholars in both fields who offered advice and support over the years as this project grew and took shape. From the English camp, I am thinking especially of Gillian Beer, Ruth Perry, Kelly Hager, Clare Walker Gore, Peter Sabor, Emily Kopley, Rae Gaubinger, Amelia Worsley, Tabitha Sparks, and Jane Levin. From the Russian camp, special thanks go to Lucy Parts, Greta Matzner-Gore, Caryl Emerson, Robin Feuer Miller, Hilde Hoogenboom, Barbara Alpern-Engel, William Wagner, Dominique ("Chai") Lieven, and Jane Taubman. These generous colleagues and friends read drafts, suggested sources, asked hard questions, and helped me understand the role of family in the novel from new angles. Linda Layne guided my reading in anthropology and sociology. Matthew Birkhold and Mary Kuhn were ideal interlocutors and fans at every stage. The foundations of the project were laid by Juliet Mitchell, who first taught me to think of the family in terms of a lateral and vertical axis, and Ruth Perry, whose *Novel Relations* inspired me to think about the family plots in relation to family history.

The first draft of the manuscript was written during my "golden year" as a Visiting Fellow Commoner at Trinity College, Cambridge. Thank you to Emma Widdis for nominating me for the fellowship, and to everyone at Trinity—from Fellows, to Porters, the Manciple, chefs, gardeners, and staff—for making it the most joyful and productive year of my life.

The research for this book touched on many fields and I could not have done it without the help of amazing librarians: Liladhar Pendse, Tatiana Bedjanian, and the team at the National Library in St. Petersburg, Russia. My research trips to Russia were supported by two generous grants from the Social Sciences and Humanities Research Council of Canada and from the Fonds de recherche du Québec—Société et Culture.

Many of the works I cite are untranslated and I am grateful to Adalyat Issiyeva and Lynne Debenedette for advice on tricky passages. John Wright revised and improved all my translations; any inaccuracies are purely my own. Audra Wolfe gave structural feedback on the first complete draft and Regina Higgins did beautiful copy editing to improve the flow of the prose. And the team at Oxford University Press did stellar work bringing the book into the world.

I would not have chosen to write a book about family had my own family not played such foundational role in my life. I feel so lucky to be part of an extensive kinship network of parents, siblings, aunts and uncles, cousins, nephews, grand-mothers, in-laws, and intentional kin who showed me the importance of lateral spread. And on the vertical axis, the rosy cheeked baby Owen's imminent arrival motivated me to "collect the scattered threads" of this project and "tie them in a seemly knot," as Trollope puts it. His arrival as I reached the final pages helped me get this book done.

Contents

Note on Transliterations and Translations of the Text

Transliterations of Russian words in the body of the text follow the Library of Congress system, except in the case of proper names, for which I have used the spelling most familiar to Anglophone readers (e.g. Alexander instead of Aleksandr). Well-known spellings are used for famous names (e.g. Tchaikovsky instead of Chaikovsky), and Tsars' names are anglicized (Nicholas II, Peter the Great). Bibliographic references adhere strictly to the Library of Congress system.

Where I have used a published English translation, the page number is indicated after that of the Russian original. If not otherwise indicated, all translations are my own, but have been edited and improved by John Wright.

Some sections of text appeared in modified form in "Dostoevsky and the (Missing) Marriage Plot," in Bowers, Katherine and Kate Holland (eds.) *Dostoevsky at 200*, 41–60. Toronto: University of Toronto Press, 2021; "The Problem with Brothers in the Nineteenth-Century English Novel," *Victorian Review*, vol. 46, no. 1 (2020), 49–66; "The Family Novel (and Its Curious Disappearance)," *Comparative Literature*, vol. 72, no. 1 (2020), 1–18; and "Lateral Plots: Brothers and the Nineteenth-Century Russian Novel," *Slavic and East European Journal*, vol. 61, no. 1 (2017), 2–28.

I am grateful to the Provost and Scholars of King's College, Cambridge, and The Society of Authors as the E.M. Forster Estate for permission to use a quotation from E.M. Forster as a chapter epigraph.

Introduction

Family History and Family Novel

The question of the day now is marriage and the family system.
—Samuel Butler, *The Way of All Flesh*

It seems to me that the novel has lost the ground it used to stand on since family-ness and everything connected with it began to change its character. The novel (at least in the form in which it has appeared up to now) is for the most part a work of family-ness. Its drama has its inception in the family, does not go beyond it, and ends there. Whether in a positive sense (the English novel) or in a negative one (the French novel), in a novel the family always plays the leading role.
—Mikhail Saltykov-Shchedrin, *People of Tashkent*

History provides the causal or correlative explanations for the social and psychological phenomena that literature reveals.
—Ruth Perry, *Novel Relations*

Family is at the heart of the nineteenth-century novel, from Austen, Dickens, and Trollope, to Tolstoy, Dostoevsky, and Turgenev. However, it would be difficult to confuse an English family plot with a Russian one. Indeed, it would not be a stretch to say that it is a truth universally acknowledged that the classic English family novel, possessed of a young heroine, must be in want of a marriage at its conclusion. It might be going too far to claim that all happy English family novels are alike, while each unhappy Russian family novel is unhappy in its own way. Yet the reality is that English family novels tend to end by reaffirming the family order with a wedding and often the birth of an heir on the final pages, while few Russian novels from this period conclude with the hero and heroine successfully united in a marriage that promises domestic bliss and family continuity. What accounts for these differences? *The Family Novel in Russia and England* looks to family history—law, social customs, inheritance and property rights, and domestic ideology—to offer an answer.

In order to make broad claims about two national traditions, this study relies on a reading of over one hundred novels—roughly fifty Russian and fifty

The Family Novel in Russia and England, 1800–1880. Anna A. Berman, Oxford University Press.
© Anna A. Berman (2022). DOI: 10.1093/oso/9780192866622.003.0001

English—written between 1800 and 1880.[1] Examining such a diverse range of novels makes it possible to trace the significant patterns that appear in each national literature, from liberal to conservative novels, sensational to Christian moralizing. Rather than explaining individual families (the Dombeys or Karenins), my approach reveals the underlying structures of kinship at the heart of each national tradition. To contextualize this large canon of novels, *The Family Novel in Russia and England* compares Russian and English conceptions of the family in the nineteenth century.

The family can be conceived upon two axes: a vertical, diachronic axis, and a lateral, synchronic axis.[2] The vertical axis represents the family's movement through time, the succession of generations—family expanding forwards and backwards in time, looking back to ancestors and ahead to progeny. The lateral axis represents kinship in the present—the family extending outward: from the nuclear core, to extended kin groups, to chosen kin. While both axes are present in any family, not all societies grant them equal weight. The thesis of this book is that the English placed primary value on the vertical, while the Russians emphasized the lateral. Or, to elaborate slightly, the English had a linear model of family that focused on genealogy, origins, and descent, while the Russians were much more interested in *all* the family in the here and now. The Russians were not concerned with amassing wealth and with its vertical transmission; they did not focus all value on anything singular—an heir or family name or title. Instead, the Russians dispersed wealth and attention in a more egalitarian model (a fact that will be true for their novels as well as their families). Evidence of this vertical/lateral distinction appears in the laws and customs each society created for the family as well as in the way authors plotted consanguineal relations, courtship/marriage, and alternative kinship constructions.

The family novel was originally an English genre and it spread from there to Russia, where the novels were almost immediately translated and published alongside their Russian counterparts in the "thick journals" of the day. Yet starting from the English model, the Russians created radically different family plotlines. These differences can be traced to the two nations' fundamentally different conceptions of what the family was.[3] English novels follow the linear family model exemplified

---

[1] See the Appendix for the list of novels considered.

[2] This approach to thinking about the family in terms of a vertical and lateral axis originated in a seminar on "Siblings in Psychoanalysis" led by Juliet Mitchell in 2011 at Princeton University. Although I do not take a psychological approach like hers, I am indebted to her for the foundational underlying structures through which I approach the family. Mitchell was the first to topple the hegemony of the vertical, parent-child axis in psychoanalysis and to make a place for the equally crucial bonds between siblings and peers. And it was in that seminar that I was first introduced to Ruth Perry's *Novel Relations*, which launched my thinking that lead to this book.

[3] In taking this approach, I am deeply indebted to the model of Perry's *Novel Relations* (2004), which provides a detailed analysis of shifts in family structure to offer a compelling explanation for the repeated family plots and tropes that appear in eighteenth-century English novels. On the evolution of English family structure, see also Davidoff and Hall, *Family Fortunes*.

by primogeniture, with single sons carrying on their family names and estates (or businesses), and daughters successfully becoming wives and mothers who will produce the next generation in plotlines that reinforce family continuity. Russian novels follow expansive kinship networks not conducive to linear plots. Most Russians at midcentury considered the family to be a backward institution characterized by wife beatings and patriarchal tyranny, and in desperate need of reform. A marriage that recreated the status quo was not a desirable outcome, and many Russian heroines succeed in avoiding this by *failing* to marry at all. The happiest outcome in a Russian novel is to create a loose family conglomeration that mixes biological, legal, and chosen kin. Our theories of "the novel" are based on the linear English model of family, and fall apart when faced with these messier Russian alternatives.

While the family is a ubiquitous theme in nineteenth-century novels, not all novels are equally suited for explaining the relationship between the historical family and novel plots. The family novels in this study are all set in their own society in the nineteenth century (some are set back in time by twenty to fifty years). They are all "realist" novels, meaning they must have at least some conceit of being set in "our" world, rather than in the world of fairytale or myth, and they do not include elements of the supernatural. The emphasis on family plots makes less relevant novels that focus exclusively on childhood or bildungsroman, where the plot is defined by the coming of age of its protagonist rather than by family concerns (for example, Tolstoy's *Childhood, Boyhood, Youth* [1852–1857]). Sometimes these boundaries can be blurry, and if a novel that begins with a child protagonist shifts into a courtship plot, as, for example, occurs in Dickens' *David Copperfield* (1849–1850) or Panaeva's *The Talnikov Family* (1848), then it has a place in the study. Family chronicles (Aksakov's *Family Chronicle*, 1856; Leskov's *A Decayed Family*, 1874) receive less attention because they are not *plotted* in the same way as a novel, but instead take a more descriptive, episodic approach. In that sense, these chronicles can serve as documents of the types of family concerns that were present in the period. While many dramas were exploring similar family themes, they, too, fall outside of the scope of the argument (but can serve as historical evidence of contemporary concerns) because plot functions differently in drama than it does in the novel.[4] Dramas tend to honor the unities of time, place, and action, focusing on a discrete moment rather than tracing progression across many years, and they cannot accommodate the same kinds of diffuse plotting that we find in novels. The only exception to the exclusive inclusion of novels is the occasional novella, because the distinction is not always so clear; some "novels" were shorter than some "novellas," and plot can function in the same way in both.

---

[4] Colleen Lucey's *Love for Sale: Representing Prostitution in Imperial Russia* is focused on prostitution rather than family, but includes a chapter on dowerless brides that explores family dynamics around marriage transactions, drawing on a range of materials from novels, novellas, and short stories, to drama, and visual arts. The same themes can be found in all of these genres and media.

Family Structure and Narrative Form

Many of the foundational theories of the novel as a genre tout its close link to the family. Family-line and story-line are presumed to move in tandem, with both novels and families structured around generational progression that reinforces the patriarchal order. These standard theories of the novel were largely penned by scholars who made the English (or English and French) novel synonymous with *the* novel.[5] Adding Russia into the picture immediately complicates this. The novel has often been labeled a "bourgeois genre," yet Russia had novels but lacked a bourgeoisie.[6] Beginning with Ian Watt's *The Rise of the Novel* (1957), the genre's modern origins have been linked with the rise of individualism that made each individual a worthy subject for literature. For Watt, the "economic individualism" of capitalism must be combined with the spread of Protestantism (and a "Puritan individualism" that found spiritual meaning in personal experience) to fuel the novel's rise.[7] Yet Russian authors criticized Europeans for their individualist outlook as they wrote their novels in "communal," Orthodox Russia.[8] My point is not that Russia has been unfairly left out, but that our theories are incomplete; including Russia in the discussion of the novel clarifies both the unscrutinized cultural assumptions on which those theories are built and the ways they must be modified to be true to "the novel," not just to a particular national tradition.

Indeed, there is nothing wrong with these Western theories, if they would acknowledge the cultural conditioning that shaped the novel traditions they study. Yet few engage this issue at all, while others attempt to sidestep it. Michael McKeon, for example, provides a caveat at the end of the introduction to his illuminating study of *The Secret History of Domesticity: Public, Private, and the Division of Knowledge* (2005): "my concentration on British texts and context in this study has no better justification than the limits of my scholarly competence; however I draw on French, Italian, and American material where needed. No presumption about the relative importance of British culture should be read into this limitation."[9] No presumption *would* be needed if McKeon confined his claims to

---

[5] France had very different inheritance laws than either England or Russia, with primogeniture having been abolished in 1790. For a careful overview of the complicated evolution of French law, see Counter, *Inheritance in Nineteenth-Century French Culture*.

[6] On the novel as a bourgeois genre, see Cohen, *The Daughter's Dilemma*; Hatten, *The End of Domesticity*; Kilroy, *The Nineteenth-Century English Novel*; Lukacs, *The Future of History*; Watt, *The Rise of the Novel*.

[7] Watt, *Rise of the Novel*, 74. A thoughtful critique of this is provided by Michael McKeon ("Generic Transformation and Social Change: Rethinking The Rise of the Novel").

[8] Many studies of the "rise of the Russian novel" have offered critiques of Watt. See, for example: Kahn, "The Rise of the Russian Novel and the Problem of Romance"; Somoff, *The Imperative of Reliability* (Introduction); Todd, "The Ruse of the Russian Novel." I discuss the communal side of Russian culture and Orthodoxy in Chapters 1 and 8.

[9] McKeon, *The Secret History of Domesticity*, xxvii. Evelyn J. Hinz provides a similar disclaimer in her study of hierogamy versus wedlock: "because the generic assumptions I am mainly concerned with questioning derive in the greater part from Anglo-American attitudes, my examples are drawn almost

the British context. In a similar instance of national myopia, the French literary critic Pascale Casanova's influential *The World Republic of Letters* (originally published in French in 1999) perhaps unsurprisingly determines that Paris is "the capital of the literary world."[10] The book has little to say about Russia, which falls at the periphery of its formulation of the world of letters. Elaine Freedgood points to the need for being broader: "If we can dislodge the aesthetic racism that has placed the British and French nineteenth-century novel at the masterful, still center of a novel history that is as contingent as the genre it tries to track, other novels might have a better chance of getting a reading that is not nineteenth-century-Anglo-Eurocentric."[11]

Too often, Russia is the odd man out, though one could hardly claim that Dostoevsky, Tolstoy, and Turgenev were *not* important contributors to the nineteenth-century novel tradition. Furthermore, while scholars of the Russian novel tend to follow, at least to some degree, English theory and criticism, the same does not often seem to be true in reverse. Many Western scholars have made bold claims about the verticality of the novel's family plot as inextricably bound up with the patriarchal order, lineage, and genealogical progression.[12] This linear, vertical structure matches the structure of the English family and English novel, but, as I will argue, it runs into problems when confronted with the Russian novel, problems that can be explained by the structure of the Russian family underlying its national tradition. Considering the Russian counter-example will help us better understand the English.

Henry James, immersed in English literature, made a passionate appeal for the novel to tell a single story. He feared that a novel with even two plots would be "so cheated of its indispensable centre as to become of no more use for expressing a main intention than a wheel without a hub is of use for moving a cart."[13] Russian novels—which often included multiple family branches and accommodated their lateral spread—were one of James' targets. He believed that without "composition" there may be "life, incontestably, as *The Newcomes* has life, as *Les Trois Mousquetaires*, as Tolstoi's *Peace and War*, have it; but what do such large,

---

exclusively from British, American, and Canadian fiction. How much my argument could profit from or will require qualification in light of the theory and practice of other nationalities and cultures is something that, for the moment, I must leave in abeyance" ("Hierogamy versus Wedlock," 902).

[10] Casanova, *The World Republic of Letters*, 24.

[11] Freedgood, *Worlds Enough: The Invention of Realism in the Victorian Novel*, 139. Despite her Anglo-centric title, Freedgood argues for a greater awareness of the wider world beyond Britain. Russia, famous for its realism, receives only a few scattered mentions. In the conclusion Freedgood addresses Margaret Cohen's idea of "fringe realisms" that would include Russia (and Germany and Italy) (137).

[12] I take this up in Chapter 2, exploring claims by Roland Barthes, Peter Brooks, Edward Said, and others. In a parallel vein, Harold Bloom has famously figured the genealogy of literary history as a series of sons fighting the influence of their "Poetic Fathers" (*The Anxiety of Influence*). Given the rapidity of Russian literature's development in a very brief space of time, these relations were more fraternal than parental.

[13] James, Preface to *The Tragic Muse*, 1:x.

loose, baggy monsters, with their queer elements of the accidental and the arbitrary, artistically *mean*?"[14] While novels like William Thackeray's *The Newcomes* (1854) and George Eliot's *Middlemarch* (1871–1872) face the same criticism from James as Tolstoy and Dostoevsky's works, there were marked differences in the way the Russians and these English outliers handled plotting. Even as Eliot disperses attention across a variety of characters with interlocking lives, for example, she relies on traditional resolutions to her family plots that still concern themselves with generational progression. In the case of *War and Peace* (1865–1869), Tolstoy was starting from a looser, baggier family structure and a related view of life as a cluster of myriad events in the present, rather than a clean, linear progression of single sons coming down through the ages. His composition matched the family structure of the nation in which he wrote.

This is not just a point about the idiosyncrasies of Tolstoy, however, for he saw his approach to form as a distinctly national trait. As Tolstoy wrote in one of the drafts of the Introduction to *War and Peace*: "We Russians in general do not know how to write novels in the sense in which this genre is understood in Europe" (13:54/1087). The Russians were more sympathetic to multiplying plots than James was, as to them containment smacked of artificiality. Tolstoy claimed that *War and Peace* was not a novel because it lacked "a plot that has growing complexity, intrigue, and a happy or unhappy denouement, at which point interest in the narration ceases" (13:54/1087–1088). Tolstoy's point here is that he was capturing the messiness of life, while the European novel looked for a clean form that simplified (artificially) this chaotic sprawl. James voiced the European view, highlighting the need to create order: "Really, universally, relations stop nowhere, and the exquisite problem of the artist is eternally but to draw, by a geometry of his own, the circle within which they shall happily *appear* to do so."[15] In interpreting this passage, Gillian Beer claims that "The artist must create by means of a counter-fiction, which will contain that which is truly not to be contained."[16]

This opposition of Russian messiness to English order is far from new, but no one has linked it to family form in the two nations. Beer's point about "containment" applies not only to narrative structure but to the English family, where—as I will show—brothers had to be "removed" and "geometry" based on the *line* of descent. While the English did write multi-plot novels (as I explore in Chapter 2), they feared allowing too many family shoots to branch out. A looser approach to plotting and nonlinear narratives came more easily to the Russians, whose tradition was not bound by the genealogical plot of the family line.

---

[14] James, Preface to *The Tragic Muse*, 1:xi.

[15] James, Preface to *Roderick Hudson*, vii (first pub. 1876).

[16] Beer, *Darwin's Plots*, 156. Frank Kermode makes a similar point with his analogy of the "tick-tock" of a clock: "the interval between *tock* and *tick* represents purely successive, disorganized time of the sort that we need to humanize" (*The Sense of an Ending*, 45).

Approaching the Family Novel through Family History

In looking at broad patterns across a wide range of novels, *The Family Novel* builds on the legacy of scholars like Ian Watt (*Rise of the Novel*) and Ruth Perry (*Novel Relations*) who looked at shifts in the family structure in England and linked them to significant plot features. Many English scholars have continued to find family history a productive avenue into understanding the novel, especially in the nineteenth century. Most studies have approached specific aspects of family in relation to changing legal and social discourse.[17] Joseph Allen Boone's oft-cited *Tradition Counter Tradition: Love and the Form of Fiction* (1987) is an early exemplar that uses the history of marriage and ideas about romantic love to explore how the ideal of romantic wedlock and related beliefs are "translated into narrative structures that at once encode and perpetuate those beliefs."[18] Boone's study aims to complicate this one-to-one congruence of ideology and literary representation by establishing the dominant paradigm and the *counter* tradition: "the persistent 'undoing' of the dominant tradition" by all the contradictions literature reveals.[19] Talia Schaffer is similarly interested in upending accepted ideas about the marriage plot being based on an idealization of romantic love, suggesting that actually, many heroines choose the *un*romantic lover, the figure who is coded more like a brother (*Romance's Rival*, 2016). Kelly Hager goes a step further, challenging the very primacy of the courtship plot and focusing attention on the many fraught marriages depicted in Victorian fiction (*Dickens and the Rise of Divorce*, 2010). Tracing the progression of British legislation about marriage and divorce in the eighteenth and nineteenth centuries, she is interested in the way these laws limited or enabled different family plots. In all these studies, the historical realities of the family serve as the context for understanding the ideological work of the novels.

Despite this growing field of scholarship for the English novel, studies of this nature—looking at novels in relation to family history—have not been done in any serious way for the Russian novel. This can partly be explained by the varied levels of interest we find in family history in the two nations.[20] The Victorian family has been a source of seemingly endless fascination for scholars. There

---

[17] James F. Kilroy has a slightly different approach, tracing the increasing threats to the patriarchal order across the nineteenth century (*The Nineteenth-Century English Novel: Family Ideology and Narrative Form*, 2007).

[18] Boone, *Tradition Counter Tradition*, 2.

[19] Boone, *Tradition Counter Tradition*, 2. Paula Cohen's study of marriage plots follows in this tradition, exploring the role of daughters in the "relatively closed, affective system" of the nineteenth-century nuclear. She argues that the courtship plot only seems to be about the heroine's passage into a new stage of life, while it is really about prolonging her time in her family of origin (Cohen, *The Daughter's Dilemma: Family Process and the Nineteenth-Century Domestic Novel*, 3, 26).

[20] I believe this difference can be explained in a large part by the women's movement in the West and the rise of women's history as a validated area of study decades earlier than in Russia. For a thoughtful overview of this history, see Pushkareva, Natalia and Maria Zolotukhina, "Women's and Gender Studies of the Russian Past: two contemporary trends."

are excellent studies of many aspects of family life, drawing on a wide range of historical sources.[21] As English family historian Steven Mintz observed in 1983:

> Perhaps a major reason why family history has been an intellectual growth industry is that the family provides a bridge between two fundamental domains of human life and experience—between social processes and psychological processes...As a social institution, the organization and structure of the family is closely connected with the organization of the realms of life, such as economics, politics and religion.[22]

While these reasons would hold for Russia as well as England, rather than a "growth industry" we find a strange gap. There is a strong body of scholarship on the peasant family and on the fate of the family under the Soviet regime, but very little has been written about the history of the gentry family.[23] One can see why Soviet scholars would not take up the topic, but outside of Russia the only monograph devoted specifically to the gentry family is Jessica Tovrov's *The Russian Noble Family: Structure and Change* (1987), which, while incredibly informative, also has some methodological shortcomings.[24]

In the absence of comprehensive studies of the gentry family, we can piece together an understanding of historical realities and debates by looking at studies of property rights, inheritance laws, advice literature, estate culture, and women's history—all of which touch in different ways on family mores.[25] Micro-histories, debates about changing imperial family law in the thick journals, writings on the woman question, articles in women's domestic journals, and discussions of the family in literary criticism fill out the picture. This range of sources reveals a set of

---

[21] A few examples: Behlmer, *Friends of the Family* (1998); Davidoff and Hall, *Family Fortunes* (2002); Davidoff, *Thicker Than Water* (2012); Gillis, *A World of Their Own Making* (1997); Mintz, *A Prison of Expectations* (1983); Nelson, *Family Ties in Victorian England* (2007); Peterson, *Family, Love, and Work in the Lives of Victorian Gentlewomen* (1989); Tosh, *A Man's Place: Masculinity and the Middle-Class Home in Victorian England* (1999); Wohl, *The Victorian Family* (1978); Wolfram, *In-laws and Outlaws* (1987).

[22] Mintz, *A Prison of Expectations*, 2.

[23] On peasants, see Engel, *Between the Fields and the City: Women, Work and Family in Russia, 1861–1914* (1994); Ransel, *The Family in Imperial Russia* (includes other topics, but much on peasants); Worobec, *Peasant Russia: Family and Community in the Post-Emancipation Period* (1991). On the Soviet family, see Friedman, *Modernity, Domesticity and Temporality in Russia: Time at Home* (2020); Goldman, *Women, the State, and Revolution: Soviet Family Policy and Social-Life, 1917–1936* (1993); Liegle, *The Family's Role in Soviet Education* (1975); Mace, D. R. and Vera, *The Soviet Family* (1963); Schlesinger (ed.), *Changing Attitudes in Soviet Russia: the Family in the U.S.S.R.* (1949); Vishnevskii, *Evolutsiia sem'i i semeinaia politika v SSSR* (1992); Ginsborg, *Family Politics: Domestic Life, Devastation and Survival, 1900–1950* (2014).

[24] There is also coverage of this topic in Elaine Elnett's rather dated *Historic Origin and Social Development of Family Life in Russia* (1926), which provides few references for the points it makes. Half of Elnett's study focuses on the pre-Petrine era.

[25] Of particular note are Barbara Alpern Engel's *Mothers and Daughters: Women of the Intelligentsia in Nineteenth-Century Russia* (1983) and *Breaking the Ties that Bound: The Politics of Marital Strife in Late Imperial Russia* (2011); William Wagner's *Marriage, Property, and Law in Late Imperial Russia* (1994); Gregory Freeze's work on marriage and divorce.

underlying (and often unspoken) assumptions authors held about what the Russian family was, as well the debates that were raging in the mid-nineteenth century about what the family *should* be.

Historical realities as well as ideology are important in understanding the treatment of family in the novels. Louis Althusser has called ideology the "imaginary relationship of individuals to their real conditions of existence," emphasizing its lack of basis in reality.[26] Yet other scholars, like Mary Poovey, argue that ideologies are more than ideas. "Instead, they are given concrete form in the practices and social institutions that govern people's social relations and that, in so doing, constitute both the experience *of* social relations and the nature of subjectivity."[27] Following Poovey, this book explores the ideals that underlie both English and Russian constructions of kinship and family, recognizing the reciprocal relationship between these ideals and the institutions and practices that the English and Russians created and which then reinforced those ideals. This historical approach does *not* mean treating the novels as a reflection of historical realities, though certainly many nineteenth-century authors and critics saw them this way. Instead, the novels were responding to those realities, sometimes through depicting what they believed to be the case, and other times reacting against it.[28] Like Poovey's study of gender ideology in mid-Victorian England, *The Family Novel in Russia and England* is aimed at "neither the individual texts (of whatever kind) nor literary history, but something extrapolated from texts and reconstituted as the conditions of possibility for those texts."[29] The *conditions of possibility* for the English family novel looked quite different than those that shaped the Russian novel.

Nineteenth-century readers also approached novels in the light of current social, political, or cultural conditions. Many articles in the English press criticized novelists for getting the law wrong or misapplying it in their novels, laying bare the assumption that the novels should accurately reflect historical realities.[30] Wilkie Collins includes an appendix to *Armadale* (1866) in which he assures readers that wherever the story touches on law, "it has been submitted before publication to the experience of professional men" (658). Readers expected to see their own world. Alexander Ostrovsky (1823–1886) made a similar claim about this assumed reflective quality of literature in Russia:

The literature of every educated people runs alongside society, following it through the different stages of its life. In what manner does art follow societal

[26] Qtd. in Poovey, *Uneven Developments*, 3.
[27] Poovey, *Uneven Developments*, 3.
[28] As Talia Schaffer cautions in her study, "the marriage plot was an imagined structure, not a documentary record. It commented on reality, often by positing a compensatory fantasy that worked very differently from real practices" (*Romance's Rival*, 41). Yet those "compensatory fantasies" are themselves conditioned by the realm of possibility made available by a given culture or society.
[29] Poovey, *Uneven Developments*, 15.
[30] Frank, *Law, Literature, and the Transmission of Culture in England, 1837–1925*, 70–71.

life? The moral life of a society, passing through different forms, gives to art this
or that model, this or that challenge. These models and challenges on the one
hand inspire the writer to create, they unsettle him; on the other hand, they give
to him ready-made, pre-shaped molds. (13:139–140)[31]

Ostrovsky's own dramas were certainly viewed as a reflection of Russian social and
family life. Some of the most famous critiques of the family in the mid-nineteenth
century appeared in Nikolai Dobroliubov's (1836–1861) "literary criticism," most
famously his reviews of Ostrovsky's dramas: "The Kingdom of Darkness" (1859)
and "A Ray of Light in the Kingdom of Darkness" (1860), which provided a
scathing attack on the merchant family.

Russians viewed their literature as part of the societal debates taking place in
salons and the periodical press.[32] As Dmitri Pisarev (1840–1868) wrote in 1861:

[Russian realist novels] have for us not only an aesthetic but also a social interest.
The English have Dickens, Thackeray, and Eliot, but they also have John Stuart
Mill; the French have journalists and socialists as well as novelists. But in Russia
the whole sum of ideas about society, about the human personality, about social
and family relations, is concentrated in *belles lettres* and in the criticism of *belles
lettres*; we do not have an independent moral philosophy, we do not have a social
science, and so we must look for all of this in literary works.[33]

Illustrative of this mixing of literary and social critique, in the middle of an 1858
review of a contemporary novel, Dobroliubov claimed: "The question of so-called
family morality is one of the most important social questions of our time...No
matter what is said about different means of improving life in society, these always
have their beginnings and ends in the relations within the family, understood not
only in the sense of marital bliss but in a much broader sense."[34]

[31] This claim is from the start of a review of Evgenia Tur's first novel, *A Mistake*, first published in
Moskvitianin №7, 1850.
[32] And an initial reviewer of *Crime and Punishment* called Raskolnikov "an authentic creation of the
everyday reality of our society" [*estestvennoe proizvedenie byta nashego obshchestva*], demonstrating
this seamless integration of literary types into social discourse. S Kapustin. "Po povodu romana g.
Dostoevskago: 'Prestuplenie i nakazanie'" *Zhenskii vestnik* №5 (1867), 1–29.
[33] Qtd in Brown, "Pisarev and the Transformation of Two Russian Novels," 155. Originally in *Sochinenii v chetyrekh tomakh* (Moskva, 1955–56), 1:192–193. De Vogüé made a similar claim in his Preface
to *Le Roman Russe* (1886) in justifying why he sought "the secret of Russia in her novelists." What would
be found in other countries under the headings of "philosophy, history, the eloquence of the pulpit and
the bar," De Vogüé claimed, "in Russia finds its way into the broader framework of poetry and the novel,
the two forms of expression which are natural to the national thought, the only ones which are compatible with the exigencies of a censorship which was formerly uncompromising and is today still quick
to take offense" ("On Russian and French Realism," 313).
[34] Qtd. in Todd, *Literature and Society in Imperial Russia 1800–1914*, 256. Originally in "Povesti i
rasskazy Voskresenskogo" in *Sobranie sochinenii* (Moscow-Leningrad, 1961), 3:223.

Intellectuals saw Russian novels as a direct critique of the state of the family. In an 1861 article criticizing imperial family law as the root of Russia's despotic, patri-archal order, the author closed with the statement: "Read all Russian literature, especially her best representatives: Pushkin, Lermontov, Gogol, Turgenev, Ostro-vsky, Goncharov, Panaev, Grigorovich, Nekrasov, Pisemsky, Tur, and others, and you will see what sort of heavy burden the morals reflected in our law(s) have placed on the whole of family life, and what a sad appearance that life has acquired as a result."[35] The Russians read English literature in the same way. In a review of Hippolyte Taine's *Histoire de la littérature anglaise*, V. Chuiko asserted that Dick-ens and Thackeray: "taken together give a clear understanding of English character and English society."[36]

While the Russians claim—to some degree rightly—the exceptional ideologi-cal weight Russian literature had to bear as the site of social and political debate in the nineteenth century, English literature was also deeply engaged with con-temporary social issues. As laws around marriage, divorce, property rights, and legal inheritance were debated and revised throughout the Victorian period, these issues featured prominently in the novels. An 1865 article in the *St. James Maga-zine* noted the "very strong connection between law and literature," and scholars have traced the way shifting laws around issues like wills, inheritance, marriage, and divorce in turn shifted plotlines.[37] For example, the question of marriage to a deceased wife's sister—which Gilbert and Sullivan playfully called "that annual blister" plaguing Parliament in their comic opera *Iolanthe* (1882)—became an explicit target of novelistic inquiry in Felicia Skene's *The Inheritance of Evil: Or, the Consequences of Marrying a Deceased Wife's Sister* (1849) and Dinah Craik's *Hannah* (1872).[38] To understand the depictions of family in both national lit-eratures, one needs to appreciate these wider debates in which the novels were participating.

---

[35] Filipov, M. "Vzgliad na russkie grazhdanskie zakony" *Sovremennik* №3 (1861), 265. Similarly turning to the novels as an illustration of the problems with Russian family law, an 1867 article in *Women's Herald* complained that until the new law that had just been passed, when a man serving in the Church died the common practice was to marry his oldest daughter off to whomever replaced him, often leading to a 30-year old women being married to an 18-year old student (*kandidat*), seeing each other for the first time only at the altar. As the author observed: "The kind of life that followed is known to many, especially after the brilliant sketches of Pomialovsky" (K—in. "Vnutrennee obozrenie" *Zhenskii vestnik* №8 (1867), 49–54 (here 54).

[36] Chuiko, V. "Angliiskie romanisty (po Tenu)" *Zhenskii vestnik* №2 (1866), 1–41 (here 5).

[37] Qtd. in Frank, *Law, Literature, and the Transmission of Culture in England*, 67. On the relation-ship between law and literature in Victorian England, see also: Schramm, *Testimony and Advocacy in Victorian Law, Literature, and Theology*.

[38] See Frew, "The Marriage to a Deceased Wife's Sister Narrative: A Comparison of Novels"; Corbett, *Family Likeness*, esp. Ch. 3. The history of this law and responses to it are examined in detail by Chase and Levenson, *The Spectacle of Intimacy*, 105–120. It is quite fitting in the context of this study that the resolution to the plot in *Hannah* is the in-law couple moving to the more sexually permissive France, marrying, and living happily ever after.

The Political Stakes of the Family

Sometimes a cigar may be just a cigar, but rarely is the family only a discrete group of individuals. In the nineteenth-century novel it carried great symbolic weight as "a prime social unit, a model of order and an essential instrument for educating the young."[39] Lynn Hunt has drawn attention to the powerful family analogies underlying the French Revolution—a shift from father as king to his replacement by a band of brothers (who did *not* conceive of themselves as "founding fathers").[40] The family stood for more than itself, making the stakes for writing about it high.[41] Both the English and the Russians regarded the family as the building block and model in microcosm for the state, "legitimating each institution by associating it with the 'naturalness' of the other."[42]

Relying on just such logic in his response to the horrors of the French Revolution, Edmund Burke (1729–1797) famously sought to justify the English system of governing by analogizing it to the family: "we have given to our frame of polity the image of a relation in blood; binding up the constitution of the country with our dearest domestic ties; adopting our fundamental laws into the bosom of our family affections; keeping inseparable, and cherishing with the warmth of all their combined and mutually reflected charities, our state, our hearths, our sepulchres, and our altars."[43] There was a religious underpinning to this view, as Victorians inherited a highly moralized understanding of the family as a microcosm of God's kingdom, with the head of the household representing God's authority within the family.[44]

Like the English, the Russians also drew many analogies between the family and the State, with the stability of the former held up as the foundation for the stability of the latter. Ilarion Vasilev, an instructor in Imperial law at Moscow Commercial School wrote in 1827: "If calm, tranquility, and peace reign in the depths of

---

[39] Kilroy, *The Nineteenth-Century English Novel*, 5.

[40] Hunt, *The Family Romance of the French Revolution*. She notes the contrast with American republican imagery of "Sons of Liberty" and "fathers of the republic" (71). The term "Founding Fathers" was actually a twentieth-century invention.

[41] Fredric Jameson makes this argument for all "third-world texts," arguing that "the story of the private individual destiny is always an allegory of the embattled situation of the public third-world culture and society" ("Third-World Literature in the Era of Multinational Capitalism," 69). Much of the argument would seem to apply to Russia as well.

[42] McKeon, *The Secret History of Domesticity*, 11. This language of analogy is also what Mary Wollstonecraft turns to in making her case for the rights of the individual in both *A Vindication of the Rights of Men* (1790) and *A Vindication of the Rights of Women* (1792). Employing the analogy of family as state, she shows how this has been used to justify domestic tyranny. See Kilroy, *The Nineteenth-Century English Novel: Family Ideology and Narrative Form*, 11.

[43] Burke, *Reflections on the Revolution in France* (first pub. 1790) (Penguin, 1983), 120.

[44] Broughton and Rogers, *Gender and Fatherhood in the Nineteenth Century*, 18. Sophie Gilmartin has noted the way fictions and myths around pedigree "reveal much about Britain's anxieties over, and defense of itself as a unified nation," linking family concerns in the novels to issues of imperial expansion and the accompanying incorporation of alien peoples and cultures (*Ancestry and Narrative in Nineteenth-Century British Literature: Blood Relations from Edgeworth to Hardy*, 4).

families, then throughout the State hostilities and revolts fall silent and security dwells."[45] Similarly, leading Russian Church father Filaret (1782–1867) declared in 1861: "The state consists of families. Disorder in the constituent parts causes disorder in the whole."[46] Sergei N. Glinka (1776–1847), who published the *Russian Herald* (1808–1825), used the journal as a platform for attacking the type of utopian, anarchist thinking that led France into its Revolution. He made the "good father" the basis for his ideas about authority, with a benevolent God ruling over humanity, just as the Tsar ruled benignly over his people, and the noble over his serfs, all father-child relations for Glinka.[47] Invoking the same familial metaphors, in 1803 Nikolai Karamzin wrote of the duty of the good Russian nobleman to be a kind landowner: "he who fulfills it serves the fatherland as a faithful son, he serves the monarch as a faithful subject."[48] This is quite a different defense of the status quo than the one mounted by Burke, but both relied on the family analogy.

The same logic held in reverse for women. In the introduction to her popular cookbook, *A Gift for Young Housewives* (1881), Elena Molokhovets reminded readers that: 'The young housewife must concern herself not only with her own family, servants, and peasants, but also with the welfare of her neighbor in the broadest sense, being both a mother to her household [*sem'yanika svoego doma*] and a citizeness in the great family of humanity."[49]

Given the frequent analogization between the family and the State, any thoughts about family reform could be seen as a social or political threat. Indeed, attempts to reform family law were often part of broader missions to revise or defend Russia's existing social and political institutions and structures.[50] Viewed in this context, the depictions of family in the novels take on greater social and political weight. The pervasiveness of the theme of tyrannical fathers and patriarchal

[45] Qtd. in Wagner, *Marriage, Property, and Law in Late Imperial Russia*, 73. There were, however, moments in Russian history when family loyalty actually subverted national stability, such as when the Decembrists' wives and sisters chose to follow their husbands/brothers into exile: "In choosing loyalty to husband over loyalty to state, these women turned the family values of Nicholas I on their head. Rather than promoting political order, wifely devotion rewarded rebelliousness instead" (Engel, *Women in Russia, 1700–2000*, 44).

[46] Filaret, qtd. in Wagner, *Marriage, Property, and Law in Late Imperial Russia*, 73.

[47] Martin, "The Family Model of Society and Russian National Identity," 35. The role of Tsar as father was enshrined in the "scenarios of power" he created to reinforce his reign. Richard Wortman illuminates the way Nicholas I crafted the "domestic scenario": "It made the family a central symbol of the moral purity of autocracy—the purest form of absolute monarchy. The association between domestic morality and autocratic government outlived Nicholas's reign and remained intrinsic to the image of Russian autocracy for the duration of the empire. To violate the principle of autocracy became tantamount to a biblical sin against the father, while violation of family morality would throw into doubt the moral foundations of autocratic rule" (*Scenarios of Power: Myth and Ceremony in Russian Monarchy*, 1:334–335). Not only was Nicholas paterfamilias for his loving and devoted wife, Alexandra, and their children, but also symbolically for all Russia.

[48] Karamzin penned this under the name Luka Eremeev, a fictional subscriber to Karamzin's journal, *Herald of Europe* (qtd. by Grigorian, *Noble Subjects*, 44).

[49] Qtd. in Kelly, *Refining Russia*, 125.

[50] Wagner, "Family Law, the Rule of Law, and Liberalism in Late Imperial Russia," 520.

oppression could be understood as the closest authors could come to critiquing the autocracy.

Comparing Russia and England

Certain features of a national tradition only truly come into focus when viewed in opposition. As Lois Bueler has observed: "Just as people living inside an ideology or a language typically do not see it and cannot describe it, for it is what they look through to the world around them, people using a literary structure are unlikely to see it, for it is the naturalized means by which they imitate the human types and actions of their world."[51] Just as English scholars, for example, give too little credence to the structural role primogenitural inheritance customs play in their plots, so too are Russian scholars perhaps too uninquisitive about the role a partible (that is, shared among heirs) inheritance structure played.

The pairing of specifically Russian and English literature is motivated by the novels themselves as well as by cultural perceptions. The family novel, as a genre, is mostly associated with England and Russia, while the other dominant literary traditions in the nineteenth century—namely the French and German—had different concerns. The genre began in England, with Samuel Richardson usually credited as its originator, and it spread across Europe to Russia.[52] While this is not a study of influence, the Russian family novel was inherently building upon the English tradition.[53] In the eighteenth century, the foreign languages spoken by most educated Russians were French and German, so English literature reached most people in translation.[54] Sometimes this meant reading the works in French or German, or else in Russian translations that themselves were based on translations.[55] *Pamela*, for example, first entered the Russian consciousness in the 1740s through its English publication, then through French translations, and ultimately in 1787 it received its first Russian translation (translated from the French).[56]

---

[51] Bueler, *The Tested Woman Plot: Women's Choices, Men's Judgments, and the Shaping of Stories*, 4. Bueler was referring specifically to the way people viewed marriage (qtd. in Schaffer, *Romance's Rivals*, 19).

[52] I explore the history of the genre in "The Family Novel (and Its Curious Disappearance)."

[53] Casanova argues that national literatures are "not a pure emanation of national identity; they are constructed through literary rivalries, which are always denied, and struggles, which are always international" (*The World Republic of Letters*, 36). In the case of Russia, I think this terminology may be overly violent and negative. The Russians fully acknowledged their indebtedness to European models and saw themselves as inheritors who were building on these great traditions, borrowing and reshaping for their own national context.

[54] For a good overview of the translation and reception of English literature in Russia in the nineteenth century, see Buckler, "Victorian Literature and Russian Culture: Translation, Reception, Influence, Affinity."

[55] From 1762–1801 (reigns of Catherine II and Paul), 382 novels were translated into Russian from French, 126 from German, and 8 from English (Cross, *The Development of the English Novel*, 38).

[56] Tikhonova, "Mariia Nikolaevna Volkonskaia (Tolstaia) '...Chto Ia Znaiu O Nei...', Ili Dvesti Let Spustia," 183.

Eighteenth-century Russians appreciated the "moral trends" in the English writing.[57] Russian translators would justify the importance and worthiness of the books they had translated with claims that, for example, the book "may be called useful by virtue of its light yet highly persuasive moralizing and pleasant in the analysis of wondrous events contained in it."[58] One Russian journal recommended to translators in 1764 "that they at any rate better make use of their labours on English works or those translated from English than on French, because in the former for the most part honesty and virtue, and in the latter mostly passions, prevail."[59]

In the nineteenth century, this belief in the virtue of English literature for inculcating good moral values continued to hold sway.[60] And indeed translators may have played into this. Irinarkh Vvedensky, when translating *Jane Eyre* (1849), for example, modified Charlotte Brontë's text to emphasize the importance of marriage for women.[61] This fits with the "branding" of English literature in Russia, which emphasized family values. A commentator in *Woman's Herald* claimed that England's greatest writers—Dickens and Thackeray—were totally unalike save for their English "love for family life."[62] An 1867 review article in the same journal praised England's female authors for their domestic and familial subjects, the "quiet family attachments" rather than "stormy passions."[63] It was not only England's domesticity that appealed to the Russians, but its whole moral and social outlook. As O. R. Demidova has argued: "Humanitarian ideas, heightened social awareness, sympathy for the 'insulted and injured' all meant that the works of the 'brilliant Pleiad of English realists' were in harmony with the literature of the Russian natural school."[64]

[57] Levin, "English Literature in Eighteenth-Century Russia," xxix; Sipovskii, *Ocherki iz istorii russkago romana*, 411. For a characteristic nineteenth-century statement on the moral quality of English literature from a French critic, see De Vogüé, "On Russian and French Realism," 332–334.

[58] *Sirota Aglinkskaia, ili o Sharlotte Summers* (St Petersburg, 1763), I, p. 3. Qtd. in Levin, "English Literature in Eighteenth-Century Russia," xxvii.

[59] Qtd. in Levin, "English Literature in Eighteenth-Century Russia," xxxv.

[60] It is certainly not only the Russians who viewed English literature this way, but also the English themselves. In his *Autobiography*, Anthony Trollope claimed that he "always thought of [himself] as a preacher of sermons," and, as Maria Frawley has noted, moralizing statements "flow thick and fast through much of George Eliot's fiction" amongst other writers (qtd. in Frawley, "The Victorian Age, 1832–1901," 397).

[61] See Syskina. "Perevody XIX veka romana 'Dzhen Eir' Sharlotty Bronte: Peredacha kharaktera i vzgliadov geroini v perevode 1849 goda Irinarkha Vvedenskogo."

[62] Chuiko, V. "Angliiskie romanisty (po Tenu)," 16.

[63] Sof'ia T...va. "Ocherki zhenskago truda. Bessi Rainer Parkes (Essays on woman's work By Bessie Rayner Parkes. Second Edition)." *Zhenskii vestnik* №7 (1867), 16–26 (here 16).

[64] Demidova, "The Reception of Charlotte Brontë's Work in Nineteenth-Century Russia," 689. Julie Buckler makes a similar claim about George Eliot's popularity: "Russian critics lauded Eliot for precisely those literary qualities most valued in Russia's own emerging national literature—seriousness of purpose, psychological realism, positivism, deep understanding of a specific socio-cultural setting, and a commitment to the moral and spiritual development of her readers." Buckler, "Victorian Literature and Russian Culture: Translation, Reception, Influence, Affinity," 218.

This praise was also, of course, meant as a contrast to the other literary tradition venerated by the Russians: the French.[65] While the Russians were avid readers of French literature in the nineteenth century, they did not associate the French with the theme of family. A commentator in an 1859 issue of *Family Circle* decried the dangers of French novels "that excite [a girl's] imagination and spoil her morals."[66] Attacking the French customs that had infiltrated Russia, he lamented, "Take a young lady from high society: her mind is not occupied by anything, she has nothing to do, no desire to read, boredom overcomes her. What kind of measures should she take against this bitter enemy of the beautiful and not-beautiful halves of the human race?—A French novel like Flaubert's *Madame Bovary*? French the-ater, balls?"[67] Another article entitled "An Admonition for Daughters," appearing later that same year advised daughters not to read French novels, but instead English and Russian.[68] As Nikolai Strakhov characteristically stated in 1870: "In many Russian families girls are taught English especially so that they are able to read English literature, which depicts the image of the English woman...England is the classic land of pure family values, just as France is the classic land of love intrigues" (138).[69]

Within the novels, we find the same views. The heroine of S. Dolgina's *Ficti-tious Marriage* (1876), for example, "read most of all English novels (as is well known, they are considered the most proper reading for high society maidens)" (30). It is no accident that Dostoevsky's greatest femme fatale, the fallen Nasta-sya Filippovna, is reading *Madame Bovary* (1856) in *The Idiot* (1868); perhaps equally significant, Prince Myshkin takes the book away from her. Or in a more egregious instance, when Amalia Potapovna is grooming an innocent girl to be seduced in *Petersburg Slums* (1864–66), she gives her a French novel, "one of those works that acts enticingly on the young imagination, revealing to it the tantalizing world of sensual images and sensations, that before it, drop by drop, sneakily pours a seductive poison into the fresh soul that is sensitive to every-thing" (1:142).[70] In England, the same belief in the dangerous values of the French held sway. In Charlotte Brontë's *Shirley* (1849), when the eponymous heroine's uncle is berating her for having faulty values about marriage, he exclaims: "You read French. Your mind is poisoned with French novels. You have imbibed French principles" (460).

[65] For a guide to Russians' responses to French literature, see Priscilla Meyer's *How the Russians Read the French*, 2008.

[66] I. Aprelev. "Zametki o zhenshchinakh" *Semeinyi krug* №4 (1859), 123–134 (here 128).

[67] Aprelev. "Zametki o zhenshchinakh,"125.

[68] Tragen. "Nastavlenie docheri" *Semeinyi krug* №11 (1859), 144–163 (here 160).

[69] In the same vein, in the epigraph to this Introduction, Saltykov-Shchedrin claimed the family was the center of the novel, in a positive way in the English novel and in a negative way in the French (10:33).

[70] Lucey notes that in Panaev's vignettes of the demimonde, the women's love of French novels is "a major indicator of [their] moral licentiousness" ("Fallen but Charming Creatures," 109).

There is a long scholarly tradition of pairing the Russian and English literary traditions.[71] Some studies have focused on specific cases of influence between two authors.[72] Others have been even more focused, looking at links between individual novels or at the influence of English literature on a specific novel (e.g. Amy Mandelker's *Framing Anna Karenina: Tolstoy, the Woman Question, and the Victorian Novel*).[73] Some explore earlier or later periods.[74] None have focused on the family. Perhaps the scholar whose interests have most closely aligned with my own is Emma Lieber, whose Ph.D. dissertation, *On the Distinctiveness of the Russian Novel*: The Brothers Karamazov *and the English Tradition* (2011), explores the formal differences between novels in the two traditions, taking as its exemplars one pairing from the eighteenth century to compare and one from the nineteenth. Lieber's approach is somewhat more spiritual and ideological, relying on the assumption of there being a "Russian point of view, with its underpinnings in Orthodox theology and its anti-empiricist epistemology" which she contrasts to an English outlook. This study is grounded in history and the concrete laws and customs each society created, rather than national sensibility, which can be more difficult to pin down or define.

Bringing together the two national traditions actually mirrors the reading practices of nineteenth-century Russians, as they were first absorbing most novels in the "thick journals," where Russian novels were published alongside translations of English.[75] For example, Tolstoy's *Family Happiness* (1859) appeared in *Russian Herald* the same year as Eliot's *Adam Bede* (though not the same months). A few years later (1868), in the same journal Dostoevsky's *The Idiot* was originally serialized in parallel with a translation of Collins' *The Moonstone* and another English novel, *My Son's Wife* (Emily Jolly, 1867). For contemporary readers this opposition of Russian and English literature was constantly before their eyes.

[71] Buckler provides an excellent "Suggested Reading" list that covers the major studies of English/Russian influence ("Victorian Literature and Russian Culture: Translation, Reception, Influence, Affinity," 225–226).
[72] See, for example: Lary, *Dostoevsky and Dickens: A Study of Literary Influence* (1973); MacPike, *Dostoevsky's Dickens: A Study of Literary Influence* (1981); Avastsaturova, V. V. "Ch. Dikkens v tvorcheskov soznanii L. Tolstogo" (1990). There are also studies looking at influence in both directions for authors like Dostoevsky (*Dostoevskii and Britain*, ed. Leatherbarrow, 1995) or Tolstoy (*Transnational Tolstoy*, ed. Foster, 2013).
[73] See also Goubert, "Did Tolstoy Read *East Lynne*?"; Jones, "George Eliot's 'Adam Bede' and Tolstoy's Conception of 'Anna Karenina'"; Cruise, "Tracking the English novel in *Anna Karenina*: who wrote the English novel that Anna reads?"; also sections of Knapp's *Anna Karenina and Others: Tolstoy's Labyrinth of Plots* (2016).
[74] Simmons, *English Literature and Culture in Russia (1553–1840)* (1935); Zhirmunsky, *Bairon i Pushkin: Pushkin i zapadnye literatury* (1978); Polonsky, *English Literature and the Russian Aesthetic Renaissance* (1998).
[75] Buckler provides information on the year and journal in which many Victorian novels were first published in Russian translation ("Victorian Literature and Russian Culture: Translation, Reception, Influence, Affinity," 216–218).

Choice of Novels

The over one hundred novels sampled for this study (see Appendix) attempt to provide representative coverage, from canonical texts by the most highly regarded authors in each national tradition—Dickens, Thackeray, Eliot, Tolstoy, Dostoevsky, Turgenev—to lesser works that were popular in their day. The novels represent a variety of styles and viewpoints, from the Christian moralizing of Charlotte Yonge to the sensation novels of Wilkie Collins and Mary Elizabeth Braddon, from the radical thought of Nikolai Chernyshevsky to the more conservative family ideals of Dmitri Begichev.

The temporal range of the study has been dictated by the evolution of the family novel genre. On the English side, this means beginning at the start of the nineteenth century with Edgeworth and Austen, who were central in shaping the tradition. In Russia, the story picks up in 1832, the year when the final chapter of *Eugene Onegin*—typically considered to be Russia's first family novel—was published (earlier chapters began appearing in 1825). This later start for Russia reflects the fact that the real rise of the novel in Russia did not come until the 1840s, but writers at that time were intimately familiar with earlier European novels; therefore, it would feel artificial and unjustified to begin looking at both traditions only at that point. The study concludes in 1880, the year marking the final novel by Dostoevsky and in many ways the close of the great Russian realists (Tolstoy at that stage had given up fiction, though he would ultimately return to it to write a final novel in 1899). On the English side, 1880 saw major advances for married women's property rights and could serve as a transitional point before the late-Victorian period. The rise of novels about the New Woman in the 1880s–1890s by women such as Sarah Grand, Mona Caird, and Olive Schreiner, as well as men such as George Gissing, Thomas Hardy, and George Moore ushered in a new and different set of family concerns.[76]

This eighty-year span in England and the fifty years in Russia were far from static times. In each country, as social and political reforms took place and as the literary tradition evolved, treatments of the family also shifted. English "social problem novels" of the 1830s–1840s often sought resolutions to economic and social strife within the domestic sphere.[77] In the second half of the century, focus would shift from emphasizing the landed estate as the goal of the marriage plot to the rise of the self-made man and new models of success. In Russia, the novels of the 1840s show a strong tie to Romantic ideology (and the influence of George Sand) in their ideals and envisionings of love and family life, while the 1860s–1870s witness the rise of radical thought and the influence of the "woman question." While

---

[76] The term "New Woman" comes from a pair of articles written in 1894 by Grand and Ouida. Many saw the New Woman as a threat to the institution of marriage and traditional domestic arrangements (Ledger, *The New Woman: Fiction and Feminism at the Fin de Siècle*, 11–12).

[77] Frawley, "The Victorian Age, 1832–1901," 396.

being sensitive to the evolution of literary trends across the decades considered, this study will address the strange fact that family plots remain remarkably consistent. The emancipation of the serfs, for example, did not cause the kind of rupture one might expect.

Social class is a complicated issue that functioned differently in Russia and England. Much of the argument that follows does not hold for all levels of society. On the Russian side, it will be confined to the gentry (*dvorianstvo*), and occasional *meshchanstvo* (petit bourgeoisie) and *raznochintsy* (literally "people of various ranks") who shared a similar intellectual milieu. Gentry ideas about the Russian peasant family will occasionally be included to shed light on what the gentry thought the traditional Russian family was or should be (there was much projection in the process of searching for Russian national identity). On the English side, this study is primarily concerned with the bourgeoisie and landed classes. As inheritance is central to parts of the argument, not all claims would hold for the working class, but, as in Russia with the peasants, they were not the primary subject of novels. Family property need not be a landed estate; some of the novels feature a family business, or church living, or some bit of capital to be passed on.

While the English canon is full of female writers in this period, Russia's significant women novelists have largely dropped from view, although some were highly regarded and played a central role in the literary scene in their day.[78] V. Krestovsky (pseudonym) (pen name for Nadezhda Khvoshchinskaya), for example, was the third-highest paid author by journals in the 1870s, after Turgenev and Tolstoy (and ahead of Dostoevsky, Saltykov-Shchedrin, and Pisemsky). I seek to redress their current absence by returning them to their rightful place among their now more well-known male colleagues.[79] The inclusion of Russian women writers is also important to the comparative aims of the project. It prevents a comparison of a predominantly female tradition in England with a male one in Russia, obfuscating which differences could be accounted for by gender versus nationality. I also concur with Rosalind Marsh's concern that "it is particularly important to look at both male and female-authored literature together, in order that literature by Russian women should not simply be regarded as an autonomous cultural experience, marginal to Russian literary history as a whole."[80] That is not the place it held in

---

[78] Gheith suggests that part of the reason they have been forgotten is their categorization in the nineteenth century. "Russian intellectuals generally considered that fiction by women did not advance social agendas," and social significance was linked with literary value in the period (*Finding the Middle Ground*, 129). Hilda Hoogenboom has suggested that the dominant male authors stayed in the canon because they had wives and families who helped support their writing, especially after their deaths, and kept their works in print, while Russia's women writers lacked this kind of support (said during questions at conference in St. Andrews, Scotland, June 2019).

[79] Sally A. Livingston is a welcome exception who includes women authors in her study of the way property rights affected narratives about women (*Marriage, Property, and Women's Narratives*). However, she only considers works that have been translated into English and received critical attention from Anglophone scholars, which significantly limits the pool.

[80] Marsh, "Introduction" to *Women and Russian Culture: Projections and Self-Perceptions*, x.

the nineteenth century. Russia's female writers tended to focus greater attention on the details of domestic life and the constraints imposed upon women by society, and critics of the period noted these differences.[81] Yet overall, Russian women's writing on the family resembles that of Russian men far more than it does English women, indicating that the salient issue is nationality, not gender.

Chapter Breakdown

Part I: *Consanguineal Kin* focuses on the English and Russian treatments of blood kin, or family of origin. While the English prioritize lineage and ancestry (progression across time), the Russians are more concerned about *all* kinship relations in the present (lateral spread).

Chapter 1, "*Contrasting Family Models*," brings readers into the worlds of Russia and England in the nineteenth century, exploring the large structural forces that shaped the two nations' differing views of the family. The English obsession with lineage was predicated on a sense of stability. Rights and titles were inherited like family estates and passed down generation to generation. In Russia, where the Tsar could (and often did) confiscated wealthy families' property, people lived with a kind of radical uncertainty that made them focus on the present. This opposition underlies the English vertical model of family and the custom of primogeniture versus the Russian partible model of inheritance that spread family concern outward in the present. The chapter also explains the different constructions of social class in Russia and England, making clear the two models for attaining gentry status in Russia (hereditary or earned through service) that also weakened the importance of ancestry in the Russian context.

Chapter 2, "*The Traditional Vertical Family Plot*," lays out the standard theories of the novel that draw a congruence between family line and story line, showing how these theories rely on the English family model presented in Chapter 1. The chapter then examines the consanguineal relations that can be accommodated in the two standard family plots identified by scholars: generational and marriage. Each follows a linear model, so sisters, for example, by marrying *out* of the family, offer no threat to this progression. Brothers, however, pose a "problem," as

---

[81] We find a characteristic example in Ostrovsky's review of Evgenia Tur's first novel: "The works of women-writers, having, almost without exception, the same societal character, differ from the works of the male pen in that, often being inferior to them in artistry, they excel in their richness of fine details, subtle psychological nuances, a special energy and fullness of feeling—very often a feeling of indignation. They lack calm creativity, cold humor, and precision in the completion of their portrayals; and yet in [their works] those portrayals are more touching, revealing, and dramatic. It could not be otherwise: a woman makes contact with society with a more sensitive side of herself than does a man. A woman, before she became a writer, for the most part either was a victim of the usual empty talk, or, having lived the better half of her life, discovered that all the most noble spiritual actions went for nothing, self-sacrifice was not valued, love was either deceived, or did not find in the emptiness of society worthy reciprocation." First published in: *Moskvitianin* (№7, 1850).

they challenge the linearity of the family. The English most often solve this by excluding brother-brother relations from their novels (there are almost no significant brothers in England's canonical novels). In presenting the accepted norm, the chapter relies on many short examples, rather than an in-depth analysis of individual novels. It draws on perennial favorites like Austen, Anne Brontë, Collins, Dickens, Eliot, Gaskell, Trollope, Dostoevsky, Goncharov, Pushkin, and Tolstoy, as well as lesser-known authors such as Julia Kavanagh, Harriet Martineau, Mrs. Henry Wood, Charlotte Yonge, Sergei Durov, Krestovsky (pseud.), and Evgenia Tur to show readers the pervasiveness of these patterns.

Chapter 3, *"Brothers,"* picks up where the previous chapter left off, exploring what happens when a novel *does* focus on brothers. In the English novel, when brothers take center stage, their standard plotline is romantic rivalry and the second brother cannot be accommodated in the novel's conclusion. Resolution most often comes through removing a brother (usually through his death). The primary novels I analyze for this pattern include Eliot's *Adam Bede* (1859), Collins' *Poor Miss Finch* (1872), Anna Drury's *The Brothers* (1865), Braddon's *Like and Unlike* (1887), Gaskell's *Wives and Daughters* (1864–1866), and Brontë's *Shirley*. The Russians, by contrast, gave brothers a central role in their reconfiguring of family plots. With an inheritance system that equalized siblings and reduced structural tensions, they were free to create plots that were not progressive—driven toward the telos of a singular heir—but instead focused on the challenges of lateral bonds in the here and now. Blood kinship (*rodstvo*) is not only about blood*line*, but also about the clan of kin who share in it. The narrative structure this creates is more of a woven mesh than a spun-out line. The chapter demonstrates that this structure is directly related to the structure of the family. The primary Russian examples come from Turgenev's *Fathers and Children* (1862), Tolstoy's *Anna Karenina* (1875–1878), Aleksei Potekhin's *Poor Gentry* (1863), Saltykov-Shchedrin's *The Golovlyovs* (1875–1880), and Dostoevsky's *The Brothers Karamazov* (1880).

Part II: *Conjugal Relations* is concerned with the historical factors that shaped the marriage plot. According to many prominent theories, courtship and marriage provide *the* quintessential plotline for the nineteenth-century novel. Comparative studies usually rely on England vs. France (courtship vs. adultery), but adding Russia into the mix reveals and upends many of the assumptions on which the theories are built.

Chapter 4, *"Family Ideology,"* explores the underlying ideas about gender roles and the domestic sphere that were crucial to shaping family plots. While there were certain similarities in women's conditions in England and Russia, in other ways they were radically opposed. Unlike their English counterparts, who upon marriage ceased to exist as their own legal entities, married Russian women could own their own property and many were involved in estate management. While this seemed to give them certain advantages, within the family they had no rights— legally obligated to live with their husbands who had the legal right to rape and beat them. By the mid-nineteenth century, the Russian family was generally agreed to be a backward institution in desperate need of reform. The Victorians, by contrast, clung to an idealized vision of the family as a space of peace and love, a retreat from the harsh outside world. The English vision relied on looking back to an idealized past for the family (whether or not such a past existed), while for the Russians the traditional past was filled with wife-beatings and patriarchal tyranny. They instead looked forward to a progressive rethinking of the family.

Chapter 5, "*Courtship and Its Promises*," builds on the historical findings in the previous chapter to understand why English and Russian novels handle courtship so differently. In theory (and in England) courtship plots should lead to a marriage, yet in Russia they rarely do. I argue that the reason for this difference lies in the way the two nations positioned the family ideal in time. For the English, looking back to an idealized family past, the marriage plot serves a conservative function, reaffirming that stable order as a primary source of continuity. Its aims are vertical: the continuation of the family line through producing a legal heir. While some scholars have challenged the hegemony of this positive portrayal of marriage, most failed marriages are superseded by or contrasted against a successful courtship plot that reaffirms the ideal. Key texts I consider include Austen's *Pride and Prejudice* (1813), Thackeray's *Vanity Fair* (1848), and Trollope's *He Knew He Was Right* (1869) and *An Eye for an Eye* (1879). Since for the Russians the family's past was a time of patriarchal tyranny and wife beatings, believing in "good family values" meant advocating progress and change. As a result, they turned courtship into a progressive plot, and progress meant *not* creating marriages that would continue the existing order. If in England the purpose of the marriage plot was to create a legal heir (valuing vertical continuity), in Russia it was to liberate the woman, focusing on her spiritual well-being in the present. In practice, this meant that she often ended up unwed, but still morally superior. Pushkin's *Eugene Onegin*, Dostoevsky's *The Idiot* (1868-1869), Tur's *A Mistake* (1849), and Pavlova's *Double Life* (1848) serve as the primary texts that ground this discussion, with additional examples drawn from Tolstoy, Turgenev, Begichev, Krestovsky (pseud.), and Shalikova.

Chapter 6, "*Marriage and Its Discontents*," is concerned with the state of marriage and its potential plots. If the goal of the marriage plot is not the vertical (English) production of an heir, but lateral—present—relations, then the actual legal state of being married loses its significance (as we see in *Rudin* [1856] or *Ursa Major* [1871] with "pure" Russian heroines who are not tainted by their willingness to become fallen women). I make the counter-intuitive claim that marriage was not actually the goal of the Russian marriage plot. The Russians separated the "form" of legal marriage from the "content" (the quality of relations between the couple), placing value on the latter. This is seen especially clearly in novels about fictitious marriages, like Chernyshevsky's *What Is to Be Done?* (1863), and Dolgina's *Fictitious Marriage*. In the English novel, marriage is typically an endpoint for plot, and marriage itself only becomes plot-worthy when the marriage has gone awry, as in novels like *Dombey and Son* (1846–1848), *He Knew He Was Right*, *The Tenant of Wildfell Hall* (1848), or *Daniel Deronda* (1876). The English, with their powerful domestic ideal of marriage as a perfect union, could not accept imperfection; any failed marriage was a threat to the institution itself. To solve this, English novels remove failed marriages (just as they remove second brothers), allowing them to be superseded or counterbalanced by successful courtship plots. In Russia, where marriage was generally understood to be a broken institution, there was room for novels to both diagnose the problems with conjugal life and to attempt repair, tolerating imperfection (take Mme Larina in *Eugene Onegin*, for example, who allows habit to take the place of bliss). Russian authors plotted the trials of married life in works like Mikhail Avdeev's *Underwater Stone* (1860) and Fyodor Stulli's *Twice Married* (1875), allowing wedlock to be a rocky state, yet still redeemable through liberalization.

Parts I and II treat the normative model of the family as married couples and their offspring, but this does not capture many of the family configurations depicted in nineteenth-century Russian and English novels. Part III: *Alternative Kinship* turns to the alternatives. There are a series of pre-conditions that enable alternative forms of family to arise and thrive in the novel, and these conditions are standard features of the Russian context. While Russian novels are full of failures of the marriage plot that provides the typical path to forming new families in the English novel, the flip-side is that these same conditions open different narrative paths that lead to new kinds of family configurations.

Chapter 7, "*Alternative Family Models in Time*," explores the role of the vertical axis in shaping alternative kinship plots. I argue that the vertical axis, with its focus on ancestry and futurity, is a conservative force that must be weakened for alternative family formations to arise. The lack of concern for producing an heir to continue the line enables family to expand in the present. Such conditions appear frequently in Russia, where many people saw a historical breakdown in the vertical family model. The exploration focuses on the works of Dostoevsky, contextualizing them with examples from Herzen, Panaeva, Tolstoy, and Tur. In England, where there was still faith in the patriarchal family model, more extreme conditions were needed to remove the emphasis from the bloodline. English novels that embraced alternative family tend to have an absent vertical (for example, an orphaned hero), or a queer challenge to reproductive futurity. The primary examples come from Craik, Dickens, Gaskell, Jewsbury, and Yonge.

Chapter 8, "*Alternative Family Models in Space*," approaches alternative kinship constructions on the lateral axis through the spatial metaphor of restriction vs. expansion. It looks at the way the English conceived of the family as a bounded sphere ("every man's house is his castle"), while the Russians allowed and encouraged family to expand by treating ever-wider circles as kin. I suggest that "intentional family"—literally *choosing* to make others kin—is often the model for successful family creation at the end of a Russian novel, taking as my primary example Tur's *The Niece* (1851), but placing it in dialogue with Turgenev's *Fathers and Children*, Dostoevsky's *The Adolescent* (1875), and other texts by Begichev, Goncharov, Krestovsky (pseud.), and Tolstoy. While in Russia alternative kinship constructions are an answer to the "problem" of the normative family, in England such alternatives most often arise as a way to accommodate queer desires that did not have a place in the standard nuclear model. The key texts considered are Craik's *John Halifax, Gentleman* (1856) and *A Noble Life* (1866), Butler's *The Way of All Flesh* (1873–1884), and Trollope's *The Warden* (1855) and *Barchester Towers* (1857).

While Part III begins from binaries that divide Russia and England, ultimately alternative kinship is where these binaries collapse. When the conditions of an English novel can be made to model the Russian norms—when the possibility of reproductive futurity has been removed—we find the same types of alternative family configurations appearing. It takes a serious obstacle, however—usually disability or hereditary illness that remove characters from the possibility of reproductive futurity—for such expansive configurations to appear in England. In both traditions, the embrace of alternative kin leads to a liberalizing of the family and to plotlines of inclusion in the present, rather than a line of descent.

The Conclusion returns to the issue of narrative form, focusing specifically on endings. The differing shapes of the family in Russia and England created different goals that motivated their family plots. These, in turn, dictated what would provide narrative closure. English endings—typified by marriage and childbirth—provided stability and continuity, "an ending that is also a beginning," in the words of Barry McCrea. Russian endings—full of unwed heroines and intentional kinship ties—often lack such English closure. The present is never finalized.

PART I
CONSANGUINEAL KIN

1

Contrasting Family Models

He was a great proficient in all questions of genealogy, and knew enough of almost every gentleman's family in England to say of what blood and lineage were descended all those who had any claim to be considered as possessors of any such luxuries. For blood and lineage he himself had a most profound respect.

—Anthony Trollope, *Barchester Towers*

"Take what I have, for your children; take me to live with you, like a son takes his own father, or come to live with me, like a son to his father, totally, with your children, so that we were all one, soul to soul..."

—Sofia Khvoshchinskaya, *Acquaintances*

Everyone is born into a family with a bloodline stretching back in time and usually with a web of relations in the present: parents, siblings, aunts, uncles, cousins, etc. Part I is concerned with this kind of consanguineal kin (as opposed to family created through marriage, which will be the subject of Part II). This chapter begins with history, looking at how the Russians and English conceived of the consanguineal family. Where did its limits lie? Which relations were most valued? What historical factors account for the different family structures in the two nations? It then turns to the role of ancestry in the novel, looking at the weight accorded to it in the English tradition and the Russian alternative model of the *rod* (literally both "line" and "clan") that expands both vertically across time and laterally amongst contemporaneous relations. Building on this groundwork, Chapter 2 will turn to novel theory, exploring how family form has shaped our ideas about narrative structure. As most of our theories of the novel were created in an Anglophone context, they closely align with English family structure based on a single line of descent, rather than expansion in the present. Some family relations can be accommodated better within them than others. Chapter 3 brings the material from the first two chapters together, looking at how family form and novel theory interact. Focusing on the example of brothers, it explores how the different conceptions of family in the two nations shaped the plotlines they created for brothers and the problems our theories have in accounting for the lateral family spread that brothers represent.

The Family Novel in Russia and England, 1800–1880. Anna A. Berman, Oxford University Press.
© Anna A. Berman (2022). DOI: 10.1093/oso/9780192866622.003.0002

Defining the Family

What did "family" actually mean in the nineteenth century, and whom did it include? Usage of the term is variable, shifting across times and having broader or narrower applications in different cultures. In England in the seventeenth and eighteenth centuries, "family" typically referred to the members of a household, which included dependents such as live-in relatives, servants, and apprentices.[1] In both English and French dictionaries from the period, family was defined by either co-residence or kinship.[2] By the late eighteenth century "family" came to refer to a married couple and their immature children (a definition that amalgamated both earlier ones).[3]

In addition to the meaning of the term changing, family structures were also in flux. Ruth Perry has argued that in England the eighteenth century saw a shift in what was considered the primary kinship group, from "an axis of kinship based on consanguineal ties or blood lineage to an axis based on conjugal and affinal ties of the married couple."[4] This is not the same as the now debunked argument that the extended kinship network was replaced by the nuclear family, as few families actually contained only parents and children. However, in Perry's words, this shift from "collateral to lineal definitions of kinship...diminished the number of relatives who counted as kin, shrinking the psychological reach of most members of kin groups."[5] In the nineteenth century, the family and the house were almost synonymous, to the point that the 1851 census included a section on "Families and Houses." For the census, family was defined as "the persons under one head," reinforcing an idea of patriarchal domesticity, even if in reality many people (for example, widows with children, or bachelors with servants) did not fit this norm.[6]

In Russia the family was also a porous concept. The term "family" (*sem'ia* or *semeistvo*) did not exist in its present sense at the time of the famous sixteenth-century domestic manual the *Domostroi*. Instead, its authors write of the homestead with many "*domochadtsye*" (household members). According to Iu. L. Bessmertny, the word for home (*dom*) was used "to designate a single economic/household [*khoziaistvennogo*] entity, a social and psychological whole, whose members are in a master-subject relationship, but are equally necessary

---

[1] Tadmor, "The Concept of the Household-Family in Eighteenth-Century England," 112. Qtd. in Perry, *Novel Relations*, 15. Randolph Trumbach explains that aristocrats in the eighteenth century distinguished between their "little and their great families," with the former referring to their children and the latter including servants (*The Rise of the Egalitarian Family*, 129). Over the course of the century, skepticism about servants grew—with stories of them introducing children to masturbation, or the maid acting as "a standing invitation to experimentation"—and the great family came to be seen as a threat to the little one (129–130).

[2] Flandrin, *Families in Former Times: Kinship, Household and Sexuality*, 4.

[3] See also McKeon, *Secret History of Domesticity*, 120.

[4] Perry, *Novel Relations*, 2.

[5] Perry, *Novel Relations*, 237.

[6] Chase and Levenson, *The Spectacle of Intimacy*, 4.

for the proper functioning of the household organism."[7] In Imperial Russia, there were various mutually exclusive meanings of "family" that were based on context. Here I draw on the five provided by Jessica Tovrov:

1. All persons recognized as related by blood and marriage within a certain degree set by the individual himself, the Orthodox Church, law, or tradition. This might or might not include dead relatives.
2. All persons recognized as related by blood (except persons born illegitimately) and/or marriage within the limits mentioned in 1. This includes affines, persons who do not share a blood relationship.
3. All persons who live together in one house (or houses which are seen as a unit of some kind). This might or might not include serfs.
4. All persons recognizing the same person as "head of the family."
5. All persons sharing a joint experience, e.g., service, school, or in a more diffuse way, a good friend.[8]

This list makes clear the conflicting or intersecting definitions of kin based on biology, legal kinship, and voluntary or elective kinship. Tovrov argues that in Russia blood ties were less important than behavior in establishing kinship, and that this flexibility was mainly used to extend kinship as far as possible.[9]

One window into understanding how far kinship is thought to extend is how a society defines incest.[10] In both England and Russia, relations with anyone in the direct line of descent were always strictly forbidden (i.e. parents and children or grandchildren), but the limits of incest in other relations were hotly debated and the definitions changed in both countries over the course of the nineteenth century. Comparing these debates brings into focus the differing political and social concerns that shaped conceptions of the family in the two countries.

Incest had been a fraught issue in England since Henry VIII repeatedly challenged and changed the laws in order to free himself of certain marriages and legally enter into others in the attempt to produce an heir.[11] The guiding logic was concern for family futurity in the form of a male line.[12] In later centuries, the debate around incest would become more economic, focusing on first-cousin marriage

---

[7] Bessmertnyi, *Chelovek v krugu sem'i: ocherki po istorii chastnoi zhizni v Evrope do nachala novogo vremeni*, 303.

[8] Tovrov, *The Russian Noble Family*, 66–67.

[9] Tovrov, *The Russian Noble Family*, 70–72. This did not extend, however, to serf mistresses or illegitimate children had with serfs, any of whom were *not* considered part of the family.

[10] Eve Kosovsky Sedgwick literally calls it "the boundary...between inside and outside the family" ("Tales of the Avunculate," 70).

[11] In the first case, this involved divorcing Catherine of Aragon (widow of his deceased brother) through tightening incest law, while later, in order to marry Catherine Howard, he needed to loosen the law and to legalize marriage between first cousins by blood or in-law (Pollak, *Incest and the English Novel, 1684–1814*, 28–31).

[12] Given all the frequent changes, by the end of his time on the throne most people in England were no longer clear on what counted as incest, so to help clarify the matter the Table of Kindred and Affinity

and the 1835 Marriage Act, which forbade a man from marrying his deceased wife's sister. The aristocracy wished to consolidate their wealth through allowing cousin marriages, particularly on the paternal side: the eldest brother's daughter to the next brother's son (keeping wealth and title together). The middle class wanted marriages between close affines (for instance, with a deceased wife's sister) as a way to move up the social ranks.[13]

Both these types of marriages indicate a weakening of consanguinial ties. Allowing first-cousin marriage "is to assume," in Perry's words, "that there is no sibling unity that transcends generations and that the sibling tie is dissolved by adulthood and marriage."[14] Marriage to a sister-in-law challenges the idea that marriage had created kinship between the original couple, making the husband and wife "one flesh."[15] Karen Chase and Michael Levenson argue that the desire for marriage to a sister-in-law also reflects the "growing isolation and detachment of the middle-class home" and a "shy unwillingness to venture beyond the cozy hearth in order to find a new wife and, often more pressing, a new mother for the children"—both of which, in turn, reinforce a bounded vision of family.[16]

In Russia, where no tsar ever used incest law to wriggle in and out of marriages like Henry, the debates about incest were played out among the intelligentsia and the Church. The focus was not on the future line, but on the present sanctity of the family, broadly construed. From the Medieval period into the nineteenth century, marriage was under the control of the Orthodox Church, which defined incest more rigidly than in Judaism or Catholicism, forbidding marriages between individuals related in the sixth degree by consanguinity (second cousins), the fourth degree by affinity (spouses' siblings), and also close spiritual relatives.[17] In January 1810, the Church loosened this, setting the limit at the fourth degree by consanguinity.[18] When the Russian government began to standardize its legal system, it essentially left marriage in the hands of the Church, and the section on incest in the first Code of Laws (*Svod Zakonov*)—which appeared in 1832—does not explicitly state which degree of consanguinity or affinity was considered acceptable, relying on Church designations. Of all the marriage annulments between 1836 and 1860,

---

was publicly displayed in every church and was printed in the Book of Common Prayer. See Hudson, *Sibling Love and Incest in Jane Austen's Fiction*, 14; Pollak, *Incest and the English Novel, 1684–1814*, 31.

[13] Trumbach, *The Rise of the Egalitarian Family*, 18–19.

[14] Perry, *Novel Relations*, 121.

[15] Perry, *Novel Relations*, 20.

[16] Chase and Levenson, *The Spectacle of Intimacy*, 109. They note that for the more wealthy, households were more expansive and when the wife fell ill, her sister was a less indispensable source of aid, as nurses, governesses and servants could be hired, so the desire for legalizing marriage to a deceased wife's sister would be weaker.

[17] Pushkareva, *Women in Russian History: From the Tenth to the Twentieth Century*, 31; M. Krasnozhen, *Tserkovnoe Pravo*, 219–223.

[18] Krasnozhen, *Tserkovnoe Pravo*, 221.

12.2% were for kinship (incest), indicating that the law was actually enforced, and therefore of consequence.[19]

During the reform era, incest was also being debated in the popular press.[20] Economics seems to have been a much lesser concern than in England. Given that Russian women had far greater property rights than English women and that the Russians did not honor primogeniture but instead split estates among their children, there was little incentive to consolidate wealth through "marrying in," making first-cousin marriages less economically desirable. The laws on incest were not based on concerns about heredity and inbreeding, as evidenced by the fact that spiritual kin (godparents and godchildren) were treated the same under the law as biological kin.[21] Instead of all these factors, religious concerns about the sanctity of the family appear to have taken precedence. Russian law was stricter about affinal ties (that is, between in-laws) than in the West, because, according to the Orthodox Church, when a couple marries, they become "flesh of one flesh," making their relatives also kin.[22] This was not the case in England, where familial relations only extended to the married couple and their kin on each side.[23] So the laws on incest reveal a more expansive vision of family in Russia that included biological, legal, and spiritual kin, versus a more restricted definition in England, with greater focus on the future of the line.

Vertical vs. Lateral Family Models

The logic governing incest laws underpins the central claim of this book: that the English emphasized a vertical, diachronic model of family, while the Russians' approach was more lateral and synchronic, expanding in the here and now. The clearest example of this vertical/lateral distinction is in the inheritance customs

---

[19] Freeze, "Bringing Order to the Russian Family," 724.

[20] See, for example: M. Filipov, "Vzgliad na russkie grazhdanskie zakony" *Sovremennik* №2 (1861): 530–531; "Vrednyia sledstviia brachnykh coiuzov mezhdu blizkimi rodstvennikami" *Dushepoleznoe chtenie* (January 1863): zametki 1–7; "Brak v blizkikh stepeniakh rodstva" *Pravoslavnoe obozrenie* 7 (July 1863): zametki 176–177. To clarify any confusions about the topic, S. Grigorovskii provided a guide for Church practitioners on which relations were legally allowed to wed: "Rodstvo i svoistvo, kak prepiatstviia k braku, po nyne deistvuiushchim uzakoneniiam" *Tserkovnyi vestnik* № 46, 47 (1892).

[21] Studies of the adverse effects of close-kin marriage were being carried out in Europe, and Russian authors frequently cited their statistics. Some, backing the strictness of Russian law, promoted findings of high rates of deaf-mutes and other types of birth defects and illnesses arising from close-kin marriages (ex. "Vrednyia sledstviia brachnykh coiuzov mezhdu blizkimi rodstvennikami" *Dushepoleznoe chtenie* [January 1863]). Others challenged the validity of the statistics (ex. "Brak mezhdu blizkimi rodstvennikami (po A. Gëtu i Dzh. Darvinu)" *Znanie* 3 [1876]: 82–116). None of this directly touched Russian law, as the studies did not compare outcomes for differing degrees of close kinship. Also, the strictness of Russian law was more in the handling of affinial and spiritual kin than blood relations.

[22] Krasnozhen, *Tserkovnoe Pravo*, 222.

[23] Wolfram, *In-Laws and Outlaws: Kinship and Marriage in England*, 17. See also: Perry, *Novel Relations*, 32, 119–120.

each society created.[24] The English practice of giving all property to the primo-genitor both reflected and enforced a linear understanding of the family; wealth and title were to be kept together and passed down to a single heir who would continue the line. According to Zouheir Jamoussi, the English viewed the custom of primogeniture as a safeguard "against the disintegration of patrimony and fam-ily."[25] He further reminds us that the system "was at the service, not of individuals but of patrilineal families. It was aimed at perpetuating the power and prestige of families over generations..."[26] Samuel Johnson (1709–1784) articulated this view when he was challenged for suggesting that the profligate owner who was ruining a great Scottish family estate should die. Replying to the accusation that he preferred the estate to its owner, Johnson claimed "Nay Madam, it is not a preference of the land to its owner, it is the preference of a family to an individual. Here is an estab-lishment in a country, which is of importance for ages, not only to the chief but to his people; an establishment which extends upwards and downwards; that this should be destroyed by one idle fellow is a sad thing."[27] Johnson's "upwards and downwards" captures the verticality of the family and its expansion on the tem-poral axis. The focus on futurity and accrual also reflects England's fully evolved capitalist economic system.

Views like Johnson's, while typical, were not universal, however. The opposite opinion was articulated by Thomas Paine (1737–1809) in his *Rights of Man* (1791), where he attacked eldest sons: "They begin life by trampling on all their younger brothers and sisters, and relations of every kind, and are taught and educated so to do. With what ideas of justice or honour can that man enter a house of legislation, who absorbs in his own person the inheritance of a whole family of children, or doles out to them some pitiful portion with the insolence of a gift?"[28] Thinkers like Paine held that second (and third) sons were like second-class citizens. What is at stake in this debate—and the fact that primogeniture remained the custom throughout the nineteenth century despite criticisms—is a system of values that

---

[24] Here I am guided by anthropologists like Jack Goody, who claims that: "The linking of patterns of inheritance with patterns of domestic organization is a matter not simply of numbers and formations but of attitudes and emotions. The manner of splitting property is a manner of splitting people; it creates (or in some cases reflects) a particular constellation of ties and cleavages between husband and wife, parents and children, sibling and sibling, as well as between wider kin" ("Introduction" to *Family and Inheritance*, 3).

[25] Jamoussi, *Primogeniture and Entail in England*, 16. Jamoussi provides an excellent summary of the debates about primogeniture from the seventeenth to nineteenth century. The custom faced criticisms and was a source of debate, but remained in practice till 1925.

[26] Jamoussi, *Primogeniture and Entail in England*, 41. Similarly, Lawrence Stone notes: "There was a strong sense of moral obligation felt by most great landowners, first that they were no more than trustees for the transmission intact of their patrimony according to the rule of primogeniture and second, that all their children were entitled to a fixed and guaranteed monetary share" (Qtd. in Nunokawa, *The Afterlife of Property: Domestic Security and the Victorian Novel*, 79).

[27] Quoted in Jamoussi, *Primogeniture and Entail in England*, 112.

[28] Quoted in Jamoussi, *Primogeniture and Entail in England*, 118.

places the family above the individual and defines the family not as a conglomeration of kin in the present, but as a linear, genealogical progression.[29] The ultimate value is the future of the line: the singular heir who will inherit this property and, in turn, pass it on to the next generation, hopefully augmented but certainly not diminished.

The growing nineteenth-century English obsession with things that could be passed down through the family provides additional evidence of the vertical family model. Take, for instance, the increasing importance of family names in this period. Up to the eighteenth century only the nobility could claim a stable family name that went back to earlier centuries, and even in the eighteenth century names were often attached to the land rather than the family (and many of the poor had only a first name or nickname). But in the nineteenth century, surnames became important to people. According to John R. Gillis, "Names became a family's symbolic link with its past and the promise of its future."[30] Along with this interest in names, people also became obsessed with family history. Pedigree had long been a concern for the aristocracy, but now the middle-class, too, became enthralled by genealogy.[31] Beginning in the eighteenth century, family portraiture became another way of recording and displaying family history, and noble families attempted to fill out their collections to provide viewers with a sense of "unbroken descent."[32] In art historian Kate Retford's words, these portrait collections "had to demonstrate or at least imply the existence of worthy ancestors and the successful and repeated passing of name, estate and title from father to son."[33] Heirlooms—another vertical link to the family across time—also came into vogue amongst the middle class in the mid-nineteenth century. The Russian language, by contrast, has no word for "heirloom."[34]

---

[29] As John Stuart Mill opined: "So much are the power and dignity of the class the first object, that to it are sacrificed the interests and wishes of the very persons who for the time being represent the class." Mill, "Speech on Land Tenure Reform," May 15, 1871 (qtd. in Jamoussi, *Primogeniture and Entail in England*, 113).

[30] Gillis, *A World of Their Own Making*, 75.

[31] James Kilroy notes ways the middle class "came to evince the same pride in family lineage to support a claim that their newly recognized status had been long deserved" (*The Nineteenth Century Novel*, 100). Practices included Scottish families wearing tartan to connect them to noble ancestry, scouring church records for illustrious ancestors, adding "Junior" to the names of eldest sons, or listing their names as "the Fourth or Fifth" to prove the family's status was not recently acquired (100).

[32] Retford, *The Art of Domestic Life*, 166.

[33] Retford, *The Art of Domestic Life*, 166. Retford points to Jonathan Richardson's *Sir Nathaniel Curzon, 4th Bt., his Wife, Mary Assheton, and their Son, Nathaniel* (1727–1730) as an example that reinforces this idea. The upper left-hand corner of the painting features an angel child whom Retford takes to represent the eldest son, Jonathan, who died at age two or three. "Thus the portrait clearly emphasises that, despite the death of the eldest son, the family name will continue down the proper route of primogeniture" (174).

[34] The closest equivalent is *famil'naia tsennost'* (family valuable), but this lacks the link to heirloom's original meaning of "A chattel that, under a will, settlement, or local custom, follows the devolution of real estate" (*Oxford English Dictionary*).

Rather than thinking across time, the Russians focused on all their kin in the present. Their traditional inheritance practice involved splitting estates amongst their children, while keeping the immovable property within the family group. Russian nobles had two kinds of property leading up to 1714: patrimonial estates that were either inherited (*rodovaia votchina*) or earned through service (*vysluzhennaia votchina*), and acquired estates (*kuplennaia votchina*)—land purchased from another clan.[35] Like the English—as epitomized in the quotation from Johnson above—the Russians considered patrimonial estates as belonging to families rather than to individuals, but they conceived of the family as a group or clan (*rod*) in the present. Thus proprietors were more like custodians than absolute owners, and the property "a resource to be used for family purposes...that provided support, however inequitable, for each of its members."[36] Acquired estates could be disposed of as the owner wished, but once they had been bequeathed to a family member they became patrimonial and then fell under the same restrictions.

The Russians' animosity toward primogeniture was brought into the open in 1714 when Peter the Great introduced a Law of Single Inheritance that upended centuries of tradition. The response was virulent.[37] Lee Farrow argues that the nobility considered the new law "an infringement on their ability to provide for their family members and protect their families' political and social interests...hurting family preservation and the future of their children."[38] In Farrow's analysis, the gentry's opposition centered on moral as well as social and political factors. Parents felt responsible for providing for *all* their children, and in Russia there were few socially acceptable alternatives to land ownership for younger sons.[39] According to the memoirist Major Mikhail Danilov (1722–1790), "inequality between children disturbed the tender parents' hearts."[40] On the social

---

[35] Marrese, *A Woman's Kingdom*, 19. The hereditary estates could only be bequeathed to a restricted circle of kin (and in order to sell, the permission of brothers and other male kin was required). There were also service estates (*pomest'e*) granted by the sovereign in return for military service, but they could only be enjoyed during the owner's lifetime and could not be sold or bequeathed. Peter the Great's Law of Single Inheritor abolished the distinction between these different kinds of property (20). See also Pushkareva, *Women in Russian History*, 106–112.

[36] Marrese, *A Woman's Kingdom*, 7–8.

[37] One of the characters in Leskov's *A Decayed Family* (1851) gives a diatribe summarizing this position (5:107).

[38] Farrow, *Between Clan and Crown*, 72.

[39] Farrow, *Between Clan and Crown*, 88. This concern was captured in a memoir-like piece in *Russian Herald*, "The Baklanov Family (From My Reminiscences)" (1875). The author described the worried thoughts of the Baklanov father as he imagines having a second son and being forced to split Baklan: "In one set of hands this is a grand (*barskoi*) estate: with it, one can maintain the brilliance of our name and preserve a completely independent position; but in this case [of a second son] Baklan will become two manor houses and will be a real representative of the Baklanov clan (*rod*). If Baklan is given in its entirety to the older son, on condition that he make a payment to the younger son in accordance with the appraisal [of the estate], would that be legal and fair?" N. G. Chaplygin. "Semeistvo Baklanovykh. (Iz moikh vospominanii). Gl. I-X.)" *Russkii vestnik* 1875, № 6 (June), 708–786 (here 716–717).

[40] Qtd. in Farrow, *Between Clan and Crown*, 88.

scale, noble families relied on having a network of well-connected kin, so partible inheritance was helpful in enabling more sons to be noble landowners and to exert influence in society and government. Women were also important representatives of their families, so parents wished to provide them with substantial dowries that could enable matches that in turn furthered the family's interests. All these family concerns were threatened by Peter's law.

Continually thwarted and sidestepped by the hostile nobility while it was in force, the Law of Single Inheritance was repealed by Anna Ioannovna in 1731, shortly after she ascended to the throne. The senate report of December 9, 1730 advising her to do so argued that "it is not only natural but also commanded by divine law that fathers reward each of their children with equal shares."[41] And further, it claimed that the law had created "hatred and quarrels among brothers and drawn out litigation involving substantial losses and ruin for both sides."[42] These moral arguments again focused on familial relations in the present, rather than future wealth. In her repeal, Anna called the law "contrary to God's justice."[43]

Even as the law was done away with, many noble families were already suffering from the kind of impoverishment Peter I had hoped to avoid. And yet, they did not seem deeply concerned about the material legacy they were passing on to heirs. According to Arcadius Kahan, the decline from 1762 to 1834 in the number of serf-owners with more than 1,000 serfs was due to spending on luxury goods, education, and travel.[44] In making economic decisions, their time horizon (the distance they were willing or able to look into the future) was low. Alexander Gerschenkron links this to Russia's economic backwardness, and further shows that in Russian literature a high time horizon—often associated with thrifty and virtuous Germans—was depicted as "downright un-Russian."[45] A visitor to Russia in 1843 noted that "money is made and spent almost immediately."[46] The nobles were not trying to increase their capital to enhance the prestige of their heirs. Their more feudal economic system was not centered around accrual and the delay of gratification. Instead of going "upwards and downwards," their concerns seemed to be more rooted in the present. This may be the reason concerns about wills and inheritance play a much less significant role in Russian novels than in English ones.[47]

---

[41] Qtd. in Farrow, *Between Clan and Crown*, 89.
[42] Qtd. in Farrow, *Between Clan and Crown*, 89.
[43] Qtd. in Farrow, *Between Clan and Crown*, 90.
[44] Kahan, "The Costs of Westernization in Russia," 46.
[45] Gerschenkron, "Time Horizon in Russian Literature," 695–696.
[46] August Haxthausen, qtd. in Kelly, *Refining Russia*, 93.
[47] Russian characters spend far less energy struggling over the fate of their relatives' property. Onegin blithely accepts his uncle's estate, just as Olga (the heroine of Shalikova's *Two Sisters*) calmly accepts that her father and stepmother are squandering her inheritance from her deceased mother. The struggle over Count Bezukhov's will at the start of *War and Peace* reads like a foreign import plot, and the central beneficiary, Pierre, fails to understand what is even going on.

The weakening of the vertical family axis in the eighteenth century was also due to government policies around education. Wishing to create an enlightened new generation, Peter the Great removed sons from their families and put them in schools. Catherine the Great would expand upon this, creating schools for girls as well as boys. In the early nineteenth century, Alexander I increased the number of institutions. As education was made affordable and provided training for government positions, many families sent their children to boarding schools, possibly "loosening the moral and spiritual ties between parents and children."[48] Handing off their children first to serf nurses and then to educational establishments set up by the crown, parents were literally not held responsible for the upbringing of the next generation.

Political Order and Stability

The English focus on futurity versus the Russian emphasis on the present can be explained by a more fundamental distinction between the two societies: stability, or lack thereof. Giving all the family's wealth to a single heir is only an effective and desirable strategy for family continuity if one can be certain that said heir will be able to maintain control of the estate. In England, the rule of law provided a foundation for everything in the gentry way of life. Edmund Burke (1729–1797) relied on this sense of stability in justifying the English system of "considering their most sacred rights and franchises as an *inheritance*" rather than them being based "on abstract principles 'as the rights of men.'"[49] Burke attempted to fortify England against the type of dangerous thinking that inspired the French Revolution in part through drawing an analogy between the state and the family. Liberties, he claimed, were "an *entailed inheritance* derived to us from our forefathers, and to be transmitted to our posterity...We have an inheritable crown; an inheritable peerage; and a house of commons and a people inheriting privileges, franchises, and liberties, from a long line of ancestors."[50] This whole line of argument is based on an unshakeable belief in the stability of the English system.[51] As E. P. Thompson writes, "Take law away, and the royal prerogative, or the presumption of the

---

[48] Elnett, *Historic Origin and Social Development of Family Life in Russia*, 60.

[49] Burke, *Reflections on the Revolution in France*, 118.

[50] Burke, *Reflections on the Revolution in France*, 119.

[51] England also had its share of instability. With rapid industrialization and a growing working class who were not reaping the benefits of the country's growing prosperity, the Chartist movement arose in the 1830s, pushing for political reform and sometimes resorting to violent tactics that created a feeling of unrest and fear of the types of revolutions that swept Europe in 1848. Jan-Melissa Schramm links the traumas endure by England in the nineteenth century—Chartist protests, repeated cholera epidemics, the Crimean War—to the desire for narratives that conclude on a note of resolution and forgiveness, "mercy rather than judgement, reconciliation rather than conflict" (*Atonement and Self-Sacrifice in Nineteenth-Century Narrative*, 36).

aristocracy, might flood back upon their properties and lives; take law away and the string which tied together their lands and marriages would fall apart."[52]

In the land of the tsars, where the Tsar could bestow fortunes but also taketh away, there was no guarantee that a family's estate one day would still belong to it the next, so such a logic was impossible. While Burke could argue that "By a constitutional policy, working after the pattern of nature, we receive, we hold, we transmit our government and our privileges, in the same manner in which we enjoy and transmit our property and our lives," Russian nobles had no guarantee to the transmission of either.[53] One must remember that the Russian Empire had *no constitution* until 1906.[54]

In the early eighteenth century, the wealthiest and most powerful aristocrats regularly fell into disgrace and had their estates confiscated at the discretion of the crown. Of the twenty-nine nobles who owned more than 3,000 male serfs, ten suffered a total confiscation of their property, and of the nobles with more than 1,000 male serfs, a quarter would experience a confiscation during their careers. In addition, forty-seven were stripped of their rank and sent to a distant post or into exile.[55] In such a system, spreading around the family's assets was actually a more adaptive strategy for family survival.[56] Informal family and patronage networks could provide some protection, but no true security if a member of the family fell out of favor.[57] At a very basic level, the lack of stability contributed to the present-oriented outlook of the Russians. If one might not be here tomorrow, if everything one has been building might be wiped out, then it becomes natural to place value on the present, rather than the future.[58]

Russian elites knew that they were always subject to the will of the autocrat, in whose interests it was to keep aristocratic families from gaining too much power. Dominic Lieven notes that, unlike in Russia, in England the aristocracy "were a ruling class in the full sense of the word," serving in Parliament and as justices of

---

[52] Thompson, *Whigs and Hunters*, 264. Thompson notes that there were occasions when the government itself lost in courts and "such occasions served, paradoxically, to consolidate power, to enhance its legitimacy, and to inhibit revolutionary movements" (265).

[53] Burke, *Reflections on the Revolution in France*, 120.

[54] This absence and the documents that filled parts of the function of a constitution are discussed by Bella Grigoryan, *Noble Subjects*, 11–12. The introduction to her book gives a solid overview of the insecurities of noble status and rights. See also Elnett, *Historic Origin and Social Development of Family Life in Russia*, 51.

[55] These statistics come from Wirtschafter, *Social Identity in Imperial Russia*, 30.

[56] I am grateful to Margarita Vaysman for first drawing my attention to this connection.

[57] Farrow, *Between Clan and Crown*, 57. Farrow also compares Russia with Western Europe, noting that noble families in the west often had "very close ties to the land, passing family property from generation to generation more or less intact, and attaching the name of the estate to the family name," while "Russian nobles never developed strong attachments to individual estates" (*Between Clan and Crown*, 69).

[58] Simon Franklin points to Russia's unstable conception of its own history. Debates about its place in the movement of "universal time" gained force in the 1830s in response to German Romantic philosophy. Petr Chaadaev's very influential "First Philosophical Letter" (1836) actually claimed Russia had "no proper history at all" (Franklin, "Russia in Time," 17).

the peace in the counties.[59] They also shared a more coherent sense of values and cultural life, an example of which is the tradition of the English country estate. With deep ties to the land going back for centuries, the English gentry was in a strong position to defend its property rights and put money and emotional investment into its country houses, which were a major source of pride. In contrast, John Randolph argues, the Russian nobility "was a service nobility of relatively recent origin" and lacked this secure base. Service obligations took gentry men away from the land and led to an "absentee-owner mentality, and little emotional or financial investment in the country estate."[60] So while the English estate was another source of stability, buttressed by centuries of tradition, Russia's estates were in a more precarious position and could not serve as the same kind of conservative anchor.

Furthermore, both political and administrative factors contributed to Russians' sense of instability. On the political front, Peter I "institutionalized instability" through decreeing that the sovereign could select his or her own successor, which immediately challenged the idea of divinely ordained power.[61] And Russia's Tsars proved vulnerable. Two were assassinated: Peter III and Paul (who was murdered after ending dynastic uncertainty by enacting an ordered succession). Nicholas I had to quell two rebellions by military officers, and—shortly after the period of this study—Alexander II was assassinated by radicals after several failed attempts. One of those attempts, by Dmitri Karakazov (on April 4, 1866), became linked in the public imagination with the Time of Troubles (1603–1613), when a series of "False Dmitris" attempted to take the throne of Russia. The 1860s–1870s saw a flourishing of interest in pretenders—most famously in Musorgsky's opera *Boris Godunov* (1869, 1872) and Dostoevsky's *Demons* (1872)—which either added to, or at the very least reflected, the feeling of political instability.[62]

Instability of the political order would bleed into problems of administering the empire. Peter I's attempt to combine personal absolutism with the rule of laws created a tension that was never fully resolved. And given the vastness of the empire and the very practical limits to the sovereign's ability to govern all that territory, much depended upon individual discretion and decisions made at the local level. Elise Wirtschafter points to the "chronic discrepancy between resources and intentions [that] perpetuated personalized authority, even as explicit rules of administration promoted uniformity and delimited arbitrariness."[63] With no clear distinction between lawmaking and administration, "administrators became de facto lawmakers ... whose pronouncements could be overturned by superiors at multiple levels of review, reaching from provincial offices all the way to the

[59] Lieven, "The Elites," 228.
[60] Randolph, "The Old Mansion," 730.
[61] Wirtschafter, *Social Identity in Imperial Russia*, 4.
[62] See Emerson, "Pretenders to History: Four Plays for Undoing Pushkin's Boris Godunov"; Frey, "Boris Godunov and the Terrorist."
[63] Wirtschafter, *Social Identity in Imperial Russia*, 7.

throne."[64] In such a context, it is understandable that the Russian gentry would not think about the family in terms of a long-term, stable progression where everything created or acquired by one generation could be passed on to the next and down through the ages. Yet such a way of thinking has long been treated as foundational to novels' family plots, and their underlying structure.

The Importance of Ancestry in the Novel

In the nineteenth-century English novel, the family into which one was born is central to defining a character's identity.[65] As George Eliot observes in the opening line of *Silas Marner* (1861), "No one knew where wandering men had their homes or their origin; and how was a man to be explained unless you at least knew somebody who knew his father and mother?" (3). So that the reader could "know his father and mother," *David Copperfield* (1849–1850) famously begins with a chapter entitled "I am born," devoted entirely to the family backstory of its protagonist. While that may be extreme, most novels rely on such a system of identification. Poking fun at this obsession with lineage as a pre-determiner of identity, Samuel Butler opines in *The Way of All Flesh* (1873–1884), "If a man is to enter the Kingdom of Heaven, he must do so, not only as a little child, but as a little embryo, or rather as a little zoosperm—and not only this, but as one that has come of zoosperm which have entered into the Kingdom of Heaven before him for many generations" (212).

The scientific metaphor is not misplaced, and can also be seen in the parallels between the genealogical obsession of Victorian fiction and the master-narrative woven by Charles Darwin about "origins" and "descent."[66] In *The Origin of Species* (1859), Darwin attempted to draw a more complete family tree, one that would, in Gillian Beer's words, "restore man to his kinship with all other forms of life."[67] Darwin himself compared the complexity of piecing together the family tree of "an ancient and noble family" with naturalists' struggle to trace the affinities between species. While telling a story about origins and genealogical progression, Darwin was also concerned with variation and interconnectedness, shifting from vertical metaphors to lateral ones that emphasized interrelations. "One of the most disquieting aspects of Darwinian theory was that it muddied descent, and

---

[64] Wirtschafter, *Social Identity in Imperial Russia*, 7.

[65] In the words of Sophie Gilmartin, "an individual's definition of self, his or her assertion of social existence, begins with the family tree" (*Ancestry and Narrative in Nineteenth-Century British Literature*, 3).

[66] In the introduction of *Darwin's Plots*, Gillian Beer describes the "process of naturalisation" through which Darwin's ideas came to "provide a determining fiction by which to read the world" (2). Later she links Darwin's theories specifically to the family metaphor: "Succession and inheritance form the 'hidden bond' which knits all nature past and present together, just as succession and inheritance organise society and sustain hegemony" (196).

[67] Beer, *Darwin's Plots*, 57.

brought into question the privileged 'purity' of the 'great family'. In terms of the class organisation of his time this is clearly a deeply unpalatable view."[68] Darwinian theory pushed against ideas that were foundational to English thought. Some novelists would follow Darwin in these concerns, but the dominant tradition still emphasized the vertical.

As with Butler's zoosperm entering the Kingdom of Heaven, so too with entering society: family background is paramount in the novel. When Miss Betty invites Miss Matty to a tea party in Gaskell's *Cranford* (1853), she explains that she has not yet asked Miss Pole, because "Of course, I could not think of asking her until I had asked you, Madam—the rector's daughter, Madam" (62). Matty's deceased father's position is enough to secure her pride of place. Mrs. Forrester will be invited to tea as well because "Although her circumstances are changed, Madam, she was born a Tyrrell, and we can never forget her alliance to the Bigges, of Bigelow Hall" (62). One's origin story becomes all-important in this vertically defined family system. Thus, as Lady Bracknell—the embodiment of polite Victorian values in Oscar Wilde's *The Importance of Being Earnest* (1895)—tries to determine whether Jack would be an eligible partner for her daughter, she is deeply dismayed by his *lack* of family origins when he admits to being found in a handbag at a train station.

LADY BRACKNELL. The cloak-room at Victoria Station?
JACK. Yes. The Brighton line.
LADY BRACKNELL. The line is immaterial. Mr. Worthing, I confess I feel somewhat bewildered by what you have just told me. To be born, or at any rate bred, in a hand-bag, whether it had handles or not, seems to me to display a contempt for the ordinary decencies of family life that reminds one of the worst excesses of the French Revolution.

As Sophie Gilmartin has noted, the irony in this exchange is that the *line* is far from immaterial; family line is Lady Bracknell's essential concern in selecting a suitor for her daughter.[69]

The truth of one's ancestry proves difficult to hide or repress in the English novel. Describing the proper choice of a bride in Trollope's *An Eye for an Eye* (1879), the narrator notes: "Sophia Mellerby was a tall, graceful, well-formed girl, showing her high blood in every line of her face" (42). Even when Bertie Cecil is serving as a common soldier under a false name in the French legion in Ouida's *Under Two Flags* (1867), everyone who meets him can immediately tell that he is a gentleman. Hidden truths will out. The neighborhood takes a strong dislike to Mr. Marchmont in Geraldine E. Jewsbury's *Constance Herbert* (1855), even though he is (falsely) introduced as a retired barrister of good family. As the local squire who

---

[68] Beer, *Darwin's Plots*, 57.
[69] Gilmartin, *Ancestry and Narrative in Nineteenth-Century British Literature*, 13.

knows that he is really the son of a horse-jockey tells him "instinct and nature cannot be deceived" (1:182). Therefore, acquiring land would do Mr. Marchmont no good: "You would never be received amongst these landed squires, had you the Chauntry lands and a dozen estates to boot" (1:183). In the world of the English novel at mid-century, one's worth flows in the blood one has inherited, though as the century progresses, this gradually begins to change.

In the Russian novel, ancestry was a fraught topic and did not carry such weight. While the English novel was considered a bourgeois genre, Russia lacked a bourgeoisie. Instead it had the gentry/nobility (*dvorianstvo*)—an estate/class notoriously difficult to define because of the tremendous range it encompassed.[70] In Russia, everyone was born into an estate/social status (*soslovie*), with girls inheriting the social rank of their father at birth and then acquiring their husband's at marriage (noble women could retain their status if they married a commoner, but could not pass it on to their children).[71] Gentry status in Russia was not only hereditary (customary), but could also be earned through service (legislated) and advancement up the Table of Ranks (such service was compulsory until 1762). While there was a small, wealthy core of aristocratic families from the seventeenth century who remained central to the ruling class through to the twentieth century, the imperial elite was still permeable and no family held proprietary control over any government office or position.[72]

With a synchronic model for gaining gentry status—present service—competing with the diachronic model of hereditary nobility, the significance and meaning of lineage had an ambivalent place in Russian culture. Under Catherine the Great, the *dvorianstvo* was turned into a "nobility" more along the lines of Western Europe, receiving greater privileges and honored status. As Catriona Kelly has shown, "Catherine's reign, then, witnessed an ambiguity creeping into the conception of upper-class status. Elevation to the *dvoryanstvo* on meritocratic grounds continued, but those with long family histories were encouraged to take pride in lineage."[73] Each province in Russia kept a genealogical listing of the local

[70] The Charter of the Nobility (1785) and the first Code of Laws (1832) identified six categories of nobility: 1. granted by the sovereign; 2. achieved by reaching commissioned officer rank (rank fourteen); 3. achieved by reaching rank eight in the civil service; 4. derived from membership in a foreign noble family; 5. belonging to a titled Russian noble family; 6. ancient wellborn untitled Russian noble family (Wirtschafter 23–24).

[71] Alison Smith provides a comprehensive analysis of the system of *soslovie*, the fluidity of the term's meaning, how the system was administered, and the procedures for and individual to change *soslovie* (*For the Common Good and Their Own Well-Being*).

[72] Wirtschafter, *Social Identity in Imperial Russia*, 22. Up until its abolition in 1861, serfdom was the primary source of labor on gentry estates, and wealth was often measured in "souls," or male serfs. Status was derived from proximity to the tsar, service rank, and number of serfs owned. Given the partible inheritance system, government service was an important source of education and salary that helped to forestall impoverishment of noble families. While at the upper end there were a tiny proportion of families with tremendous wealth, the vast majority of the gentry were poor, with many living at the same level as the peasants.

[73] Kelly, *Refining Russia*, 13.

families (*rodoslovnaia kniga*).[74] In the early nineteenth-century, Pushkin represented an ambivalence that would grow in society as a whole during the reform era. While he linked refinement and aristocratic status in "To a Grandee" (*K vel'mozhe*, 1830) in the same year, he wrote "My Family Tree," in which he "assult[ed] both the aristocracy's claim to hereditary legitimacy and its claims to cultivation" with biting parodies of many noble families.[75]

By the second third of the nineteenth century, the whole division of Russian society into levels was in flux, increasing the ambivalence about lineage. The genteel lifestyle of the true "aristocracy" was only affordable for a tiny minority, while the rest of the gentry who tried to maintain this type of gentility were rapidly outspending their annual incomes and sliding down the ladder in terms of wealth, leading to increased stratification.[76] And at the same time as the gentry were in decline, the richest merchants could afford many of the same accouterments of genteel existence that were rapidly slipping out of the grasp of most *dvoriane*, blurring the distinction (in terms of lifestyle) between the *dvorianstvo* and *meshchanstvo* (petit bourgeoisie or middling classes).[77]

In addition, there was a growing new category of *raznochintsy* (literally "people of various ranks") who are difficult to define, except that they were not members of other categories or communities. This group's members ranged from the sons of clergymen who did not follow their father's occupation, to non-noble civil servants, single householders, retired soldiers, the children of nobles who did not have hereditary nobility, scholars, artists, and others who fell outside the standard system of categorization.[78] With the *raznochintsy* added into the mix, the traditional boundaries of the estates began to break down and affiliations to form across them. The people who found themselves in this ambiguous middle were not, however, in concordance in their outlook on the significance of lineage. The Russian radicals would reject the importance of family origins and bloodline, while Slavophiles would fight to protect the importance of the *rod*. Dostoevsky explores this issue in *The Adolescent* (1875), where the protagonist, Arkady, is the legal son of a former serf, Makar Dolgoruky (and thus bears this princely name), but the biological son of Makar's former master, Versilov. *Not* a Dolgoruky prince, but also *not* a Versilov, Arkady struggles with the question of identity and the different

---

[74] I am grateful to Barbara Alpern-Engel for bringing this to my attention.

[75] Kelly, *Refining Russia*, 89.

[76] See Kahan, "The Costs of 'Westernization' in Russia." While Davidoff places the number of high society families in England at this time at 300–400 (*The Best Circles*, 20), Kelly argues that Russia had only a few dozen (*Refining Russia*, 101). In 1834 there were only 1,453 nobles who owned over 1,000 male serfs, and only 2,273 who had between 500–1,000 (the categories that qualified as well-to do). In 1858 they still account for 3% of serf owners, with 1,382 owning over 1,000 serfs and 2,421 owning 500–1,000. See Blum, *Lord and Peasant in Russia: From the Ninth to the Nineteenth Century*, 367–369. Smith notes that even with "significant economic downward mobility" it was hard to exit the gentry (*For the Common Good and Their Own Well-Being*, 9).

[77] Kelly, *Refining Russia*, 92–101.

[78] Wirtschafter, *Social Identity in Imperial Russia*, 63–64.

ways of conceiving kinship based on legal versus blood ties. He is a classic embodiment of the uncharacterizable and ephemeral middle class that Russia seemed to lack because it was small and difficult to classify.

Even when one's family origins are clearly delineated, characters in novels question their importance. In Natalia Shalikova's *Two Sisters* (1858), a countess trying to convince her young protégée to marry a wealthy man remarks "I'm not saying he's an aristocrat...but what does birth mean?" (1:280).[79] This question of "what birth means" receives open debate in Nikolai Leskov's *A Decayed Family* (1874), subtitled a "Family Chronicle." The novel/chronicle opens with the statement "Our kin-group (*rod*) was one of the most ancient kin-groups in Rus': all Protozanovs descended in a direct line from the first ruling princes, and under our family coat of arms one can see that it was not given to us in kindness, but belongs to us 'not by the charter' [i.e. not for service]" (5:5).

Yet while the chronicle begins by asserting the importance of the family's hereditary status as nobility, the central figure—the narrator's grandmother, Princess Varvara Nikanorovna—actively challenges this idea. She is greatly upset when a count claims that "true fidelity, like you want, Princess, can only be found in hereditary aristocracy" (5:106). This prompts the Princess—with whom the reader is meant to sympathize—to launch into a long speech attacking the behavior of Russia's great families—Tavrichesky, Dolgoruky, Tolstoy, Menshikov, Odoevsky, etc.—culminating in a description of Odoevsky's fall into abasement (renting out his serf choir and swiping cash off card tables) and the exclamation "If even a descendent of Rurik has sunk that low, then forgive me, but how are you supposed to get any sort of aristocracy out of that! No, that song and dance is of no profit to us: we need to remember that woe be it to him whose name is more important to him than his deeds" (5:107). The Princess' speech encapsulates the crucial opposition between family models I am arguing for; in choosing to value actions in the present over bloodline, the Princess epitomizes the Russian stance.

If value and self-definition are to be rooted in the present, and not inherited through the bloodline, this opens up new narrative possibilities for the family. Lateral bonds take on greater weight in the Russian novel, and characters are identified more by their present connections and conditions than their genealogy. For example, in *Anna Karenina* (1875–1878) Stiva Oblonsky introduces Levin to his colleagues as "A zemstvo activist, a new zemstvo man, a gymnast, lifts a hundred and fifty pounds with one hand, a cattle-breeder and hunter, and my friend, Konstantin Dmitrich Levin, the brother of Sergei Ivanych Koznyshev" (18:21/18). Stiva places all emphasis on attributes in the present, and the one family relation he mentions is brotherhood (to a half-brother with a different family name), rather

---

[79] Shalikova published *Two Sisters* under her pen name, E. Narskaya. Grigoryan humorously notes that "it is reported that [Kostanzhoglo,] the model landowner [in Gogol's *Dead Souls* Part Two] finds his ancestry irrelevant, because it has no application in agriculture" (*Noble Subjects*, 90).

than lineage. Similarly, we never learn anything about Anna Karenina's parents; her one defining consanguineal tie is to her brother, Stiva (who shares a penchant for adultery).[80] Explaining Bakhtin's views on Dostoevsky, Caryl Emerson makes a similar point that could hold for Russian literature generally: "What matters is not the evolution of an individual biography, but 'coexistence and interaction'—or as Bakhtin rapturously overstates the case, 'there is no causality in Dostoevsky's novels, no genesis, no explanations based on the past, on the influences of the environment or of upbringing ... Every act a character commits is in the present tense' (Bakhtin 28–29)."[81] Belonging to family also happens in the present.

The Russian Alternative to Family *Line*: the *Rod*

The closest term for family line in Russian, *rod*, can be translated as line, kin, clan, or genus, and is the root of the words "birth," "relative," "parent" (*roditel'*, literally: one who births you). So it refers to both the line of descent and to the expansive network of consanguineal kin. According to Judith Armstrong, the concept of the *rod* accounts for the centuries-old tradition of using kinship names in addressing strangers as well as the continued use of patronymics.[82] As George Fedotov (1886–1951) has famously argued, through using kinship terms for non-kin "all social life is shaped as an extension of family life and all moral relations among men are raised to the level of blood kinship."[83] We see this enacted in *War and Peace* (1865–1869) when Nikolai Rostov shows up in Voronezh in 1812 and the governor's wife "received Rostov like a close relation" and starts matchmaking for him, while he, in turn, calls her "*ma tante*," despite the lack of any legal kinship (12:17, 19/946, 948). Emphasizing the need for connection in the present, Nikolai Fyodorov (1829–1903) laid out a characteristically Russian doctrine of relatedness as the true goal of the human race. Fighting against the idea of progress—or any kind of futurity—he argued that people should strive not for self-preservation, but for the restoration of the life of the forefathers, a goal "opposed to progress."[84] His views had an important impact on writers like Tolstoy and Dostoevsky.

Not only was a wider kin-group given value, but the individual was also devalued in Russian society. Yuri Corrigan reminds us that there is no term for "self" in Russian, explaining that "The absence of such a term has been attributed to Russia's

---

[80] I do not mean to ignore the importance of characters' pasts. Diane Thompson's study of memory (*The Brothers Karamazov and the Poetics of Memory*) or Yuri Corrigan's study of repressed past trauma in Dostoevsky (*Dostoevsky and the Riddle of the Self*), for example, both indicate the importance of what a character has *lived through*. But that is different to an inherited worth via lineage.

[81] Emerson, "Polyphony and its Discontents."

[82] Armstrong, *The Novel of Adultery*, 39.

[83] Fedotov, *The Russian Religious Mind: Kievan Christianity*, 16. See also Tovrov, *The Russian Noble Family*, 72.

[84] Fyodorov, "The Question of Brotherhood or Relatedness," 51. The essays was originally published in 1906.

unique history in which the concept of individualism emerged later and with many more attendant difficulties than in Europe."[85] If in England, the rise of the Renaissance concept of "self" has been linked to matrimony coming to signify "the apex of the protagonist's growth," then it is significant that in Russia the individual was part of the larger whole of the *rod*.[86] This is not to suggest that Russian novels were not interested in individual selves, but that these selves are positioned in a lateral web of connections, not as singular representatives of a family line (characters who attempt to isolate themselves from such webs, like Raskolnikov or Anna Karenina, face dire consequences).

While this book focuses on a higher stratum of society, studies of peasants and rural gentry offer insights into the traditional roots of Russia's expansive kin networks. Paul Fredrich, for example, has found that extended households were common and "the status of relatives could be achieved by sharing in the daily work."[87] Furthermore, analyzing semantic structures, he shows that cousins were often referred to as siblings (cousin in Russian is literally "second-kin-sister" or "-brother," but the "second-kin" part can be dropped).[88] So a "cousin" could become a "brother" and "Brothers were bound by what appear to have been the strongest ideals of loyalty. Furthermore, the Russians had developed a number of analogous relationships, among them ritual siblinghood (*pobratimstvo*), which was sealed by exchanging the cross worn around the neck (*natél'nyi krest*). A total of fourteen alternative terms, some of them situationally definable, are listed by Dahl for the single status of ritual siblinghood."[89] The Slavophiles would latch onto this more traditional family model in defining Russia's uniqueness vis-à-vis the West.

Slavophile views of the family are often contrasted with those of Russia's radicals, but despite their vast differences they share an emphasis on the present. While the Slavophiles gave great importance to the *rod*, the radicals were dismissive of given family ties. In their more individualistic outlook, "pride in one's descent was considered absurd, and even familial piety was suspect, relationships of affect being regarded much more highly than ties of blood."[90] Slavophile depictions of the family highlight the need for an expansive network of kin in the here and now, rather than emphasizing *rod* as ancestry. Even Sergei Aksakov's *Family Chronicle* (1856), which, as a chronicle, must follow the progression of time, still shows the crucial role played by siblings and cousins in shaping family realities in the present. In the same way, rejecting familial piety as the radicals did also means defining oneself in the present. This emphasis on the present is a consistent feature in Russian texts.

---

[85] Corrigan, *Dostoevsky and the Riddle of the Self*, 12.
[86] Boone, *Tradition Counter Tradition*, 48.
[87] Friedrich, "Semantic Structure and Social Structure," 137–138.
[88] Fredrich, "Semantic Structure and Social Structure," 139–141.
[89] Fredrich, "Semantic Structure and Social Structure," 142.
[90] Kelly, *Refining Russia*, 104.

The Slavophiles also turned to Russian Orthodoxy to reinforce their communal vision. They made *sobornost'* (togetherness, "a spirit of universal brotherhood, a kind of noninstitutional, universal church"[91]) a central tenet of the religion.[92] As multiple scholars have noted, this idea of *sobornost'* was actually a mid-nineteenth-century invention. According to Steven Cassedy, the language of freedom and universal brotherhood that the Slavophiles used to describe Russian Orthodoxy actually derived from Hegel's descriptions of Lutheranism (which he claimed to be uniquely *German* in spirit).[93] For my purposes, it does not matter so much whether *sobornost'* was "authentic" to Russian Orthodoxy; the fact that it came into vogue and that many people *believed* it to be central to the religion is enough to indicate their belief in a communal Russian spirit.

This communal spirit is relevant to understanding the family because in Russia the family was less divided from the rest of the world than in the West, often viewed on a continuum, rather than placed in opposition.[94] Reinforcing this idea, a recent Russian literary critic noted that "[t]he great Russian novelists contrasted the family as an island—harmonious, but isolated from the rest of the world—with the concept of the family *as world* and the *universal* family, the family *as a small church* (S. Telegin), the family *as temple* (V.V. Rozanov) ... they each conceived of the ideal family not as cut off from the world of valleys and mountains, but wide open to it with all its human 'agitation and sorrows' (I. Goncharov)."[95]

Contrast this with the description of the English family provided by Dr. Carus in the introduction to the 1851 census report. He closes by explaining the importance of a separate dwelling as an expression of "that long-cherished principle of separation and retirement, lying at the very foundation of the national character." It is "that proud feeling of personal independence," Carus maintains, "which is stereotyped in the phrase, 'Every man's house is his castle.'"[96] In the English system, which emphasized family *line* and attempted to keep wealth and title together for a single heir to be passed down through the ages, the family had every incentive to guard its borders. Additional members meant the dissolution of property (even if only in the form of dowries or maintenance allowances for junior members and dependents). For the present-oriented Russians, everyone should be kin *now*.

[91] Cassedy, *Dostoevsky's Religion*, 25.
[92] See Esaulov, "*Sobornost'* in Nineteenth-Century Russian Literature"; Zenkovsky, "The Spirit of Russian Orthodoxy."
[93] Cassedy, *Dostoevsky's Religion*, 10.
[94] Tovrov, *The Russian Noble Family*, 108.
[95] V. A. Nedzvetskii, *Istoriia russkogo romana XIX veka*, 48.
[96] Qtd. in Chase and Levenson, *The Spectacle of Intimacy*, 3.

2

The Traditional Vertical Family Plot

But to have squandered the acres which have descended from gener-
ation to generation; to be the member of one's family that has ruined
that family; to have swallowed up in one's own maw all that should
have graced one's children, and one's grandchildren! It seems to me that
the misfortunes of this world can hardly go beyond that!
                                          — Anthony Trollope, *Framley Parsonage*

The nineteenth-century novel's principal subject matter and structuring mechanism is the family. And families, in turn, are shaped by the societies to which they
belong. In England, the family served as a primary mechanism for continuity and
stability with both private property and institutional rights being inherited and
passed down generation to generation. In Russia, with an all-powerful autocrat
and no constitution, such stable progression was not an assumed right. Families relied more on their present composition than on an inherited legacy. These
factors had a profound impact on shaping the novels of the two countries.

The first theorizers of the novel as a genre studied the English novel, and consequently our standard theories are in turn shaped by the English conception of
the family. These theories emphasize linear progression, rather than lateral expansion, in identifying two traditional plots: one focused on marriage and the other on
genealogy. This chapter will begin by exploring how scholars have linked family
and plot in the novel, first examining theories that emphasize a linear model, and
second theories that offer a lateral alternative. I will then turn not to the marriage
plot (to be discussed in Part II), but to consanguinal kin. Parent-child relations
have been the traditional focus for scholars, but I look instead to sisters and brothers, who seem to fall outside our standard family plots. The integration of siblings
into these plots can serve as a test case to reveal the narrative limits and possibilities for lateral expansion in each national tradition. How do our theories—and
the novels—account for them? Looking at the three possible dyads (sister/sister,
brother/sister, brother/brother) reveals the way English novels fit siblings into
their vertical plots. Russian novels were not restricted by the linearity of inheritance, thus challenging our standard theories and opening new plot potential for
siblings.

The Family Novel in Russia and England, 1800–1880. Anna A. Berman, Oxford University Press.
© Anna A. Berman (2022). DOI: 10.1093/oso/9780192866622.003.0003

Family Plots and Theory of the Novel

What constitutes a "family plot"? If we begin from Robert Belknap's most basic formulation, plot is "the organization of the incidents in a literary work," and, as he rightly notes, while the *fabula* may be "a multidimensional, intricately intercon- nected array where events may happen simultaneously," in a novel the *siuzhet* (the way the incidents are related in the text) must be linear because this is the manner in which the reader literally takes in the words of a text.[1] Most literary studies of the family have been guided by the linearity of the *siuzhet*, treating family plots as progressions from A to B: either from single to married or from one genera- tion to the next. These are the two standard family plots discussed by critics: the marriage plot and the generational plot. Both involve a legal act: matrimony, or the transfer of property and title through inheritance.[2] The marriage plot is tradi- tionally associated with women and tends to focus on the domestic sphere.[3] It is guided by passionate romantic love, which has a clear storyline from first meet- ing to courtship, engagement, and finally marriage, which presumes a new cycle of birth and maturation (its inverse is the adultery plot that moves from union to rupture). There is a clear conclusion and consummation to this plot that is built into its very structure.

The generational plot also has an organic progression, in this case from parents to children.[4] Indeed, many western scholars have claimed that the paradigmatic family plot of the nineteenth-century novel is vertical: tracing the progression of lineage, of one generation begetting the next, which will gradually supplant it.[5] Peter Brooks asserts that "the nineteenth-century novel as a genre seems to be inseparable from ... the issues of authority and paternity, which provide not only the matter of the novel but also its structuring force, the dynamic that shapes its

---

[1] Belknap, *Plots*, 17.

[2] Sharon Marcus summarizes these two approaches: "Some equate the novel's formal capacity to generate a sense of closure with its embrace of marriage as a social institution (Boone, DuPlessis). Others define the genre in terms of oedipal quests and conflicts that fuel narrative momentum (Barthes, Brooks)" (73).

[3] Classic studies that focus on the marriage plot include Boone, Calder, Hinz, and Tanner. This linking of the domestic sphere with women has led to men's role in the home often going overlooked (Tosh, *A Man's Place*, 2). Similarly, in studies of the English novel, men's role in the marriage plot tends to take second place.

[4] Studies that focus on the generational plot include Beizer, Brooks, Ragussis, Said, Shideler, and Tobin.

[5] As Roland Barthes rhetorically asks, "Doesn't every narrative lead back to Oedipus?" (*The Plea- sure of the Text*, 47). See also Broughton and Rogers, "Introduction: The Empire of the Father," esp. 6. *Dombey and Son* exemplifies this generational model of plotting. As Michal Peled Ginsburg writes of Mr. Dombey, he "sees history as a repetitive process by which a son joins and then replaces his father, to be then joined and replaced by his own son, to the end of time" ("House and Home," 59). While the novel undercuts this idea by showing that Dombey and Son "is indeed a daughter," this daughter restores the male line through her son Paul: "from his daughter, after all, another Dombey and Son will ascend," as Mr. Toots remarks (912, 946).

plot."[6] Others have noted the "congruity between time-line, family-line, and story-line," and the way themes around paternity, authority, legitimacy, and genealogy relate to formal aspects of the novel such as "mimesis, order, coherence, linearity, unity, closure and totalization."[7] Edward Said sees the project of novel writing itself as paralleling these concerns, emphasizing "the novel's paternal role—to author, father, procreate a rival reality" to our own.[8]

The generational plot focuses on traditionally male concerns about property, inheritance, and the continuity of the family name and family honor; these are male because it is men who carry on the family name, while women marry *out* of the family (thus Mr. Dombey is so focused on "and son" as to forget the existence of his daughter).[9] We find a bald explication of this inheritance theme in Geraldine Jewsbury's *Constance Herbert* (1855), where the novel's villain—the son of a jockey—is motivated by one ambition: "he determined that he too would found a family [like the noble ones around him], become a landed proprietor, and leave children, who should take root and establish themselves as a 'country family'" (1:218). In what I am calling the "generational plot," the drama comes either from the interloper trying to improve his family's future by worming his way into a higher class, creating a clash of classes, or from the conflict of generations within a family, creating clashes in ideology or values that either lead to a new order being ushered in or a reaffirmation of the patriarchal order (e.g. Turgenev's *Fathers and Children*, 1862).

Often the marriage and generational plots are inextricably intertwined, with the former running up against obstacles from the latter, as they rely on different values systems. The generational plot puts a premium on family name and standing above matters of the heart, favoring tradition and continuity over individuals' desires. For example, in Trollope's *An Eye for an Eye* (1879), the protagonist, Fred Neville, struggles between his duties as heir to the Earl of Scroope and his love of a penniless Irish Catholic beauty whom he has seduced. As he laments to his brother, "If it were only myself, I would give up all to her. I would, by heaven. But I cannot sacrifice the family" (257). While these values can clash, in many novels the marriage and generational plots are two sides of the same coin because they share an

---

[6] Brooks, *Reading for the Plot*, 65. Brooks calls paternity "a dominant issue within the great tradition of the nineteenth-century novel ... a principal embodiment of its concern with authority, legitimacy, the conflict of generations, and the transmission of wisdom" (63).

[7] Patricia Tobin, *Time and the Novel: The Genealogical Imperative*, ix; Janet Beizer, *Family Plots: Balzac's Narrative Generations*, 3.

[8] Said, *Beginnings: Intention and Method*, 152. Following canonical figures like Harold Bloom, Jane Spencer writes of the genealogy of literary history: "At the rhetorical level, kinship metaphors were an organizing principle of literary history. Literary tradition was understood as a genealogy in which individual writers figured as fathers and sons ..." (*Literary Relations*, 5). Russian literature is known for its belatedness and the incredible rapidity of its rise, which put its foundational figures in a fraternal, rather than parent-child relationship.

[9] See Sadrin, *Parentage and Inheritance in the Novels of Charles Dickens*, 9–12; Schor, *Dickens and the Daughter of the House*, 51.

ultimate goal: the formation of new nuclear families that will produce heirs and continue the family line.[10]

There are, however, alternatives to this linear, patriarchal model, ones that emphasize lateral bonds. The master family plot at the heart of the nineteenth-century Russian tradition embraced lateral spread. To some degree, this was due to Russian Realists' skepticism about linear plots. In Milton Ehre's words, they "viewed plot and tightly knit form as smacking of artfulness and artificiality …'[P]lots' could only obfuscate the rendering of 'real life.'"[11] Tolstoy is a prime exemplar. He explained his structuring idea for *Anna Karenina* (1875–1878) to Nikolai Strakhov as a "labyrinth of linkages," where his collection of thoughts are "linked to each other for their expression, but each thought, expressed in words separately, loses its meaning, is horribly decreased when it is taken alone from the linkages in which it was located" (62:269). Tolstoy focused on adjacencies rather than linearity, and on meanings that arise through these lateral linkages rather than through a linear plot progression. In family terms, *Anna Karenina* is built on three plots that are woven together through sibling bonds (Anna Karenina's brother, Stiva, is married to Dolly, whose sister, Kitty, ultimately marries Konstantin Levin).

Some scholars see this kind of expansive plotting in the Victorian multi-plot novel as well. Peter K. Garrett argues that the multi-plot form, which became popular in the 1840s–1870s, was aimed at "inclusiveness": "the large and densely populated worlds of most Victorian multiplot novels, the expansive effects produced by differences of situation and mode between their narrative lines, and the generalizing effects produced by similarities are all ways of achieving inclusiveness through multiplication."[12] Perhaps the best exemplar of this kind of expansiveness is the novels of George Eliot, and especially *Middlemarch* (1871–1872). As Gillian Beer has argued, Eliot "interrupts the movement toward resolution by revealing further and further affinities of event and feeling between characters who have no close personal relationship to each other."[13] This sounds much like Tolstoy's description of *Anna Karenina*'s labyrinth of linkages. Eliot was interested in diversity of experience; as she notes in the "Prelude" of *Middlemarch*, "the limits of variation are really much wider than anyone would imagine from the sameness of women's coiffure and the favourite love-stories in prose and verse" (4). The novel traces this Darwinian variation, beginning with two Brooke sisters who chart radically different courses. Yet even with all Eliot's attention to lateral variation and

---

[10] Tat'ianina, *Proza molodogo L. N. Tolstogo i problema semeinogo romana*, 136.

[11] Ehre, "A Classic of Russian Realism," 4.

[12] Garrett, *The Victorian Multiplot Novel*, 2. Similarly fighting against the view of the Victorian novel as "integrated, coherent, and conservative," Elaine Freedgood's *Worlds Enough: The Invention of Realism in the Victorian Novel* (2019) aims to "restore the Victorian novel's formal problems and its lack of formal coherence" (ix, x).

[13] Beer, *Darwin's Plots*, 152.

Darwin's "web of affinities," in her family plots she ultimately returns to a traditional model in her conclusions.[14] Both Brooke sisters end up happily married with children. While pushing boundaries with the form of her novels, Eliot still conforms to the propulsion toward wedlock and procreation that is the topic of Part II.

Despite the prevalence of multi-plot novels in England, most were not tracing "further and further affinities" like Eliot; instead they were simply multiplying the number of linear family plots they included. Trollope's *He Knew He Was Right* (1869), for example, has many strands, but they all are tied off with conjugal knots. This is not lateral plotting. As regards the English tradition, I agree with the general consensus among scholars that lateral plots were a modernist invention.[15] Exemplifying this view, Robert Caserio argues that the nineteenth-century novel displays "an analogy between family line and story line," while the modernist novel breaks with this, relying not on "the 'repressive central authority' of what we may call the family plot" but instead on making "the parts of a fictional discourse become adjacencies, juxtapositions."[16] Caserio's description of the modernist novel sounds like Tolstoy's description of *Anna Karenina*: "What truth the parts of such discourse reveal or uncover is not deliberately formed; their truth results from a disclosure rising up from the mutuality and adjacency of the parts."[17] While Caserio claims the shift from vertical to lateral was initiated by the modernists, clearly the Russians (and Eliot) were already relying on "fraternal" adjacencies in the nineteenth century.[18]

Reflecting perhaps these non-linear, Russian priorities, Mikhail Bakhtin created theories much more laterally driven than those of the great Western theorists. Caserio's conception of a novel based on adjacencies and juxtapositions resonates with Bakhtin's idea of the polyphonic novel—a genre he claims Dostoevsky created: "*A plurality of independent and unmerged voices and consciousnesses, a genuine polyphony of fully valid voices is in fact the chief characteristic of Dostoevsky's novels.*"[19] According to Bakhtin, the "fraternal" parts in Dostoevsky's novels (to use Caserio's term) are the ideas, each embedded in a human personality. "The idea begins to live, that is, to take shape, to develop, to find and renew its verbal expression, to give birth to new ideas, only when it enters into genuine dialogic relationships with other ideas, with ideas of *others*."[20] Polyphony also creates its

---

[14] On Eliot and Darwin's "web of affinities," see Beer, *Darwin's Plots*, 154.

[15] Fredric Jameson has argued for a shift from diachronic to synchronic in the Victorian novel, "not the fateful destiny of this or that privileged or at least narratively favored protagonist, but rather the immense interweaving of a host of such lots or fates" ("The Experiments of Time: Providence and Realism," 119).

[16] Caserio, *Plot, Story, and the Novel*, 234.

[17] Caserio, *Plot, Story, and the Novel*, 235.

[18] Caserio, *Plot, Story, and the Novel*, 235.

[19] Bakhtin, *Problem of Dostoevsky's Poetics* 6.

[20] Bakhtin, *Problem of Dostoevsky's Poetics* 88.

own novelistic structure. Like Tolstoy's "labyrinth of linkages" and Caserio's adja-cencies, Bakhtin's polyphonic novel is based on this lateral coexistence, rather than a linear sequence directed by a paternal, monologic source.

Bakhtin suggests that the very relationship between author and hero changes in the polyphonic novel. Rather than Said's dictatorial vision of author as father, "Dostoevsky, like Goethe's Prometheus, creates not voiceless slaves (as does Zeus), but *free* people, capable of standing *alongside* their creator, capable of not agreeing with him and even of rebelling against him."[21] Bakhtin and Caserio (and Tolstoy in his comments to Strakhov) are focused on laterality that is achieved through narrative form, but the idea of a plot built of "fraternal" adjacent parts can intrigu-ingly be applied more literally to the way Russian novelists constructed their own unique version of the "family plot" through their use of brothers.

Siblings do not have an integral role in linear family progression. Therefore, their integration into family plots helps lay bare the narrative limits and possi-bilities for lateral expansion in each national tradition. A sibling plot does not follow the Aristotelian progression of beginning, middle, conclusion, but creates meaning through a focus on the present. There is no designated goal or endpoint to being a sister or brother, no consummation of the bond. And unlike vertical structures, lateral conglomerates can keep expanding outward without movement forward. Such expansion was more of a structural challenge for the English than the Russians.

Accommodating Sisters

Scholars have widely acknowledged the significant role sister-sister relationships play in the English novel, but there is general agreement that sisters do not have their own plot. Sisterhood is expected to be stable—it exists before the novel begins, is usually unchallenged by the events that are unfolding, and will con-tinue after the happy resolution or tragic denouement has passed.[22] Even where the bond proves complicated, as, for example, in Harriet Martineau's *Deerbrook* (1839), there is no progression to a new state, but rather Hester learns more self-control and finds happiness in her marriage and ceases to test Margaret's love. Most scholars see sisters playing a role in the marriage plot. For example, even in

---

[21] Bakhtin, *Problem of Dostoevsky's Poetics* 6. This is a departure from his earlier ideas, expressed in *Author and Hero in Aesthetic Activity*, where he suggested that "The hero's consciousness, his feeling, and his desire of the world …are enclosed on all sides, as if within a band, by the author's *consummating* consciousness of the hero and his world; the hero's self-utterances are encompassed and permeated by the utterances of the author about the hero" (13).

[22] Sisters often provide a steady backdrop for the heroine. In *Daniel Deronda* (1876), "They hardly seem to matter at all in the plot, although their presence is crucial in the definition of Gwendolen's character" (Levin, *Suppressed Sister*, 30). The same could be said of the Meyrick sisters. Gwendolen's sisters follow Alex Woloch's pattern for minor characters: "continual subordination by the narrative and … resilient utility within it" (*The One vs. the Many*, 47).

her chapter entitled "The Sister Plots," Amy Levin suggests that the sister "plot" that interests Austen is indeed the sisters' role in the marriage plot.[23] Similarly, when Susan Lanser claims that in both *Sense and Sensibility* (1811) and *Pride and Prejudice* (1813), "Austen creates double plots, generating marriages for the sisters that preserve sisterhood," "plots" refers to marriage plots.[24] Lanser argues that heterosexual love had to be the driver of plot: "the conventions of fiction ... defined the heroine ... in terms of romantic ... intrigue. Had Austen even imagined the possibility of writing stories about contented single women with close female relationships, she would have earned hardly a shilling for her effort."[25] The Russians may not have gotten rich, but they certainly frequented this plot (though the women were not always so contented).

Sisters often serve a powerful if subordinate purpose in Austen's novels, what Sharon Marcus calls "the motor rather than the subject of the [marriage] plot," fulfilling this role in different ways.[26] For positive heroines, rescuing a sister or resolving her difficulties in the marriage plot can serve as proof of moral fortitude and worthiness while also advancing that plot (for example, Marian rescuing Laura in *The Woman in White*, 1859–1860; Molly Gibson rescuing her half-sister, Cynthia, in *Wives and Daughters*, 1864–1866; Nettie supporting her sister's family in Margaret Oliphant's *The Doctor's Family*, 1863).[27] Often, a sister's own marriage plot can directly facilitate or inhibit those of her sisters. Lydia Bennet's escapade with Wickham nearly ruins the prospect of the other Bennet sisters ever marrying (*Pride and Prejudice*), while in the inverse, as Mrs. Bennet anticipates a much-desired proposal from Mr. Bingley for her eldest, she congratulates herself that "It was, moreover, such a promising thing for her younger daughters, as Jane's marrying so greatly must throw them in the way of other rich men" (99). Reaping such a benefit, Nora Rowley is able to return from the Mandarins to England—and to the prospect of finding a husband—because she can live with her sister, Emily, after Emily's brilliant marriage to Mr. Trevelyan (*He Knew He Was Right*). In many cases like this, the sister controls proximity. Good sisters bring suitors closer; bad sisters keep suitors away through hurting the family name or standing.

[23] "Austen only sketches out the connections between the sister story and the marriage plot in *Sense and Sensibility*; she reserves a fuller treatment of the theme for *Pride and Prejudice*" (Levin, *The Suppressed Sister*, 37). Many of Sharon Marcus's astute observations about plots for female friends apply to sisters as well, again highlighting their auxiliary role in the marriage plot: "Like the donor and helper in Vladimir Propp's analysis of the folktale, the female friend is not a static or dispensable secondary character but one with a crucial role to play in achieving the marriage plot's ends" (Marcus, *Between Women*, 79). Sisters could be what Marcus terms a "narrative matrix": "a relationship that generates plot but is not its primary agent, subject, or object" (79).
[24] Lanser, "No Connections Subsequent: Jane Austen's World of Sisterhood," 54.
[25] Lanser, "No Connections Subsequent," 65.
[26] Marcus, *Between Women*, 82. She is writing of female friends, not sisters, but the point could apply to both.
[27] For sister rescue, see Brown, *Devoted Sisters*, 44–59; Cohen, *Sisters: Relation and Rescue in Nineteenth-Century British Novels and Paintings*.

Two sisters can end up in the same marriage plot, but this is usually resolved without conflict. *Middlemarch* and *Tess of the D'Urbervilles* (1891, slightly after the end of my study)—both with very positively portrayed heroines—offer models of a suitor's peaceful transfer of affection from one sister to another. True romantic rivalry between sisters is reserved for those who lack sisterly love and a proper sense of morals and manners (for example, Maria and Julia Bertram in *Mansfield Park*, 1814). The rivalry between Mercy and Charity Pecksniff (*Martin Chuzzlewit*, 1843–1844) offers a comic version of this plot trope without turning their sororal jealousy into a "seriously destructive force,"[28] while that destructive force appears comic when the vacuous Camilla French threatens to stab her sister, Arabella, before letting her marry Mr. Gibson (*He Knew He was Right*).[29]

Triangles that link sisters with the same man can be resolved by differentiation of roles. In Wilkie Collins' *The Woman in White*, for example, half-sisters Marian Halcombe and Laura Fairlie are so close, and Laura is so trusting of the stronger Marian, that Marian's friendship with Laura's beloved Walter Hartwright is of almost equal force and importance to his relationship with Laura herself.[30] This appears to be a classic case of what René Girard calls "mimetic desire," with the beautiful Laura as a mediator for the intense connection between Marian and Walter (or he as mediator for the sisters' bond).[31] Girard, focused primarily on triangles that included two men, saw such desire as a source of jealousy. However, for sisters, English novelists found more amicable resolutions to these triangles that validated the different forms of desire on each axis of the triangle.[32] At the end of *The Woman in White*, when the three are reunited after many adventures, Marian tells Walter "You and I are together again; and the one subject of interest between us is Laura once more" (558). After he weds Laura, Walter worries that they are selfishly keeping Marian, but she claims "After all that we three have suffered together ... there can be no parting between us, till the last parting of all ... Wait a little till there are children's voices at your fireside ... the first lesson they say to their father and mother shall be—We can't spare our aunt!" (621). Becoming an aunt could be seen as the culmination of the sister's role in the marriage plot.[33]

There is no obstacle, however, to both sisters marrying and forming families; this need not weaken their sisterly bond. Jane and Elizabeth Bennet marry best

---

[28] Brown, *Devoted Sisters*, 126.

[29] On the last page peace is restored, and Camilla "is now rather fond of being a guest at Mr. Gibson's house" (930).

[30] Corbett explores examples where jealousy does exist on the part of the wife who realizes her husband is better suited for her sister (*Family Likeness*, 57–85).

[31] See Hofer and Kersh's thoughtful analysis of their sororal bond and its potential erotic component ("The Victorian Family in Queer Time").

[32] See Chambers for the potential problems in applying Girard's model to sisters ("Triangular Desire and the Sororal Bond," 21).

[33] Similarly, in *He Knew He Was Right* Pricilla laments that she will have no love after her sister weds, and Dorothy replies "Oh, Priscilla, do not say that. If I have a child will you not love it?" essentially offering her sister the role of aunt (914).

friends and settle only thirty miles apart, and in *Sense and Sensibility* "between Barton and Delaford, there was that constant communication which strong family affection would naturally dictate" (380).[34] In *Deerbrook*, Margaret has promised frequent return visits before her marriage and departure at the novel's close. So as auxiliaries in each other's marriage plots, the sisters have a continued place at the novels' conclusions.[35] English novels comfortably accommodate multiple sisters within their standard, vertical family plotlines.

We find similar patterns for sisters in Russian novels as well. *Eugene Onegin* (1825–1832) set up a model of sisters as foils for each other (one that would be repeated by many female authors who described soulful, bookish elder sisters and light-hearted, gregarious younger ones).[36] The sororal relationship is often a stable background, rather than an instigator of plot. In *Anna Karenina*, Kitty and Dolly play an important role in each other's lives, but as regards the plot their relationship could be seen as reinforcing the marriage and generational plots. Dolly makes predictions about Kitty's suitors and attempts to reunite her sister with Levin (requesting a saddle, inviting him to a dinner), while Kitty helps care for Dolly's sick children and hosts her family in the country, helping to secure the survival of the next generation. In the multi-plot structure of *Anna Karenina*, where the main plots are defined by the romantic couplings (Anna/Vronsky, Kitty/Levin, Dolly/Stiva), only brothers fall outside this structure.[37]

Romantic rivalry is not a salient feature of sororal plots, but when it occurs in the Russian novel, it follows the same model as with brother rivals (explored in the next chapter): placing the sororal bond above personal happiness. For example, both Maria Zhukova's *Two Sisters* (1843) and Evgenia Tur's *Two Sisters* (1851) center on a love triangle where two sisters fall in love with the same man, but struggle not to win the beloved but rather to make their beloved sister happy. In Zhukova's novel, this involves each sister trying to sacrifice her own happiness so that the other ends up with the sought-after groom. In Tur's novella, Elena Bertina falls in love with Evgeny Arbenev only because he reminds her of her beloved half-sister, Ida. She explains to Arbenev: "my sister is my one love; she is everything on earth for me" (46). Awaiting Ida's arrival and Arbenev's first introduction to her, Elena begs Arbenev: "Love her, if you want me to love you," and Arbenev claims: "I will love her for the fact that she is your sister. I want to love all who are dear and important to you" (a classic case of Girardian mediated desire) (47). When

---

[34] See Corbett, *Family Likeness*, 47.

[35] Here I disagree with Levin's claim that sisters "ultimately form part of that darker underside, the reverse weave of the novel—what has to be suppressed, distanced or unfulfilled in a heroine for her to accept a traditional marriage and for the novelist to create a conventional ending" (*Suppressed Sisters*, 52–53).

[36] Versions of this appear in Tur's *A Mistake* (1849), Shalikova's *Two Sisters* (1859), and even Goncharov's *The Precipice* (1869).

[37] Anna and Stiva aid each other in their respective marriage plots, but Nikolai Levin's and Koznyshev's relations with Konstantin Levin do not relate to marriage or generational concerns.

Arbenev proposes to Elena and faces opposition, he triangulates his pleas: "We will be two, and together we will love and care for your sister" (50). He agrees to take second place to Ida: "love your sister more than me if that is necessary for your peace of mind, love her, I give her first place in your heart" (52). Elena agrees to accept his proposal on the condition that it is kept a secret until he finds favor with Ida. Not knowing that Arbenev is Elena's fiancé, but seeing his incredible kindness and attempts to win her good opinion, however, Ida falls in love with him. When Elena realizes what has happened, she forces Arbenev to give her up and to marry Ida instead, keeping Ida blissfully ignorant of the sacrifice she (and Arbenev) have made. The sisters' love is a stable constant in this marriage plot whose drama comes from the exchange of roles.

Brother-Sister Bonds

Like sisters, brother-sister relationships do not typically create their own plot, but serve as part of the matrix of other family and romantic plotlines.[38] There is no Aristotelian progression or climax to the brother-sister bond; the resolution at the end of a novel is never "and the brother and sister continued to be brother and sister and to love each other dearly."[39] *Cranford* (1853) provides a strange exception, where the generation in focus is long past the marriageable age, and Matty is relieved from economic woe by the return of her beloved brother from India. Usually, in cases where the brother-sister relationship resembles a companionate marriage, it either remains in the background as a stable constant (i.e. Faith and Thurston in Gaskell's *Ruth*, 1853) or the sister must ultimately give way to replacement by a "true" wife (for example, Kate in Julia Kavanagh's *Daisy Burns*, 1853, and Cornelia in Ellen Wood's *East Lynne,* 1860–1861). Living with a brother was one of the few economically viable alternatives to marriage for many women, but aside from *Cranford* I know of no novels that center on it as their plot.[40] Theodora in Charlotte Yonge's *Heartsease, or Brother's Wife* (1854) imagines herself remaining unwed and living with her brother's family—"She would be the maiden aunt,

---

[38] Valerie Sanders sees sibling relationships not as a driver of plot, but as a locus for the airing of societal concerns. In her reading, the same issues faced in the marriage plot or generational plot are often displaced onto siblings—a realm where they can be more safely discussed (*The Brother-Sister Culture in Nineteenth-Century Literature*, 10). This makes siblings a corollary of existing familial plots, a site for addressing concerns and anxieties that are really the product of other relationships.

[39] The exception to this would be incest, which would follow a romantic love plot. While sibling incest was a fascination among the Romantics (for example, Byron's "Manfred") and provided the ultimate horror in Gothic literature, it became a less explicit focus later in the century in the realist or family novel. For a discussion of the often murky distinction of "familialization" (making someone *like* kin) which leads to a sexualized bond (a common pattern in nineteenth-century novels) versus actual incest, see Shaffer, "Familial Love, Incest, and Female Desire."

[40] Nelson discusses the historical realities of such living arrangements (*Family Ties in Victorian England*, 100).

the treasure of the family, and Arthur's house should be the center of her usefulness and attachments"—yet like so many other heroines, she instead ends up in her own marital union (276).[41]

Sisters and brothers often aid each other in the marriage plot, with access to members of the opposite sex coming through friendship with the same-sex sibling. As a minor character in *Shirley* (1849) quips, "Every sister, with an eligible single brother, is considered most kind by her spinster friends" (340). Caroline Bingley in *Pride and Prejudice* is just such a sister, and Jane Bennet increases her intimacy with Mr. Bingley through Caroline's invitation to visit Netherfield Park (as does Elizabeth with Darcy through Georgiana's invitation to Pemberley). Similar examples can be found in *The Tenant of Wildfell Hall* (1848), and *Can You Forgive Her?* (1864). Eliot's Daniel Deronda is drawn to Mirah by his spiritual bond with her brother. Even his initial marriage plans involve "taking Ezra and Mirah to a mild spot on the coast, while he prepared another home that Mirah might enter as his bride, and where they might unitedly watch over her brother" (682). Here we find an example of Girard's point that "the impulse toward the object [Mirah] is ultimately an impulse toward the mediator [Ezra]."[42] Yet these triangles can remain stable (like the sister-triangle in *Woman in White*).[43]

If the sibling bond is too highly valued by a sister, it can block her possible marriage plot(s) completely. Yonge's *The Daisy Chain* (1856)—a sibling novel par excellence with eleven May children left motherless and turning inward to their family for comfort and support—offers consanguinial kinship as an alternative to the conjugal knot. Ethel May chooses *not* to enter a marriage plot with her rich Scottish cousin, who shares the name of her beloved brother, Norman. Instead of replacing the fraternal Norman with a conjugal one, she continues devoting herself to her first family. Eliot's *Mill on the Floss* (1860) provides the most striking example of a sister-brother bond that prevents the sister from moving on from her first love object.[44] While Maggie adores Tom and seeks his approval throughout the novel, the relationship is mostly *not* characterized by the ideal harmony with which the Victorians typically endowed novelistic sibling bonds. Claiming "compliance from his sister on the basis of his role as preserver of the family" and usurping the role of the father,[45] Tom forces Maggie to give up her attachment to Philip Wakem by making her choose between friend and brother, and he exiles Maggie from his affections (and the family home) for her near elopement with

---

[41] Other siblings who consider this include Kate and Nicholas (*Nicholas Nickleby*, 1839), and Rex and Anna (*Daniel Deronda*, 1876).

[42] Girard, *Deceit, Desire, and the Novel*, 10.

[43] I explore this in greater depth in Chapter 8 in relation to "in-lawing," pp. 216–217.

[44] In Corbett's words, "the tie between Maggie and Tom Tulliver ... provides supreme testimony to the persistence of the first-family bond in the nineteenth-century English tradition" (*Family Likeness*, 115).

[45] Kilroy, *The Nineteenth-Century English Novel*, 126. Maggie rebels against this, telling Tom "I will submit even to what is unreasonable from my father, but I will not submit to it from you" (389).

Stephen Guest.[46] Yet despite the love she receives from these other men and the harsh treatment from Tom, they cannot supplant him in her heart. When Philip laments that Maggie will "never love me so well as you love your brother," she agrees (344). Ultimately, Maggie meets her end in the attempt to rescue Tom during a flood, "brother and sister [going] down in an embrace never to be parted" (588). Brother has virtually replaced lover for Maggie, creating the ultimate barrier to her possible marriage plots.[47] If siblings were to have their own plot, it would appear to be here, yet the conflicts that fuel their plotline all relate back to the marriage and generational plots; she wishes to follow her heart, while he wishes to preserve what he sees to be the family honor.

Sisters are often expected to sacrifice for brothers, and these sacrifices can direct their choices in the marriage plot. In *Hard Times* (1854), Louisa Gradgrind marries Mr. Bounderby in in no small part because she wishes to aid her beloved brother, Tom. Such marital sacrifices often aim at advancing the family fortunes. In *The Tenant of Wildfell Hall*, Milicent explains her acceptance of a not entirely desirable proposal: "Mr. Hattersley, you know, is the son of a rich banker, and as Esther and I have no fortunes and Walter very little, our dear mamma is very anxious to see us all well married ... she assures me it will be a good thing for the family as well as for me. Even Walter is pleased at the prospect" (222). Flora May (*The Daisy Chain*) is partly marrying from her own desire to enter higher society, but she also uses a sibling justification: "out of six sisters some must marry, for the good of the rest" (334). Thinking hard about "the good of the rest," Hardy's Tess ultimately agrees to give herself to Alec D'Urberville because her little siblings are starving and "the necessity of applying herself heart and soul to their needs took her out of her own cares" (346). In each of these cases, the sister's choices about the marriage plot are inflected by lateral, sibling concerns.

As with the similar treatment of sisters in Russian novels, we also find comparable patterns for the sister-brother relations. Like Tess sacrificing herself to help her starving siblings, in *Crime and Punishment* (1866) Sonya Marmeladova enters prostitution to provide for her penniless step-siblings, while Dunya is planning to marry Luzhin to help advance her brother's prospects (not unlike Louisa Gradgrind). Varya Ardalionovna marries Ptitsyn in *The Idiot* (1868–1869) because in doing so "she was also providing a corner for her mother, father and brothers. Seeing her brother [Ganya] in misery, she felt like helping him, in spite of all their earlier domestic perplexities" (8:388/544). Like English brothers and sisters, Russian ones often play a role in each other's marriage plots. In *Anna Karenina* Kitty Shcherbatskaya initially becomes intimate with Levin because of his close friendship with her brother (who has died before the novel begins), just as Dunya

---

[46] See May, *Disorderly Sisters*, 82–83.

[47] Like this slippage between the brother and lover roles, the plot trope of literally mistaking a sibling for a lover could create a temporary barrier to the romantic plotline (e.g. *North and South*, 1854; *The Tenant of Wildfell Hall*; *East Lynne*).

Raskolnikova meets and is attracted to Razumikhin in *Crime and Punishment* because of his friendship with Raskolnikov.[48] In a corrupted version of this type of sibling intervention in the marriage plot, Hélène Bezukhova helps bring her profligate (and secretly married) brother Anatole together with Natasha Rostova.[49] Russian brothers and sisters can also become obstacles in each other's marriage plots. Raskolnikov's first action in relation to Dunya is to help break off her engagement to Luzhin, and had Natasha Rostova married Prince Andrei in *War and Peace* (1865–1869), her brother Nikolai would have been unable to wed Andrei's sister Princess Marya (this would have qualified as incest).

The brother-sister relationship also serves a purpose in preparing characters for future marital relations. Sisters and brothers often model the kinds of compassion and support amongst themselves that they will later exhibit with their spouses in what Valerie Sanders calls "innocent training in the roles children would ideally adopt as adults."[50] In plot terms, this makes siblinghood an early step in the process of preparing for married life and creating new families. The element of the plot this engenders is the shift from consanguineal ties to conjugal. We see this shift enacted in *Crime and Punishment* as Raskolnikov transfers his allegiance from Dunya to Sonya. In *War and Peace* this shift is prepared for a long time as Natasha and Nikolai contemplate each other's future marriage partnerships, and it is realized in the first epilogue when Natasha sides with her husband, Pierre, against her brother in a family dispute.

Thus sister-brother relationships (like sister-sister) had a comfortable place in both the English and Russian novel within the standard family plotlines of marriage and genealogy. Kate and Nicholas Nickleby can both marry and form families without this challenging their affection for each other or the future of the Nickleby line. With a sister and a brother there is no threat to the linear model of family progression at the heart of the classic novel, as theorized by English scholars because only *one* sibling—the brother—represents the future of the family.

The Problem with Brothers in the English Novel

If one's conception of the family is a vertical line, and one's favored plotline is the marriage plot, brothers become a "problem." Among the English landed classes

---

[48] I explore the Girardian, incestuous underpinnings of this triangle in "Incest and the Limits of Family in the Nineteenth-Century Russian Novel," 98–99.

[49] In the adultery version of the opposite-sex-sibling-as-auxiliary-in-the-marriage-plot, Anna Karenina comes to Moscow help mend the rift in her brother's marriage after Dolly learns of his affair. And in a parallel gesture, he will go to Petersburg to beg Karenin for a divorce after Anna has left her husband for Vronsky. Sibling relationships are untouched by adultery; a fallen woman by necessity usually fails as a mother too (e.g. Anna must leave her son), but she is no less of a sister (Tanner, *Adultery in the Novel*, 17).

[50] Sanders, *The Brother-Sister Culture in Nineteenth-Century Literature*, 5.

and those with a business to pass on, the salient issue that distinguished brother-hood from the sister bond was that of inheritance and primogeniture. While there is no limit to the number of eligible suitors with landed estates who could appear in a novel to marry a group of sisters, only one brother can offer his bride such a family manor. Thus, in *East Lynne* the narrator explains that of the (briefly men-tioned) four sons of Baron von Stalkenberg, "The young Baron von Stalkenberg was at liberty to marry; three Counts von Stalkenberg were not—unless they could pick up a wife with enough money to keep herself and her husband. In this creed they had been brought up: it was a perfectly understood creed, and not rebelled against" (385). A young lady in *Tenant of Wildfell Hall* complains: "I saw one or two gentlemen in London that I might have liked, but they were younger sons, and mamma would not let me get to know them" (374). Or as scheming Mrs. Gibson quips in *Wives and Daughters* after meeting the Hamley brothers and imagining the elder as a match for her daughter, "Somehow, I always do like eldest sons. He will have the estate, won't he?" (210). Because of primogeniture, only one brother had a desirable place in the English marriage plot.[51] In Russia, by contrast, with property divided among siblings, this was not such an impediment.[52]

There were plotlines available for the cadets of the family, but they were not in the family novel. As Zouheir Jamoussi observes, "the centrifugal force exerted by primogeniture on the younger sons of manor houses turned them into ide-ally mobile individuals, forced into outward-bound paths."[53] Consequently, they became the heroes of travel or adventure novels (*Robinson Crusoe*, 1719; *Gulliver's Travels*, 1726), while family novels focused on eldest sons or heirs.[54] Edward John Trelawny begins his *Adventures of a Younger Son* (1831) by lamenting the wretched conditions of second sons that forced them out into the world:

> My birth was unpropitious. I came into the world, branded and denounced as a
> vagrant, not littered by a dram in a ditch but still worse; for I was a younger son

[51] Although primogeniture was standard practice, it was not required by law, except when a father died without leaving a will, and this only became law in 1833 (Cecil, *Primogeniture: A Short History of Its Development in Various Countries and Its Practical Effects*, 53). Deeds of entail, however, were commonly used to assure that a "man of expensive tastes" could not mortgage or sell the family house or reduce the size of land holdings, protecting these fundamentals for future generations (Nelson, *Family Ties in Victorian England*, 73).

[52] We find an interesting parallel example in anthropology with the practice of Tibetan polyandry, where brothers marry the same wife. This practice appears most common amongst the social groups with the most land. As explained by Melvyn C. Goldstein, "The application of this norm was motivated by the strong desire to prevent partition of the corporate unit with its lands. Given the basic inheri-tance rule which held that all males in a family were coparceners [joint heirs] with demand rights to a share of the family's corporation's land, Tibetans considered situations with two conjugal families in a given generation (i.e., join families) unstable. Situations such as this produced serious conflicts of interest between the two conjugal families (and their two sets of heirs) and were thought likely to lead to partition between the two units" ("Stratification, Polyandry, and Family Structure in Central Tibet," 68).

[53] Jamoussi, *Primogeniture and Entail in England*, 197.

[54] Jamoussi, *Primogeniture and Entail in England*, 197, 201–202.

of a family, so proud of their antiquity, that even gout and mortgaged estates were traced, many generations back, on the genealogical tree, as ancient heir-looms of aristocratic origin, and therefore reverenced. In such a house a younger son was like the cub of a felon-wolf in good King Edgar's days, when a price was set upon its head. There have been laws compelling parents to destroy their puny offspring; and a spartan mother might have exclaimed with Othello, while extinguishing the life of her yet unconscious infant,

> 'I that am cruel, am yet merciful,
> I would not have thee linger in thy pain;'

which was just and merciful, in comparison with the atrocious law of primogeniture. (1)[55]

As exemplified in this pseudo-novel (purported autobiography), the younger brother's plot required him to be alone on adventures geographically far from the manor house where an older brother's marriage plot would unfold. This geographical necessity essentially keeps brothers in separate novels. Thus, Ouida's *Under Two Flags* (1867) traces the exploits of Bertie Cecil as he suffers under a false name in the French Legion in Africa while his elder brother inherits the estate and title of Royallieu (given its military setting, it is decidedly an adventure novel, *not* a family novel). Or in reverse, in Martineau's *Deerbrook* the central figure, Dr. Hope, carries on a correspondence with his younger brother, Frank, who is off in India and never appears in the novel outside of his letters. With the brothers kept separate in this way, their *relationship* is not a central focus.

While the reigning ideology in England was one of family harmony and love, given the inheritance practice of eldest-takes-all, rivalry and competition were built into the structure of the brother-bond, making it a tricky subject for family novels to navigate. As the narrator of William Makepeace Thackeray's *Vanity Fair* (1848) boldly proclaims:

My dear sir, you ought to know that every elder brother looks upon the cadets of the house as his natural enemies, who deprive him of so much ready money which ought to be his by right. I have often heard George Mac Turk, Lord Bajazet's eldest son, say that if he had his will when he came to the title, he would do what the sultans do, and clear the estate by chopping off all his younger brothers' heads at once; and so the case is, more or less, with them all. (596)

[55] The title, which placed so much emphasis on birth order, was not actually Trelawny's choice (he wanted *A Man's Life*), but came from Mary Shelley, who helped get the work published. Trelawny claimed the book was autobiography, but it quickly veers off into adventure fiction very much inspired by Byron and his *Corsair*. For a discussion of the publication history and veracity of the tale, see the "Introduction" by William St. Clair in Trelawny, *Adventures of a Younger Son*.

This is hardly material for English domestic fiction, yet such tensions simmer in many an English novel where multiple brothers appear.

When second-born Theobald Pontifex produces a male heir before his older brother John in *The Way of All Flesh* (1873–1884), Old Mr. Pontifex's pursuant "interview with his solicitors" causes "dismay" to the John Pontifexes (58). Sometimes the feelings go far beyond dismay. References to Cain and Abel appear in Charlotte Brontë's *Shirley*, Dinah Craik's *John Halifax, Gentleman* (1856), Hardy's *Far from the Madding Crowd* (1874), and Ouida's *Under Two Flags* among other novels.

Novels could only portray family harmony if they managed to excise the rivalry and envy that would be caused by a younger brother. Claudia Nelson has observed that the ill-will produced by primogeniture is the subject of Yonge's *The Heir of Redclyffe* (1853) and Mary Elizabeth Braddon's *John Marchmont's Legacy* (1863), but in both cases the conflict is between cousins, not brothers. She suggests this is "a literary device likely to be less disturbing to the sentiments of readers conditioned to revere the sibling tie."[56] As the novel was meant to help form morals, "[a] literature that only rarely acknowledges the possibility that siblings may feel indifference, jealousy, or hatred for one another is a powerful tool in encouraging readers to repress such feelings in their own lives."[57] By avoiding brothers or pushing them to the margins, many authors essentially enacted such repression in their novels.

Alex Woloch's *The One vs. the Many* (2003) provides perhaps the most comprehensive and compelling theory of character marginalization, but it fails to account for this pattern for brothers. His theory of "character-space" (each character's position within the narrative as a whole) and the "character-system" that arranges these different character-spaces into a unified narrative structure has no place for the *family*-system in which they are embedded. Analyzing the opening lines of *Pride and Prejudice*, he claims that "'Possession of a good fortune' is the precondition for the 'want of a wife' both because marriage requires property—only a wealthy man is an eligible husband—and because property requires marriage, as the stable form of its transmission."[58] This "precondition" has a major impact on second (and third) brothers and the narrative space they can occupy. While at the start of *Pride and Prejudice* any of the sisters could turn out to be the central figure (Woloch details how the narrative ultimately focalizes on Elizabeth), a brother's possible plotline—and centrality—are dependent on his position in the birth order. In Trollope's *An Eye for an Eye*, when Fred Neville tries to trade places with his younger brother Jack because he has become entangled in a *mésalliance*, Jack reminds him:

---

[56] Nelson, *Family Ties in Victorian England*, 118. Along these lines, Trollope directs the older brother's animosity at his step-mother in *Orley Farm* (1862), not at his small half-brother.

[57] Nelson, *Family Ties in Victorian England*, 107.

[58] Woloch, *The One vs. the Many*, 57.

"My dear Fred, you can't change the accidents of birth" (286). In other words, brothers cannot exchange plots.[59]

Focusing narrative attention primarily on one brother, I suggest, served as a technique for avoiding, obfuscating, or downplaying fraternal rivalries and tensions—and could thus explain brothers' frequent marginalization. For example, Austen keeps her second brothers in the background as minor characters, though their impact may be great. The denouement of *Sense and Sensibility* hinges on the very "minorness" of the second Ferrars brother, priming Elinor (and the reader) to assume that the new "Mrs. Ferrars" *must* refer to the wife of her beloved Edward. And in the same novel, Colonel Brandon is seeking Marianne's hand because she reminds him of his first beloved, Eliza, who was forced to marry his older brother (who never appears in the novel). In *Mansfield Park*, the minor brother's significance is economic: Edmund Bertram's church position must be sold to pay his older brother Tom's gambling debts. In *Emma* (1815), we see little of Mr. Knightly's brother John, but his marriage to Emma's sister creates the familial closeness that allows the couple to become intimate. By keeping John in the background, Austen never has to explore his feelings about being deprived of the family estate as "a brother whose home it had equally been the longest part of his life, and whose attachments were strong" (100). A similar tactic of marginalizing a brother—or keeping a pair in the background—can be found in countless other works, making it understandable why the brother-bond would not become a major focus of scholarship in these texts.

Brothers provide the ultimate test of vertical family plots and the narrative theories they have engendered. The next chapter takes up what happens when an English novel attempts to accommodate two brothers at the heart of its plot ... and how this differs from a Russian brother-plot.

---

[59] In *Heartsease, or Brother's Wife*, Sir Anthony's elder son, Pelham, is mentally weak, so characters discuss the possibility of his settling the property on the younger, Percy. Arthur (another second son) comments: "He could not do a wiser thing. But of course it is entailed—there's always a provision of nature for starving the younger branches" (229). Later, another character comments: "It is quite in their power, you know, to do the only rational thing under the circumstances—make an eldest son of Percy, and set poor Pelham aside, with enough to make him happy" (262).

3

Brothers

Two brothers of whom it had been our boast that from babyhood they had never been known to lift a hand against each other—now struggling together like Cain and Abel. And from the fury in their faces, the quarrel might have had a similar ending.
— Dinah Mulock Craik, *John Halifax, Gentleman*

That all men should be brothers is the dream of people who have no brothers.
— Charles Chincholle

Consanguineal kinship is a central subject and structuring device in the novel. Yet as the previous chapter explored, not all relationships fit comfortably in the structure provided by the progressive movement from one generation to the next. Among lateral relations—those between siblings—sisters and sister-brother relations can easily be accommodated because, as sisters marry *out* of the family, they pose no threat to the linear progression of family or plot. Brothers, however, offer a challenge to the vertical family plot. When they take center stage, they necessarily call for their own plot that is not about family futurity, but about relations in the present. This chapter uses them as a case study for understanding the way the family structures in England and Russia shaped such lateral plots. English novels about brothers tend to maintain the linearity of the family by placing the brothers in a single marriage plot, where only one can come out producing heirs. Russian brothers—each with their own inheritances—have more space for self-individuation and their futures are less dependent upon each other. Their plots can focus more upon present relations, rather than resolving the structural "problem" of a potential branch in the family tree.

The English Brother Plot and the Love Triangle

The fact that almost no canonical English novels focus on a pair of brothers is indicative of their fraught place in the tradition. Plots thrive on conflict, and the brother-bond would seem to be an ideal venue for dramas based on rivalry and jealousy (the route Thackeray the satirist takes), but this would clash with

The Family Novel in Russia and England, 1800–1880. Anna A. Berman, Oxford University Press.
© Anna A. Berman (2022). DOI: 10.1093/oso/9780192866622.003.0004

readers' desire to believe in an ideal of fraternal love.[1] In his *Sermon to Young Men* (1771), Reverend William Dodd claimed that "the Duty of Fraternal Love [is] a duty not less inforced by nature, than by religion, and by every consideration of present advantage and comfort. Next to filial love, it is certainly one of the most natural propensities of the human heart."[2] Dodd's quotation illustrates a prevailing ideology of the *naturalness* of familial love on both the vertical—filial—and lateral—fraternal—axes. English novels tended to reinforce this view of fraternal affection. Rather than creating a new lateral plot for brothers, as I will suggest occurred in the Russian novel, the English repeatedly attempted to include multiple brothers in their existing, vertical family plots. The novels reveal the lack of a sustainable place for them. This failure to accommodate multiple brothers in the novels' conclusions, in turn, reinforces the linear structure of the novel that has been theorized by scholars.

It may be a surprise to discover that the most disparate of novels—from highly-regarded authors like Charles Dickens and George Eliot to un/little-knowns like Anna Drury, from the Christian moralizing of Charlotte Yonge to the sensation novels of Wilkie Collins and Mary Elizabeth Braddon—actually follow the same basic plotline for brothers. At its most essential, two brothers—the "most faithful of friends"—fall in love with the same woman.[3] Stuck in a single marriage plot that cannot contain the two, the one who loses the romantic tussle is ultimately removed from the linear progression of the family plot to restore harmony at the novel's close. Told another way: the novel opens with a pair of brothers as its primary unit and must transform this into a conjugal pairing by its close. While multiple sisters can make this shift from consanguineal to conjugal without disrupting their sororal attachment, in English novels it appears that only one brother can marry and the other—if he survives—must have chosen brotherly love *at the expense* of connubial bliss.

To elucidate this classic pattern, I turn now to close readings of the novels, beginning with Eliot's *Adam Bede* (1859). The novel opens with a scene that demonstrates the warm bond between Adam and Seth, establishing the older Adam as Seth's protector. Indeed, Seth almost owes Adam his life, as Adam used his savings to pay for a replacement, thus freeing Seth from "going for a soldier" (41).[4] Although their mother openly favors her beloved firstborn, Seth never experiences resentment, instead replying to one of her characteristic observations that "Th' Methodies'll niver make thee half the man thy brother is" with the "mild"

[1] Davidoff notes that "The moral injunction for brothers and sisters to care for and support each other, to sacrifice their own interests, or even their own lives for each other was a strong theme in prescriptive and fictional literature" (*Thicker than Water*, 109).

[2] Dodd, *Sermons to Young Men*, 54.

[3] I will not discuss them here, but this pattern also appears between the eldest two sons, Guy and Edwin, in Dinah Craik's *John Halifax, Gentleman* (1856), which serves as an epigraph to this chapter.

[4] Similarly, in Collins' *Poor Miss Finch* (1872), Oscar owes his life to Nugent, who found evidence to clear him in a murder trial.

remark: "Adam's far before me, an's done more for me than I can ever do for him" (42). When Adam is shown favor by a local landowner and is asked to dine separately from his family at a celebration, Seth encourages him: "thy honour's our honour ... The further I see thee above me, the better, so long as thee feel'st like a brother to me" (235). In the working-class Bede family, there is no estate or title to be inherited, but presumably the house and carpentry business will go to Adam, and Seth's deferential submissiveness befits his place in the hierarchy.

Their comfortable inequality relies upon Seth playing a more feminine role in the family, and, ultimately, in the plot. He slips easily into domestic roles typically associated with women in the Victorian novel. For example, after a sleepless night Adam falls asleep in the workshop (a male domain), while "Seth was in the back kitchen making a fire of sticks that he might get the kettle to boil, and persuade his mother to have a cup of tea" (95).[5] He speaks to her "tenderly," saying, "I'll put two or three of these things away, and make the house look more comfortable," all tasks and attributes associated with the female sphere (96). When Adam is expecting happiness with Hetty Sorrel and wishes Seth were as happy as he, Seth claims contentment, cheerfully suggesting "I'll be an old bachelor, belike, and make a fuss wi' thy children" (351), typically a woman's activity.

This gendering of the brothers has a powerful impact on their roles in the marriage plot. As is the case in the majority of English novels about brothers, Adam and Seth will fall in love with the same woman, Dinah Morris. Yet through emasculating Seth, Eliot has primed the reader to accept that he will be able to resign his beloved to his more virile brother, as his love seems to lack amorous desire.[6] Seth tells Dinah, "I think it's something passing the love of women as I feel for you, for I could be content without your marrying me if I could go and live at Snowfield, and be near you" (33).

While the brothers had always relied on "halving iverything" (127), romantic love cannot be "halved," foregrounding the problem of having two Bede brothers in the marriage plot. Scholarship on the novel has similarly struggled with acknowledging the place of the second brother, with one critic dismissing Seth as "supernumerary."[7] Even in an article specifically about Seth, R. E. Sopher claims that "Seth's role in the novel ... must be understood primarily in relation to Adam and his moral progression," and treats him as "an obstacle—but a minor one—to

---

[5] Sarah Brown claims that "although both Adam and Seth live at home, Adam is so engaged by his work that we are scarcely aware that he shares a home with his brother" (*Devoted Sisters*, vii). I would suggest that we are keenly aware of the shared home, but the differentiated roles make them seem to be in separate realms. Seth's association with "Victorian femininity" via housework is discussed in R.E. Sopher, "Gender and Sympathy in *Adam Bede*," 12.

[6] John Reed calls Seth a model of "'castrated' masculinity" ("Soldier Boy," 274), and Sopher suggests that "sympathy like Seth's is incompatible with sexually desirable masculinity like Adam's" ("Gender and Sympathy in *Adam Bede*," 5).

[7] Wolff, "*Adam Bede*'s Families," 67.

Dinah and Adam's marriage," rather than as an independent being.[8] Most scholars ignore the character of Seth entirely.[9]

It is Adam and Seth's sense of unity that ultimately enables them to resolve their love triangle. When Adam's mother tells him of Dinah's love and suggests a marriage, his first thought is for Seth: "Would the lad be hurt?" However, he immediately reassures himself: "Hardly ... there was no selfish jealousy in him; he had never been jealous of his mother's fondness for Adam" (449). As Adam had predicted, Seth shows an almost miraculous lack of jealousy as he shifts from the role of lover to that of brother-in-law to Dinah. I believe that Seth's ultimate contentment comes partly from his deep identification with his brother. When Adam asks Seth if he would be hurt if Dinah loved him (Adam), Seth answers "warmly" in the negative: "Have I felt thy trouble so little that I shouldna feel thy joy?" (451). This answer hints at an overlap of identity between the brothers, as if Seth believes they could occupy the same place in the marriage plot and both benefit from Dinah's acceptance of Adam.[10]

Ultimately, the brothers *do* both benefit, but not through filling the husband role. The conclusion of *Adam Bede* finds a way to harmonize Adam and Seth through shifting Seth's place structurally in the family. I suggest that the emasculated Seth moves from the role of brother to that of sister. In the Epilogue we find the Bede family living contentedly together, with Seth in the role of child-caretaker that he predicted for himself: "to walk by Dinah's side, and be tyrannized over by Dinah's and Adam's children, was Uncle Seth's earthly happiness" (479). Tara MacDonald links this outcome to his "extreme, even selfless model of compassionate masculinity," which made it a struggle for Eliot "to find a place for him socially or domestically," so that she left him "as merely an observer of a happy family."[11] I would suggest he more than observes, but that in structural terms he has been turned into a maiden aunt, much like Marian in *The Woman in White* (1859–1860).[12] This triangulation allows Seth to maintain his closeness with

[8] Sopher, "Gender and Sympathy in *Adam Bede*," 2.

[9] Tara MacDonald has actually enumerated the cases of scholars ignoring Seth, and claims it is "surprising that Seth's role as an alternative husband for the independent preacher, or even his role as brother-in-law, has not been further explored," yet she links the issue only with conceptions of masculinity, not with family structure (*The New Man, Masculinity, and Marriage in the Victorian Novel*, 76).

[10] MacDonald similarly notes that "Dinah benefits by having them both, just as they benefit from each other" (*The New Man*, 60).

[11] MacDonald, *The New Man*, 3.

[12] I am in accord with Ellingson and Sotirin, who call "aunting" a "practice" and "a choice that is available to *everyone*" ("Aunting," 4). This also accords with how some nineteenth-century readers thought about effeminate male characters who ended up in care-taking roles. An 1858 review of *John Halifax, Gentleman* made this point about the invalid narrator, Phineas, who lives with his best friend, John, and John's family. The critic noted that although "Phineas professes to be an uncle, the reader is aware constantly that he is really an aunt" ("Novels by the Author of John Halifax" *North British Review* 29 [1858], 466–481; qtd. in Furneaux, "Negotiating the Gentle-Man," 117).

Adam, just as Marian remains with her sister Laura. "Sister-Seth" has a comfortable place in the English novel, as he will not bifurcate the family lineage.

The trope of turning a brother into a sister is even more explicit in Yonge's *Heartsease, or Brother's Wife* (1854). The primogenitor, John Martindale, has recused himself from the marriage plot after the early death of his fiancée, and he ends the novel by literally replacing his sister in caring for their mother. He shows his mother "the necessity of relinquishing her daughter [so she could wed], intending to offer himself as her companion and attendant" (486). John is eager for his younger brother's family to live with them, claiming that "a home is all that I can ever want; and that for Arthur to afford me a share in his, and in his children's hearts, would be the greatest earthly happiness that I can desire" (487). Only one brother marries, and John, like Seth Bede, closes the novel in the role of aunt. This trope of turning one brother into a maiden sister allows for the family to maintain primacy over the individual; rather than the extra brother creating a new branch to the family tree, he can remain united with the central shoot, maintaining the familial and narrative linearity the English novel craved.

Sharing a Beloved

In many brother-novels like *Adam Bede*, the linearity comes from having only one object of desire. I believe this pattern of choosing the same beloved hints at the primacy of the brother-bond over the romantic in the two-brother-one-lover triangle. Mary Elizabeth Braddon's *Like and Unlike* (1887)—another novel where one brother wins away the other's beloved—makes this explicit.[13] While Eliot's and Braddon's styles could not be more dissimilar, the gendered dynamics for the Bede brothers are remarkably akin to those between twins Adrian and Valentine Belfield. In both novels, the virile son wins in love and the effeminate son surrenders his beloved and remains true to his brother.[14] Ceding his fiancée, Helen, Adrian writes in a parting letter to Valentine: "it is a quality of my nature to love you, and, even while smarting under the sense of a deep wrong, you are still to be something more than a brother. You are a part of myself" (1:276).

Sibling loyalty prevails over romantic heartbreak because the fraternal bond is actually dearer to Adrian than his romantic love. Shortly after becoming engaged,

---

[13] The novel falls slightly beyond the temporal scope of this study, but given its close resemblance to the pattern under discussion, I felt it would be artificial to exclude it.

[14] The "effeminate" Adrian loses the romantic rivalry because he has been outmanned. When he recognizes the attraction between Valentine and Helen, Adrian reflects "'Nature made him to rule and me to serve,' he told himself. 'How could I ever hope to be victorious where he could be a competitor. He has beaten me in all things in which men care to conquer. He has left me my books, and my music: a woman's occupation, not a man's" (1:264). After marrying Valentine, Helen tells him of her earlier feelings for Adrian: "He had been to me as a kind and dear friend, never as a lover" (2:69), and Valentine concludes: "In other words, you loved me because I was a man" (2:70).

at a time when one would expect him to be consumed by love for Helen, Adrian tells her "Even with your sweet companionship I begin to weary for [Valentine's] return" (1:175). In characterizing this love of Valentine to his doctor, he explains "it is more than mere fondness. I am a part of himself, feel with him in almost all things, am angry with him, sorry with him, glad with him; and yet there is antagonism. There is the misery of it. There are times when I could quarrel with him more desperately than with any other man upon earth; and yet I declare to you, doctor, he is as it were my second self" (1:24). Like Seth Bede, Adrian can be content losing the romantic rivalry because it is his rival—"My brother—my beloved brother, the second half of myself"—whom he most adores (3:136).

Just as brothers' rivalry and antagonism is a threat to the family, so too is brothers' love. Scholars have explored the potentially erotic component of close sister-attachment in this period, but as Leonore Davidoff notes, "[t]he possibility of such erotic feelings between brothers has received less coverage ... perhaps because of the emphasis on fraternal rivalry and hatred that has so often been invoked."[15] The potential for erotic feelings between brothers introduces a form of triangulation that complicates earlier theories. Rephrasing René Girard, Eve Sedgwick has famously suggested that "in any erotic rivalry, the bond that links the two rivals is as intense and potent as the bond that links either of the rivals to the beloved," yet she does not specifically consider brothers.[16] Sedgwick adds to Girard the possibility of an unbroken "continuum between homosocial and homosexual," opening a new understanding of the male desire at play on the third axis of these love triangles.[17]

I would suggest that the brother-lover-triangle is designed to fail, but in such a way that the linearity of the family will be maintained. Collins' Poor Miss Finch— about identical twins vying for the love of a blind girl—offers an ideal illustration. The rivalry comes directly from the closeness—virtually overlapping identities— between the twins. This hints at the fact that structurally the ideal position for them in the family is actually to be singular, to occupy a totally overlapping place as one sole heir. In psychoanalytic terms, Juliet Mitchell suggests that within the family structure, the sibling "stands exactly in the same place as oneself," as both are "the baby" in relation to the parents.[18] This structural problem of overlap creates the sense of both annihilation and also intense self-love—both of which we find English brother-novels struggling to resolve. In Poor Miss Finch, on receiving word of Oscar's engagement, Nugent writes "Your happiness is my happiness. I feel with

---

[15] Davidoff, Thicker than Water, 221.

[16] Sedgwick, Between Men, 21. Her discussion of Adam Bede, for example, mentions the bond of Adam and Arthur Donnithorne (rivals for Hetty Sorrel), yet is curiously mute about Adam and Seth.

[17] Sedgwick, Between Men, 1.

[18] Mitchell, Siblings, 43. Similarly, human evolutionary biologist Joseph Henrich claims "brothers usually occupy the same role within a kinship network, so they are interchangeable, from the kingroup's point of view" (The WEIRDest People in the World, 171–172).

you" (125). This claim is echoed by Valentine's first words to his brother's fiancée in *Like and Unlike*: "You cannot be greatly loved by him without being a little loved by me. We are two halves of one whole, and I am the stronger half. You cannot be wax to him and marble to me; melt at his touch, and freeze at mine. Our natures are too closely interwoven. To love one of us is to love the other" (1:189). The brothers *almost* act as a single entity; their desire is inseparable. In *Poor Miss Finch* Oscar is delighted when Nugent is taken with Lucilla because "[h]is brother's opinion ranked above all human opinions in his estimation" (143), or in Girard's formulation, "The mediator's prestige is imparted to the object of desire."[19] In these two-brother-one-lover triangles, the attachments are potent along all the axes.

This configuration is an inversion of what Holly Furneaux calls "in-lawing," the common pattern whereby "prohibited desire for a member of the same sex is often quite transparently redirected or extended to an opposite-sex sibling" (107) (for example, Smike transferring his affections from his friend Nicholas Nickleby to Nicholas' sister Kate). With brothers, the love of the same-sex sibling is transferred to the sibling's opposite-sex lover. When—in novel after novel—brothers who describe their relationship as "something more than affection" and consider the other to be "an angel" fall in love with the same woman, it opens room for speculation that such romantic triangulation might be a strategy for displacing an illicit form of desire onto a "safe" object.[20] The brothers' romantic rivalries could be seen as a way of neutralizing an initial threat of incestuous, homosexual desire entering the family by replacing it with the more openly addressable threat of jealousy and hatred, which could then, in turn, be resolved.

This resolution constitutes the plot of the English brother-novel. The most common "solution" to these rivalries—the easiest path to narratively removing this threat to familial unity—is to "remove" a brother. *Adam Bede* and *Heartsease* remove him only from the possibility of marriage, but the more common ending is to remove him altogether, through death. We find this at the end of Anna Drury's *The Brothers* (1865), Collins' *Poor Miss Finch*, Yonge's *Three Brides* (1876), Gaskell's *Wives and Daughters* (1864-1866), and Braddon's *Like and Unlike*. All these novels symbolically indicate their discomfort with the laterality of brothers and their need for vertical order by replacing the brothers with a father-son pair on the final pages. Literally, one brother dies and the surviving brother names his son after the deceased.

[19] Girard, *Deceit, Desire, and the Novel*, 17.
[20] In Drury's *The Brothers*, Roland and Harcourt Clarendon are bound by "an affection, whose tenderness was known only to themselves" (1:36). Speaking of his younger twin in Braddon's *Like and Unlike*, Adrian Belfield claims "Fondness can hardly express our feeling. It is something more than affection. It is a sympathy so close that his vexations and his pleasures move me almost as strongly as my own" (1:175). Collins' *Poor Miss Finch* opens with Oscar calling his twin brother Nugent "the noblest creature that God every created!" and "an angel!" (49). In *Wives and Daughters* Mr. Gibson says of the Hamley brothers, "whatever those lads may be to others, there's as strong a brotherly love as ever I saw, between the two" (227).

Drury's *The Brothers* offers perhaps the clearest illustration. The novel opens with the protagonist, Roland, living with his older brother, Harcourt, and managing the family estate of Morlands, which his brother has inherited. While the brothers are content with this arrangement, everyone around them continually tells them the situation is unsustainable, as it proves to be when Harcourt falls in love with Roland's beloved, Marion Egerton. The novel closes with the ultimate act of restoring order to the family plot: Marion bears Roland a son and heir to Morlands and they name the child after Harcourt, who has (conveniently) died in a fire. *Poor Miss Finch* has the same ending: Oscar and Lucilla wed, and Nugent leaves England, requesting that if Oscar have a boy, "call him by my name—for my sake" (425). In the final pages, he dies at sea and Lucilla's eldest son is named Nugent. The exact same dynamic plays out between the eldest two sons in Yonge's *Three Brides*: the eldest dies, and the second names his son for him.[21] In all these cases, the plot is resolved through the removal of one brother and his replacement by a son. Lateral has again been made vertical and order—the linear order of family line paralleling story line—has been restored.[22]

In Dickens' *A Tale of Two Cities* (1859), Sydney Carton is only metaphorically a brother to Charles Darnay, his "double" who looks like his twin. But as in other brother-novels, the two fall in love with the same woman, Lucie, and the resolution is the same: Carton's death and Darnay making his son Carton's namesake, the classic brother-ending. Carton's final reflection before the guillotine reveals the triangulation of his desire, as he imagines the future and longs equally for a place in Lucie's and Darnay's heart: "I see her and her husband, their course done, lying side by side in their last earthly bed, and I know that each was not more honoured and held sacred in the other's soul than I was in the souls of both. I see that child who lay upon her bosom and who bore my name, a man, winning his way up in that path of life which once was mine" (441–442). Believing that his name will be "made illustrious" by this child (who also bears Darnay's last name), Carton almost fuses himself with Darnay, and gives them a shared heir.

The Love Triangle *à la Russe*: Turgenev and the Displaced Duel

Such brother-love triangles are not absent from Russian literature, but Russian authors approached the theme with a different set of priorities that led

[21] In Dinah Craik's *Hannah* (1871), the primogenitor is sickly and expected to die young, so his younger brother is raised as heir. But here too, when the elder brother dies the younger names his son for him.

[22] In Margaret Oliphant's *The Doctor's Family* (1863), the profligate elder brother, Fred, begins the novel living off the hardworking Doctor Edward Rider. But by the end of the novel Fred has died, Dr. Rider has married Fred's sister-in-law, Nettie, and they are raising Fred's son, Freddy. "Where Fred once lay and dozed, and filled the doctor's house with heavy fumes and discreditable gossip, a burden on his brother's reluctant hospitality, little Freddy now obliterated that dismal memory with prayers and slumbers of childhood" (192). This is an inverted version of naming the son after the deceased brother; here, too, the lateral has been replaced by vertical to restore harmony.

to quite different plots and outcomes. The brothers' love carries greater weight than romantic attachment, and never leads to open rivalry. Nor does it contain the homoerotic element that appears in many English novels. In *The Brothers Karamazov* (1880), for example, Dmitri and Ivan Karamazov are romantically entangled with the same woman, Katerina Ivanovna. But in this case Ivan confirms that "[Dmitri] himself solemnly handed her over to me, with his blessing" (14:211/232), and, as their younger brother Alyosha notes, it is not clear whether either brother is *truly* in love with her. Dmitri is ready to run off with Grushenka; Katerina Ivanovna, exemplifying true Dostoevskian psychology, both loves Dmitri and considers him a reptile [*gad*]; and Ivan "loved her madly, though it was true that at times he also hated her so much that he could even have killed her" (15:48/611). What this love triangle notably does *not* do is create actual rivalry between the brothers, as in the English novel. If anything, it brings them closer. Before Dmitri's murder trial, Ivan realizes his negative feelings toward Dmitri did not stem "from Katya's 'reversions' to him, but precisely *because he had killed their father!*" (15:56/619). In other words, it is his respect for familial bonds and not romantic rivalry that make Ivan dislike Dmitri. By contrast, father and son *are* overcome by jealousy as they struggle feverishly for Grushenka.

Turgenev's *Fathers and Children* (1862) contains a more elaborated instance of brothers as rivals for the same woman, yet neither the narrator nor the brothers ever openly acknowledge that this is what is going on (and the "winning" brother remains oblivious that such a rivalry ever existed). Unlike their English counterparts, Nikolai and Pavel Petrovich Kirsanov jointly inherit their family's property and choose not to split the estate. This enables them to remain allies in the conflict-of-generations plot, living together and helping each other financially. Thus during their cohabitation they face none of the inequalities of Roland and Harcourt in Drury's *The Brothers*. There, primogenitor Harcourt asserts his authority during their romantic tussle, telling his brother during a disagreement about who will drive what carriage: "Now, Roland, if you say any more, I shall have to remind you that I am master, after all. Sit where you please, but not in my place" (1:172).

The Kirsanov brothers do not face any material rivalries or resentments, but, like their English brethren, they fall in love with the same woman—Nikolai's peasant mistress, Fenechka. Turgenev introduces an early hint of this rivalry on the first night after Arkady's arrival, as Pavel Petrovich stares into the fire with an "intense and gloomy" expression. The narrator writes coyly: "God knows where his thoughts wandered, but it wasn't only the past," and then immediately mentions Fenechka in her back room (8.1:211/15). A few chapters later, after Pavel is interrupted by Nikolai during a visit to Fenechka, he returns to his study, throws himself on a sofa, "and sat there motionless, staring at the ceiling almost in despair" (8.1:233/33). Again, the narrator claims not to know what is troubling Pavel. In Turgenev, the brothers' rivalry is never explicitly mentioned by the narrator, while in the English novels both narrator and characters openly discuss it.

Caught in the same kind of love triangle we find in *The Brothers* or *Poor Miss Finch*, Pavel Petrovich so strongly desires to maintain brotherly relations that he displaces the romantic rivalry plotline onto another character. Instead of acknowledging his competition with Nikolai, who clearly has Fenechka's heart, he fights a duel with Bazarov over her. Scholars have interpreted the duel in many ways—a fight over ideology or values, or even a form of projection—but none have acknowledged the force of this displaced sibling rivalry.[23] While all their explanations are partially true, they overlook the fact that Bazarov *knows* they are fighting over a woman, not over philosophy, ideology, class conflict, or any of these other motivations. He realizes that he is a replacement rival: "But can he really be intervening on his brother's behalf? What's so important about a kiss? There must be more to it. Bah! Could he be in love with her himself? Of course he is; it's as clear as day" (8.1:349–350/122). He is the only one willing to openly state this. Thus, the romantic rivalry plotline is carried out between men who are allowed to dislike each other and have—as all the scholarship on the duel has shown—many other legitimate reasons for wishing to shoot at each other. Nikolai Petrovich's brotherly love shields him from awareness of the rivalry and jealousy, even when the wounded and feverish Pavel admits that Fenechka looks like his former beloved, Princess R., and then says "Ah, how I love that silly creature!" Nikolai "didn't even suspect to whom these words might pertain" (8.1:357/128).

Pavel Petrovich wishes for Bazarov to be his competitor because he feels fully justified in hating Bazarov, whereas he could never hate his brother. But after testing Fenechka, who affirms her love for Nikolai Petrovich, Pavel can no longer pretend. He magnanimously tells Nikolai to marry Fenechka, but putting brotherly love above personal desires comes at a cost. As in the English novels where the losing brother must ultimately give way to his successful rival, Pavel Petrovich decides to go away after the wedding. The narrator comments, "Lit by the bright daylight, his handsome, emaciated head resting on the white pillow looked like the head of a dead man ... In effect, he was a dead man" (8.1:363/133). The resolution of the brothers' plotline in Turgenev is the same as in the English novels about two brothers in the marriage plot—the "removal" of one of the brothers. Unlike in the English versions, however, here the secret of the rivalry is maintained, and Pavel preserves Nikolai's blissfully ignorant happiness with Fenechka

---

[23] Richard Freeborn claims that seeing Bazarov kissing Fenechka "supplies [Pavel] with the grounds for challenging Bazarov to a duel," but that the "inner meaning of this episode" is its ideological significance, as Bazarov is "prepared not only to reject the *dvoryanstvo* [nobility], but also to devote his life to working for the peasants" (*Turgenev*, 72). Wasiolek takes issue with this reading, arguing that "Bazarov's flirting with and stealing of a kiss from Fenechka and his acceptance of the duel all seem a voluntary immersion of himself in what he had held in the highest scorn ..." (Fathers and Sons: *Russia at the Cross-roads*, 106). Milton Hindus calls "the incident with Fenitchka" the "needed excuse" for a duel that is really about their conflict over values and manners ("The Duels in Mann and Turgenev," 309). Similarly, Phillip Atteberry notes Bazarov's kiss as a pretense, but claims that "more symbolically, and more significantly, the duel provides both with an opportunity to attack the worst qualities they see within themselves" ("Regenerative and Degenerative Forces in Turgenev's 'Fathers and Sons,'" 53).

(just as Elena keeps Ida ignorant of their rivalry in Tur's *Two Sisters*, 1851, as discussed in Chapter 2).

Sofia Smirnova's *Strength of Character* (1876) has a radically different plotline, but again a character ultimately sacrifices himself to keep his brother ignorant of their rivalry. In this case, the younger Solovoi brother, Nikolai, is trapped in an unwanted affair with his older brother's wife. He falls in love with the marriageable young heroine at the start of the novel, but he is blackmailed by his sister-in-law as he tries to escape the affair. Driven to a half-crazed state, he decides to kill her. With no clear plan for the murder, the only thing he is set on is that "His brother should not know about their relations—, even after her death ... It was the only, but a very important, condition" (387–388). Nikolai ultimately takes his own life after the murder, leaving a suicide note that keeps people from connecting the two events. With his suicide, he is able to protect his brother from ever learning of his betrayal of brotherly trust.

Resolving the English Two-Brother Problem *à la Russe*

A very small number of English novels did find ways to include multiple brothers with families in their conclusions, and these offer clues to what was needed for lasting fraternal harmony: two sources of income, a condition that was standard in the Russian context. When the sense of rivalry inherent in the inheritance structure is removed in an English novel, as well as the expectations that come with being an eldest son, this can enable brothers to marry and live peaceably side-by-side. Yonge's *Three Brides* was mentioned above in relation to the first and second sons fitting the standard pattern where the oldest dies and the second names his son for the departed brother. Yet it is about *three* married brothers (with two additional unwed brothers), and the end of the novel sees the second and third—Miles and Julius—happily raising families near each other, with Miles replacing his deceased brother, Raymond, as MP, and Julius as a curate. I believe Miles and Julius are aided in their fraternal harmony by having both been raised with the same expectations: "Slight as had been his seniority, poor Raymond had always been on a sort of paternal pinnacle, sharing the administration with his mother, while Miles and Julius had paired on an equality" (396). There is no primogenitor in this situation (psychologically speaking). Younger brothers needed a stable career and more modest ambitions, something Yonge's didactic, moralizing fiction was happy to provide.

Charlotte Brontë's *Shirley* (1849)—a historical novel set in 1811–1812—explores a more radical, gender-bending path to fraternal harmony that again culminates in two sources of income. While most scholarship frames *Shirley* as "a novel about two women"—focusing on the development of Shirley and Caroline—insufficient attention has been given to the pair of brothers these women marry.[24] Indeed, one scholar goes so far as to claim that "Robert and Louis are not particularly important in the novel."[25] I will suggest that their roles in the love triangles that structure the novel are equally as important as the women's. The primogenitor, Robert Moore, has inherited a family business mired in debts, which he struggles to revive (causing him to resist his attraction to his penniless cousin, Caroline), while Louis "had, when the blight of hereditary prospects rendered it necessary for him to push his own fortune, adopted the very arduous and very modest career of a teacher" (55). In economic terms, Louis would seem to be ineligible for a marriage plot, as he has nothing to offer a bride. And for this very reason, he feels inhibited from revealing his affections to his former pupil, the wealthy heiress Shirley Keeldar.

Scholars have discussed the love triangle at the heart of this novel as two women—Caroline and Shirley—around Robert Moore, focusing on the female bond as the most potent.[26] Terry Castle offers up a series of diagrams that rework Sedgewick's *Between Men* theories—moving from a two man/one woman triangle through a tetrahedron to a two woman/one man triangle—to suggest that "within this new *female* homosocial structure, the possibility of male bonding is radically suppressed."[27] Yet the novel has *two* Moores, which would belie this triangular conclusion. It seems that our existing theories cannot accommodate the second brother. Indeed, if we follow the progression of Castle's diagrams, we conclude with a triangle where one of the men has been "removed," just as the novels discussed above do in their own conclusions. Similarly, Julia Gardener essentially eliminates Louis, turning the two brothers into one when she claims "Louis in particular is so peripheral that he comes to function as little more than a near clone of his brother. It is almost as if the women are marrying the same man."[28] She wishes to turn this into a single brother novel, suggesting that the double wedding's function at the end is to unite the two women: "Rather than being exchanged between the two men, Caroline and Shirley bond together, collapsing Robert and Louis into one entity" (ibid), a claim that echoes scholars' treatment of the Bede brothers.

Louis and Robert are distinctly *not* one entity, yet this push to treat them as singular by scholars is also exactly what needs to happen—structurally—in all English brother novels: there is only a place for *one*. Since the brothers cannot literally "stand in exactly the same place"—and the two women cannot literally marry the same man—*Shirley* must resolve the issue by taking one of the brothers

[24] Taylor, "Class and Gender in Charlotte Brontë's 'Shirley,'" 85.
[25] Gardner, "'Neither Monsters Nor Temptresses Nor Terrors': Representing Desire in Charlotte Brontë's *Shirley*," 417.
[26] Castle, "Sylvia Townsend Warner and Lesbian Fiction," 133–134; Gardner, "Neither Monster Nor Temptress."
[27] Castle, "Sylvia Townsend Warner and Lesbian Fiction," 133.
[28] Gardner, "Neither Monster Nor Temptress," 417.

out of this problematic construction. As there are two heroines, removing a brother through death or putting him in a sister-role would not be a satisfying resolution, but Brontë offers a different kind of gender-flipping solution.

Louis' plotline—which is rarely (if ever) discussed as such, as his story has been treated by scholars as an auxiliary of Shirley's—is a rewritten *Jane Eyre* (1847), reversing the roles of hero and heroine. Louis finds himself in the traditionally female role of a dependent in the household, while Shirley, "a woman who should have been a man" in the words of one critic, is his rich Rochester.[29] As Shirley herself famously announces, "They gave me a man's name; I hold a man's position: it is enough to inspire me with a touch of manhood" (172). Shirley may be playing the "male" role in a courtship of sorts with Caroline, but she is also in love with a man who is positioned in the feminine, dependent role economically.[30] The great challenge at the end of the novel is for Shirley to relinquish her dominant, masculine position and to make Louis the "master," as her property becomes his upon marriage.[31]

While feminists may be horrified at this shift in Shirley's once strong and assertive character, she resolves the "two-brother-problem" by giving the brothers two sources of income. The "tidy but disappointing double marriage plot" that restricts these women to traditional roles at the conclusion also makes a place for two brothers to harmoniously coexist.[32] Instead of treating the two brothers as one in order to make a clean triangle, I am suggesting that—as in the other brother-novels—we need to recognize the intense homosocial bonding that has not fitted into our standard theories. The brothers do not become one, but they remain united. With the economics resolved, the brothers can imagine a shared future, and Robert asks Caroline "What would you think if, one day—perhaps ere another ten years elapse—Louis and I divide Briarfield parish betwixt us?" (539). This idea of splitting the estate offers a very un-English twist and keeps the two brothers together in a way we find in many Russian novels, which suggests that the distribution of property is a central factor in determining whether such a novelistic outcome is possible.

It is more difficult to speak of the ending of Gaskell's *Wives and Daughters*, as she did not live to complete it, but even without its final chapter it hints at a more modern resolution for brothers that would be coming later in the century.[33] In some ways the novel follows the pattern explored above: as in *The Brothers, Poor Miss*

---

[29] Taylor, "Class and Gender in Charlotte Brontë's 'Shirley,'" 89.

[30] On the romance between Shirley and Caroline, see Gardner, "Liminality and Antiliminality in Charlotte Brontë's Novels"; Keen, "Narrative Annexes in Charlotte Brontë's *Shirley*."

[31] Boone, *Tradition Counter Tradition*, 13–14.

[32] Keen, "Narrative Annexes in Charlotte Brontë's *Shirley*," 107.

[33] First published serially in the *Cornhill Magazine* (August 1864—January 1866), the novel was not quite complete when Mrs. Gaskell died suddenly in 1865.

Finch, and *Three Brides*, the elder brother dies.[34] However, here the brothers have different beloveds, and Osborne's death and Roger's growing successes—scientific and romantic (presumed to be coming in the missing final chapter)—do not fully re-establish the patriarchal order and provide the neat plot resolution we find in the other novels. In *Wives and Daughters* it is as if the wrong brother has sired the son. Just as Oscar Dubourg and Roland Clarendon name their sons after their brothers, Osborne decides "if we have a boy, I will call it Roger" (390).[35] Thus, at the end of the novel there are two Rogers; rather than restoring the clear linear progression of fathers and sons, this naming carries over the problem of doubling into the next generation. Osborne's child ensures that his brother Roger will not become the heir to Hamley Hall. The family line is still branched.

It seems that Gaskell was seeking an alternative path for younger brothers, based not on family continuity, but on progress. Early in the novel, when Osborne is in financial difficulties, Roger hopes for a fellowship from Trinity College, Cambridge, promising Osborne "then we'll have a purse in common" (355). This is a progressive development for the younger brother to find a source of income outside of the family inheritance structure, based purely on talent (unlike the Church, army, or law, which still often relied on family connections). On the final page of the last completed chapter, adult Roger—a proto-Darwin figure—departs on a dangerous six-month voyage to Africa for research, leaving the problem of his future and his ability to marry the heroine unresolved. The *Cornhill Magazine* editor, Frederick Greenwood, assured readers that this marriage most certainly would have taken place. As to the problem of inheritance, Greenwood suggested that Roger "has no need to draw upon the little fortune which is to go to poor Osborne's boy, for he becomes professor at some grey scientific institution, and wins his way in the world handsomely."[36] Linda Hughes sees in this a modern twist, as "Roger's destiny is an international career; [Hamley] Hall is to be owned by the offspring of an international and cross-class union."[37] With Roger's scientific career, the novel looks ahead to a time when two brothers would be able to more stably coexist in a plot because there would be alternative paths open to them. This is something authors like Austen had already begun to explore with their second-son clergymen and officers, but those fields still relied on being given a post or living and were not just about independent talent and hard work. But it would only

---

[34] Many scholarly interpretations of the novel link his death with Darwinian themes, as "Osborne, the fragile poet, nurtured by the exclusively classical education of Rugby ... is 'weeded out', failing examinations, falling into debt, then dying prematurely" (Debrabant, "Birds, Bees and Darwinian Survival Strategies in *Wives and Daughters*," 17). See also D'Albertis, *Dissembling Fictions*, 142; Henson, "History, Science and Social Change," 27; and Yeazell, *Fictions of Modesty*, 215. D'Albertis refers to "Gaskell's insistence on Osborne's effeminacy" (153), and Sparks writes of his "distinctly feminine persona," which links his portrayal with that of Seth Bede and Adrian Belfield (*The Doctor in the Victorian Novel*, 78).

[35] His father is also named Roger, but at the moment of this decision he is thinking of his brother.

[36] See Henson, "History, Science and Social Change," 30.

[37] Hughes, "*Cousin Phillis, Wives and Daughters*, and Modernity," 97.

become realizable with "the erosion of property in land as the principal foundation for one's social identity," something which "coincided with industrialization,
imperialism, and the rise of commodity culture" toward the end of the century.[38]
With Gaskell's death and the final chapter missing, *Wives and Daughters* never
fully resolved the brothers issue.

Shirley and *Wives and Daughters* both point to a key element in an English
novel trying to accommodate multiple brothers—multiple sources of income. In
the earlier *Shirley*, this must be two estates. *Wives and Daughters* looks ahead to
a time when men—at least exceptional ones like Roger Hamley—could pursue
careers based on intellect and talent, independent of their family ancestry. Sharing was only possible for English brothers who had no heirs, and consequently
no conflicting duties to family futurity. For example, Dickens' Cheeryble brothers in *Nicholas Nickleby* (1838–1839) happily run their counting house together,
but both are unwed and they share a single heir—their nephew. In Russia, with its
partible inheritance, either splitting an estate or sharing its profits gave brothers
their own income, and this opened up for them new plot possibilities.

Brothers and the Russian Literary Tradition

There are very few brothers in Russian literature from the first half of the nineteenth century, before the rise of the Great Russian novel.[39] Griboedov, Pushkin,
Lermontov, Gogol, and early Turgenev all focused on defining Russian literature
and the Russian literary hero, and this quest centered on a solitary (retrospectively
labeled by Turgenev "superfluous") type. Chatsky seems to have no family of his
own to visit when he returns to Moscow and dashes impetuously to his beloved
Sophie ("Woe from Wit," 1823). Pechorin feels alienated from all his peers, and
is never seen with his family members, nor does he often recall them (*Hero of
Our Time*, 1842). The narrator mentions the death of Onegin's father in the third
stanza of *Eugene Onegin* (1825–1832) and then never refers to any family ties for
his hero, aside from the dying uncle whose estate Onegin inherits at the end of
the first chapter. Turgenev's Rudin, too, has no family ties to ground him (*Rudin*,
1856). In pointing out the "Russian disease" with superfluous men like Pechorin,
Onegin, and Rudin, these authors depicted a state of alienation that comes, in part,
from being cut off from kinship bonds. It is no accident that all these superfluous
men are only children. They do not have brothers and do not know how to participate in a broader sense of brotherhood, be it biologically, socially, or spiritually
constructed.

---

[38] Frank, *Law, Literature, and the Transmission of Culture in England, 1837–1925*, 45.
[39] Exceptions: Pushkin's "*Brat'ia razboiniki*" (1822); Gogol's *Taras Bulba* (1835) has a significant
brother pair, but the relationship between the brothers is not emphasized.

For many Russian authors, the question of brotherly love was tightly bound up with the ideal of Russia herself. In his "Selected Passages from Correspondence with Friends" (1844), Gogol suggested that without loving Russia, one could not love one's brothers:

> But how can we love our brothers, how can we love men? The soul desires only to love the beautiful, and poor men are so imperfect, there is so little beauty in them! How shall we do it? Thank God, above all, that you are Russian. For the Russian, at the present time, there is a way; that way is Russia herself. If only the Russian loves Russia and everything there is in Russia! It is to this love that God Himself now directs us.[40]

Similarly, for Dostoevsky the "cure" to the "Russian disease" infecting characters like Onegin and Pechorin was based on the combination of Russianness and brotherhood. In his famous "Pushkin speech" (1880), Dostoevsky preached Russia's mission to bring brotherhood to the rest of Europe, exclaiming euphorically "To become a real Russian ... means just (in the final analysis—please bear that in mind) to become a brother to all people, a *panhuman*, if you like" (26:148/2:1294).[41] And further, he suggested that "the Russian heart is more plainly destined, among all the peoples, for universally human and brotherly unity" (26:148/2:1295).

On the literary front, I believe this "cure" is to be found in the families in which authors embed their characters during the second half of the century. Even in the early examples Dostoevsky draws upon, the family-less Aleko and Onegin are his models of the negative, isolated Russian type, while Tatiana, his "apotheosis of Russian womanhood," is firmly rooted in the Larin family. Beginning in the 1860s, Russian authors would place the next generation of superfluous men—Andrei Bolkonsky, Bazarov, Raskolnikov—in families where kinship duties would challenge their sense of purposelessness and alienation. And it is no accident that Dostoevsky delivered his "Pushkin speech" about brotherhood in the same year he published *The Brothers Karamazov*—his greatest masterpiece about brotherly bonds. The thematic links between the two reveal the same set of pressing concerns. In his fiction, Dostoevsky used a family of brothers to embody his philosophical claims.

In order to find belonging, characters in the Russian novel must work out their relationships with their siblings, and most important in this quest are the relationships between brothers. I believe brothers are more significant than sisters in this respect because the "seeker" characters in the works of the Great Russian realists—Turgenev, Dostoevsky, Goncharov, and Tolstoy—tend to be men. These novelists

---

[40] Gogol, *Selected Passages*, 111.
[41] The "Pushkin Speech" was published in Dostoevsky's *Writer's Diary*.

reserved the deepest philosophical and existential soul-searching for their male protagonists, while women, like Sonya Marmeladova or Turgenev's strong heroines, who already have answers to these questions, do not go through the same process of *seeking* truths. Additionally, as Leonore Davidoff has noted, "Moving from the single dyad to the group, the idea of a sibling relationship has long figured as *brotherhood* and, less frequently, *sisterhood*."[42] Brothers, rather than sisters, provide the more accepted path to universal brotherhood (which includes both men and women)—a principal obsession of the Russians.

Loving Thy Brother: Failure or Ongoing Spiritual Struggle

One way to demonstrate the importance of fraternal harmony is to depict the dire consequences of its absence. Aleksei Potekhin did just this in his once popular *Poor Gentry* (1863). The novel traces the fate of the Ostashkovs, who are descended from an old gentry family (*stolbovoi dvorianin*) but live in poverty like the peasants around them. Fraternal rivalry, the lack of a legal division of property (and fears about or desires for such a division), and failures at familial unity help lead to the family's ruin. At the start of the novel, Ivan and Nikanor are living with their father and there is an agreed upon division of the land between two brothers, but nothing has been legally split. Their father has always favored the lazy Ivan to the hard-working Nikanor, but upon Nikanor's marriage he promises to legally give him a portion. Instead, however, he and Ivan sell half of it without Nikanor's knowledge, and then, while Nikanor is away in town, Ivan mows his remaining land, leaving Nikanor's family with nothing. When an alcoholic uncle (the father's brother) suddenly returns from fifteen years in the army, he makes the situation worse by fanning the flames of family discord around the division of property. Focusing on a lower strata of society than most novels, Potekhin captures the same sense of rivalry that we find in the English novel, where brothers perceived that there was not enough property or wealth to comfortably accommodate all.

In *Poor Gentry*, the English and Russian inheritance systems are directly contrasted by two members of the provincial nobility who discuss the fall of the Ostashkov family into total poverty. Their comments offer a critique of the Russian partible inheritance practice:

"Uneducated, wild, raised like a peasant!" exclaimed Palenov. "But such a decline, such pulverization/degeneration [*izmelchanie*] of gentry clans [*rodov dvorianskikh*], you must agree, is possible only in Russia, with our destructive system of breaking up estates. Look at the English aristocracy with its law of primogeniture ... Another reason for this decline, it seems, is that we don't

---

[42] Davidoff, *Thicker than Water*, 38.

have that concentration and exclusivity of class, by which every member of a known social class looks on each other member as on his fellowman/co-brother [*sobrata*], and offers his hand in help when he falls, supports him and rescues him, and by which this social class also fastidiously receives all newcomers, and aliens." (63–64)

While speeches like this seem to defend the importance of ancestry and nobility, the novel as a whole offers a rebuke.

Much like Hardy's later *Tess of the D'Urbervilles* (1891) would test the dangers of making too much of one's family descent from a higher class status, Potekhin's novel also challenges the importance of class/estate origins. Problems begin in earnest because of Nikanor's aunt wishing for him to live like gentry, and especially to raise his son like a true member of his noble estate. When she first sends Nikanor to town to work on this project, he is initially met with solidarity, as two local gentry tell him "Monsieur Ostashkov ... you understand that you are our co-brother [*sobrat*] by blood, that in you flows ancient gentry blood, the same as in us" (64). Yet from this propitious start, he comes to be used as a laughingstock and the butt of pranks. Ever more desirous of the luxury dangled before him by these "co-brothers," Nikanor becomes a hanger-on and a lackey in town, ceases to work on his farm, and ultimately leaves his family in far greater poverty than when they began. Present actions, rather than blood lineage, are what carries true value. Nikanor was successful when he worked his fields and cared for his wife and children. When he made his brother envious through the initial noble patronage he found and ceased working, the family was set on a path to ruin. In both generations—between father and uncle and between Nikanor and Ivan—laziness, alcoholism, and envy tear the family apart.

In *The Golovlyovs* (1875–1880), Saltykov-Shchedrin similarly illustrates the importance of brotherly love by depicting its utter absence. The novel was originally conceived as a series of short stories/satirical sketches that would form a cycle, "Well-meaning Speeches" (*Blagonamerennye rechi*), and even when Saltykov-Shchedrin reworked the original stories for book publication, the novel still maintained the feel of a series of vignettes about family life.[43] However, one can identify a clear plotline for the Golovlev family: decline that takes place over three generations.[44] It is easy—and correct—to blame Arina Petrovna and her horrific

---

[43] They were published in *Otechestvennye zapiski*, beginning in 1875 (for publication history, see the commentary to the *Sobranie sochinenii* 13:668–671). It was Turgenev who suggested that Saltykov-Shchedrin create a full novel about the Golovlevs (Foote, *Saltykov-Shchedrin's* The Golovlyovs, 143, 146).

[44] Milton Ehre claims *The Golovlyovs* "is the story of the disintegration of a family of the Russian provincial gentry—the Golovlyovs—which is implicitly the story of the decline of their class." Yet one sentence later, he claims the novel is "virtually 'plotless,' if we understand plot in the conventional sense of a story arranged so as to arouse curiosity about impending events" ("A Classic of Russian Realism," 3–4). For its links to degeneration and the works of Zola, see Holland, "The Russian *Rougon-Macquart*."

mothering for the family's tragedy, but it is also in no small part due to the fail-ures of brotherly relations in the first two chapters.[45] In "Family Court" (*Semeinyi sud*), the two younger Golovlyov brothers, Pavel and Porfiry—also known as Judas (Iudushka) or "Blood-Sucker"—come home to the family estate to cast judgment on their prodigal eldest brother, Stepan. Openly playing on the biblical idea of the last judgment (*strashnyi sud*), Shchedrin depicts a world in which mother calls upon brothers to essentially disinherit one of their own. However, even Arina Petrovna is horrified by the lack of brotherly love Porfiry displays: "Can it be that he is really such a bloodsucker that he would cast his own brother out on the street?" (13:43). Given no reprieve, Stepan wastes away at Golovlyovo and soon dies. While it is Arina Petrovna who under-nourishes him and leaves him without even candles for light, Stepan's brothers play a crucial role in his destruc-tion. Porfiry's judgment—which Pavel passively accepts—is the first incident in the sequence that creates the plot of family decline.

Rather unusually among Russian novels, *The Golovlyovs*, like *Poor Gentry*, focuses on the way property is divided.[46] The second chapter, "As Relatives Do" (*Po rodstvennomu*), has a *King Lear*-like plot as Arina Petrovna's husband has died, and the property has been split between their two sons. The plot of this chapter hinges on Pavel's death from alcoholism and the ensuing question of what will hap-pen to his estate. As long as there is no will, it will pass into the hands of Porfiry (Pavel has no descendants). The plot for the brothers is essentially that of a vul-ture hovering, waiting to devour his brother's remains. Iudushka races to Pavel's estate, and, using religion as a cover for acting "as relatives do," he appears at his brother's bedside to torment him. "Little Judas' eyes looked brightly, as relatives do, but the sick man saw clearly that these hid a 'noose' in them that in a moment would leap out and wrap around his throat" (13:77). All that is truly left of acting "as relatives do" is the legal aspect of inheritance; being a brother is reduced to being the inheritor of the estate. The failures of brotherhood on the spiritual and emotional planes are responsible for winnowing away at the family. Each chapter removes another branch until, finally, Porfiry is left alone at the end. The ultimate plotline of decline stems from these early failures of brotherhood when there were still three robust future lines for the Golovlyovs.

While Tolstoy did not write about such familial failures, he did not idealize the brother-brother bond or the ease of creating loving relations on the lateral axis.[47] But he did show the incredible spiritual weight of brotherhood. In *Anna*

---

[45] On Arina Petrovna's failures, see Kaminer, *Women with a Thirst for Destruction*, 32–44.

[46] This theme also features in a minor way in Krestovsky (pseud.)'s *In Hope of Something Better* (1860), where two cousins, Ivan and Vasia, are set against each other as rivals for their grandmother's inheritance (666–668).

[47] Brothers were a consistent theme for Tolstoy. *Childhood* (1852), *Boyhood* (1854), and *Youth* (1857) all make a brother-brother relationship central to the family dynamics. The last of Tolstoy's Sevastopol stories, "Sevastopol in August" (1855), also centers on two brothers. While writing *War and Peace*, Tol-stoy focused primarily on brother-sister relationships, but the first plan for the novel actually contained

Karenina (1875–1878), Nikolai Levin brings Konstantin to his spiritual crisis that comprises the body of the final Part VIII. After describing a loving, domestic scene of Kitty and baby Mitya, the narrator opens a new section with the words "From that moment when, at the sight of his beloved brother dying, Levin had looked at the questions of life and death for the first time through those new convictions as he called them ... he had been horrified, not so much at death as at life without the slightest knowledge of whence it came, wherefore, why, and what it was" (19:367/785). Brotherhood forces Levin to face the inescapable realities of life and death.[48]

The domestic ideal of the English novel—attained with wife and child—is trumped by the spiritual concerns raised by the brother bond. Even after his spiritual awakening prompted by a conversation with a peasant who reminds him of living for God, Levin still struggles to love his half-brother Koznyshev—the immediate test of brotherly love. They encounter one another right after Levin's moment of revelation: "the brothers' eyes met, and Levin, despite his usual and now especially strong desire to be on friendly and, above all, simple terms with his brother, felt it awkward to look at him" (19:384/802). There is no linear progression to their brotherhood and can be no ultimate resolution, no completed state of unity (like marriage for lovers). This seems to eliminate them from linear plot, but I believe they create a new kind of lateral plot, one that does not develop across time, but links characters to the ongoing challenge of living in harmony with their fellow humans.[49]

Levin's ultimate realizations—reached through argument with Koznyshev—are about the limits of brotherhood and our duties to legal or biological family versus the abstract neighbor. When Koznyshev claims that the Turks are "killing our brothers, of the same blood, of the same religion" and that it is a natural response that Russians "run to help stop these horrors," Levin counters "there is not and cannot be such an immediate feeling about the oppression of the Slavs," removing the word "brothers" from the discussion (19:387, 388/805). He cannot accept the existence of truly *familial* bonds with perfect strangers. If he struggles to love even Koznyshev as a brother, how could that concept of brotherly love be expanded to such abstract extremes? The question of brotherly love is the crux of Tolstoy's moral concerns.

---

many more brother-brother relationships. It opened with the words: "There were two brothers and two sisters in the Mosalsky family." The older brother had died, but the younger also had two sons (13:13).

[48] In Anthony Thorlby's words, "Nikolay has always disturbed Levin's conscience ... because he embodies so inescapably, by virtue of being a brother with unbreakable ties of blood and memory, those basic facts of illness, misery, and death, which Levin finds so hard to assimilate" (*Leo Tolstoy*: Anna Karenina, 72). There are also important autobiographical resonances here with Tolstoy's loss of his own brother, which forced him to confront the issue of death.

[49] Thorlby suggests that the brothers "make little difference to the plot—plot is relatively unimportant as an organizational principle of *Anna Karenina*—but they contribute considerably to the novel's realism and theme" (*Leo Tolstoy*, 72). See also Knapp, Anna Karenina *and Others*, 95.

Brotherhood as Plot: *The Brothers Karamazov*

Of all the novels written in the nineteenth century, *The Brothers Karamazov* prob-
ably gives the most central place to brothers. Both the marriage plot and the
generational plot are present in the novel, but Dostoevsky sidelines them, making them the catalyst for relationships between the brothers, which are the true
heart of the drama. The generational plot has received by far the most attention,
so I will not revisit it here; certainly one of Dostoevsky's concerns was to depict
the breakdown of the patriarchal order and the failure of the father.[50] In addition,
each brother does have a potential marriage plot.[51] However, a plot summary that
focused on these would leave out the primary concerns of the brothers and would
fail to explain the true driving force of the novel (Ivan's "Rebellion," the Grand
Inquisitor, and Father Zosima, for example, would not appear). The brothers' relationships are entwined with the key philosophical and moral questions the novel
raises about the possibility of universal brotherhood and harmony in the face of
human antagonism and weakness.

The role of brothers in the plot is directly related to the type of "accidental" family to which they belong: three legitimate and one illegitimate brother, the children
of three mothers (all now deceased) and a buffoon father, who were raised mostly
apart and come to know each other only as young adults.[52] The plot for these
brothers hinges on defining the very nature of brotherhood. As in *Anna Karenina*, this task is ongoing. Accidental families remain accidental. Unlike Tolstoy's
brothers, however, the Karamazovs do not have warm childhood memories to
fall back on; their ties must be formed in the present, even in the face of forces
that could threaten to drive them apart. As I have explored elsewhere, Ivan challenges Alyosha's faith and love by laying bare all the darkness in his soul during his
"Rebellion" and recitation of his Grand Inquisitor *poema*.[53] Expecting rejection,
Ivan is unprepared for Alyosha's brotherly love—demonstrated by his silent kiss—
and instead finds himself drawn closer to his brother. And as mentioned above,
Dmitri and Ivan are almost romantic rivals for Katerina Ivanovna, yet rather than
this potential challenge creating a division, it actually seems to bring the brothers
closer.[54]

---

[50] Dostoevsky was explicit about this in his *Writer's Diary* (e.g. 22:7).

[51] I explore these in "Dostoevsky and the (Missing) Marriage Plot."

[52] As is well known, Dostoevsky formulated his conception of the family in part as a reaction against
Tolstoy's (see 25:173). He continued the polemic with Tolstoy in the final pages of *The Adolescent*, and
in even greater depths in the drafts (e.g. 17:142). I am grateful to Chloë Kitzinger for bringing this to my
attention by quoting this passage in her paper at ASEEES (November, 2015). For more on Dostoevsky's
response to the Tolstoyan family, see Bem, *U istokov tvorchestva Dostoevskogo*; Holland, *The Novel in
the Age of Disintegration*; Kliger, "Russia (18th–19th Century)."

[53] Berman, *Siblings in Tolstoy and Dostoevsky*, 115–119.

[54] It can be easy to overlook the closeness of this bond because, as I argue in *Siblings in Tolstoy and
Dostoevsky*, the narrator deliberately hides it from view, but other characters allude to it (122).

The Karamazov brothers are not rent asunder by romantic rivalry or differences in their degrees of faith, nor are they in competition over their inheritance—another primary English concern. Dmitri fights with his father about his rights to his deceased mother's money, but the brothers never seem to even think about their shared inheritance. Ivan actually needs the Europe-obsessed Smerdyakov to explain why this could have been a motivation for wishing Fyodor Pavlovich dead. "After your parent, each of you three good brothers [*bratsev*], would then get nearly forty thousand, and maybe even more," Smerdyakov tells him, adding that if Fyodor Pavlovich had married Grushenka, she would have transferred the money to herself, leaving the brothers with nothing (15:52/615). Smerdyakov goes on to note that if Dmitri is found guilty, then he will be stripped of his rights as nobility and his inheritance, so his brothers will get sixty thousand, not forty. It is the envious, illegitimate Smerdyakov (who will inherit nothing), who creates this Western inheritance plot. Ivan is so disgusted by the idea that he immediately plans an escape for Dmitri, which will use up his share of the inheritance, in order *not* to profit by his brother's loss.[55]

Dostoevsky's characters actively reject the concerns at the heart of the English novel, avoiding rivalry and the plotlines it engenders. Instead, I believe the real plot for the brothers in *The Brothers Karamazov* is to learn to be one's brother's keeper. This adds a spiritual component to the family novel. The attempts and failures of the Karamazov brothers—and their unacknowledged, illegitimate brother, Smerdyakov—to enact Christ's teachings of brotherly love amongst themselves are a test of Dostoevsky's ideals.[56]

The rejected Smerdyakov fails at this test. When Alyosha asks him if "brother Dmitri" will soon be returning, Smerdyakov answers "Why should I be informed as to Dmitri Fyodorovich? It is not as if I were his keeper" (14:206/226).[57] Smerdyakov makes a veiled biblical reference to Cain's "Am I my brother's keeper," yet alters the statement so as not to use the word brother. A few pages later, when Alyosha asks Ivan what will happen between their father and Dmitri if he leaves, Ivan angrily replies "Am I my brother Dmitri's keeper or something? ... Cain's answer to God about his murdered brother, eh? Maybe that's what you're thinking at the moment?" (14:211/231–232). In *Adam Bede*, by contrast, it is Dinah Morris, not one of the brothers, who quotes this biblical passage. She does not link it to literal siblinghood, while Dostoevsky's characters actively *live* the question. Ivan's ambivalence about his duty to his brother and the possibility of brotherly love are at the heart of his spiritual crisis. He even begins his rebellion with the question of loving one's neighbors, in Russian literally one's "close ones" (*svoikh*

---

[55] Arkady Kirsanov is similarly upset in *Fathers and Children* when Bazarov suggests that a second heir (his illegitimate baby brother) is a threat.

[56] This is the topic of much of Ch.4 of my *Siblings in Tolstoy and Dostoevsky*.

[57] This passage is discussed by both Meerson, *Dostoevsky's Taboos*, 187–188 and Morson, "Verbal Pollution in *The Brothers Karamazov*," 241.

blizhnikh), (14:215), choosing his little brother as the "close one" upon whom to test out his ideas. Can a brother—one who is coming to know him for the first time as an adult—love him in the face of all his inner darkness? This is, again, a way of *living* the question of brothering.

What must be central to the Russian family, as Dostoevsky reconceives it, are spiritual ties.[58] *This* is what draws Alyosha to kiss Ivan after hearing "The Grand Inquisitor." On the night before the murder trial, Alyosha prays for his brothers, Dmitri and Ivan. During the trial, Katerina Ivanovna describes how "for those two whole months Ivan Fyodorovich had been driving himself nearly out of his mind over saving 'the monster and murderer,' his brother" and claims that "he could not bear it that his own brother was a parricide!" (15:121/690–691). These statements indicate both that the tie he felt to his brother transcends personal preferences and also Ivan's reverence for the family, despite everything else he may claim. In the trial Ivan, still struggling with himself, *does* attempt to be his brother Dmitri's keeper. He produces Smerdyakov's money, and declares "It was he who killed father, not my brother. He killed him, and killed him on my instructions ..." (15:117/686). From his hospital bed after his conviction, Dmitri worries about Ivan's health. Prayers and love, not money or worldly connections, are what brothers must learn to provide each other in Dostoevsky's new vision of the family. And while the Karamazov brothers succeed to some degree, in the end they fail in the most important challenge—recognizing that "the lackey" Smerdyakov is also their brother and just as much a part of their "accidental family" as they themselves are.[59]

Many commentators have analyzed the ways Dostoevsky implicates the reader in his novels, and his treatment of Smerdyakov's place in the family—and the novel as a whole—certainly contributes to this.[60] Specifically, readers are easily lulled into believing (like the legitimate Karamazov brothers) that Smerdyakov has no place in their family because the narrator removes him from the novelized, plotted version of that family. He is not mentioned a single time in Book One: "The Story of One Little Family" (*Istoriia odnoi semeiki*).[61] When he finally does appear, it is first in passing as "the servant Smerdyakov" (Dmitri's words) and then more fully

[58] This is partly a response to Tolstoy's depiction of loving gentry families with their years of shared experiences on the family estate (see note 52).

[59] This failure is epitomized by Ivan's statement (just cited) that Smerdyakov killed Fyodor Pavlovich, "not my brother," and by Alyosha's similar claim that "The lackey killed him [Fyodor Pavlovich], my brother is innocent" (15:189/768). See Meerson, *Dostoevsky's Taboos*, 197; Berman, *Siblings in Tolstoy and Dostoevsky*, 126. Althought it was never proved that Fyodor Pavlovich was Smerdyakov's father and Lizaveta may well have been violated by many others, everyone—including Fyodor Pavlovich—assumes his paternity.

[60] For examples of such studies, see Miller, *Dostoevsky and the Idiot*; Marintsen, *Surprised by Shame*; Belknap, *Plots*, 106–107. Meerson explores Smerdyakov's place in *The Brothers Karamazov* and the failure to acknowledge him as a brother in the brilliant final chapter of *Dostoevsky's Taboos* (183–209). See also Morson, "Verbal Pollution in *The Brothers Karamazov.*"

[61] Here I am in agreement with Greta Matzner-Gore, who calls the question of Smerdyakov's inclusion "a *narrative* conundrum," asking "Will we recognize Smerdyakov as one of the brothers, and thus

in the chapter "Stinking Lizaveta," which in family terms links him to his mother, but not to his father and half-brothers. It is not just the Karamazovs who fail to see him as a brother; the plot is constructed to make this a failure in the novel itself, or, as Olga Meerson formulates it, "his story is the main line of the plot, which Dostoevsky chose to mask as deviation."[62]

Smerdyakov is only really given a place in "the story of one little family" during Dmitri's trial, which is like a family novel of its own. The case opens with the servant Grigory retelling the story of the Karamazov family, or essentially the material of Book One (*Istoriia odnoi semeiki*). The prosecutor, Ippolit Kirillovich, claims in his closing "We are reproached with having invented all sorts of novels. But what has the defense attorney offered if not novel upon novel?" (15:174/748). In these new "novels" by the defense attorney, we essentially get a re-plotting of *The Brothers Karamazov*: what it would have looked like if told from the point of view of the minor and overlooked brother, Smerdyakov. The plot of *The Brothers Karamazov* demonstrates the dangers of leaving such a brother out of the family and the family novel (again, Smerdyakov goes unmentioned in the *narrator's* version of the "Story of One Little Family"). In narrative terms, Smerdyakov claims his fraternity with the legitimate Karamazovs by committing the parricide of which they only dreamed.[63]

Conclusion

In their treatment of consanguineal kin, the English favored a linear model of family not conducive to the branching caused by multiple brothers. Focusing on the on-going struggles of family love in the present—particularly amongst brothers—the Russians turned such traditionally vertical family plots on their side. With an inheritance system that equalized siblings and reduced structural tensions, they were free to create plots that were not progressive—driven toward the telos of a singular heir—but instead focused on the challenges of expansive bonds in the here and now. Blood kinship is not only about blood*line*, but also about the clan of kin who share in it. The narrative structure this creates is more of a woven mesh than a spun out line.[64] In *Anna Karenina*, Tolstoy used brothers and sisters to link the strands of a multi-plot novel, with virtually all of the main characters becoming siblings-in-law by the conclusion.[65] The same year its serialization began, the

one of the titular protagonists of the novel? Or will we dismiss him as nothing more than the villain, a second-tier character?" ("Kicking Maksimov out of the Carriage," 422).

[62] Meerson, *Dostoevsky's Taboos*, 184.

[63] Emma Lieber suggests this in her psychoanalytic reading of Smerdyakov ("Smerdyakov and Parricide," *Dostoevsky Studies*).

[64] I was originally introduced to the idea of plot functioning as a mesh by Caryl Emerson when I served as her teaching assistant for a course on Tolstoy (Princeton University, 2011).

[65] I discuss the kinship network in *Anna Karenina* and this linking in *Siblings in Tolstoy and Dostoevsky*, 79–103. Knapp explores how the multi-plot structure fosters the question "What does my life have to do with the lives of others?" (Anna Karenina *and Others*, 5).

lesser-known N. Aleeva (pseud. for Natalia Utina) published *Two Worlds* (1875), where she similarly connected her plotlines through kinship bonds, making her representatives of the "old world" and the world of "new people" two brothers, a sister, and their female cousin. The chapters are linked by opening sentences that set up the oppositions between the family members' fates, most frequently contrasting the two brothers.[66] At stake are their present experiences.

Yet despite fundamental differences in the two traditions, consanguineal plots also show us that there can be points of sameness. When there is not enough property for all—as in Potekhin—Russian brothers can become rivalrous like the English. And when multiple sources of wealth could be found in an English novel, or brothers could be put on a more equal footing—as with the Cheeryble brothers or in *Wives and Daughters, Shirley,* and *Three Brides* (with the second and third brothers)—we find plotlines that come closer to the Russian model, making a place for brothers to coexist. We will see the same pattern in Part II with marriage plots and Part III with alternative kinship; when conditions can be made to resemble each other, the same kinds of family plots emerge in both national traditions, suggesting that family structure is indeed a crucial determinant of the plotlines each nation embraced.

---

[66] For example, Ch.7: "While Alexander divided his time between occupations and love, Viktor spent the whole summer on the composition of his writings" (124); Ch.11: "Evidently both brothers found themselves in a not completely happy period. Alexander was vexed by his love squabbles; Viktor found much unsatisfying in his intellectual career" (168).

PART II
CONJUGAL RELATIONS

4

Family Ideology

For she's so simply, subtly sweet,
My deepest rapture does her wrong.
Yet is it now my chosen task
To sing her worth as Maid and Wife;
Nor happier post than this I ask,
To live her laureate all my life.

—Coventry Patmore, *The Angel in the House*

You still remained a slave and servant,
Without rights, without a voice, insignificant and weak,
Although praised by a crowd of admirers,
Eternal queen and eternal slave!

—L. Palmin, "To woman"

In 1834 Russia's greatest literary critic, Vissarion Belinsky (1811–1848) proclaimed "he who wants to know any nation, before all else should study it in its domestic and familial way of life" [*ego semeinom, domashnem bytu*].[1] Social relations all come back to relations in the home. And familial relations around the teapot or samovar are themselves determined by ideology about gender roles and the domestic sphere. This chapter explores the underlying assumptions about the family and the family novel that shaped the courtship and marriage plots explored in the next two chapters. In part, this means understanding family history: what were the realities in the home in each nation? It also means exploring the ideology: what did each nation project as its ideal? And it also means looking at novel theory: how were the nations using their novels? What were the genre expectations for the family novel to which each nation was either conforming, or from which it attempted to break free? While my analysis of the novels will be reserved for the following chapters, I use literary examples here to demonstrate 1) novels' explicit comments that reveal assumptions about the family, and 2) their representations of the domestic norm/ideal.

Much of the history in this chapter is not new, but for readers not versed in both national traditions an overview of the opposition can clarify the foundations for

---

[1] From his "Articles about Aleksandr Pushkin. Article Eight" (7:443).

The Family Novel in Russia and England, 1800–1880. Anna A. Berman, Oxford University Press.

England and Russia's radically opposed marriage plots. The prevailing ideology in England was benevolent paternalism that relied on an idealized past that should be reinforced and recreated (affirming the vertical axis). The Russians, by contrast, largely wrote of their traditional family as a backward institution based on patriarchal tyranny. This negative view—while not universal—was heightened in the novels because the patriarch could serve as a stand-in for the autocrat, who could not be openly criticized. Advocating good family values for the Russians meant throwing off the yoke of the past (which carried clear political symbolism for contemporary readers). This positioning of the family in relation to time—with the English looking back and trying to reaffirm an ideal and the Russians rejecting an old model and trying to create a liberalizing alternative—relates to the same vertical/lateral distinction discussed in Part I around inheritance patterns and consanguineal kin. English stability enabled a sense of genealogical progression and continuity and made preservation a desirable aim. The Russians did not trust in such smooth progressive processes, were less enamored with their own past (or current political situation), and, consequently, placed less emphasis on reaffirming it.

Theorizers of the family novel have started from the English model, taking its preservationist aim as a key feature of the genre. The received wisdom is that the family novel is a conservative genre meant to reaffirm the existing order. And certainly this is the role many English novels served. But if we explode the national framework in which these theories were conceived by including Russia, we see that the family novel can serve very different aims. The Russians turned it into a progressive force: rejecting a backward past and emphasizing the possibility of change in the present. This chapter provides the background for understanding how and why this difference occurred. Chapters 5 and 6 turn to the novels themselves, where we see the results.

English Conservative Family Ideology: the Idealized Past

As many scholars have shown, the Victorians promoted an idealistic view of the family and domestic sphere as a haven from the worries of the world.[2] It was a view tinged with nostalgia, looking back to an unblemished past for the family and cherishing what had been inherited from previous generations. This rosy idea of the past appears clearly in Mary Elizabeth Braddon's *Like and Unlike* (1887) when Colonel Deverill learns that his daughter has eloped and immediately thinks that he "would have taken her back to his heart as tenderly as the Vicar of Wakefield received his deluded daughter, could he have found her in remorse and abandonment" (3:16). Deverill's model—the Vicar—is the archetypal benevolent father of eighteenth-century fiction. Although people knew not all families succeeded in

---

[2] An excellent overview of English family ideology and how it evolved across the nineteenth century is provided by James Kilroy in the introduction to his *The Nineteenth-Century English Novel*.

living up to the ideal of the Vicar and his loving relations who end in harmony around the fireside, the prevailing idea that the family *was meant to be* the ultimate source of support and comfort went largely unchallenged. Fathers should be wise and benevolent, wives loving and submissive, and children humble and obedient.

In *Home is Home: A Domestic Tale* (1851), Mr. Dalton returns home after a day of work to find "his most snug and comfortable sitting rooms, where his pretty wife and fine curly headed boy of some three years old hailed his entrance with delight. A bright fire, tea ready, and the kettle sending forth its full puffs of steam, all announced that he had been for some time expected."[3] Mr. Dalton has brought home a copy of the latest installment of Dickens, which earns him the appellation of "dear good man" from his wife, and at the same time reminds readers of all the classic Dickensian tropes encapsulated in the scene. This is Victorian family ideology writ large. It is what Peter Gaskell dreamed of in 1833 when he called the home "the haven to which [man] may retire when driven about and persecuted by the storms of fortune."[4] It is what the Ibbotson sisters are fantasizing of in Harriet Martineau's *Deerbrook* (1839) while decorating the house they will move to upon Harriet's marriage: "On this table, and by this snug fireside, will the cheerful winter breakfast go forward, when each is about to enter on the gladsome business of the day; and that sofa will be drawn out, and those window-curtains will be closed, when the intellectual pleasures of the evening—the rewards of the laborious day— begin" (138). In both non-fiction and novels, the Victorians cherished an ideal of the family home as a space of peace and love.

The eighteenth-century English novel had been much more candid about family strife, and there is no reason to believe Victorian families were truly happier. Fielding, Defoe, and Smollett filled their pages with extra-marital liaisons, illegitimate children, cruel parents, and familial rupture. As Samuel Butler humorously reminds readers in *The Way of All Flesh* (written 1873–1884), "at the beginning of the nineteenth century the relations between parents and children were still far from satisfactory. The violent type of father, as described by Fielding, Richardson, Smollett, and Sheridan, is now hardly more likely to find a place in literature than the original advertisement of Messrs. Farlie & Pontifex's 'Pious Country Parishioner,' but the type was much too persistent not to have been drawn from nature closely" (16). Fathers were not always "dear good men," nor were husbands always wise and benevolent protectors. It is the Victorians who *wished* to make them so and who used their novels to reinforce this ideal.[5]

---

[3] Sibthorpe, *Home is Home: A Domestic Tale*, 2. Qtd. in Chase and Levenson, *Spectacle of Intimacy*, 8.

[4] Qtd. in Poovey, *Uneven Developments*, 77. This quotation also reminds us that the father was deeply connected to the domestic sphere. As Tosh argues, "For most of the nineteenth century home was widely held to be a man's place, not only in the sense of being his possession or fiefdom, but also as the place where his deepest needs were met" (*A Man's Place*, 1).

[5] Kilroy suggests that the English focused on the family ideal so much in this period precisely because they perceived it to be under threat (*The Nineteenth-Century English Novel*, 22–23).

Unhappy families do not disappear from the nineteenth-century novel, but their failures are treated as deviations that do not undermine the ideal.[6] For example, Mr. Dombey's coldness and cruel neglect of his angelic daughter Florence (*Dombey and Son*, 1846–1848) is not an indictment of Victorian fatherhood, but of *this* father. As one of the servants explicitly tells him, "there an't no gentleman, no Sir, though as great and rich as the greatest and richest of England put together, but might be proud of her and would and ought" (666). Dombey's failings are an aberration, while the shadow of the ideal remains constant before readers' eyes—and Florence's own—as she daily watches through her neighbors' windows the tender interactions of a loving father with his four daughters: "they would climb and clamber up stairs with him, and romp about him on the sofa, or groupe themselves at his knee, a very nosegay of little faces, while he seemed to tell them some story" (275). Such family love is still what is expected of a healthy family, even as Dickens acknowledges how it can go abysmally wrong. The failures as well as the successes served a didactic purpose.[7] Literature's role was typically to reinforce the ideal, not to mirror actual marital outcomes or to reflect the true state of the English family. As Trollope quips in the conclusion of *Barchester Towers* (1857), "The end of a novel, like the end of a children's dinner-party, must be made up of sweetmeats and sugar-plums" (421). The majority of novelists were ready to oblige.

All these happy English endings had a larger social and political significance, as the family was seen as the building block for creating a stable nation.[8] As a commentator in *Eliza Cook's Journal* proclaimed in 1848, "It is really the Home which governs the world, for it is there that those principles of conduct and action are imbibed which men afterwards carry with them into active life," with woman as "the chief director of this home power."[9] Marriage stood at the basis of society for larger structural reasons as well. Joseph Boone reminds us that "the marriage rite in almost all cultures plays a central role in sustaining a structured social order.

[6] Anny Sadrin notes that this ideal is embodied in God the Father, and thus is inviolable. "Worldly fathers hardly ever come up to the ideal, but the ideal remains and brings comfort to those whom their fathers on earth have unfairly or unwillingly forsaken" (*Parentage and Inheritance in the Novels of Charles Dickens*, 28). Daughters acknowledge this great father of all in *Little Dorrit, Bleak House,* and *Dombey and Son.*

[7] As Charles Hatten argues, "In its nineteenth-century form, familial literature continues to celebrate the joys of familial life and to anathematize its pitfalls, to elucidate the character of an idealized familial life, and to serve as a handbook for readers to guide and admonish them in their personal lives...Domestic texts [...] are] designed to intervene in the social world by molding the sensibilities of individuals and by influencing the families of readers. Domestic literature emphatically takes sides, not merely for families, but for specific forms and ideals of the family" (*The End of Domesticity*, 14–15).

[8] As the Vicar of Wakefield puts it in the opening lines of Goldsmith's novel (1766), "I was ever of opinion, that the honest man who married and brought up a large family, did more service than he who continued single, and only talked of population" (9). Consequently, he marries early and considers the six children his wife gives him "a very valuable present made to my country" (10).

[9] "Home Power," *Eliza Cook's Journal* 2 (1849), 129. Qtd. in Waters, *Dickens and the Politics of the Family,* 19.

Aside from its sexual and sacramental functions, marriage forms a crucial socioe-conomic variable because of the value placed on legitimate progeny to ensure the passage of property from one owner to the next, a drawing of boundaries prereq-uisite to organized community."[10] While this may be true across cultures, Boone places the significance of marriage in its uniquely English context when he explains that "The concurrent development of a contractual, secular definition of mar-riage in the civil sphere—reflecting the political reformulation of monarchy after the Glorious Revolution as a voluntary agreement between subject and king—also helped validate the practice and claims of companionate marriage."[11] Family parallels State.

In novels, too, we find the family structure reinforcing that of the nation. The stodgy Lady Milborough voices this view in Trollope's *He Knew He Was Right* (1869) when—miffed at the romantic choices of a young protégée—she was "of the opinion that young ladies ought to have their hearts under better control, so that the men entitled to the prizes should get them. It was for the welfare of England at large that the eldest sons of good families should marry the sweetest, prettiest, brightest, and most lovable girls of their age" (890). This thought succinctly links the concerns of the marriage plot with the fate of England's great families and by extension with the nation itself, elevating the stakes from romantic love to the sta-bility of an entire civilization. This role that English novels highlight for the family as a cornerstone of their civilization parallels the discourse on the family and State in other spheres, as explored in the Introduction.

Many scholars of the "family novel" believe that such conservatism is inherent to the genre.[12] Liisa Saariluoma links this conservatism with the bourgeois nature of the family novel, suggesting that "The stability and continuity of a family is based on collecting the family property, managing it and handing it over to the next generation."[13] This obsession with property and continuity reinforces the patriar-chal order.[14] Mikhail Bakhtin puts a similar emphasis on property and stability, arguing that that the family's primary goal is to sustain and recreate itself.[15] Mar-riage, of course, is at the heart of this process. Tony Tanner calls marriage "a means

[10] Boone, *Tradition Counter Tradition*, 36.

[11] Boone, *Tradition Counter Tradition*, 59.

[12] Philip Thody argues that "to write about the family rather than the individual is, implicitly, to plead for continuity and tradition as against radicalism and innovation" ("The Influence of Genre on Ideology: The Case of the Family Novel," 68). Tanner draws a similar link between novels, family, and conservatism (*Adultery in the Novel*, 369). See also Thody, "The Politics of the Family Novel: Is Conservatism Inevitable?"; Hatten, *The End of Domesticity*, 15.

[13] Saarilouma, "Virginia Woolf's The Years: Identity and Time in an Anti-Family Novel," 279.

[14] In consonance with this idea, Enid Duthie, writing on Elizabeth Gaskell, comments that her "insis-tence on the importance of the family is in tune with her acceptance of a social hierarchy...The family meant stability and peace" (*The Themes of Elizabeth Gaskell*, 90).

[15] Bakhtin claims that "what is important about the classic family novel is precisely the stable family and material goods belonging to the heroes, how they overcome elements of change (random meetings with random people, random situations and occurrences) in which they had initially found themselves, how they create fundamental, that is *family* connections with people, how they limit their world to a

by which society attempts to bring into harmonious alignment patterns of passion and patterns of property; in bourgeois society it is not only a matter of putting your Gods where your treasure is (as Ruskin accused his age of doing) but also of putting your libido, loyalty, and all other possessions and products, including children, there as well."[16] I will suggest, however, that this conservatism is not inherent to the family novel genre, but is a distinctly English trait.[17]

"Conservative" literally means the wish to conserve, to cling to a past time and mode of existence. And it was the English who embraced the view of a "lost haven," a "pastoral age" that had "vanished during the era that has already ended."[18] Waxing poetic, Robin Gilmour argues, "[C]arried forward into the future at breakneck speed on the Great Victorian Express, [the Victorians] looked back wistfully and anxiously at the familiar landmarks they were leaving behind, and their writings sought to develop a continuity between past and present, to uncover what Tennyson in another context called 'A link among the days, to knit / The generations each with each' (*In Memoriam*, lyric 40)."[19] Many Victorian novels are set back several decades from the time when they were written: *Shirley* (1849) is set in 1811–1812, *Adam Bede* (1859) is set just before the turn of the century, *Middlemarch* (1871–1872) is set in 1831–1832, and *Wives and Daughters* (1864–1866) is set in the 1820s. Gilmour links this inclination not with a desire for "comfortable detachment" from the historical setting, but with "memory and nostalgia" and the desire to be oriented "in relation to a past and present by discovering, or more precisely uncovering, a sense of personal and social continuity and stability."[20] I would add that scholars rarely discuss these novels as "historical novels," which again reinforces the idea of stable continuity persisting in England across the nineteenth century.

Russia Pushing Against Its Past

Like the English, the Russians drew many analogies between the family and the State, with the stability of the former held up as the foundation for the stability of the latter. Yet their novels did not fill the same conservative role. Metropolitan Filaret proclaimed in 1837 that in order for the State to be strong and to produce the fruits of societal well-being, family life must be "strong in blessed spousal

---

well-defined place and a well-defined narrow circle of relatives, that is to the family circle" ("Forms of Time and of the Chronotope in the Novel," 232).

[16] Tanner, *Adultery and the Novel*, 15.

[17] Bakhtin himself was not thinking about Russian novels when he made this claim. For indeed, many of the novels we now consider to be Russia's great "family novels" were not considered family novels in his day because they did not conform to this model. See my "The Family Novel (and Its Curious Disappearance)."

[18] Schaffer, *Romance's Rival*, 91.

[19] Gilmour, *The Novel in the Victorian Age*, 35.

[20] Gilmour, *The Novel in the Victorian Age*, 58.

love, sanctified parental power, children's respect and obedience," and that following from this respect for parents would be born and grow reverence for the Sovereign.[21] And in 1861 he declared "[t]he state consists of families. Disorder in the constituent parts causes disorder in the whole."[22] An attack on the power of the father/husband, by this logic, was tantamount to an attack on the autocratic order. Given this belief, one might well expect to find endings of Russian novels like the ones we find in England: secure, happy families where father (like Tsar) knows best, and where heirs are being produced who will carry on this stable order.

This is not, however, the dominant pattern in Russian novels.[23] Drunken fathers and abusive or downtrodden mothers people their pages; painful, suffering-laden childhoods abound. Avdotia Panaeva's semi-autobiographical *The Talnikov Family* (1848)—set in a *meshchanstvo* (petit bourgeoisie) family—offers a case in point. Panaeva begins her novel with the haunting image of the heroine Natasha's dead baby sister lying on the table and no one grieving. Only later, when Natasha sees a mother lamenting over a dead infant, does she realize that family love is possible: "For the first time in my life I saw such strong grief and was very surprised at how one could cry so bitterly for a little child, remembering the death of my sister, for whom no one cried" (116). Beatings were regular occurrences, and Panaeva's heroine grows up with the understanding of parental rights: "that they could not only punish, but kill [their] children" (106). In 1848 the censors refused to publish Panaeva's novel because of this negative depiction of family. The head of censorship, Dmitri Buturlin (1790–1849), himself wrote at the end of the manuscript "I forbid it on account of [its depiction of] immorality and the undermining (*podryv*) of parental power."[24]

Buturlin's view represents the conservative side of the family debate, the side reinforcing the autocratic order. This side was supported in Orthodox juridical writings. For example, Ilarion Vasilev, who taught Imperial law at the Moscow Commercial School, argued that "[t]he father is the monarch, his wife and children are his subjects," and consequently it would be "ruinous" to "introduce a republican order into the family."[25] Similarly, the author of an instructional essay on the family from 1844 noted that while the wife was a helpmate to her husband, not a servant, "she nonetheless must submit completely to her husband" or there

---

[21] Filaret, *Slovo i rechi, Tom IV 1836–1848*, 76. See also Wagner, "'Orthodox Domesticity: Creating a Social Role for Women."

[22] Filaret, qtd. in Wagner, *Marriage, Property, and Law in Late Imperial Russia*, 73.

[23] Of course some novels depict idealized childhoods (or early childhoods), like Dostoevsky's *Poor Folk* (1846), or Goncharov's *Oblomov* or *An Ordinary Story* (1847). But often seeds of future family trouble are already present, or the happy childhoods are counterbalanced by miserable ones, as in *The Insulted and Injured* (1861).

[24] Qtd. in Chukovskii, "O 'Semeistve Tal'nikovykh,'" 97. On the role of the Third Section as guardian of "family morality and peace," see Engel, *Marriage, Household, and Home*, 33.

[25] Qtd. in Wagner, *Marriage, Property, and Law*, 73. Original source: I. Vasil'ev, "Nechto o semeistvennykh obiazannostiakh v otnoshenii k dolzhnostiam i obiazannostiam obshchestvennym," *Damskii zhurnal* 17 (1827), 199, 200.

would be "no order, unity, and peace in the domestic community."[26] The type of family these authors were describing did not become a dominant subject for literature, however. Conservative actors in the government and Church may have wished for novels to support the existing order, but *belles-lettres* largely failed to live up to their desires. Among the more famous texts, we have only to remember Herzen's *Who is To Blame?* (1845–1846), Dostoevsky's *Netochka Nezhvanova* (1849), *The Insulted and Injured* (1861), *The Adolescent* (1875), and *The Brothers Karamazov* (1880), Tur's *The Niece* (1851), Krestovsky (pseud.)'s *The Boarding School Girl* (1861), Saltykov-Shchedrin's *The Golovlyovs* (1875–1880), and Tolstoy's *Anna Karenina* (1875–1878) to be convinced that the Russian family and its past—even among the gentry—were often not depicted in a rosy tint. What cannot be overlooked, however, is that these novels were pushing against another body of sacred and juridical literature supporting the conservative status quo.

Andrew Wachtel has made an influential case for the "myth of the happy gentry childhood" based on the model of Tolstoy's pseudo-autobiography, *Childhood* (1852), or Aksakov's *The Childhood Years of Bagrov's Grandson* (1858). But if we look more closely into these sources, it appears that it is specifically the *mother* who is the object of reverence (and she herself may be suffering).[27] Wachtel's claim that "practically all Russians felt that their childhoods were (or, at least, should have been) happy" may apply to memoir accounts, but it is not borne out by the novels.[28] While many scholars have followed Wachtel's lead and emphasized the nostalgic gentry vision of the country estate with the idealized mother figure presiding over her adoring children, I would suggest that such a vision is far from the rule; the dominance or centrality of the happy childhood myth might indeed be something of a myth itself.

I believe the real question is *when* to place the golden age for the Russian family: was it really in bygone days? Or was it yet to be attained? Wachtel suggests that the answer to this question breaks down along social class/estate lines, with the gentry placing the golden age in the immediate past and the non-noble intelligentsia putting it in the immediate future.[29] When we turn to literature, I am less certain that this temporal distinction breaks down along class divisions, as Wachtel makes out. Few Russian novelists seem to have believed that the family's past was golden.

For most Russians, the idea of the "traditional Russian family" was exemplified in the *Domostroi*, a sixteenth-century domestic manual about life in Old Muscovy. This is not to say that realities matched this depiction, only that it shaped common

---

[26] Qtd. in Wagner, "Orthodox Domesticity," 122.

[27] On positive memoir accounts of mothers in the eighteenth century, see Pushkareva, *Women in Russian History*, 168.

[28] Wachtel, *The Battle for Childhood*, 84.

[29] *The Battle for Childhood*, 203. Wachtel points to Vera Pavlovna's fourth dream in Chernyshevsky's *What Is to Be Done?* as an example of the future utopia the *raznochintsy* looked to for their golden age.

conceptions of the traditional family. While conservatives approved of the traditional, hierarchical model it put forth, many educated Russians saw it as a sign of Russia's backwardness. In the sections devoted to family relations, the *Domostroi* author relied on frequent quotations from the Old Testament to lay out a rigid, patriarchal structure. For wives: "Whatever her husband orders, she must accept with love; she must fulfill his every command" (124).[30] And drawing on Proverbs (29:17), the author informed parents: "Love your children. Protect them and save them with fear. While teaching them and considering their needs, lay stripes upon them. Correct your son, and he will be a comfort to you and bring you delights of every kind" (93). Though it may be impossible to determine how closely people actually followed its teachings, the *Domostroi* was a powerful source of ideology, and wife beating among the gentry did remain widespread throughout the eighteenth century and into the nineteenth.[31] The text itself was frequently referenced in the nineteenth century, becoming a shorthand for patriarchal oppression. Even in Tolstoy's *The Kreutzer Sonata* (1889), when an old man who represents traditional family values advocates wife beating (claiming "The first thing that should be required of a woman is fear!"), his fellow train passengers call him "a living *Domostroi*" (27:10/137).

When Russia's first official code of laws was enacted in 1833, it followed the same patriarchal spirit, leaving all power in the hands of fathers and husbands.[32] Wives were legally required to live with their husbands who faced no legal prohibition against raping or beating them. For many people, the "traditional family" in Russia evoked images of drunken, abusive patriarchs who ruled tyrannically over their subjugated kin.[33] As Herzen's narrator observes in *Who Is to Blame?*:

It is remarkable that there are folks who consider Russians in general, and provincial Russians in particular, as patriarchal people, primarily devoted to family life. The truth is that we are unable to drag the Russian family across the threshold of education ... If husbands didn't abuse their wives and if parents didn't oppress their children, then it would be quite impossible to understand what these people had in common, why they continued to live together and annoy each other. (4:125-126/192-193)

[30] Translation by Pouncy (1994).

[31] Engel, *Women in Russia, 1700-2000*, 34; Engel, *Marriage, Household, and Home in Modern Russia*, 6; Pushkareva, *Women in Russian History*, 102.

[32] In William Wagner's words, "Reflecting the autocratic socio-political order generally, the Imperial *Digest of Laws* defined family relations in terms of authority, obedience, filial duty, and paternalistic obligations. Conversely, the concept of personal rights for individual family members received only weak recognition" (*Marriage, Property, and Law*, 62).

[33] The peasant family was regarded in an even harsher light. Pushkareva notes that "historians and ethnographers of the nineteenth century attributed an atmosphere of hatred, violence, and intrafamilial scandal to peasant households," whether or not such a characterization was just (*Women in Russian History*, 167).

The first third of Herzen's novel is dedicated to describing the unhappy family backstories of its various characters.[34] When doctor Semyon Ivanovich encounters the central couple, he tells the wife, Lyubonka, "in all my sixty years your home is the first place I have encountered an example of family happiness outside of fiction or poetry" (4:129/196). Yet this family soon crumbles.

Even seemingly conservative novels show hints of skepticism about an earlier family ideal or myth of the "happy gentry family." *Eugene Onegin* (1825–1832) is famed for its cozy image of rustic Russian life on the family estate, yet we see what it costs Tatiana's mother to find contentment in her lot (forced into marrying a less cultured man whom she does not love). Dmitri Begichev's very popular but immensely didactic *The Kholmsky Family: Some Characteristics of the Morals and Way of Life, Familial and Single, of the Russian Gentry* (1832) offers a moral ideal in its central couple, but this is balanced against dozens of less successful characters whom Begichev chastises for their failings while analyzing the reasons for their marital strife. Tolstoy's historical *War and Peace* (1865–1869) perhaps comes closest to depicting a rosy past (set in 1805–1820). But even here, Princess Marya is tormented by her all-powerful father and grows up in terror. And amidst the family harmony of the First Epilogue (set in 1820), there are already notes of discord. Pierre Bezukhov is clearly en route to becoming a Decembrist, setting him up to be on opposite sides of the political divide from his brother-in-law Nikolai Rostov. Tolstoy closes the First Epilogue with the forgotten orphan, Nikolenka Bolkonsky, who is precariously placed in the family order, ready to side with Pierre against his legal guardian.[35] So even this past family idyll is not so fully idyllic.

Turgenev launched a very different kind of assault on the "traditional Russian family" in *Fathers and Children* (1862) by including the peasant family, but one deserving of note, given the way the intelligentsia looked to the peasants for the essence of "Russianness." In one of the most heated debates in the novel, the young nihilist Bazarov dares the older Pavel Petrovich to find "even a single institution of contemporary life, either in the family or in the social sphere, that doesn't deserve absolute and merciless rejection" (8:248). When Pavel Petrovich suggests "the family as it exists among our peasants!" Bazarov quickly destroys his argument with the reminder "You've no doubt heard of *snokhachi*" (*snokhachestvo* was the practice of incest between the father-in-law and his son's wife, and was reportedly quite widespread).

---

[34] Herzen was a vocal critic of Russia and his views certainly cannot be taken as representative of the norm, but many other novels follow this pattern of including negative family backstories.

[35] Liza Knapp also points to Marya "bemoaning her inability to love even her nephew as her own," darkening what "is often taken to be a celebration of family happiness" ("Tolstoy's Unorthodox Catechesis," 66).

This is an interesting instance to pause on, because while Russians associated incest with the "traditional" peasants and a backward past, in England there were actually fears that it was a by-product of modernization. As the traditional agrarian family structure was torn apart in England with the rise of industrialization and people moving to cities, modern life—with its crowded tenements—was feared to *cause* incest.[36] Again here we see that for the English, "good family values" was a thing of the traditional past (whether or not such a past ever in fact existed), while in Russia, for many people fighting for good family values actually meant believing in progress and change. If there was a golden age for the Russian family, it lay not behind, but ahead.

Attempting to Reform the Family

To understand the reasons for Russia's realism about the family, as opposed to England's idealism, we need to understand how the family had been evolving and the debates about its future path. In Russia, entrenched values and customs of patriarchal oppression went back centuries. Peter the Great was the first to attempt to reform the Russian family in the early eighteenth century as part of his broader modernizing agenda. Appalled at the coarseness and ignorance of the nobility (in comparison with what he saw in Europe), he tried to instill Western, enlightened values through taking over the education of their sons. Wishing to move Russia beyond the *Domostroi* model, Peter brought women out of the *terem* (space of female seclusion) and allowed young people more say in the question of their marriage partner. In 1702 he instituted a six-week betrothal period during which they were allowed to see each other daily, and after which they had the right to reject each other, an effort to prevent ill-suited matches.[37] His attempts at reshaping family life met with mixed results, the effects of the clash of new ideas with traditional laws and customs.[38] These contradictions were not soon resolved.

Throughout the eighteenth and early nineteenth centuries, the tsars struggled against the perceived backwardness of the Russian family by continuing to take education out of its hands. Schools for both boys and girls were central to their mission of creating model citizens.[39] While this resulted in some progress, it also

---

[36] Bailey and Blackburn, "The Punishment of Incest Act 1908: A Case Study of Law Creation," 710.

[37] Elnett, *Historic Origin and Social Development of Family Life in Russia*, 46; Pushkareva, *Women in Russian History*, 157.

[38] Elaine Elnett summarizes the contradictions: "On the one hand, the old basic family traditions and customs were cast away; on the other, the new form of marriage often proved to be a failure because legislation still adhered to the Code of Tsar Alexey. While it was preached that love was a necessary moral condition in marriage, it was at the same time asserted that the young people had to accept their elders' choice because love is blind and treacherous. The wife was represented as a friend and assistant, not a slave; yet the husband was to remain the head of the family and not to fall under her influence" (*Historic Origin and Social Development of Family Life in Russia*, 53).

[39] See Elnett, *Historic Origin and Social Development of Family Life in Russia*, 54–62.

created massive rifts between parents and children, while still not fully establishing a new norm. As Barbara Alpern Engel reminds us, "New ideals that elevated the status of wives and mothers took root only gradually. At the end of the eighteenth century, many nobles lived much as their parents and grandparents had done; for them, the *Domostroi* ... or books with similar principles served as the primary guides to conduct, if they consulted books at all."[40] Western ideas and practices never fully replaced Russia's traditional model.[41]

A fresh assault against Russia's repressive patriarchal system came from the followers of George Sand, as she became wildly popular in Russia in the 1830s–1850s.[42] Sand's novels offered models of pure and virtuous heroines rising above their circumstances, breaking free of oppressive marriages, and following their hearts. Placing a premium on love, freedom of sentiment, and purity of soul, Sand offered a new values system for more enlightened Russians. Her novels' idealism spoke to a new generation of Romantics eager for more soulful, spiritual connection. Sand's novels—and her own life—provided a model for real life as well as fiction, serving, for example, as a basis for the intense friendships and love affairs between the Herzens and Herweghs (1848–1852). The parties involved made frequent references to Sand's novels as they described the union of souls, spiritual friendship, and adultery that bound them as a quartet.[43] Herzen relied on the same Sandian ideology in *Who Is to Blame?*, which critiques the family through exploring the devastating results of a love triangle composed of a loving husband and a virtuous wife who has fallen in love with another man. Apropos the title, Herzen's point seems to be that *none of them* are to blame, but instead that guilt lies with the rigid, patriarchal structure in which they are trapped.[44] For the Romantics and idealists of the 1830s–1840s, Sand offered a new model of family based on mutual love and respect, rather than patriarchal absolutism.[45]

Cries for reform became more urgent in the 1850s and 1860s. With the same rhetoric being used for the master ruling over his serfs and the husband over his wife, the emancipation of the serfs in 1861 led to calls for a similar emancipation of women. The "woman question," which burst onto the scene, involved the

[40] Engel, *Women in Russia, 1700–2000*, 28.

[41] Engel, *Women in Russia*, 38.

[42] See Elnett, *Historic Origin and Social Development of Family Life in Russia*, 63–64; Engel, *Mothers and Daughters*, 22, 36. Upon Sand's death (1876), Dostoevsky praised her as having been more popular in Russia than even Dickens.

[43] As Irina Paperno reminds us, "Both before and after the Gercens, experiments with love relations were a matter of social theories embodied in family novels, and they were put into practice by families and communities" ("Introduction: Intimacy and History. The Gerzen Family Drama Reconsidered," 49). She offers a thoughtful exploration of the way the participants explained their own experiences via Sand's novels.

[44] In his discussion of *Natasha Podgorich* (cited above), Dobroliubov notes that "the content of Mr. Voskresensky's novel revolves around the same difficult question that all our writers so often come up against: who is to blame?" (3:223).

[45] On the rising importance of sentiment in marriage choices, see Engel, *Marriage, Household, and Home*, 26–28.

interrelated issues of economics, education, and roles within the family. Arguably, the family was paramount. As Mikhail Mikhailov (1829–1865)—one of the greatest proponents of women's rights—wrote in 1860, "The complete rebuilding of society is impossible without remaking its foundation, the family."[46] Many writers saw women's lack of economic options as deeply connected to their sexual vulnerability (a topic Dostoevsky explores in his literature). Others, inspired by Sand, were interested in female sexual liberation and exploring the ménage à trois and various forms of free love as alternatives to repressive patriarchal marriage. Engel catalogues three approaches to the woman question: 1) liberalizing the family and relations between the sexes within politically acceptable limits, 2) the "nihilist" call for radically altering the family, or even abolishing it, and 3) focusing on social and political rather than personal change, and holding out for a socialist future in which the woman question, along with others, would be resolved.[47]

Different social and political actors followed each of these approaches, with liberal jurists pushing a new, more egalitarian vision of family in their rewriting of imperial family law and radicals writing novels and setting up communes that modeled alternative family formations. Their assaults had similarities to those of the Sandists a generation earlier, but with different philosophical underpinnings. They based their critique not on romantic idealism, but on more rational arguments about societal good. For example, the liberal jurist Mikhail Filippov (1828–1866), lamented at the close of an 1861 article critiquing family law:

When this corner stone sank into the swamp and the filth; when in this institution, despotism, tyranny, and violence reign in place of love, equality and Christian brotherly love; when wives are given as slaves to their husbands and along with that are implicitly allowed by them to fornicate; when children, especially daughters, are given up to the complete and unlimited power of their parents; when the sins of parents fall entirely on their innocent illegitimate children, – in such a family union it is impossible to hope to obtain/derive [*pocherpat'*] healthy members, and one can find neither patriotic self-sacrifice, nor sincere Christian love, nor hatred for sin and despotism.[48]

The periodical press was flooded with articles about the family from legal, sociological, and memoiristic perspectives, with conservatives pushing back against this drive for change.

Outside of conservative circles, articles typically started from the assumption that their readers already agreed that the family was in crisis. For example, an unsigned article in *The Voice* (1871) opened with the characteristic claim:

---

[46] Mikhailov, M. L. "Zhenshchiny, ikh vospitanie i znachenie v sem'e i obshchestve," 3.
[47] Engel, *Mothers and Daughters*, 46.
[48] Filippov, "Vzgliad na russkie grazhdanskie zakony" *Sovremennik* №3 (1861): 217–266 (here 265).

No matter how much we try to prove the excellence of our laws about marriage; no matter how much we shield ourselves with the obviousness of arguments that these laws are strengthened in the form of those church definitions, which follow directly from the essence of the sacrament itself; finally, no matter how much we point to the patriarchal nature of our daily life [*byt*], in which supposedly all internal relations between family members rest on moral sources—real life, as we see, is far from reflecting this instruction.[49]

There followed a typical list of family cruelties brought to public attention in recent court cases.[50] Beatings, neglect, and inhumane treatment all defined the Russian family for the reading public. A writer for *The Stock Exchange Herald* (1870) found it terrifying that under current laws "no kind of cruel treatment or spiritual torture from her husband gave a wife the legal right to free herself from her tormentor."[51] Similarly, in his *Writer's Diary* (1877), Dostoevsky lashed out against the deplorable state of both the family and family law. After describing in gory detail a case of child abuse for which the parents were acquitted, he lamented "Who—what court—could have found them guilty, and of what? ... not a criminal court with jurors who judge by written law. And nowhere in written law is there any article that makes a father's laziness, incompetence, and heartlessness in raising his children a criminal offense. If so, we would have to condemn half of Russia—a lot more than half, in fact" (25:183/2:1048).

Dostoevsky was only one of many novelists and literary critics who jumped into the debate. In the middle of a review of a contemporary novel in 1858, the radical critic Nikolai Dobroliubov made the claim "The question of so-called *family morality* is one of the most important social questions of our time ... No matter what is said about different means of improving life in society, these always have their beginnings and ends in the relations within the family ..."[52] In Nikolai Pomialovsky's *Molotov* (1861), a wife reflects on all the family cruelty she has heard of and on her powerless legal status: "she knew very well that there was no power on earth [that could come] between husbands and wives, there was no one to complain to, no court that would hear her complaint, that husband and wife were so bound to each other that any punishment of him would be a punishment of her as well, and the children and all her descendants to come" (72). Later in the same novel, the protagonist, Molotov, recounts a legal case of husband murder for

---

[49] "Nashi zakony o brake." *Golos* №158 (1871).

[50] The use of court cases as a window into the state of the Russian family was a common device. N. Sokolovsky, for example, began an article on the woman question with the claim that the new courts opened "a wide field for the observation of a whole mass of female persons, belonging to the most varied levels of society and caught at the most interesting moment of their existence" (Sokolovskii, "Sovremenyi byt russkoi zhenshchiny i sudebnaia reforma. (Iuridicheskiia zametki.)" *Zhenskii vestnik* №9 [1867]: 57–83 [here 57]).

[51] Untitled article in *Birzhevye vedomosti* №170 (July 3, 1870).

[52] Qtd. in Todd, *Literature and Society in Imperial Russia 1800–1914*, 256. Originally in "Povesti i rasskazy Voskresenskogo" in *Sobranie sochinenii* (Moscow-Leningrad, 1961) 3:223.

which he was recently called to court. When Molotov took pity on the murderess, she recounted her story: her lover had forced her to marry his serf, who then hated her and beat her. After they had a son, he started to hate the son, and with no way out, she ultimately killed her husband and fled to the woods. Asking his colleagues at the court what should happen to the poor woman, Molotov takes a progressive, liberal stance that goes against the law: "She has suffered so much: why should she suffer more?" he asks (104). Clearly readers are meant to agree (and real life jurists took this sympathetic tack).

Pomialovsky's novel directly engages with the law, while jurists turned to the novels in making their case for reform. As noted in the Introduction, Filippov's article criticizing imperial family law as the root of Russia's despotic, patriarchal order, closed with the statement: "Read all Russian literature, especially her best representatives [followed by a list of all Russia's great authors], and you will see what sort of heavy burden the morals reflected in our law(s) have placed on the whole of family life, and what a sad appearance that life has acquired as a result."[53] The social and literary spheres were indivisible. In a land where literature was the primary site of social critique and where "traditional family" to many critics meant wife beatings, child abuse, and drunken husbands with unlimited power to tyrannize over their households, the family novel carried great ideological weight, and it could hardly idealize hearth and home. But at the same time, lurking behind the critiques was an understanding that progress was possible, and perhaps already underway. Fictional families in novels also served authors larger social and political aims.

England's "Separate Spheres" and the Role of Women

In England, too, the family came under assault in the nineteenth century, though the condemnation came from the minority of the educated population, not the majority, as in Russia. For the English, the status of women was central to all the debates. While many novels still relied on marriage as their "sweetmeats and sugar-plums" happy ending, Valerie Sanders rightly calls Victorian middle-class marriage "a highly uneasy norm, constantly under attack from lawyers, reformers, moralists, and feminists."[54] England had seen a massive shift in the eighteenth century as agrarian kinship networks were broken up with the rise of industrialization and urbanization (sped along by the Enclosure Acts, which left many smaller farmers landless).[55] The new bourgeois family of the nineteenth century was based on a strict understanding of gender roles, and a woman's place was

[53] Filippov, "Vzgliad na russkie grazhdanskie zakony" *Sovremennik* №2 (1861), 265.
[54] Sanders, "Marriage and the antifeminist woman novelist," 25.
[55] On shifts in the eighteenth-century family model and their impact on literature, see Ruth Perry, *Novel Relations*.

in the newly idealized domestic sphere. Yet this structure came with inherent tensions.[56]

Sexual difference was believed in the nineteenth century to be biologically conditioned, with women defined by their reproductive capability.[57] According to William Acton in his popular *The Functions and Disorders of the Reproductive Organs* (1857), "Love of home, children, and domestic duties are the only passions [women] feel."[58] Such domestic ideology was disseminated to English households through conduct manuals and the immensely popular "family-magazines," like *Family Herald* (1842–1939), *London Journal* (1845–1912), Dickens's *Household Words* (1850–1859), *Eliza Cook's Journal* (1849–1854), *Family Friend* (1849–1921), and *Family Economist* (1848–1860).[59] Coventry Patmore's *The Angel in the House* (1854) set the domestic ideal in verse, placing the wife on a pedestal of virtue, modesty, and selflessness. Her maternal instinct became central to the definition of a woman's role as the nurturing caretaker, guardian of the hearth and of the domestic sphere.[60] In line with Patmore, John Ruskin articulated women's role in making the home "the shelter, not only from all injury, but from all terror, doubt, and division" in his popular lecture "Of Queens' Gardens" (1864).[61]

Thomas Carlyle expressed a similar view in an 1871 letter, in a description that parallels what we find in many Victorian novels:

I have never doubted the true and noble function of a woman in the world was, is, and forever will be, that of being Wife and Helpmate to a worthy man; and discharging well the duties that devolve on her in consequence, as mother of children and mistress of a Household, duties high, noble, silently important as any that can fall to a human creature; duties which, if well discharged, constitute woman, in a soft, beautiful, and almost sacred way, the Queen of the World, and, by her natural faculties, graces, strengths, and weaknesses, are every way indicated as specifically hers. The true destiny of a Woman, therefore, is to wed a man she can love and

---

[56] As Mary Poovey argues, "the ideology of separate spheres both generated and depended on an arrangement of social and property relations that positioned women as moral superiors *and* economic dependents" (*Uneven Development*, 52).

[57] This "European 'discovery of the sexes'" spread to Russia as well, where it appeared in the criminal law code. According to Marrese, "the growing significance of motherhood in official and public discourse prompted officials to spare pregnant women and nursing mothers from corporal punishment until their children could be weaned. In the 1830s, the Senate decreed that children should not be separated from exiled mothers" ("Gender and the legal order in Imperial Russia," 340).

[58] Qtd. in Springer, "Angels and Other Women," 127.

[59] See Waters, *Dickens and the Politics of the Family*, 16–21; Shoemaker, *Gender in English Society*, 23–43.

[60] Spontaneous ovulation was first observed in a mammal in 1843, giving scientific grounds for regarding female pleasure as irrelevant to reproduction and helping give rise to the idea of maternal instinct (Poovey, *Uneven Development*, 6–7).

[61] Ruskin, *Sesame and Lilies*, 77.

esteem; and to lead noiselessly, under his protection, with all the wisdom, grace, and heroism that is in her, the life prescribed in consequence.[62]

Or as Sarah Stickney Ellis (1799–1872) put it more concisely, "The love of woman appears to have been created solely to minister; that of man, to be ministered unto."[63] Of course, not all women (or men) were content with this division of gender roles. Not all marriages (perhaps none) looked like the idylls described by Patmore and Ruskin, and women had little recourse to aid if their husbands failed to treat them as "queens" of the domestic sphere. Under English law, when a woman married she was united with her husband, meaning she ceased to exist as her own legal entity, and thus she was not able to transact business and any property she might own would come under his possession.[64]

As an increasing number of women entered into the labor market as wage earners, concerns about their property rights became more urgent because, under existing laws, a husband had the right to take all his wife's salary and use it at his own discretion. Reformers pushed for greater women's rights. Caroline Norton (1808–1877), who suffered years of physical abuse at the hands of her husband (from whom she could not obtain a divorce), published multiple influential pamphlets about legal obstacles to women obtaining justice.[65] John Stuart Mill's "The Subjection of Women" (1869) attacked the very basis of separate spheres, declaring it "presumption in any one to pretend to decide what women are or are not, can or cannot be, by natural constitution. They have always hitherto been kept...in so unnatural a state, that their nature cannot but have been greatly distorted and disguised."[66] To understand the natural differences between the sexes, Mill claimed they must first be put in conditions of equality. In his assault on marriage laws, he famously declared "there remain no legal slaves, except the mistress of every house."[67]

---

[62] Qtd. in Springer, "Angels and Other Women in Victorian Literature," 129–130. Jeff Nunokawa may not be putting a fine point on it when he states that "Anyone who has ever read a Victorian novel or lived on the family plan it helped devise has felt the force of its conviction that a man's home is his castle, a shelter from the mean streets of the cash nexus, and that a woman—a wife, a mother, a daughter—oversees this estate. And a woman's work is never done: the angel of the house is the spirit of this domain not only because she supervises it, but also because she constitutes it" (*The Afterlife of Property: Domestic Security and the Victorian Novel*, 6).

[63] Ellis, *The Wives of England* (1843). Excerpted in *Women, The Family, and Freedom: The Debate in Documents*, 193.

[64] This principle was put in law in 1765, initially as a protection for women who ostensibly would not know how to manage their wealth (Poovey, *Uneven Developments*, 71). For the very wealthy, however, a separate law was introduced enabling property to be settled on a woman in a trust, which would be overseen by a man (usually a male relative, sometimes the woman's husband). This law did not, however, extend women's rights, but instead protected the property of the man designated trustee.

[65] Her most significant was "English Laws for Women in the Nineteenth Century" (1854). See Poovey, *Uneven Developments*, 64.

[66] Mill, "The Subjection of Women," 493–494.

[67] Mill, "The Subjection of Women," 522.

To address issues around women's rights, a series of bills came before Parliament at mid-century. The Matrimonial Causes Bill that finally passed on August 28, 1857 (becoming law on January 1 of the following year) did *not* ultimately give married women property rights and acknowledge them as legal entities (one of the issues it might have attempted to resolve), but it did provide protection against assault, cruelty, and desertion as well as creating the first divorce court in London.[68] Property rights would be addressed in the Married Women's Property Acts of 1870 and 1882. The debates surrounding these bills revealed a deep-seated suspicion of the strong-minded woman who would recklessly waste her fortune (while nothing was said of the potential for a man to make unwise investments). Fears abounded that women's property rights would be the nail in the coffin of family life. Sir John Butler argued, for example, that "There was no greater source of dissention in married life ... than the existence of separate property."[69] So while the nineteenth century saw some progress for women's rights to property and to escape abusive marriages, the overarching system of separate spheres resisted significant change. There were increasing acknowledgments of problems faced by women, but the domestic ideal proved resilient *as an ideal*.

Gender Roles in Russia: Sameness and Difference

For the English, whose whole economic, political, and social system was based on sexual difference and the belief that biology had dictated different capabilities for the sexes, the realities of Russian society at the start of the nineteenth century provided a shock. Spending several years in Russia at the turn of the century, the sisters Catherine (1773–1824) and Martha (1775–1873) Wilmot were simultaneously horrified by the coarse and unfeminine manners of Russian women, and baffled by their engagement in business dealings.[70] The sisters' views of Russia reveal their English outlook that required women to be shielded from the "male" sphere of economic and business concerns. Similarly, the Frenchman Charles-François-Philibert Masson (1762–1807), was taken aback by the "masculineness of [Russian] women" who were managing estates, commanding troops in their husbands' absence, and engaging "in business by no means suitable to their sex."[71] Some Europeans blamed serfdom for the loss of sexual difference, as it institutionalized women's power over the men they owned.[72]

---

[68] The law still "enshrined the sexual double standard," as wives could only divorce their husbands for adultery if it was "aggravated by cruelty, bigamy, willful desertion for four years or incest" (Waters, *Dickens and the Politics of the Family*, 6).
[69] Qtd. in Poovey, *Uneven Developments*, 74.
[70] Their writings are discussed by Judith Vowles in "Marriage à la russe" (discussed in Chapter 5).
[71] Charles-François-Philibert Masson (1762–1807), qtd. in Vowles, "Marriage à la russe," 55, 57.
[72] See Vowles, "Marriage à la russe," 69–71.

Depending on to which sources you give greater credence, conditions were either fundamentally similar or radically different for women in England and Russia. As eloquently summarized by Engel:

In some ways the position of Russian women was more independent, because they retained their rights to property even after marriage and, depending on social position, fulfilled a variety of responsibilities that were vital to maintaining the family's economic and social status. Yet from another perspective, women were more helpless: Because the authoritarianism that characterized Russia's autocratic political system also shaped family relations, the law and custom subordinated Russian women to men more absolutely than was the case for their European sisters.[73]

Russian women were both more powerful and powerless at the same time. This seeming paradox or contradiction needs probing. What accounted for the lesser subordination of women in England, despite their lack of property rights? And how did the Russians balance the greater responsibilities they gave women with the tyrannical power fathers and husbands wielded over them? The roots of these contradictions lie in the disparate, conflicting sources of Russia's ideology around gender and domestic life. The laws were largely a remnant of Russia's past, while many customs were imported from a more enlightened West.

Russians in the mid-nineteenth century were absorbing many ideals about domestic life from Europe, although the legal situation for women was not equivalent. Some models of women's roles came via Germany through the upper-class girls' boarding schools (*instituty*), like Smolny (est. 1764), set up by the German-born empresses Catherine II, Maria Fyodorovna, and Alexandra Fyodorovna.[74] Another source of domestic ideology was the European conduct manuals that were being translated into Russian and reviewed in the periodical press. Katherine Antonova has drawn parallels between the "images of family closeness and happiness, and recommended piety, purity, and submissiveness" that girls would find in the Russian periodical press and advice literature, and the "borrowed model of domesticity as embodied in the (German-born) Empress Alexandra, as model to all mothers of the empire."[75] In addition to these sources, European novels—and particularly English—offered a model of domestic harmony. As I discussed in the Introduction, English novels were seen as a form of moral education to train girls in family life. Russian thick journals regularly published serialized English novels in translation alongside Russian ones. In women's journals, English novels received greater prominence. The first issue of *Women's Herald* for

---

[73] Engel, *Mothers and Daughters*, 6–7. This situation is also summarized clearly in Livingston, *Marriage, Property, and Women's Narratives*, Ch. 7.
[74] Greene, "Mid-Nineteenth Century Domestic Ideology in Russia," 79.
[75] Antonova, *An Ordinary Marriage*, 136–137.

1866, for example, included installments of A. Mikhailov's *In the Intoxication of Deep Thoughts* (*V chadu glubokikh soobrazhenii*), along with Gaskell's *Ruth* and Georgiana Craik's *Faith Unwin's Ordeal*.[76]

Some scholars believe that Western ideology was readily accepted in Russia because of the similar status of upper and middle-class women in the two societies—the division of "separate spheres" and women's subjugation to men.[77] In light of this, it should not be surprising that some of the domestic ideology written by Russian women reads as if it could have been penned by a Victorian. For example, in 1856 Raida Varlamova directly invoked Coventry Patmore when she suggested that "The wife and mother is the honour of the home, a peaceful angel in the house, the visible spirit of domestic order and prosperity."[78] Maria Antonovna Korsini (1815–1859), a Russian noblewoman who graduated from the Smolny Institute, wrote that:

> To a wife are entrusted the responsibilities that are particular to her abilities and her character. Her dominion is kindness and gentleness. She looks after the domestic tranquility of her husband, so that when he returns home after his labors he finds order and sees the desire of his friend to afford him pleasure in important matters as well as in minor ones. She raises her babies and is the first to pronounce for them the name of God and to make them pray. She also ensures that the servant performs her duties and that quietude and peace reign in her house. A woman is given inexhaustible patience, which helps her to endure the screams of children, lack of sleep, and many minor domestic unpleasantries.[79]

While the roles and attributes Korsini assigns to the wife are the same as we find in Victorian writings, her vision of the model home with its screaming children and "domestic unpleasantries" is far less idealized. Tolstoy's model mother—Dolly Oblonskaya in *Anna Karenina*—too struggles with the quotidian realities of disobedient children and housekeeping mishaps. This realism seems ingrained in the Russian outlook.

---

[76] A. Mikhailov was the pseudonym of Alexander Konstantinovich Sheller (1838–1900).

[77] Memoir-like accounts of childhood were a not-infrequent appearance in the thick journals, and the description of the father in one of these accounts reveals the inherent assumptions about gender roles that underlie it: "In domestic life he was neither a despot, nor a petty tyrant [*samodur*]; in family matters he allowed his wife the right to speak, took into consideration her reasonable requests, in other cases even carried out her whims and follies; but in more weighty and serious questions he reserved the last word for himself and, having once made a well-considered decision, he would not change it. In general he was a good family man, an attentive and tender father, but he couldn't speak about his feelings and if he did speak about them, he did so in his own way; so, he dearly loved his son, but his relations with him smacked of some kind of military discipline,—just as if he wanted to accustom him in his childhood years to the military chain of command." N. G. Chaplygin "Semeistvo Baklanovykh. (Iz moikh vospominanii). Gl. I–X.) "*Ruskii vestnik* 1875, № 6 (June), 708–786 (here 710–711).

[78] Raida Varlamova (qtd. in Kelly, *Refining Russia*, 125).

[79] M. Korsini, *Mysli i povesti, posviashchennyia iunoshestvu* (St. Petersburg, 1846). Qtd. in Bisha, *Russian Women, 1698–1917*, 28.

For some writers, the idealization of women's domestic calling was also a way of limiting their penetration into "male" domains. Belinsky, for example, voiced many of the same views as Korsini in an attack on women writers: "The field of woman is to arouse the energy of man's soul, the ardor of noble passions, to support feelings of duty and aspiration for the elevated and the great—that is her destiny, and it is great and sacred! For her—the representative on earth of beauty and grace, priestess of love and self-sacrifice—it is a thousandfold more praiseworthy to inspire 'Jerusalem Liberated' than to write it herself..."[80] Orthodox writers, too, had assimilated western ideas like "natural motherhood" and the ideology of separate spheres, so their writings reinforced these transplants on Russian soil, keeping women in the home.[81]

However, while the Russians, like the English, glorified women's domestic calling, the "domestic" in Russia was more broadly construed.[82] Unlike in England, Russian married women could own property, and many had their own estates.[83] In fact, in the provinces property management often supplanted the idealized role of the mother, and gentry women relegated many of the childcare tasks to peasant nurses, governesses, and tutors.[84] As one member of the landed gentry explained in an 1848 article entitled "The Importance of the *Khoziaka* [mistress/master's wife] in the Home," "The man has a purpose for the most part to direct affairs outside the home...who then would preserve concord if not for the mistress of the home, whose title is not less respectable, and whose activity is not less laborious, than that of the head of the family himself[?]"[85] Women of urban estates—merchants, artisans, etc.—were also able to operate independently.[86]

Thus Russian women were in the paradoxical position of having greater property rights than women in the rest of Europe, but virtually no rights within the family. While court records show that women successfully engaged in litigation about property, they also include women being beaten or tormented by husbands who were trying to force them into mortgaging or selling their dowries and husbands who dissipated their wives' property without their knowledge.[87] As one observer noted, "Tho a married Woman has compleat power over her Fortune she has not over her person."[88]

---

[80] Belinsky, "Review of *A Victim*," included in *Russian Women, 1698–1917* (trans. Sibelan Forrester), 30. First published 1835.

[81] See Wagner, "Orthodox Domesticity: Creating a Social Role for Women," 122.

[82] Engel, *Women in Russia, 1700–2000*, 35.

[83] Leading up to emancipation, women owned one third of the estates in private hands (Engel, *Women in Russia, 1700–2000*, 35).

[84] Engel, *Women in Russia, 1700–2000*, 36.

[85] Andrei Chikhachev, "Vazhnost' khoziaiki v dome," *Zemledel'cheskaia gazeta* 53 (1847): 417–419. Qtd. in Antonova, *An Ordinary Marriage* 137–138.

[86] I am grateful to William Wagner for bringing this point to my attention.

[87] Engel, *Women in Russia, 1700–2000*, 36

[88] Qtd. in Michelle Lamarche Marrese, "Gender and the Legal Order in Imperial Russia," 330.

The great responsibility afforded to Russian women complicated their ability to follow English models of womanhood they were receiving through conduct manuals and literature, as it clashed with the idea of separate spheres. In sum, Russian women, like English women, were in a subservient role to the men in their families—either as daughters, sisters, or wives. They had absorbed a certain amount of Western ideology about domesticity and women's roles, not all of it compatible with the realities of Russia. Starting from this position that historians want to see as both the same as and different from their English counterparts, women in Russian novels have a vastly different fate, especially as regards courtship and marriage.

5

Courtship and Its Promises

*It is a truth universally acknowledged, that a single man in possession
of a good fortune, must be in want of a wife.*
—Jane Austen, *Pride and Prejudice*

*…he told himself over and over again that the manner in which unmar-
ried men with incomes were set upon by ladies in want of husbands was
very disgraceful to the country at large.*
—Anthony Trollope, *He Knew He Was Right*

Romantic love—the kind that could lead to marriage—is a central plot motivator
in both the Russian and English novelistic traditions. Such love, like plot in Peter
Brooks' famous definition, is "a form of desire that carries us forward, onward
through the text."[1] The desire of the reader parallels that of the characters, as all
await the satisfaction of tying the conjugal knot; yet such fulfillment must be
delayed or there would be no story.[2] Brooks' conception of plot—with its built-in
emphasis on narrative closure—maps comfortably onto the English novel, which
is famous for concluding with wedding bells and the birth of an heir. But what of
the Russian novel, which is famous for its *failures* to provide such endings? While
English novels problematize the marital ideal in various ways, most ultimately satisfy desire with the sought-after love-match of virtuous and deserving heroine and
hero; Russian novels frequently leave the reader—as well as the characters—with
the ache of irresolution. Most often no knots—conjugal or otherwise—have been
tied to give the gratification of fulfillment and a tidying up of loose ends.

The reasons for and meaning behind these differences come into focus when
viewed in the context of the historical conditions of the family and marriage in the
two countries. Talia Schaffer argues that "Because the marriage plot is intimately
enmeshed with particular cultural traditions and legal and political developments,
it must be read as a national story and [the English version] cannot be extended to,
say, France or America, which had their own marital histories."[3] Chapter 4 examined the legal and social structures that shaped the "national story" in England and
Russia: the idealism with which the English regarded their traditional family and

---

[1] Brooks, *Reading for the Plot*, 37.
[2] Brooks, *Reading for the Plot*, 111.
[3] Schaffer, *Romance's Rivals*, 15.

The Family Novel in Russia and England, 1800–1880. Anna A. Berman, Oxford University Press.
© Anna A. Berman (2022). DOI: 10.1093/oso/9780192866622.003.0006

the domestic sphere, and the Russians' more realist view of their "backward" family model. This chapter explores the plotlines that resulted: some leading to the altar, others to singledom, some challenging the family structure, others affirming it.

The standard English marriage (or courtship) plot moves characters through a defined progression: from first encounter, to falling in love, various obstacles to the union (either external or caused by one or both of the lovers), to an ultimate declaration, a proposal, and often a closing wedding ceremony and some mention of a new arrival in the nursery. While the emphasis may be on romantic love, the ultimate function such a plot progression serves is to create new conjugal families. In its traditional (English) form, the marriage plot is conservative—reinforcing the vertical and recreating the status quo. In saying this, I do not disregard the vast body of scholarship that explores challenges to the English marriage ideal, which will be discussed in the next chapter. Many novels critique *aspects* of wedlock, or *specific* marriages, but they stop short of trying to topple the whole institution. At the stage of courtship, characters and readers are meant to believe that if the right couple weds, their nuptials will mark the start of "happily ever after"; any failed marriages around them do not undermine this ideal. On the whole, England's marriage plots reaffirm the normative, patriarchal family model, where achieving wedlock meant that the devoted wife would now live under the protective care of her wise and benevolent husband and raise children to repeat this pattern.

In Russia, where the educated public widely understood marriage to be a form of patriarchal tyranny, and weddings often marked the start of a life of oppression (and possibly state-sanctioned physical violence), marriage plots could not be so readily assumed to lead to the same kind of happily-ever-after. Rather than placing value on the future family that would be created, the Russians focused on the state of the characters in the present and the type of relations they shared. The trajectory of the courtship plot for women most often leads not to marriage, but to a greater degree of awareness (of both self and the world), and this awareness typically makes a union with the hero *not* the desirable outcome. Successful courtships tend to be in the background of Russian novels, while narrative attention focuses on the process of a romantic union failing to come together. Authors often gave these failed courtship plots a progressive or even radical function as a critique of gender roles, marriage, and the families it creates.

The Centrality of Marriage in Novel and Theory

In one of the most famous studies of the novel from the last half-century, Tony Tanner claimed "marriage is *the* central subject for the bourgeois novel."[4] Tanner— and the theorists like him who proclaim the centrality of marriage—use Europe

---

[4] Tanner, *Adultery and the Novel*, 15. See also Hinz, "Hierogamy versus Wedlock," 900.

as a proxy for the world. Comparative studies of marriage in the novel have largely focused on England and France. It is a truism among literary historians that eighteenth and nineteenth-century French novelists wrote adultery novels, where the narrative interest commences *after* the marriage, while the English wrote courtship plots that culminate with the wedding.[5] There are historical reasons for this; in France, girls went straight from the convent school into a marriage arranged by their parents, so the courtship phase was largely absent and the search for love manifested in adulterous affairs. Niklas Luhmann cautions: "It cannot be emphasized enough that the freedom to choose someone to love [in a French novel] applies to the *extra-marital* relations of *married* persons. Unmarried daughters were protected quite effectively against seduction, and seducing them would have hardly added to the '*glorie*' of the hero. Freedom thus began with marriage."[6] In England, by contrast, the girl was given greater freedom in choosing her spouse, so the search for love manifests as a courtship plot.[7]

Placing the rise of the novel in England, Ian Watt's seminal (but much contested) *The Rise of the Novel* (1957) made a similar foundational claim to Tanner's: "the great majority of novels written since *Pamela* (1740) have continued its basic pattern, and concentrated their main interest upon a courtship leading to marriage."[8] Watt compellingly links the rise of the novel with the growing choice in marriage for women, which created the possibility of the marriage plot as we know it. He argues that "The values of courtly love could not be combined with those of marriage until marriage was primarily the result of a free choice by the individuals concerned ... The rise of the novel, then, would seem to be connected with the much greater freedom of women in modern society, a freedom which, especially as regards marriage, was achieved earlier and more completely in England than elsewhere."[9]

Watt's claims might help explain why the rise of the novel came almost a century later in Russia than in England, but in other ways the Russian tradition provides a stumbling block to the "truths" he proclaims (as explored in the Introduction). Russia never had the courtly love tradition, and the concept of romantic love was a foreign import in the eighteenth century. Europeanized Russians would struggle

---

[5] This view is summarized by Hager (*Dickens and the Rise of Divorce*, 12). We find similar views in the nineteenth century. For example, in a review of Taine's study of the English novel, when comparing the English outlook (typified by Dickens) with that of George Sand, the reviewer noted that Sand wants to make readers love, but does not care about marriage. Chuiko, V. "Angliiskie romanisty (po Tenu)" *Zhenskii vestnik* №2 (1866), 1–41 (here 25).

[6] Luhmann, *Love as Passion: The Codification of Intimacy*, 50. Boone links the origins of this Continental/English divide to the ways in which the concept of amorous desire evolved on the two sides of the Channel: the "Continental ethos of courtly love, theoretically grounded in the irreconcilable opposition of passionate desire and utilitarian marriage, and the specifically English ideal of romantic wedlock uniting these poles" (*Tradition Counter Tradition*, 32). It is easy to see how the Continental division of passion from marriage would lead to the adultery plot.

[7] Hager, *Dickens and the Rise of Divorce*, 24.

[8] Watt, *The Rise of the Novel*, 148–149.

[9] Watt, *The Rise of the Novel*, 138.

to adapt it to their social and cultural realities. Many of Russia's classic novels, although featuring marriage plots, could hardly be said to center upon them (e.g. *A Hero of Our Time, Dead Souls, Oblomov, Fathers and Children, War and Peace, Crime and Punishment, Demons, The Golovlyovs, The Brothers Karamazov*, etc.). So in trying to understand the marriage plot and its place in "the novel," including Russia can help us to rethink our assumptions and to view the English novel in a new light.

Watt's theories have come under significant challenge and revision from within the English literary establishment as well, but none of these challenges ultimately dislodge marriage from its throne of centrality. Watt's theories have been attacked for failing to account for the prevalence of women writers in England or to acknowledge the political meaning of sexuality and marriage, for overlooking the essential relationship between public and private, and for ignoring failed marriage plots.[10] Yet while these critiques throw into question the marriage plot's meaning, they still give it pride of place. In a 1927 lecture, E. M. Forster claimed that "If you think of a novel in the vague you think of a love interest—of a man and woman who want to be united and perhaps succeed."[11] Almost one hundred years later, scholars continue to make similar claims.[12] This does not mean other relationships were absent from the novels; they are just not the primary plot motivators or the center of novel theory.[13]

This pressure toward wedlock often manifests within the world of the novel, with societal and literary expectations reinforcing each other. Even as characters may critique the centrality of marriage (often as mouthpieces for the author), they still fall into it. For example, when the orphaned Ibbotson sisters arrive in Deerbrook at the start of Harriet Martineau's eponymous novel (1839), the whole village begins concocting marriage plots, with one local remarking that "He should not wonder if some work for the rector should rise up before long, for, where there were pretty faces, weddings might be looked for" (38). That statement seems to apply to novels more than life, where not all "pretty faces" find a suitable match waiting in the quaint villages they visit. But within *Deerbrook*, this dictum proves true, and soon, the village—and the reader—can think of little else. Margaret

---

[10] On ignoring women writers, see Armstrong, *Desire and Domestic Fiction*, 14. Pushing back against "existing histories of the novel," Armstrong argues that "the history of the novel cannot be understood apart from the history of sexuality" (16). Michael McKeon's *The Secret History of Domesticity* (2005) offers its own thesis on the rise of the novel, based on rethinking the relationship between public and private. On Watt's failure to engage with failed marriage plots, see Hager, *Dickens and the Rise of Divorce*, "Ch. 1: Contextualizing the Failed Marriage Plot."

[11] Forster, *Aspects of the Novel*, 61.

[12] See also Gorsky, *Femininity to Feminism*, 21.

[13] Even in a book devoted to female friendship, Sharon Marcus acknowledges that "Victorian novels do indeed depend on the union of a man and a woman for their narrative structure" (*Between Women*, 76). Maia McAleavy shows the place of marriage within that structure when she notes that "The Victorian novel's plot structure was crucially tied to marriage as an ending, and it therefore formed the nineteenth-century's most important site for explorations of marriage as narrative" (*The Bigamy Plot*, 14).

Ibbotson complains to a friend that "all girls are brought up to think of marriage as almost the only event in life. Their minds are stuffed with thoughts of it almost before they have had time to gain any other ideas" (159).[14] Yet even while Margaret criticizes the idea, she and her sister both find a match by the end of the novel and most of the narrative attention is devoted to their marriage plots.

Resistance is futile, both for characters and authors. Trollope's *He Knew He Was Right* (1869) is constantly critiquing standard literary tropes around courtship and marriage, even as Trollope fulfills the expectations they raise. Early in the novel, Emily Trevelyan chides her younger sister Nora for saying she will not marry a wealthy suitor:

> "You can't be otherwise than a woman. And you must marry. And this man is a gentleman, and will be a peer. There is nothing on earth against him, except that he does not set the Thames on fire ..."
>
> "All the same, I shall not marry Mr. Glascock. A woman can die, at any rate," said Nora.
>
> "No, she can't. A woman must be decent; and to die of want is very indecent. She can't die, and she mustn't be in want, and she oughtn't to be a burden." (40)

In other words, marriage is the *only* option for the English heroine in the standard view Trollope is mocking ... but then conforms to (Nora ultimately weds a journalist who better suits her tastes). The multi-plot structure of *He Knew He Was Right* weaves together the breakdown of Emily's marriage with a series of three successful courtship plots (and a fourth—Mr. Gibbon being overcome by the two Miss Frenches—for comic value). As Trollope quips later in the same novel, "It is rather hard upon readers that they should be thus hurried from the completion of hymeneals in Florence to the preparations for other hymeneals in Devonshire; but it is the nature of a complex story to be entangled with many weddings toward its close" (826).

While *He Knew He Was Right* epitomizes a typical pattern of English novels making marriage their end goal, I would stress again that I am not suggesting English novels always glorified wedlock. The next chapter will explore the pattern of *un*happy marriages, like that of Emily Trevelyan, whose husband develops a paranoid belief in her infidelity and ultimately goes mad. Yet even while the English engaged with the darker sides of wedlock, their courtship plots were still based on the assumption that getting to the altar marked a happy ending for the pair. They might chip away at the armor of the marriage ideal by showing individual failings, but the body of ideology underneath remained unscathed. The Russians,

---

[14] In reality, girls in families with means had few prospects besides marriage. As one real-life Victorian brother wrote, watching his six sisters attend balls and dinners in search of suitors, "There was absolutely nothing else to do or live for." Source: Edward Carpenter (1844–1929), qtd. in Heilbrun, "Marriage Perceived," 166.

by contrast, would attack the very ideal itself. When I turn to the Russian tradition in the second half of this chapter I will make two claims. First, on the whole, rather than using the marriage plot to reinforce the existing order, the Russians used it to make a progressive statement, pushing *against* Russia's traditional family past. This liberal stance defied all expectations about the family novel genre. And second, I argue that this shift in socio-political outlook was fostered by Russia's ethics of time: placing value on the present rather than on the past or future. The goal of the marriage plot was not to produce an heir and continue a family line, but to improve life in the here and now. And marriage was not often an improvement.

England's Vertical Marriage Plot

Some aspects of the English marriage plot are so ubiquitous as to have been treated as essential, yet when viewed against the Russian alternative their uniquely English roots are revealed. One such aspect is the marriage plot's verticality: its ultimate aim is family continuity. This vertical thrust comes most fully into view when individual desire cannot be reconciled with duties to the family's past and future. In Trollope's *An Eye for an Eye* (1879) for example, Fred Neville represents the future of his line as heir to his uncle, the Earl of Scroope, but he has also seduced and impregnated the beautiful Kate O'Hara. Not only is Kate a penniless Irish Catholic, but it also turns out that her father (originally believed to be dead) has actually been in the galleys in southern France and returns to beg. His uncle does not need to forbid Fred's marriage to Kate because Fred himself has internalized the family's values: "He knew that it was not fit. He believed in the title, in the sanctity of the name, in the mysterious grandeur of the family ... He understood, almost as well as did his uncle, that Kate O'Hara ought not to be made Countess of Scroope" (165, 172). When discussing the situation with his younger brother—whom Fred wishes could take his place as heir—he laments "If it were only myself, I would give up all to her. I would, by heaven. But I cannot sacrifice the family. As to solemn promises, did I not swear to my uncle that I would not disgrace the family by such a marriage?" (257). Fred would willingly bind himself to Kate permanently, but he will not make her Countess of Scroope. "He was still willing to sacrifice himself, but his family honours he would not pollute" (306). These are classic English values.

In this impasse, Trollope turns to a radical solution that allows the vertical family axis to win out. Fred is removed from the family progression in the only way possible: through death (murdered by Kate's mother, who suspects that he is trying to turn her daughter into a mistress). Fred's younger brother marries the woman his uncle and aunt had wished for Fred, and they settle as the respectable Lord and Lady of Scroope Manor. Thus, Fred's disastrous and deadly marriage plot is followed by one that tidily restores order to the family and ensures its linear succession. Such conflicts are so common as to virtually disappear into the fabric of *the* novel; yet the tension between individual desire and vertical family needs is rarely such a powerful plot motivator in a Russian novel, suggesting it is the English emphasis on lineage that generates this kind of plot.[15]

The opening line of *Pride and Prejudice* (1813), which served as an epigraph to this chapter, exemplifies the vertical emphasis of the English marriage plot. Focusing on "the stable transmission of private property," Alex Woloch argues that "'Possession of a good fortune' is the precondition for the 'want of a wife' both because marriage requires property—only a wealthy man is an eligible husband— and because property requires marriage, as the stable form of its transmission."[16] This characterization of the marriage plot as a linear transmission of property is indicative of its ultimate verticality. It is not (just) a story of romantic love in the present; rather, it is the way the family maintains its stability. And as we saw in Part I, this property requirement ensures that the marriage plot is only available to one brother—reinforcing the linear structure of the narrative (and family).

Although I am far from the first to note the importance of property and its passage from one family member to another, many critics have framed this in purely economic terms, rather than thinking about the ethics of time being reinforced.[17] The transmission of property facilitated by the marriage plot is vertical (from generation to generation), rather than lateral (within a generation); marriage provides the legal heirs who will inherit. Underlying English concerns about marriage and property is a time perspective that places value on the family's past and future (the weight of ancestry and the duty to progeny), rather than emotional concerns in the present. This is why Fred must choose the Scroope family honor over the woman he would otherwise gladly have married. Perhaps this time perspective has gone largely uncommented upon because scholars regard it as an essential feature of *the* marriage plot—a necessity the Russian example will challenge.

With a satirist like Thackeray, the desire for family advancement manifests in baldly economic terms that reinforce our standard theories about transmission. *Vanity Fair* (1848) lays this bare in a scathing passage describing Maria Osborne's engagement to "Frederick Bullock, Esq. of the house of Bullock, Hulker & Bullock." After Maria's brother is disinherited, Frederick hopes for an increase in his fiancée's dowry and to have half her father's property left to Maria, but Mr. Osborne refuses, saying Frederick had agreed to take her with £20,000. A feud ensues and the engagement is temporarily broken off, but ultimately "Fred's father and senior

---

[15] Of course there are exceptions, like Nikolai Rostov's early love for his penniless cousin Sonya (*War and Peace*), though he grows out of it on his own and not because of family pressures.

[16] Woloch, *The One vs. the Many*, 57.

[17] A fascinating study that engages the relationship of economics to the family is Elsie Michie's "Rich Woman, Poor Woman: Toward an Anthropology of the Nineteenth-Century Marriage Plot." Michie is interested in the trope of the hero choosing between "the heiress and a poorer but more desirable rival," for example Mr. Darcy rejecting Miss de Bourgh in favor of the impoverished Elizabeth Bennet (423).

partners counselled him to take Maria, even with the twenty thousand settled, half down, and half at the death of Mr. Osborne, with the chances of the further division of the property" (538). They are literally approaching the engagement as the vertical transmission of Osborne wealth.

Meanwhile, the Osbornes are thinking about the Bullock lineage. Despite offenses, Mr. Osborne (*not Maria!*) accepts the reestablishment of the engagement because "Hulker and Bullock were a high family in the city aristocracy, and connected with the 'nobs' at the West End. It was something for the old man to be able to say, 'My son, sir, of the house of Hulker, Bullock & Co., sir; my daughter's cousin, Lady Mary Mango, sir, daughter of the Right Hon. The Earl of Castlemouldy'" (538–539). The engagement reads more like a business dealing between the men, where what is to be gained is not connubial bliss, but future family wealth and prestige.[18] This is a capitalist transaction. The collateral relations acquired through the marriage are a benefit not for the sake of their kinship or support in the present, but for upward mobility, which, of course, has a future thrust. Comparing this to the way Russian novels treat the relatives around their newlyweds shows that in-laws, cousins, uncles, aunts, etc. could instead be valued for their companionship and love in the present.

Pride and Prejudice demonstrates that vertical family concerns need not be as crudely economic as Thackeray made them out to be in *Vanity Fair*. Mr. Darcy, who is not greedily seeking wealth, still feels a duty to his family's past and the need to preserve its dignity into the future. Faced with the prospect of his heiress cousin, Miss de Bourgh (the family's preference) or the impoverished but desirable Elizabeth Bennet, Darcy's choice is less about wealth (he will end up rich either way), but about family honor. When Mr. Darcy initially proposes to Elizabeth Bennet, his failure stems in a large part from giving too great a credence to the vertical: "His sense of her inferiority—of its being a degradation—of the family obstacles which had always opposed to inclination, were dwelt on with a warmth which seemed due to the consequence he was wounding, but was very unlikely to recommend his suit" (189). Shocked at her stinging refusal, Darcy asks "Could you expect me to rejoice in the inferiority of your connections?—to congratulate myself on the hope of relations, whose condition in life is so decidedly beneath my own?" (192).

What Darcy lays bare is that among the gentry (and bourgeois classes who emulated them) marriage is not about joining two individuals, but two families whose antecedents are expected to align or complement each other as well as the couple's natures do in the present. Darcy must learn to resist these vertical

---

[18] Here I am in agreement with the influential argument put forward by Gayle Rubin in "The Traffic in Women: Notes Toward a Political Economy of Sex." This type of exchange is explicit in Charlotte Brontë's *Villette* (1853), where the young lover tells his beloved's father "I did truly regard you as the possessor of the most valuable thing the world owns for me. I wished for it; I tried for it. Sir, I ask for it now" (516). The men ultimately withdraw to the study to finalize the transaction, exchanging Paulina from one to the other.

pressures—including active attempts at intimidation by his aunt—to find personal fulfillment.[19] In England it was far more acceptable for a wealthy husband to raise a wife to his level than for the woman to descend in marriage.[20] Mr. Bennet was a gentleman, and Darcy ultimately recognizes that Elizabeth's innate gentility will ensure that he has not "lowered" himself or his family by the marriage. As Elizabeth herself declares, "He is a gentleman; I am a gentleman's daughter; so far we are equal" (356). While this statement "demystifies the great gentry," serving reformist aims, as Claudia Johnson has noted "it leaves the social structure radicals had assailed substantially intact."[21] Even if "the 'shades of Pemberley' are 'finally polluted' by Elizabeth" and her middle-class relations, "the majesty of Pemberley itself is still affirmed, and any suspicion on our part that it may have been tarnished is soon set to rest by our confidence that the new properly proud Darcy would never permit any real compromise of its integrity."[22] The vertical axis of family lineage is still affirmed.

It is comforting to believe that the world's Darcys could recognize the worth of the Elizabeth Bennets, and that heroes and heroines should not have to choose between love and money. Johnson calls *Pride and Prejudice* "almost shamelessly wish fulfilling," yet it is hardly alone; many English novels supported this same wish.[23] Treating the marriage plot anthropologically, Elsie Michie points to "an unceasing negotiation between the material appeals readers knew individuals felt and the immaterial values novels wanted to insist they desired."[24] One might naturally want the wealth of the heiress, but in the world of the novel the poor but virtuous heroine should hold greater worth.

Eschewing reality, English novelists tended to let their heroines have their cake and eat it too: a love match and sufficient wealth. Many, like Elizabeth and Jane Bennet, conveniently fall in love with men of or above their own station. While background figures like the heroine's mother in *Mansfield Park* (1814) might be shunned for an imprudent love match, when it is the impoverished heroine whose choice falls upon a man of little means she is still able to follow her heart while ending up comfortably provided for; church livings, London jobs, and inheritances were always to be found by authors when needed to smooth the path into

---

[19] Johnson points to the fact that Austen structures the conflict between aunt and nephew, not parents and son, "avert[ing] a more politically potent ... conflict" (*Jane Austen: Women, Politics, and the Novel*, 89). In her words, "the family is spared a frontal attack" (89). This helps to maintain the family ideal, just as not including multiple brothers relieves authors of the need to address inherent structural tensions between them.

[20] This is why Florence Dombey rejoices at being disowned and poor when she marries Walter Gay (*Dombey and Son*, 1846–1848): "It makes my heart swell with such delight to know that those who speak of you must say you married a poor disowned girl, who had taken shelter here; who had no other home, no other friends; who had nothing—nothing! Oh Walter, if I could have brought you millions, I never could have been so happy for your sake, as I am!" (853).

[21] Johnson, *Jane Austen: Women, Politics, and the Novel*, 88.

[22] Johnson, *Jane Austen: Women, Politics, and the Novel*, 89.

[23] Johnson, *Jane Austen: Women, Politics, and the Novel*, 73.

[24] Michie, "Rich Woman, Poor Woman," 423.

comfortable wedlock (for example, Elinor and Edward Ferrars in *Sense and Sensibility*, 1811). In *He Knew He Was Right*, after Nora chooses the journalist, Hugh Stanbury, over Mr. Glascock, Trollope assures the reader that the pair were able to settle in a comfortable part of London, describing in detail their financial situation (the amount of Stanbury's life insurance, their savings, their annual budget, and other pertinent details). English novels did all they could to provide stability and continuity for the families they created.

Producing an Heir

The primary meaning of the marriage plot lies in what comes after it: the production of a legal heir. Barry McCrea claims "The English nineteenth-century novel from Austen on seems, structurally at least, to be in the thrall of a sort of fertility cult, where all sense of beginnings and endings are predicated upon marriage and procreation."[25] This procreative force is not aimed at fecundity and expansion, but at futurity represented by a singular line of descent. Thus in Thackeray's *Vanity Fair* when George Osborne's father anticipates his son marrying a rich girl, "His blood boiled with honest British exultation, as he saw the name of Osborne ennobled in the person of his son, and thought that he might be the progenitor of a glorious line of baronets" (250). It is noteworthy that Thackeray makes this exultation a "British" trait, again hinting at the cultural conditioning of this obsession with family line.

While Osborne is looking forward, an heir also bears the burden of two families' pasts. In *He Knew He Was Right*, the minister's wife holds the view "that a man of family should strengthen himself by marrying a woman of family. It was so necessary, she declared, that a man when marrying should remember that his child would have two grandfathers, and would be called upon to account for four great-grandfathers" (815). This immediate and automatic (con)fusion of marital choice with the lineage of the future heir is symptomatic of the function marriage plays in the English novel; it reinforces family lines and social stability.[26]

The wife is the one who provides the family's future. When Lady Glencora Palliser, the wife of the future Chancellor of the Exchequer, becomes pregnant in Trollope's *Can You Forgive Her?* (1864)—in a chapter duly titled "Great Moment to all the Pallisers"—she tells a friend "It seemed as though I were destined to bring nothing but misery to everybody, and I used to wish myself dead so often. I shan't wish myself dead now" (614). Glencora, who had been miserable in her marriage and was contemplating adultery, now experiences joy and fulfillment as the means of providing a new little Palliser to this illustrious family line. The news of his wife's

---

[25] McCrea, *In the Company of Strangers*, 7. See also Gorsky, *Femininity to Feminism*, 23.
[26] The social stability provided by marriage is emphasized by Tanner (*Jane Austen*, 105).

condition leaves Mr. Palliser in a state of "almost unconscious exaltation" (the same word Thackeray used for Osborne's father) (612). Mr. Palliser tries to explain why this is a matter of "such immense importance" to his friend Mr. Grey, who assures him "Oh yes! When there's a dukedom and heaven know how many thousands a year to be disposed of, the question of their future ownership does become important" (614, 615). The vertical transmission of property is inextricably linked with the vertical transmission of blood, and all is made possible by the wife.

In a contrasting example that illustrates the same point, in *Daniel Deronda* (1876) Sir Hugo's second wife, Lady Mallinger, feels guilt "as the infelicitous wife who had produced nothing but daughters, little better than no children, poor dear things, except for her own fondness and for Sir Hugo's wonderful goodness to them" (379). Despite the family's happiness in the present, Lady Mallinger has failed to provide a *future* for the family line, and, as a result, all the property and title will go to a nephew, Mallinger Grandcourt. Lady Mallinger's guilt reminds us that marriage in the English novel is supposed to be synonymous with the futurity provided by a male heir. In McCrea's words, "With its implicit promise of biological reproduction, marriage is the embodiment of the happy end, i.e., an end that is also a beginning ..."[27] It contributes to the cycle of generations, such that *Dombey and Son* (1846–1848) can end with a Paul and Florence sibling pair, just like it began.

The flip-side to valuing marriage and reproductive futurity is devaluing consanguineal kin. Wedlock is meant to replace the family of origin in the English tradition. This kinship hierarchy dates back to the eighteenth century, when we see "a movement from an axis of kinship based on consanguineal ties or blood lineage to an axis based on conjugal and affinal ties of the married couple. That is, the biologically given family into which one was born was gradually becoming secondary to the chosen family constructed by marriage."[28] Richardson's Clarissa Harlowe laments that marriage means "To be given up to a strange man; to be engrafted into a strange family; to give up her very name, as a mark of her becoming his absolute and dependent property: to be obliged to prefer this strange man to father, mother—to everybody" (148). This, again, is a way of reinforcing the vertical model of family. Women have married *out* into a new line that their children will be continuing. As Ruth Perry has noted, the dowry was actually a form of *dis*inheritance, designed to get the daughter off the family's hands.[29]

---

[27] McCrea, *In the Company of Strangers*, 8. The list of novels that end with a child (or expectancy) includes Anne Brontë's *The Tenant of Wildfell Hall* (1848); Mary Elizabeth Braddon's *Aurora Floyd* (1863) and *Like and Unlike* (1887); Wilkie Collins' *The Woman in White* (1859–1860) and *Poor Miss Finch* (1872); Craik's *Hannah* (1871); Dickens' *Nicholas Nickleby* (1839), *David Copperfield* (1850), *A Tale of Two Cities* (1859) and *Our Mutual Friend* (1864–1865); Drury's *The Brothers* (1865); Eliot's *Adam Bede* (1859) and *Middlemarch* (1871–1872); Thackeray's *Vanity Fair*; and Trollope's *Barchester Towers* (1857) and *Can You Forgive Her?*.

[28] Perry, *Novel Relations*, 2.

[29] Perry, *Novel Relations*, 52.

Marriage means entering the vertical and continuing a family line, while devaluing the family of childhood as merely a temporary unit. Consanguineal kin often
perceive this as a loss, as is remarked upon in Charlotte Brontë's *Villette* (1853),
Gaskell's *Wives and Daughters* (1864–1866), and Charlotte Yonge's *Heartsease, or
Brother's Wife* (1854) and *The Daisy Chain* (1856). The only way for the heroine to
resist this severance is to marry someone within her family of origin, and scholars
have explored the pattern of marriages to close kin.[30] Fanny Price's marriage to
her cousin at the end of *Mansfield Park*, for example, allows her to remain in the
home in which she was raised, while in reverse in *Wives and Daughters*, Molly Gibson becomes an accepted daughter of the Hamley family, so it will not really be a
break with her past to marry Roger and take the Hamley name. Only by marrying
a figurative "brother" could the heroine continue to make such a figure the center
of her world, otherwise he would be superseded by a husband (only secondary
characters manage to remain as brother-sister companionate pairs).

In Russia, we find the opposite hierarchy of values. In *Crime and Punishment*
(1866), when Dunya is trying to judge her fiancé after he has fallen out with her
brother, Luzhin becomes deeply offended and complains to her "'Either you or
him,' you say, and thereby show me how little I mean to you ... I cannot allow it, in
view of the relations and ... obligations existing between us.'" This enrages Dunya.
"'What!' Dunya flared up. 'I place your interests alongside all that has so far been
precious in my life, all that has so far constituted the *whole* of my life, and you
are suddenly offended because I attach so *little* value to you!'" (6:231/302). Dostoevsky makes it clear that the reader is not meant to agree with Luzhin's claim that
"Love for one's future life-companion, a future husband, ought to exceed the love
for one's brother," which is pronounced "sententiously" by a thoroughly unworthy
character (6:231/302).

For the Russian heroine, the brother does not need to lose value, and ties to
the consanguineal family are not severed in the same way as in the English mind-
set.[31] Dunya stays devoted to Raskolnikov even after her marriage to Razumikhin,
and part of what draws her to her future husband is that he shares this devotion. Examples from history also reveal this balancing of marital and blood ties

---

[30] Corbett, *Family Likeness*, vii. See also Clark, "The Family in the Novels of Sarah Harriet Burney,"
77. Paula Marantz Cohen goes further, arguing that the courtship plot is not actually about the heroine's
transition to new family, but the deferral of such movement (*The Daughter's Dilemma*, 26).

[31] I do not wish to oversimplify the case or to suggest that Russian women stayed fully connected
to their family of origin upon marriage. We can see in the debates and changing laws around dowries,
for example, that the daughter was seen as entering a new *rod* upon her marriage. After a review of
numerous eighteenth-century court cases, Lee Farrow concludes "All of the property issues discussed
[... here] point to the conclusion that a woman's place within the clan was tenuous and not always
supported by law once she married and took another clan's name" (*Between Clan and Crown*, 140).
The idea that a woman was leaving her *rod* underlies laws like that passed in November 1731, which
only allowed acquired property, not family property, to be given in a dowry (Farrow, *Between Clan and
Crown*, 122). The same logic underlies Peter's Law of Single Inheritance, which required that if the last
surviving member of a *rod* willed property to a female member, her husband and heirs in perpetuity
were required to attach her family name to theirs (134).

in Russia. We see it in the Bakunin family, where the youngest brother, Alexander, lived on the family estate with his parents, trying to keep it going, while his older brother, Mikhail, led a successful career in St. Petersburg. Writing to Mikhail in 1793, Alexander requested "Please send money in the future when you can ... but always remember that you must found a fortune for your wife and children."[32] Alexander acknowledges the coexistence of both consanguineal and conjugal kin. A broader range of kinship ties can remain potent in the Russian novel as well, as family expands outward, offering an alternative to the English model based on amassing all value in a singular heir and line of descent.

Reader, I Didn't Marry Him

With a family model that emphasizes the present, rather than the future, the lateral spread of kin, rather than ancestry and progeny, Russian novels did not have the same end goal to their marriage plots as English novels did. And the function these plots served in public discourse became one of critique rather than affirmation of the existing norm. Authors focused their attentions on the inner lives of their characters and on their conditions within their families and society. They did not start from the assumption that for a heroine, getting married would bring a life of domestic bliss, and rejected the wedding as the ultimate goal. Instead, the purpose of their marriage plots was to interrogate Russia's courtship practices and to reveal why they produced so many *unhappy* families. In practice, this often led to heroines remaining single, but given the sorry state of marriage in Russia, a failed courtship plot might ultimately be the happi*er* ending.

From 1825–1832 Pushkin published his novel-in-verse, *Eugene Onegin*, which became a touchstone for all that followed. Often credited as Russia's first family novel,[33] it follows a simple plot: living on her family's rural estate, the dreamy, melancholy Tatiana encounters the dashing and disaffected Onegin, a society fop who inherits a neighboring estate. Inspired by reading European novels, Tatiana falls in love with Onegin. She writes a letter confessing her feelings, and he coldly but honorably rejects her. Out of ennui Onegin provokes a fight with her sister's fiancé, Lensky, kills him in a duel, and then leaves to wander abroad. Several years later Onegin re-encounters Tatiana—who is now a married, high-society lady—and falls madly in love. In a parallel gesture to her original letter, he writes to her, then appears at her home to plead his case. Despite the love she still feels for him, Tatiana rejects Onegin to remain faithful to her husband. Pushkin's novel laid the foundation for a pattern found in many later works: the strong, morally superior

[32] Qtd. in Randolph, *The House in the Garden*, 54.
[33] Authors who have claimed *Eugene Onegin* is the first Russian family novel include Eikhenbaum, *Tolstoy in the Seventies*; Proskurina, *Russkie pisateli XIX veka o sem'e*.

woman (Dostoevsky called Tatiana "the apotheosis of Russian womanhood") falls in love with the weaker, "superfluous man," yet the pair fails to unite.[34] Variants of this appear in almost half the Russian novels in my study. Plot comes precisely from the *failed* attempt at a union.

Chernyshevsky famously blamed this pattern of romantic failures on Russian men's weakness and indecision. In his essay "Russian at the *Rendez-vous*" (1859) he laments that "the hero is very daring so long as there is no question of action and one need merely occupy spare time, fill an empty head or empty heart with conversation and dreams; but when the time comes to express one's feelings and desires directly and precisely, the majority of heroes begin to waver, and are stricken dumb."[35] Notably, this interpretation puts emphasis on the *men* in the courtship plot, reminding us that in Russia, unlike in England, such plots are often narrated from their point of view.[36] Chernyshevsky turns the failure of Russian marriage plots into a critique of Russian liberals and a whole generation who needed to be replaced by "new people." His attack was aimed as much at Turgenev (whose *Asya* he was ostensibly reviewing) as it was at the fictional characters mentioned in the review.

Weak, over-intellectualizing men became a Russian trademark, and not one that was conducive to producing weddings. Russian men's sense of inadequacy, according to Judith Armstrong, is socio-culturally conditioned, deriving from their lack of purpose and their guilt over serfdom.[37] There was no Russian Charles Grandison or Mr. Darcy. Whether or not we agree with Chernyshevsky and Armstrong, their arguments should remind us that the literature and contemporary debates about gender and marriage were inseparable. Literary tropes were not *only* literary, and a weak suitor could represent the failures of Russian men writ large.

Eugene Onegin provided not only subject matter to be emulated (weak man, strong woman), but also a structural model; the failure at romantic union is at the heart of the plot, while successful courtship goes largely un-narrated. The novel is about Tatiana and Onegin *not* ending up together, and we never even see the man she *does* marry. Similarly, after Lensky dies, we learn only in passing of Olga's quick recovery and marriage to an unnamed other. And thus it will be in many a Russian novel to follow: the narrative interest is in the couple who do *not* wed.

---

[34] Dostoevsky's claim appeared in his "Pushkin Speech" (1880) and Turgenev first used the term in his "Diary of a Superfluous Man" (1850). Colleen Lucey notes that Tatiana is taken to Moscow "to the marriage market" (*na iarmanku nevest*, Ch.7, Stanza XXVI) to be married off. Her experiences in Moscow represent an early example in Russian literature of a woman being regarded in terms of "her value as a potential bride" (*Love for Sale: Representing Prostitution in Imperial Russia*, 115).
[35] Chernyshevsky, "The Russian at the Rendez-vous," 112.
[36] In Schaffer's discussion of the English "neighbor plot," in which the heroine marries the local squire instead of the dashing stranger, she notes that the squire is usually used only instrumentally, and we have little access to his interiority or why *he* wants to marry the heroine (*Romance's Rival*, 116). Indeed, she links the disappearance of this plot with the increased attention being given to male characters' thoughts and feelings in the late Victorian period.
[37] Armstrong, *The Novel of Adultery*, 82, 94.

The bulk of Turgenev's *Rudin* (1856)—which responds directly to *Onegin*—focuses on Natalia's failure to unite with the titular hero, while only a letter another character receives in the conclusion informs us of Natalia's ultimate marriage to Volyntsev.

Turgenev keeps the successful courtship plot in the background of *Fathers and Children* (1862) as well, focusing most narrative attention on the failed union of Bazarov and Odintsova, while Arkady and Katya's budding romance hovers unacknowledged (even by them) until near the novel's close.[38] In Dostoevsky's *The Idiot* (1868–1869), the potential for a marriage between Aglaya and Prince Myshkin is a central narrative focus, but after this fails there is only a brief mention at the end of the novel that she has married a Catholic (a "fate practically worse than death" for Dostoevsky).[39] Similarly, Krestovsky (pseud.)'s first novel, *Anna Mikhailovna* (1849), traces the eponymous heroine's failed romance with Okolsky, and we only learn of Anna's ultimate marriage on the final page when someone mentions ending up on a train with her husband. The narrator shows surprise to hear that she is married and asks for details, and the novel closes with the line "He told me a long story …" (165). The reader, however, never hears this story; it falls outside of the novel, as do all these other "successful" courtships that crossed over into wedlock. We never actually *see* the married couples together, just as we never see Tatiana Larina's husband, only hear his clinking spurs.

After that litany of examples, one might ask: why do the Russians avoid narrating the courtships that succeed? Why do they return again and again to the trope of the failed romantic union? To answer this, we must put Russia's marriage plots back into their historical context, where debates about the form of the family and the role of women shaped plot outcomes. The novels both reflected and intervened in these debates. The remainder of this chapter will suggest two things hinted at above: first, that the dominant pattern in Russia was to make the marriage plot a progressive force, pushing against a backward family past. This liberal tendency broke with standard expectations for the family novel genre. And second, I link this shift in socio-political outlook to Russia's ethics of time, where value was focused on the present, rather than on ancestry or progeny. Consequently, the goal of the marriage plot was to ameliorate the conditions of life in the present, and marriage was not often the way to accomplish that.

Marriage Ideals in Flux

When the marriage plot has clear vertical aims, those aims prescribe the values that guide courtship. Exemplifying the English model, in Mrs. Henry Wood's *East*

---

[38] See Gary Saul Morson's analysis in "Genre and Hero."
[39] Matzner-Gore, *Dostoevsky and the Ethics of Narrative Form*, 124 (fn. 49).

Lynne (1861), Mr. Sympson boils down the socially accepted definition of an eligible suitor to three qualities: "A fine unencumbered estate; real substance; good connections" (393). Or, as Major Bagstook explains a "good match" in *Dombey and Son*, "she had beauty, blood, and talent, and Dombey had fortune; and what more could any couple have?" (411). While this claim is undercut by the disastrous failure of Dombey's marriage (which lacks love and respect), blood and fortune remain powerful motivators for English wedlock. Tolstoy gently mocks the simplicity of this model in *Anna Karenina* (1875–1878), equating "English happiness" with "a baronetcy and an estate" in the novel Anna reads on the train (18:107/100). If this "English" happiness is not the desired goal, however, then the criteria for selecting a partner become less obvious. With all the societal reforms taking place at mid-century, Russian novels frame the aim of the marriage plot as an open question.

Dostoevsky explores this uncertainty in *The Idiot* when the Epanchin parents consider the possibility of Prince Myshkin—descended from a noble line and with wealth, but of questionable mental and emotional stability—as a suitor for their youngest daughter, Aglaya. General Epanchin reflects on the potential engagement to his wife:

> "Of course, it's all very strange, if it's true, and I don't dispute that, but…" (another silence.) "But on the other hand, if one looks at the matter directly, then the prince is, after all, quite honestly, a most splendid young fellow, and … and, and—well, at last, our name, our family name, all this will have the appearance, as it were, of keeping up our family name, which has fallen in the eyes of society, that is, if one looks at it from that point of view, because … of course, society; society is society; but the prince is not without a fortune, though it's not much of one. He has … and … and …" (Prolonged silence and decided anticlimax [*osechka*].) (8:421/591)

The stumbling, silences, and ellipses reveal the murkiness of the criteria. Ivan Fyodorovich has no accepted system of values to guide him.

His wife is equally conflicted, attacking her husband's tentative conclusions, yet also questioning her own statements:

> First of all there was the fact that "this wretched little prince was a sickly idiot, secondly, a fool with no knowledge of society and no place in it: to whom could one show him off, even were one to get him in? He was some kind of impossible democrat, didn't even have a civil service rank, and … and … what would Belokonskaya say? And was this the kind of husband we imagined and intended for Aglaya?" The last argument was, of course, the main one. The mother's heart trembled at this thought, was bathed in blood and tears, though at the same time something stirred within her heart, which suddenly said to her: "But why isn't the

prince the kind of man you want?" Well, it was these objections of her own heart that were most troublesome of all for Lizaveta Prokofyevna. (8:421/591–2)

Connor Doak reads this exchange as a reflection of "Myshkin's indefinability, his resistance to categorization and his queer challenge to society."[40] Certainly, he is a unique case, as a former "idiot" who openly announces that his doctor has said he is in every way a child and that he cannot marry because he is unwell (which presumably means he is unable to sire children). He breaks all social conventions, but with a winning naïveté. This is all on the Epanchin parents' minds, though they do not have the language to articulate their concerns in this area.

At a more fundamental level, however, the Epanchins' thought processes also reflect a value system not based exclusively—or even primarily—on rank and status. While both parents begin with these concerns, the "main one" has to do with Myshkin's character and suitability for Aglaya at a deeper level. The objections *of her own heart*, not her reasoning about society, trouble Lizaveta Prokofyevna the most. Devaluing the vertical, she is less concerned with family line or rank (or lack thereof), but with something of deeper, more spiritual worth in the here and now. Aglaya's sister, Alexandra, defends Myshkin's eligibility, telling their mother that "after all God only knew what would be the criterion of the social standing of a decent man with us in Russia in a few years' time: obligatory success in civil service, as previously, or something else? In response to all this the mother at once snapped that Alexandra was 'a freethinker, and all this is that accursed woman question of theirs'" (8:422/592–593).[41] In her discomfort, Lizaveta Prokofyevna blames the contemporary debates that threaten a more traditional—and consequently familiar and secure—social and familial structure.

The disagreement between daughter and mother also highlights shifting norms and the generational rift this created. Scholars often discuss the "conflict of generations" theme in terms of political outlook or broad societal concerns, but the shift from the more old-fashioned generation of the 1830s and 1840s to a more liberated youth is also reflected in views on love and marriage.[42] Many young heroines fall in love with men who do not meet their parents' traditional criteria (these include the heroines of Turgenev's *Rudin* and *On the Eve*, 1860). N. Aleeva lays these tensions bare in *Two Worlds* (1875), where the young and idealistic Polina falls in love with a brilliant but penniless intellectual, Vetlov. When Polina asks her mother for permission to wed, her mother cries and says Vetlov will be forbidden to come to the house. Polina asks if her mother likes him and believes him to be an honest man, revealing her values for selecting a spouse. But her mother replies "What is

---

[40] Doak, "Myshkin's Queer Failure," 10.

[41] The importance of wealth and rank are discussed by Farrow, *Between Clan and Crown*, esp. 61.

[42] Barbara Alpern Engel notes that "generational conflict between daughters and parents, as compared with the conflict between fathers and sons, was far more intense and tended to be more personal than ideological" (*Mothers and Daughters*, 68).

it to you if I respect him or not! This has nothing to do with my feelings about him" (329). To Polina's mother, what matters is what the rest of the extended family and society at large, will say. The question of defining the eligible suitor is not affirmatively answered, perhaps because there was no one societally accepted set of values to determine it. Although wealth is often mentioned in general terms, we find none of the details about income levels and marriage settlements that appear so frequently in English novels.

Courtship practices are specific to each nation and provide the framework within which marriage plots are conducted. In Russia, these practices were also in flux. As mentioned above, the traditional opposition in scholarship is between the French model of arranged marriages after convent school and the English model of courtship plots based on a girl's free choice. Russia, which had absorbed so much European culture and thrown off its traditional model of match-making was left without a clear system—or a clean path from courtship to marriage for its novels. Kitty's mother explicitly laments this uncertainty in *Anna Karenina*:

> The French custom—for the parents to decide the children's fate—was not accepted, and was even condemned. The English custom—giving the girl complete freedom—was also not accepted and was impossible in Russian society. The Russian custom of matchmaking was regarded as something outrageous and was laughed at by everyone, the princess included. But how a girl was to get married or be given in marriage, no one knew. (18:49/44–45)

Kitty's first attempt—which her mother encourages—ends in a disaster so humiliating that she falls gravely ill.

Novelists explored the plots that derived from both extremes: parents trying to choose for their children, and parents who gave their daughters full liberty. A flood of novels in the early 1860s were plotted around daughters' rebellion against their parents' choice of suitor or refusal to sanction a love match: Turgenev's *On the Eve*, Krestovsky (pseud.)'s *Boarding School Girl* (1861), Nikolai Pomialovsky's *Bourgeois Happiness* (1861), Marko Vovchok's *Three Sisters* (1861), and Chernyshevsky's *What Is to Be Done?* (1863).[43] Dostoevsky's Epanchin parents in *The Idiot* adopt the opposite system, not hurrying their daughters into wedlock, but instead relying on them to make their own choices. General Epanchin believes "their parents would merely need to keep a more watchful and unobtrusive eye on

---

[43] Evgenia Tur blamed daughters' rebellious escapes on their mothers. In a polemic exchange with Natalia Grot about Turgenev's *On the Eve*, she proclaimed "In life, as in novellas, daughters run away from their parents' homes, but in Turgenev's novella this phenomenon is a lesson that relates not to daughters but to mothers. Let mothers like Anna Vasilevna Stakhova remake themselves and take care of their children. Then, of course, they will inspire love and respect in their daughters, gain their trust, and, in that case, they will certainly not be abandoned" (Tur, "A Few Words Regarding 'The Russian Woman's' Article, 'Elena Nikolaevna Stakhova,'" trans. Jehanne M. Gheith, in *Russian Women, 1698–1917*, 47).

them, lest any strange choice or unnatural aberration occur, and then, seizing the proper moment, do all that they could to help them and direct the matter with all their influence" (8:33/45). All this seems fine and good until, suddenly, the eldest reaches twenty-five still unwed—and they see that this system too has its flaws.[44]

At mid-century in Russia, courtship practices were an object of attack, with social critics and novelists telling the same story about their failures. An 1859 article in *Family Circle*, for example, argued that Russia's unhappy marriages resulted from young people not having the opportunity to learn each other's character before becoming engaged. "People quite unacquainted with each other often come together at balls and in drawing rooms where affectation [*iskusstvennost'*] alone holds sway; here you will never see or come to know truth [*istina*], but at the same time, it is here that young people become closer, and here that they stealthily play out endearing comedies that end with a tragic denouement."[45] Kitty's initial attachment to Vronsky in *Anna Karenina* is of this mold (she is saved from the "tragic denouement" by his sudden passion for Anna).

Russian women writers—perhaps more attuned to the strict regulation of girls' intercourse with men—picked up on this critique of the restricted nature of social interactions with particular force. The description in *Family Circle* sounds like a plot summary of Karolina Pavlova's *Double Life* (1848). The wealthy and pampered heroine, Cecilia, is raised by a mother who shelters her from any knowledge of the real world. When she is wooed by the charming Dmitri Ivachinsky (whose name, as Diana Greene reminds us, "recalls the *samozvanets* or false Dmitrii of Russia's time of troubles"), she lacks the resources to judge his true character.[46] As the narrator laments, "She who had lived her whole life in this all-pervading atmosphere of banality could not be struck by Ivachinsky's banality, just as a pallid artisan who never leaves his dirty workshop does not notice the oppressive airlessness of his dwelling" (94).

Dmitri is looking for a wealthy bride and does not truly love Cecilia, but she has no opportunity to learn who he really is, only seeing him in society settings "where affectation alone prevails." Only the reader knows that he promised friends to resume his debauchery within a week of the wedding. This is one of the rare novels in which the heroine marries the central male character at the end, and the result promises to be a "tragic denouement," not the "sweetmeats and sugar-plums"

---

[44] Perhaps playing on these English narrative conventions, in an 1859 literary sketch the Russian F. Matveev's narrator describes the need for caution on returning to his village: "Everywhere there were daughters, dear sisters, nieces, and creatures of the female sex slated for marriage, searching at every step for connubial happiness, ready to spin a whole story about love, suffering, matchmaking, and unstoppable striving toward married life—all from one careless movement, accidental glance, or superfluous word." F. Matveev. "Moe sosedstvo. Ocherk pervyi. Semeistvo Garinykh" *Semeinyi krug* №9 (1859), 48–82 (here 51). These daughters, sisters, and nieces had presumably been reading English literature, like the narrator who himself references *Romeo and Juliet* in the sketch.
[45] Tragen. "Liubov' i brak" *Semeinyi krug* №10 (1859), 163–176 (here 171).
[46] Greene, "Gender and Genre in Pavlova's a Double Life," 564.

offered by the English wedding bells. Evgenia Tur's *The Niece* (1851) follows this same pattern of courtship in society settings, misjudgment of the hero, and an unhappy marriage.

Failure as a Form of Critique

When even "success" in the courtship plot can—and often does—lead to unhappiness, we must re-evaluate the meaning of "failure." Many Russian courtship plots that do not culminate in a marriage provided social critique of both gender roles and societal values. Tur's *A Mistake* (1849) was read in this light by its original reviewers and serves as a characteristic example.[47] The plot of *A Mistake* is simple: after years of loving each other, Olga Fyodorova and her beloved Alexander Slavin are finally going to be able to wed. Alexander is already twenty-eight and legally in possession of the fortune he inherited from his father, so he has independence, but he wants his mother's blessing. She is against the match, because Olga's mother (a distant cousin) married down and Fyodorov is a "petty bourgeois name" (*meshchanskoe imia*). The Princess believes Olga is unfit for society and that Alexander will ultimately be unhappy with her, but she writes to him that if he stays in society for one more winter, in the spring she will bless his marriage to whomever he chooses. Readers can guess where this is going. Over the course of that winter, Slavin is seduced away from Olga by Nadinka Gorskina, who is adept at shining in society, though she lacks Olga's elevated and poetic soul. Olga at first senses she has lost Alexander's affections, then learns the truth that he has fallen for someone else. She releases him from their engagement and leaves Moscow. On the final page, readers learn that Alexander and Nadinka have wed.

Woven into this straightforward story are deep engagements with both literary predecessors and with contemporary debates about the family that were just taking off in this period. On the literary front, Tur essentially rewrote Pushkin's *Eugene Onegin*, with Olga as a modern-day Tatiana. Both are living with their mother and a younger, more gregarious sister. Both are bookish and alone, even in their loving families. The worldviews of both are shaped by their reading. The problem in Olga and Alexander's relationship is similar to that faced by Tatiana and Onegin: they are living in different literary scripts from each other. While Onegin was immersed in Bryon and is compared to Childe Harold, Alexander's mother accuses him of playing the role of "a faithful Arcadian shepherd or the hero of an August Lafontaine novel" on his visits to the little Fyodorov *domik* [cottage] (9). Olga, meanwhile, has been reading Shakespeare and Schiller. Here again we have a strong, morally pure woman paired with a weak, cowardly man.

---

[47] See Ostrovsky's review originally published in: *Moskvitianin* (№7, 1850). Gheith has noted this object of Tur's fiction as well, claiming she "offered specific challenges to common nineteenth-century constructions of family" (*Finding the Middle Ground*, 142).

Men were not alone, however, in taking the blame for the failures of Russian courtships and marriages. *A Mistake* is equally critical of women's roles.[48] Tur devotes sufficient attention to the successful Nadinka to make clear to readers why she chooses to seduce Alexander away from Olga, *even though she does not love him*, laying the foundations for another unhappy family. While Olga lives outside the social world of visits and balls, Nadinka is in the midst of it with an oppressive society mother, Princess Gorskina, watching and criticizing her every action. She is miserable at home and knows that her only escape is marriage. Nadinka is not in love with Alexander, but she understands that with him she will have more freedom than with her mother, and this is all she cares about.[49]

Princess Gorskina, meanwhile, is happy to do her part in aiding along her daughter's seduction of Alexander because he is rich and she wishes to see her daughter high-placed in society: "The princess allowed Slavin enough familiarity for him to take a fancy to her daughter, but did not allow him that easygoing intimacy, in which days flow by serenely and the wearied feeling dies down" (151). The seduction is a calculated move, and achieves both of their ends: a brilliant match and an escape. Nadinka has no other options. In this one sense alone, she is like Tatiana Larina, who marries not for love, but because it is the only way forward. Alexander, meanwhile, falls victim to the same flawed system of courtship as Cecilia in *A Double Life* ("unacquainted people com[ing] together at balls and in drawing rooms where affectation alone prevails ..."), and we have every reason to believe that he will recognize his "mistake" (of the title) after the novel closes.

The groom was weak, the bride was trapped, but ultimately the critique in *A Mistake* extends far beyond these individuals. Tur uses their typical plotline to push against the idea that marriage is by necessity the ideal outcome. As Jehanne Gheith has argued, "Ol'ga does not go mad or die, as was common in the earlier works; rather, she chooses a life of integrity outside of marriage. This choice and the way it is validated in the novella again suggest that women may be better off alone or in their families of origin rather than in a loveless union."[50] The novel is an attack on the marriage ideal that is central to the English tradition.

The Russian Ethics of Time

Underlying all the Russian examples in this chapter is a values system that prioritizes the present over the past or future. Russian courtship plots resist the

---

[48] I am in agreement with Jehanne Gheith, who has made this claim about Tur's works more broadly (*Finding the Middle Ground*, 142).

[49] The same dynamics play out in Apollinaria Suslova's short story "For the Time Being" (*Pokuda*, 1861) where Zinaida makes a very ill-suited match simply in order to gain freedom from her oppressive mother.

[50] Gheith, "Women of the 1830s and 1850s," 90.

progressive drive of the English to focus instead on relations as they exist here and now. In *A Mistake*, the denouement of Olga's failed courtship plot is a scene of rapprochement with her mother, who was upset at her for calling off her engagement. The pair are reunited in a tearful moment of intimacy in which Olga's mother "forgot about the advantageous marriage, she saw only her daughter, her own first child," who was painfully suffering (215). The consanguineal family takes primacy over conjugal, as their love is reaffirmed in the present, with no future aims accomplished.

This present-oriented values system is consistently reinforced throughout *A Mistake*. The narrative hints that Alexander's mother and the false values she instilled in him contribute to his mistake in succumbing to Nadinka. Her teachings emphasized the family lineage, and Alexander was often reminded that:

> the Slavin name was an ancient one, that they all had served from olden times and all obtained high rank; that he was born in order to carry on the name of his ancestors and to give to his children the name and fortune in the same state as he received them: the name irreproachable, and the fortune undiminished, and that in his turn he should achieve honors and ranks, and that whatever happened, he should occupy a prominent place in society side by side with others. (8)

These teachings may seem to contradict my argument about the Russian novel not being concerned with the vertical axis. However, Tur undercuts this teaching by highlighting the *falseness* of Slavin's education:

> But there was no humane feeling developed in him and could not be. Often his mother spoke to him of rank and ambition, but never 'of sincere love for the motherland'; often of God and religion, never of the essence of it ... They often explained to him his bloodline (*rodstvo*) and reminded him about connections and friendship in society, [but] never spoke to him about connections based on sincere feeling, about friendship as selflessness, [or] about friendship as striving with another or with many for the common good, an unselfish benefit for the good of humanity." (16–17)

This passage makes very explicit the opposition between caring about *rodstvo*—which Tur conflates with all kinds of petty and selfish concerns like luxury, rank, and high status in society—and a kind of true, spiritual concern for others in the world. The values on the vertical axis are vilified here, while how one lives *in the here and now* is what matters. In other words, the logic of ancestry is false to the logic of true honor in this novel. Olga is of greater value because of her spiritual worth than a woman with a noble name, fortune, and position in society. These are the same values we saw in Pushkin: Tatiana Larina's worth lies in her pure soul and strong morals, not the status in high society that she ultimately attains.

Natalia Shalikova's *Two Sisters* (1858) rewrote *Eugene Onegin*, providing commentary through elaborating on the fates of Tatiana and Olga Larina.[51] Shalikova's reinterpretation of the characters and their situations highlights the importance of family expanding in the present, rather than the linear drive toward reproductive futurity. Just as in Pushkin's novel, the elder sister, Olga Eladina, is dark and thin, thoughtful and quiet, ill at ease in society, and often dreaming, while the younger, Elena, is blond and gregarious. During a romantic season in Odessa, Olga falls in love with Yuri Dolitsky, whose early idealism was destroyed by falling in love with a woman who broke his heart. She accepts his proposal, but their happiness is short-lived, as the woman from his past re-appears and he abandons Olga, leaving her crushed. Elena, meanwhile, chooses to captivate a rich but boring and unintelligent man whom she marries, and he takes her off to a life of empty luxury.

After her heartbreak, Olga is committed to living an independent life, supporting herself and her dying father through her work as an artist. She creates a family sphere around her without marriage, accepting as her ward the child of an impoverished neighbor who has died, and, after her father's death, living for a time with a doctor and his wife who have befriended her. Ultimately, a worthy suitor, Aleksei Grigorevich Alimov, rescues Olga and her young ward during a rainstorm, and this aid leads Olga to feel justified in coming to care for his mother when she falls ill. This brings her into Alimov's home and family life: "How many pleasant evenings Olga passed with them! How much comfort she found in these friendly, family relations, to which her heart had become unaccustomed" (2:281). The doctor acts as Alimov's advocate to Olga, and she ultimately acknowledges her readiness to accept a proposal from him.

While waiting for Alimov to arrive, Olga is rereading one of Yuri's old letters when he suddenly appears, penitent and begging for the renewal of her love. We are witnessing the final scene between Tatiana and Onegin again, and Yuri's words bring back hints of Pushkin: "You're crying, Olga! my adored Olga! my guardian angel [*angel khranitel'*]! my life!" (2:297). Yet here the heroine is not *yet* wed, so the choice involves no breaking of vows; it is not a moral choice, but a question of what she most values. In making her decision, she is guided by thoughts not only of the two men, but also of broader family ties. After three days of solitude and reflection, Olga rejects the poetic and passionate lover of her youth (in a letter that also addresses Yuri's kindly mother), committing herself instead to the steady, faithful man. This is Tatiana's choice. But Shalikova goes further than Pushkin, justifying that this is also the happier outcome.

Olga and Alimov's success lies in all the familial ties they enjoy in the present. After telling the doctor that she is going to accept Alimov, the first thing Olga does is make sure her ward, Nadia, will be happy: "You love Aleksei Grigorevich very

---

[51] Natalia Shalikova (1815–1878), a sister-in-law of the publisher Mikhail Katkov (1818–1887), published under the pen name E. Narskaya.

much, right?" to which Nadia affirms that she loves both him and his mother and will be thrilled to live with them (2:313). The match is not just about the lovers, but also about this wider family web. When the doctor brings Alimov to claim his beloved, they immediately call for Nadia. And then they all rush to Alimov's mother. Cousins and friends bring congratulations. "What a pleasant evening was passed in this happy family!" (2:321). Unlike the concerns about family networks that we saw in *Vanity Fair*, where they were purely used for advancement ("It was something for the old man to be able to say, 'My son, sir, of the house of Hulker, Bullock & Co., sir; my daughter's cousin, Lady Mary Mango, sir, daughter of the Right Hon. The Earl of Castlemouldy'"), here there are no economic benefits to be gained from an aging mother and penniless ward. Success in the marriage plot is about creating this kinship web in the present, choosing family—in-laws, wards, extended family, chosen kin—over the narrative of an idealized past of romantic dreams.

While the Russians are more focused on kinship in the present, I do not go so far as to suggest that there is *no* concern for heirs. We see almost the same state of "exaltation" experienced by Mr. Palliser (*Can You Forgive Her?*) and Osborne's father (*Vanity Fair*) at the thought of an heir in the protagonist of Dmitri Begichev's once immensely popular *The Kholmsky Family* (1832). When Pronsky learns that his wife, Sofia, is expecting, "the thought that he would be a father brought him to ecstasy [*privela ego v voskhishchenie*]" (155). When asked if he wants a son or a daughter, "A son, a son!"—cried Pronsky.—It seems to me that I will go out of my mind with joy when I have a son" (156). He sounds quite like an English hero, but his wife is still able to reply with a laugh: "If that's the case, then I will bear you a daughter." This was no laughing matter for Glencora or Lady Mallinger (discussed above), whose husbands can only pass on their estates and titles to a male. Sofia does fall into a faint from the extreme joy at learning that she has borne her husband the wished-for boy, but the subject is treated with none of the seriousness of the English novel.[52]

Escaping the Marriage Plot: Narrative Possibilities

When marriage is often a backward state of patriarchal tyranny, when what has value is spiritual not legal bonds, personal growth, not producing heirs, then marriage ceases to be the desirable option for many Russian heroines, and other narrative possibilities can replace it. Shalikova's *Two Sisters* explores this

---

[52] In one of the secondary couples in *The Kholmsky Family*, the husband shows far less concern for his obnoxious and demanding wife during her second pregnancy because "He already had an *heir* (*naslednik*), thus it followed, that there was hope to collect a million after the death of the Famusovs. So why should he make a bother now?" (162). While the comment places emphasis on the importance of inheritance and heirs, the tone, however, suggests we are not meant to sympathize with this view.

possibility in Part II, as Olga supports herself as an independent artist, but the novel ultimately falls back on marriage. In other novels, the path of the female artist leads to a more lasting state of independence (for example, *The Boarding School Girl* and *Two Worlds*). The heroines who escape the marriage plot and forge their own liberated course challenge conservative models of family and women's roles and offer a liberalizing new vision of the possible paths for an unmarried heroine. In cases with a poor heroine (the "dowerless bride," *bespridannitsa*), they also highlight the commodification of women and their economic exchange, with older relatives marrying them off (or attempting to) for financial gain (including Dostoevsky's *Poor Folk* [1846], Chernyshevsky's *What Is to Be Done?*, and Panaeva's *A Woman's Lot* [1862]).[53]

Much has been written about Varenka in *Anna Karenina*—who either fails to elicit or actively wards off a proposal from Koznyshev—and remains single. Scholars have debated whether this was a valorized escape of traditional women's roles, a broadening of the sphere of possibility for women, or a mark of failure in Tolstoy's matricentric values system.[54] Krestovsky (pseud.) put such a debate directly into *The Boarding School Girl*, allowing the characters themselves to air this clash of ideologies. The novel presents two women: Lolenka, who has chosen a liberated path *away* from family, and Sofya, who has taken the conservative path of marriage and submission. Lolenka is proud at the end of the novel that she has escaped the marriage her parents wanted to push her into and is supporting herself as an artist in St. Petersburg.

Krestovsky, however, closes by directly questioning whether this escape was truly a victory. The final conversation of the novel contrasts Lolenka's fate with that of the hero Veretitsyn's beloved Sofya, who married a landowner she does not love and remained in the provinces caring for him and making peace in his family. Lolenka attacks Sofya's choice:

> But look at it from a present-day point of view, what is it? Slavery, the family!... A more elevated woman is subjected to some nice fellow; she sacrificed herself at the whim of her egotistical mother; she reconciled—that is, reunited again—two bad people so they could cause even more harm together! Somehow, amid the constraints, despite the derision, she passes something humane on to the children ... but is it really humane, is it healthy? She passes on to them the same unfortunate precepts of selflessness that are destroying her! Precepts of submission to

---

[53] On this economic aspect of the "exchange of women," see Lucey, *Love for Sale* (esp. Ch. 4).

[54] To my mind the best analysis of Varenka's avoidance of marriage is in Amy Mandelker's *Framing Anna Karenina*. Mandelker analyzes the botanical symbolism of the mushroom hunt to argue for Varenka's active agency in preventing Koznyshev's proposal (*Framing* Anna Karenina, Ch. 6). This interpretation is challenged by scholars like Rosalind Marsh ("An Image of Their Own?: Feminism, Revisionism and Russian Culture," 37, fn. 76).

tyranny! ... She's guilty, your Sofya. She serves evil, teaches evil. She's training victims! (3:847/133)

By contrast, Veretitsyn defends Sofya and the traditional, sacrificial role she has chosen in the patriarchal family: "She set out against vulgarity, egotism, the half educated, insults, cruelty; she set out the way martyrs have gone to profess their faith and meet their death! This is the fulfillment of responsibility which imposes a consciousness of truth and thirst for goodness! There's no higher deed in our age" (3:849–850/136).

Krestovsky herself does not take a side in this debate, but even if we are to side with Veretitsyn it may give Sofya the kind of "terrible perfection" Heldt identifies in her feminist reading of Russian literature, but it offers little hope for the Russian family. Being a dutiful wife is still a form of martyrdom. Sofya is reproducing the highly flawed status quo. Gheith provides a list of the unhappy marriages in Krestovsky (pseud.)'s work, including eight novels (that often had more than one unhappy marriage each). She concludes that "to make a broad generalization, the female characters in Krestovsky's work must choose between an unhappy marriage and an unhappy singlehood, but, as in Tur's fiction, when they are single, they more often maintain a sense of self and of moral integrity. This sense of moral integrity is partly based on resisting the dominant or expected plot."[55] It is also a way of pushing back against a family system in need of reform.

Dostoevsky's *The Idiot* may be his most *semeinyi roman* (family/ial novel), but it too toys with the idea of female emancipation. In the middle of the novel, Aglaya's ambiguous marriage plot with Myshkin takes a twist toward becoming a plot of female liberation as she turns the standard courtship tropes on their head. Writing Myshkin a note and calling him to a secret tryst, Aglaya then proposes "friendship" to him. She explains that she has rejected another suitor "because I don't want them to keep trying to marry me off!" and then announces: "I want ... I want ... well, I want to run away from home, and I've chosen you to help me" (8:356/500–501). What began with the trappings of an amorous tête-à-tête has suddenly veered off the courtship tracks. Parroting the ideas of the liberated woman, Aglaya explains to Myshkin:

I don't want to go traipsing around their ballrooms, I want to be of some use. I've wanted to go away for a long time now. I've been corked up with them for twenty years, and all that time they've been trying to marry me off ... all this last year I've been preparing myself and studying and have read an enormous number of books ... I've told my mother and father long ago that I want to change my social position entirely. I've decided to train to be a teacher, and I'm relying on

---

[55] Gheith, *Finding the Middle Ground*, 166.

you because you said you love children. Can we both train to be teachers together, if not now, then in the future? (8:356–358/501)

While Aglaya's statements are comical in their illogic and naïveté (Dostoevsky's classic device of having a character misquote the views of a group he is attacking), and we know her parents had chosen the tactic of specifically *not* trying to marry her off, the challenge to the wedlock tradition underlying her words is real. Aglaya is dreaming of independence, not of matrimonial bliss. This "a-traditional" wish unites her with a broad cohort of Russian heroines.

There are also a group of English novels in which the heroines do not wed, but in most cases this is not because she does not *desire* marriage. For example, in Geraldine Jewsbury's *Constance Herbert* (1855), the eponymous heroine is convinced to reject a suitor and never marry because of the hereditary insanity that runs in her family and the horrors of passing this on. After taking her to see her lunatic mother for the first time, Constance's aunt lays it to her: "I appeal to you whether you will transmit this terrible heritage, or whether you will endure your own lot alone, to prevent another being made as wretched as you are at this moment?" (2:130). The sacrifice of giving up her suitor nearly kills Constance, but ultimately her purpose comes in a very "Russian" form: she inherits an estate, and, as an heiress, she takes over the management of it. Indeed, a gentry farmer who aids her "thought Constance one of the most enviable women in the world, to be able to manage her estate for herself, and have all her own way as though she were a man" (3:296). She adopts her goddaughter as an heir, and little Constance spends part of every year with her, so she creates family for herself, a common pattern for the Russian novel that will be explored in Part III. With her estate and her chosen family, Constance ends up filling a role much more typical for Russian women; but in the English context, it takes extreme obstacles to the traditional wedlock path to get her there.

The value system in Yonge's *The Daisy Chain*—a novel admired by Tolstoy— also resembles what I am arguing we find in many Russian novels, with emphasis on kinship in the present rather than the future of the line. And here, too, the heroine makes the moral choice not to wed. Ethel May has the opportunity to marry her beloved cousin, but she flees this tempting prospect in order to stay with her father. She was "dazzled" by "the misty brilliant future of mutual joy" a marriage would bring her, "But there was another side: her father oppressed and lonely, [her oldest sister] Margaret ill and pining, Mary, neither companion nor authority, the children running wild; and she, who had mentally vowed never to forsake her father, far away, enjoying her own happiness" (369–370). Just like Ivan Karamazov—who rejects founding human happiness on the suffering of an innocent—Ethel cannot build her personal joy at the expense of her first family, where she is still needed. She puts consanguineal before conjugal.

At the end of the novel, when her closest brother, Norman, has married and left her, Ethel still reaffirms the selfless choice she has made: "Her dear father might, indeed, claim her full-hearted devotion, but, to him, she was only one of many. Norman was no longer solely hers; and she had begun to understand that the unmarried woman must not seek undivided return of affection, and must not set her love with exclusive eagerness on aught below, but must be ready to cease in turn to be first with any" (563). The pious, Christian Ethel has sensed something higher than the call of family love. In her reflections on the closing page, she rejects the idea of marriage in favor of serving the needy: "My course and aim are straight on, and He will direct my path" (564). In both these examples, where the heroine gives up on conjugal aspirations and prioritizes family in the present, her life comes to resemble that of Russia's unmarried heroines.

Rethinking the Theory

While courtship is a central plot for both the English and Russian nineteenth-century novel, it serves a different function in each tradition. The Russians turned courtship into a progressive plot, and progress meant *not* creating marriages that would continue the existing order. If in England the purpose of the marriage plot was to create a legal heir—reinforcing continuity across time—in Russia it was to liberate the woman, focusing on her spiritual well-being in the present. In practice, this meant that she often ended up unwed, but still morally superior to her potential suitor. Marriage, in the Russian novel, never achieved the valence it enjoyed in England, but this opened up narrative possibilities both for courtship and for the married state itself, as Chapter 6 will explore.

Russia's literary tradition of failed courtships and non-unions challenges received wisdom about the family novel and its conservative aims discussed in the previous chapter. In light of what we find in Russia, we can see that Philip Thody's argument that "to write about the family rather than the individual is, implicitly, to plead for continuity and tradition as against radicalism and innovation," is based on the assumption that there is a positive tradition to continue (the English case).[56] Other scholars have noted the ways novels could push against this family tradition, especially in their treatment of adultery. In his famous study, Tanner points to this challenge: "Very often the novel writes of contracts but dreams of transgressions, and in reading it, the dream tends to emerge more powerfully."[57] Even Tanner's claim, however, is based on the idea of the contracts as a positive and breaking with "the authority of the Father" as a sinful transgression. But in Russian

---

[56] Thody, "The Influence of Genre on Ideology: The Case of the Family Novel," 68. See also Thody, "The Politics of the Family Novel: Is Conservatism Inevitable?"

[57] Tanner, *Adultery and the Novel*, 368.

novels this break with continuity and tradition was not an illicit transgression, but a positive moral action. Virtuous heroines remained single to avoid degradation, oppression, or tyranny. As the next chapter will explore, many devoted themselves to serving others in need.

What the Russian tradition reveals is that our theories of *the novel* are based on a normative model of the family that is not universal. If Tanner is right that "the novel had a conservative drive, serving to support what were felt to be the best morals and manners and values of the period," it does not necessarily follow, as he assumes, that it would support the traditional family.[58] In Russia, "the best morals" were pushing for progress, for breaking the mold of patriarchal tyranny. When we modify our assumptions by recognizing that the traditional family could be seen as a negative force, a source of immoral action, when we recognize that marriage was not presumed to be the happy outcome of Russian courtship plots, we must also modify our standard theories. Rather than calling the family novel conservative, a more accurate statement would be that the family novel, as a genre, pushes for thriving families, and this is only a conservative drive when there is a family ideal worth conserving. When the family itself needs reform in order to thrive, we find the genre taking on a more liberal or even radical stance as novels push for meaningful change.

---

[58] Tanner, *Adultery and the Novel*, 369.

6

Marriage and Its Discontents

"There is no happiness in love, except at the end of an English novel."
—Anthony Trollope, *Barchester Towers*

Happiness is found not only in the pleasures of love, but also in the higher harmony of the spirit.
—Fyodor Dostoevsky, "Pushkin Speech"

Despite scholars' insistence that "marriage is *the* central subject for the bourgeois novel," unless they are about adultery, most novels stop short before describing married life.[1] The plot of "being married" lacks a built-in narrative structure; there is no climax toward which it is driving.[2] The previous chapter explored the standard courtship plot that leads its English hero and heroine to the altar (or fails to in Russia), treating marriage as an end goal. The plot arc this creates is based on the assumption that the difficulties and narrative interest lie on the path to the church, and then once the vows are taken, the couple will live happily, with little of interest to be said about them.[3] Many theories of the novel, from Ian Watt onward, treat wedlock as a form of resolution that provides narrative closure.[4]

This conception of novel plotting was so firmly engrained in the nineteenth century that Tolstoy actually used it in the 1860s to explain why *War and Peace* (1865–1869) was *not* a novel. He claimed novels confine characters within given limits, "a marriage or a death after which the interest in the narration would cease," while for him, "a marriage seemed more like a source of complication than diminution of the reader's interest" (13:55). George Eliot voiced a similar view in *Middlemarch* (1871–1872):

Marriage, which has been the bourne of so many narratives, is still a great beginning, as it was to Adam and Eve, who kept their honeymoon in Eden, but had

---

[1] Tanner, *Adultery and the Novel*, 15. See also Heilbrun, "Marriage and Contemporary Fiction," 310. A crucial exception that describes married life is Part II of Richardson's *Pamela*, yet scholarly attention tends to focus on Part I.

[2] See Boone, *Tradition Counter Tradition*, 113–114.

[3] See Gorsky, *Femininity to Feminism*, 18.

[4] Tamara S. Wagner's study of sidestepping conventional marriage plots in Yonge and Oliphant ironically comes to a similar conclusion, as all the novels she analyzes in depth ultimately conclude with marriages ("Marriage Plots and 'Matters of More Importance': Sensationalising Self-Sacrifice in Victorian Domestic Fiction").

The Family Novel in Russia and England, 1800–1880. Anna A. Berman, Oxford University Press.
© Anna A. Berman (2022). DOI: 10.1093/oso/9780192866622.003.0007

their first little one among the thorns and thistles of the wilderness. It is still the beginning of the home epic—the gradual conquest or irremediable loss of that complete union which makes the advancing years a climax, and age the harvest of sweet memories in common. (832)

While Eliot might seem to be contradicting Tolstoy's point that marriage must conclude a novel, ironically (but not by chance), this passage comes right at the end of *Middlemarch* in the section duly titled "Finale." Despite Eliot's words, it does not feel like a premature ending to exclude the tale of advancing years for Dorothea and Ladislaw.

The many novels that *do* explore the "home epic" feature couples far less well suited for each other than the Ladislaws (Dorothea's first unhappy marriage to Casaubon is a prime example). For marriage to have a plot, it must be imperfect; there is no story to unvaried spousal harmony and contentment. D. A. Miller explains this in terms of the "narratable" versus the "nonnarratable": "What defines a nonnarratable element is its incapacity to generate a story."[5] This is Tolstoy's "all happy families" that are alike, or the "perfect union" of Emma and Mr. Knightley. For "each unhappy family [that] is unhappy in its own way," there is generative potential for plot; unhappy family—and by extension unhappy marriage—is "narratable."

While many scholars write of failed marriage as emerging with modernism, some have drawn attention to the darker, more plottable side of marriage that appears in the Victorian novel.[6] Joseph Allen Boone's *Tradition Counter Tradition* (1987) argues that alongside the novelistic marriage tradition in England (and America) we find "a simultaneous counter-narrative: the persistent 'undoing' of the dominant tradition by the contradictions concealed within the specific forms that its representations of 'life' and 'love' have assumed."[7] In other words, there is a tradition of challenging the tradition. Despite this early acknowledgement, and a wave of studies beginning in the 1990s that problematized literary depictions of the Victorian family ideal, it took almost thirty years before Kelly Hager attempted to give failed-marriage a place in novel theory.[8] She argues that it was critics following Watt's lead (even those who challenged his work while still subscribing to its courtship bias), not the novels themselves, who created the pressure to see marriage as the ultimate source of closure.[9] For Hager, the novels themselves

[5] Miller, *Narrative and Its Discontents*, 5.

[6] Hager notes that scholars are willing "to admit the existence of the failed-marriage plot from Hardy on" (*Dickens and the Rise of Divorce*, 22).

[7] Boone, *Tradition Counter Tradition*, 2.

[8] Many of these studies have focused on Dickens, e.g. Sadrin, *Parentage and Inheritance in the Novels of Charles Dickens* (1994); Schor, *Dickens and the Daughter of the House* (1999); Waters, *Dickens and the Politics of the Family* (1997).

[9] In Hager's words, "even when critics do notice the conservative basis of our theory of the novel, they attribute the conservatism to the novels they are reading rather than to our theoretical conclusions about them" (*Dickens and the Rise of Divorce*, 21). See also Mintz, *The Prime of Life*, "Chapter 4. I Don't:

tell a different story, focused as often on the "unraveling" of a marriage as on the "plotting" of a courtship.[10] While this is undoubtedly true, adding Russia into the picture puts the English failed-marriage plot in perspective. Relatively speaking, the English tradition as a whole still comes out looking happy, thereby helping to explain the theories (as they apply to the English novel).

Critics who ascribe to Watt's theory and the ideal of stable marriage may be eliding some of the complexity—the tensions within the novels and struggles against the reigning domestic ideal—but they are true to the spirit of how these English novels are structured and the values that claim to win out in their conclusions. As Hager herself acknowledges, "the domestic novel does often encourage us to believe that marriage ensures a happily-ever-after, even as it portrays the failure of marriage in its subplots, for instance, or even as it suggests—while plotting a successful courtship—how naïve we are to succumb to such wish fulfillment."[11] Here Hager puts failed marriage side-by-side with successful courtship, reminding us that they usually come together. I argue that in the Russian novel we often find a reversal of this structure. Many Russian characters fail to make it to the altar at all (failed courtship), while those who *do* marry can have more success in navigating the difficulties of wedlock because they have more realistic expectations for what it will offer.

How marriages go wrong, and how novels plot them, are specific to each national tradition. This chapter takes up the function marriage serves in the English and Russian novel and the plots it generates. In both nations, marriage only becomes "narratable" when problematic. Its plot is shaped by historical factors around the legal and social conditions of marriage, literary factors around genre expectations, as well as the interaction of these two. The English, with their powerful domestic ideal of marriage as a perfect union (Chapter 4), could not accept imperfection; any failed marriage was a threat to the institution itself and had to be somehow sidelined or removed by the novel's end. In Russia, where marriage was generally understood to be a broken institution, there was room for novels to both diagnose the problems with conjugal life and to attempt repair. In other words, English idealism called for an all-or-nothing approach to marital success (often putting the two extremes beside each other in the same novel), while Russian realism accommodated a grey zone of compromise.

Marriage also served different ends in the two traditions. For the English, wedlock was necessary for the vertical, as the foundation for producing legal heirs (and so, for instance, Dombey must have a wife to produce "and Son"). The Russians were less concerned about legal sanction and more focused more on the state of relations between the couple and their lived experience in the present (not what

---

Alternatives to Marriage." Mintz is mostly concerned with America, but makes some helpful comments about England and the English novel.

[10] Hager, *Dickens and the Rise of Divorce*, 5.

[11] Hager, *Dickens and the Rise of Divorce*, 21.

it could lead to). The final sections of this chapter will isolate the legal institution, or "form" of marriage, and separate it from "content," the emotional, physical, or spiritual relationship the couple shares. For the family's progression through time, form is essential (it legitimates heirs), while in the present what matters is the state of connection. The Russian emphasis on the here and now rather than the vertical had the consequence of devaluing the legal institution of marriage and elevating the spiritual bond regardless of official sanction.

English Idealism *Despite...*

There is a paradox in the English novelistic depiction of the family: the novels are full of unhappy or dysfunctional marriages, yet *despite* all the abuses, we come away with an impression of marital bliss and domestic felicity. Mismatched temperaments, tyrannical husbands, bigamy—there are many forms the challenge to the marital ideal can take, but despite the frequency with which they occur, authors present these as individual failures; they do not ask readers to reject the institution of marriage or the patriarchal family.[12] We still come away with an impression of the Victorian novel idealizing the family sphere.

This paradox is encapsulated in the legacy of Charles Dickens. Since his own day, Dickens has been famous for his depictions of family love.[13] As Margaret Oliphant exclaimed in an 1855 review, "nowhere does the household hearth burn brighter—nowhere is the family love so warm—the natural bonds so strong [as in the middle class]; and this is the ground which Mr Dickens occupies *par excellence*—the field of his triumphs, from which he may defy all his rivals without fear."[14] Such praises abounded in the writings of his contemporaries— in both England and Russia—and in criticism up to the present day. And yet, as Catherine Waters reminds us, "Dickens's reputation as a purveyor of cosy domestic bliss would seem to be at odds with the relatively small number of happy and harmonious families depicted in his fiction."[15]

English novels did not hold back on revealing the potential horrors of wedlock. Dickens lays them in the open when describing Paul and Edith Dombey's

---

[12] Even in novels with unhappy outcomes, Boone claims the "narrative patterns" of the fictional marriage tradition "almost uniformly uphold the *concept* of romantic wedlock as their symbolic center and ideal end" (*Tradition Counter Tradition*, 9). Building on Richard Kiely, he argues that "within the logic of the novelistic tradition of marriage ... even when the outcome is tragic a bad union is 'never to be blamed on the institution itself'" (115). Quoting Kiely, *Beyond Egotism: The Fiction of James Joyce, Virginia Woolf, and D.H. Lawrence*, 86.

[13] This is why Hager's focus on the dysfunctional marriages in his works is so provocative and persuasive in reshaping our understanding of the Victorian tradition.

[14] Oliphant, "Charles Dickens" *Blackwood's Magazine* 77 (1855), 451–466, qtd. in Waters, *Dickens and the Politics of the Family*, 15

[15] Waters, *Dickens and the Politics of the Family*, 15.

marriage (*Dombey and Son*, 1846–1848): "Ill-assorted couple, unhappy in them-selves and in each other, bound together by no tie but the manacle that joined their fettered hands, and straining that so harshly, in their shrinking asunder, that it wore and chafed to the bone, Time, consoler of affliction and softener of anger, could do nothing to help them" (699). Mr. Dombey seeks every way of humili-ating Edith and crushing her pride, while she admits that "I despise him hardly less than I despise myself for being his!" (678). Grandcourt's total subjugation of Gwendolen, reducing her to "miseries" in *Daniel Deronda* (1876), is another case in point: "Already, in seven short weeks, which seemed half her life, her husband had gained a mastery which she could no more resist than she could have resisted the benumbing effect from the touch of a torpedo" (363). Grandcourt destroys her spirit to the point that when he falls overboard in a sailing accident and she is standing on board holding the rope, she later recalls "I held my hand, and my heart said, 'Die!'" (596). In *The Tenant of Wildfell Hall* (1848), Helen Huntingdon wishes to escape her abusive husband, but he steals her private journal, discovers her plans, and confiscates the little money she had saved up through selling her possessions and paintings. It is only when he begins teaching their innocent child to drink and curse that she takes to desperate flight.

These examples might seem like the ultimate condemnation of Victorian mar-riage, laying bare the subjugation of wives and the power imbalance on which the system was built (as discussed in Chapter 4). But if we contextualize these failed marriage plots within the novels as a whole, there is always a "despite." Dickens, Eliot, and Anne Brontë all hold back from trying to topple the institution of mar-riage. Each novel is carefully structured so that *despite* the darkness they show, they still end with a glorification or vindication of wedlock.[16] Alongside Gwendolen, we have Daniel Deronda who enters a model marriage with Mirah. Dombey and Edith's failure is supplanted not only by Florence and Walter's idyllic union, but by a crowd of three more happy marriages (and the comic overpowering of Bunsby by Mrs. MacStinger, proving that a woman can have the upper hand in wedlock). Brontë's Helen has the chance to re-marry the tender and loving Gilbert. In English novels, the individual failures may reveal problems with the system but do not indict it wholesale. This fact could partly explain why the horrors are painted in such extreme colors: the worse the marriage, the further *outside* the norm it is in the English context. In Russia, by contrast, horrors often *are* the expected norm, and readers would recognize them as part of Russian reality (vivid descriptions of court cases involving family abuse were all over the press).

Much of the scholarship on the nineteenth-century English family novel in recent decades has been devoted to challenging the supremacy of marriage and

---

[16] I agree with Marlene Springer, who notes that "The ramifications of and deviations from the cul-tural ideal are a major concern of Dickens, George Eliot, Thackeray, Meredith, and Hardy," but then argues that their forays into depicting the darker side of marriage and family life were another way of reaffirming the ideal ("Angels and Other Women in Victorian Literature," 136–137).

the traditional, heteronormative family as well as the earlier theories that tout its centrality. Scholars have sought to uncover or reveal the social and political critiques encoded in authors' treatments of marriage and the domestic sphere, to read in "a fashion which is alert to the silences and the gaps" in order to find "another novel buried beneath the surface of the fiction we are accustomed to reading."[17] Beyond the insights they produce, what interests me in these studies, some of which I will engage with here, is the amount of work they require: both on the part of the critic (who must find the message the author could not explicitly state) and of the author (who—assuming these interpretations are correct—must struggle to affirm an ideal, even while revealing the traces of dissent that the critic has admirably discovered).

Kelly Hager's astute reading of *David Copperfield* (1850) as a novel of divorce exemplifies this new wave of scholarship that chips away at the supremacy of marriage. It is an ideal sample because the reading is so clear and persuasive, and, at the same time, the very power of Hager's argument hinges on showing the ways Dickens attempted to smooth over or elide his own critique. Claiming *David Copperfield* is a novel of divorce is an "estranging" reading to be sure, as divorce was not made legal until *after* the time when the novel is set. Yet Hager looks at the pattern of marital separations and second marriages, either enacted or fantasied about: Dora "effects her own divorce and paves the way for her husband's marriage to Agnes";[18] Mrs. Micawber repeats over and over that she will "never desert Mr. Micawber" though no one ever suggested she would, and re-reads her marriage vows by candlelight to confirm that she has no right to do so and is trapped; "married Miss Trotwood" *does* leave her unnamed husband, yet insists that she is still in love with him. Parsing this last example, Hager notes that "Although Dickens thus presents us with a woman who does leave her husband, he nevertheless insists that that woman remains in love with the husband she leaves ... Thus, the significance of the Miss Betsey plot is buried beneath the narrative convention of the loyal wife."[19] In other words, Dickens brings her back into a traditional script of dutiful wife, allowing her to fill this role when her husband passes away and is buried. "While he presents us with a novel in which all wives seem to want to leave their husbands," Hager argues, "he insists upon the existence of love in all these failed marriages."[20] Hager lays bare the gulf between what Dickens is explicitly telling us and what he is implicitly showing us. Russian novelists will be far more direct in their critiques.

The Betsey Trotwood pattern of love and reunion is repeated in other abusive marriages; Emily Trevelyan (*He Knew He Was Right*, 1869) and Helen Huntingdon (*Tenant of Wildfell Hall*) will both return to and nurse their husbands on

---

[17] Hager, "Estranging *David Copperfield*: Reading the Novel of Divorce," 1015.
[18] Hager, *Dickens and the Rise of Divorce*, 140.
[19] Hager, *Dickens and the Rise of Divorce*, 144.
[20] Hager, *Dickens and the Rise of Divorce*, 147.

their deathbeds, re-entering the conservative marriage script once their abuser is enfeebled and needs them (Jane Eyre, too, follows a similar model). By contrast, in Marko Vovchok's *Three Sisters* (1861), Olga escapes her abusive husband after he is incapacitated by a stroke and she allows him to die alone, despite everyone's entreaties that she return. No myth of the loving wife is maintained in the Russophone example.[21] The English authors, however, attempt to hide the very flaws they are revealing through an ultimate vindication of the marriage ideal.

Dickens strives to make readers believe in the ideal even as his novel problematizes it. Michal Peled Ginsburg's earlier reading of *Dombey and Son* makes a similar argument to Hager's, showing Dickens' attempt to depict the ideal domestic sphere and to make it seem natural through erasing all the labor and care that are required for its maintenance in reality. Yet, as she persuasively argues, to accomplish this, Dickens must transform home "from a physical space to an idealized affective state," such that "the idyll of family love that marks the end of the novel cannot take place in a real house where time and care are always present."[22] It takes great labor on Dickens' part to maintain the ideal in the face of what his novel is simultaneously revealing: that domestic harmony is *not* natural and effortless. Even as "estranging" readings like this point us to the implicit critique lying beneath the surface of novels that end with glorifications of marriage, at the same time they show how hard English authors were working to maintain the very myth they were simultaneously unveiling.

This tension of concealing and revealing the critique is built into the structure of the novels and the way they integrate their multiple plots. Failed marriages and successful courtships typically appear together, with the failed-marriage plot as a corollary that buffers our faith in the romantic prospects of the new couple. This is why studies of dysfunctional marriage have failed to dislodge the ideal. Take, for example, Christopher Herbert's study of the "Male Tyrant" figure (Betrothed, Brother, or—most often—Husband). Herbert uses Trollope's *He Knew He Was Right* to analyze the way Victorian ideals of marriage "attempted to fuse two antithetical ideals ... into a single ideological structure": the principle of male supremacy and that of the companionate marriage.[23] While this incompatibility leads to disastrous results for Emily and Louis Trevelyan, the multiplot structure of Trollope's novel embeds their relationship amongst many other romantic pairings that culminate in (seemingly) happy companionate marriage, and thus reinforce the norm. In addition to Emily's struggles, we follow the fate of her younger sister,

---

[21] Marko Vovchok was the pen name of Maria Alexandrovna Vilinskaya (1833–1907), a Ukrainian writer of Russian descent. She wrote *Three Sisters* in Russian and published it in a Russian journal, and therefore I include her in this study with the Russians.

[22] Ginsburg, "House and Home," 71.

[23] Herbert, "*He Knew He Was Right*, Mrs. Lynn Linton, and the Duplicities of Victorian Marriage," 451. Kathy Psomiades is thinking along similar lines when she claims that *He Knew He Was Right* uses the "language of tyranny and consent" to "characterize the narrative of marital cruelty, making clear its role as an analogue for larger questions of legitimate rule" ("The Marriage Plot in Theory," 55).

Nora, who successfully weds her beloved Hugh Stanbury, while Nora's friend, Caroline Spalding, marries the wealthy suitor Nora rejected, and Hugh's sister Dorothy marries the man for whom Hugh was disinherited by his aunt. Taken all together, the novel's many plots glorify marriage and reinforce its traditional role as plot-closer (since these are successful marriages, they mark a cessation of narrative interest). The narrator even apologizes near the end of the novel for the speed with which the reader must move between weddings, adding "In this little history there are, we fear, three or four more to come" (826). This sounds like the ending of *Dombey and Son* with its chapter titled "Chiefly Matrimonial"; in each case, the sheer quantity of happy marriages helps to balance out the one catastrophic failure. In other words, authors do not negate the marital ideal as a *dominant norm* or *guiding ideology* for the English novel, but instead seek ways to shore it up *despite* problems or threats.

The institution is also reaffirmed by the way in which English novels resolve their failed marriages. Rather than allowing the central characters to remain in a state of domestic distress, authors tend to remove the painful marriage, usually through the death of a spouse. The plot trajectory for Emily and Louis Trevelyan epitomizes the standard model. All starts happily, but once the seeds of discord have been sewn (Louis' false belief in Emily's infidelity), rupture becomes increasingly hard to mitigate. Emily flees with her child and seeks protection from an uncle. Trevelyan kidnaps the child and takes him to Italy. His mind becomes increasingly deranged, and he ultimately falls ill, reigniting Emily's love and compassion: "She was his wife, and nothing should entirely separate her from him, now that he so sorely wanted her aid" (814). There is no chance of returning to their happier past, and Trevelyan ultimately dies (having admitted his wife's innocence), with Emily by his side as comforter. The failed marriage is resolved through literally being removed. We find the same pattern in *The Tenant of Wildfell Hall*, only with Trevelyan's mania replaced by alcoholism and debauchery. Helen takes her child and flees her abusive husband, Mr. Huntingdon, but then, when he is dying, she returns to nurse him. He, like Louis Trevelyan, ultimately dies, ending this failed marriage. The abusive Mr. Grandcourt who tyrannizes over Gwendolen in *Daniel Deronda* comes to the same end, though without a final rapprochement.

Other types of marital failure are likewise resolved through the death of the erring partner. Mrs. Henry Wood resolves the adultery plot of *East Lynne* (1860–1861) in this manner, with Isabel's death and ultimate forgiveness by her former husband. Amelia's ill-conceived marriage to George Osborne (*Vanity Fair*, 1848), David Copperfield's marriage to Dora, Laura Farlie's marriage to the odious Percival Glyde (*The Woman in White*, 1859–1860), and Cecil's to Raymond (*Three Brides*, 1876) are all resolved by the death of the spouse, freeing the heroes to make a successful match. From sensation novel to domestic fiction, in authors as diverse as Wilkie Collins, Dickens, Thackeray, and Charlotte Yonge, we find the same pattern. In plot terms, the deaths of the spouses serve a similar function to the death of the elder brothers discussed in Chapter 3: removing these characters allows the English to maintain their ideal without accommodating any deviations from it. Fraternal tension that would threaten family harmony is removed by removing a brother; the solution to a failed marriage that would threaten the domestic ideal is to remove the marriage by getting rid of one of its members. The relationship itself cannot be salvaged, for to attempt finding some compromised state of coexistence would be to compromise the whole marital ideal. Instead, the failure is simply supplanted in what Hager calls a "second-chance plot," where an unhappy marriage is replaced by a more felicitous one (Amelia's marriage to Dobbin, David's to Agnes, Laura's to Walter, etc.).[24] Or if the hero or heroine does not remarry, as is the case for Emily Trevelyan or Gwendolen Grandcourt, the novel juxtaposes the failure that ended with a host of positive beginnings. Thus while these novels demonstrate that any individual marriage is not a guarantor of closure, when we look at their structures as a whole they still rely on a marital union to close their pages.

A slew of Victorian novels went beyond "second chance" marriages to explore the threat of having multiple contemporaneous spouses, another category of "despite" that challenged the marriage ideal. Maia McAleavy's study of the ubiquitous "bigamy plot" reveals a Victorian fascination with this trope that destabilizes the linearity of plot and the idea of marriage and death as finalities. In bigamy novels, supposedly dead spouses frequently reappear, while marriages turn out not to be valid or not to be the end point of a drama, but rather the beginning of a forking path. Bigamy is destabilizing on two levels: to social structure, where marriage represents stability, and to narrative structure, where the wedding should be the "inescapable ending."[25] While plot is often treated as a progression, for characters caught in a bigamous triangle, their past returns, disrupting linearity. In novels like *Jane Eyre* (1847) or *East Lynne* two (almost) wives can occupy the same dwelling, threatening the idea of the house as "the most important metonym of marital happiness and monogamous seclusion."[26] McAleavy argues that the bigamy plot thus forces us to think of plot not as the drive toward a resolution, as Peter Brooks argues, but "plot as a pattern rather than a line."[27] Bigamy challenges ideas about both space and time.

Even if the bigamy novel destabilizes death and marriage as secure endings, like the other forms of failed marriage discussed above, it tends toward a restitution of order on its closing pages. For example, in Mary Elizabeth Braddon's *Aurora Floyd* (1863), after sensational pages of bigamy, assault, and murder, the novel leaves

---

[24] Hager, *Dickens and the Rise of Divorce*, 14.
[25] McAleavy, *The Bigamy Plot*, 8.
[26] McAleavy, *The Bigamy Plot*, 47
[27] McAleavy, *The Bigamy Plot*, 25.

Aurora—her first husband *truly* in the grave and all suspicions of her guilt in land-
ing him there removed—lovingly united with her second husband and "bending
over the cradle of her first-born" (459). Superfluous spouses have a way of dying
off (for real) and even the most sensational of bigamy novels often close with a
monogamous couple and legitimate offspring. Viewed in that light, the Victorians'
repetition compulsion—returning to bigamy and other forms of marital failure literally hundreds of times in the literature of mid-century—could actually be seen
as a way of reaffirming again and again *in the face of threat* the stable order at each
novel's close.

English novels are not trying to offer up a radical alternative or overthrow the
institution of marriage, something we will see in the Russian novel. Even Eliot—
who challenged the marital ideal—ultimately offered few positive alternatives for
her female characters.[28] One exception to this might appear to be the contented
spinster, but even she tends to find a place in a family based on the conjugal
model. For example, Marian in Collins' *The Woman in White* does maintain an
active sphere, but her energies are directed toward arranging her sister's (two) marriage plots. She remains united with Laura in a single family unit that is ultimately
resolved by Laura's marriage to the worthy Walter, with whom the two settle. So
Marian's singledom is in no way an attack on the primacy of wedlock.[29] Spinsters
helping their sisters marry is also a common occurrence in Yonge's novels, again
highlighting the surprising degree of similarity between family plots in sensation
and domestic novels.

Russian Realism: Accepting Marriage's Discontents

While the "failed-marriage plot" English scholars write of is literally the failure
of the marriage, in the classic Russian novel the hero and heroine rarely get to
this plot because their failure comes earlier: they never even manage to wed (see
Chapter 5). Barbara Heldt observes that "Gogol', Turgenev, Goncharov, Tolstoy,
Dostoevsky, and Chekhov all describe marriages that don't happen, often against
the background of bad or ordinary ones that do."[30] Before this section explores
those "bad or ordinary ones," I want to highlight their positioning in the text and
how they fit into the overall form of the novel.

The Russian novel reverses the narrative structure of the English novel. In the
double-plot formulation described by Hager above, the heroine on the path to
a glorious marriage that promises a happily-ever-after ending is typically in the
foreground, while somewhere behind her or off to the side is a marriage that has

---

[28] See Frank, *Law, Literature, and the Transmission of Culture*, 126.
[29] I consider the possible erotic component to the sisters' relationship in Chapter 2, p. 54.
[30] Heldt, *Terrible Perfection*, 21. She notes that Rozanov has made a similar point.

gone awry.[31] Or there is a chronological progression; the unhappy/unsuccessful version is dealt with early in the novel and is superseded by the idealized conclusion. In the Russian novel, as we saw in the previous chapter, failed courtship is at the center of the plot while authors withheld narrative attention from the happy pairings that hovered in the background (Alexandra Pavlovna and Lezhnev in *Rudin* [1856], or Arkady and Katya in *Fathers and Children*), or an ultimate union was tacked on at the end and left undescribed, so readers do not know whether or not it is successful.

The English novel required the ideal of marriage to be maintained if the edifice were not to crumble, but the Russian novel had a more realist view of marriage as an imperfect state. The story Russian novels tell about marriage is one of accepting imperfection and working toward liberalization. If the English "counter tradition" is an attack on marriage (Boone), in Russia—where the "tradition" is composed of heart-broken but superior heroines—the "counter tradition" might be said to be an attack not on marriage, but on the romantic *ideal* of marriage, the version Russian heroines would have read about in novels. Gary Saul Morson calls the alternative to the "ideology of transcendence and desire" characterizing the romantic love tradition "prosaics."[32] While many Russian maidens would hold their dreams of a "perfect union," from the time of Pushkin's *Eugene Onegin* (1825–1832)—which founded the tradition of the Russian family novel—Tatiana's mother initiates a powerful counter-narrative of marriage as prosaic acceptance of reality. Raised under the influence of European literature, "She loved the fictions and the fancies / Of Richardson and of Rousseau."[33] In *Onegin*, Pushkin highlights the fact that the whole idea of romantic love is a western import that took hold particularly among gentry girls (Tatiana's peasant nanny claims not to have heard of love when she married). Tatiana's mother, smitten with a dashing cadet whom the narrator refers to as her "Grandison," is forced instead to marry Tatiana's father.

Yet rather than treating this loveless marriage as a disaster, Pushkin shows that imperfect marriage can still create prosaic contentment:

> The clever husband chose correctly
> To take his grieving bride directly
> To his estate, where first she cried
> (With God knows whom on every side),
> Then tossed about and seemed demented;
> And almost even left her spouse;

---

[31] Noting that Gaskell's *Ruth* is a major exception, Boone makes a similar point about seduction being a subplot in Victorian novels (e.g. Em'ly's in *David Copperfield* and Hetty's in *Adam Bede*). "Its secondary status as such could thus 'safely' be used to enhance the exemplary status and appeal of the wedlock ideal touted in the narrative's major development" (*Tradition Counter Tradition*, 113).

[32] Morson, *Prosaics and Other Provocations*, 25.

[33] «Она влюблялася в обманы / И Ричардсона и Руссо» (Ch. 2, stanza 29, translation by James Falen).

But then she took to keeping house
And settled down and grew contented.
Thus heaven's gift to us is this:
That habit takes the place of bliss.[34]

Along with idealistic and passionate heroines like Tatiana, we find a counter-current of these adapters to the conditions of Russian life and love. They have a clear-eyed view of marriage with all its imperfections. The English analogue would be Charlotte Lucas, but *Pride and Prejudice* (1813) portrays her marriage in a comic and critical light, while the Russian novel applauds its adapters to prosaic reality.

This counter-tradition would be picked up on by Nikolai Pomialovsky in *Molotov* (1861), where Anna Andreevna reflects on the need to love her husband:

Her love was mandatory, dictated by law, consecrated by the church, and there-fore, inescapable. It was not permitted for her to hate her husband, otherwise she would perish. In other layers of society a wife could say to her husband: "I do not wish to live with you," and drive off to an apartment where she could be free, but here it was impossible even to think about that ... Run away?. where to? And the damnation pronounced by her mother, who would have no mercy on her? And the hatred of her relatives? And poverty? And the children?—would she have to desert them? And the passionate desire to live as people do? And, finally, the strength of marital obligations? Everything had come together in Anna Andreevna's life so that she was obliged to love her husband, and she had managed to love his soul, appearance, and social status. For this, she had sought out good sides of her husband, had invented them and forcefully deluded herself, which was possible only thanks to her cold and sedate character. It goes without saying that Dorogova's mandatory love could not be passionate and novelesque. (74)

This is a totally realist outlook on the legal and economic ties binding women in marriage. Knowledge of Russia's laws and customs helps characters like Anna Andreevna avoid the despair or poor choices that come from unrealistic expecta-tions. Had she sought a life with Mr. Darcy at Pemberley, she would have been sorely disappointed by her husband, who quickly fell out of love with her after their marriage and took to carousing. But instead, she finds the best way to keep him in line and to maintain a level of tranquility in their home, contenting herself with this minimum level of peace.

---

[34] «Разумный муж уехал вскоре / В свою деревню, где она, / Бог знает кем окружена, / Рвалась и плакала сначала, / С супругом чуть не развелась; / Потом хозяйством занялась, / Привыкла и довольна стала / Привычка свыше нам дана: / Замена счастию она.» (Ch. 2, stanza 31, translation by Falen).

English characters who subscribe to the ideology of marriage as a "perfect union" can be led to pursue the wrong aims and then struggle to make peace with their lot. For example, Dorothea's misguided marriage to Casaubon in *Middlemarch* is based on an idealized notion of the wife's role as helpmate to an older, wiser husband. In part, her failure comes from expecting marriage to be the happily-ever-after of the classic novel. While English mothers like Mrs. Allarby (*The Way of All Flesh*, 1873–1884), who "never looked at a young man without an eye to his being a future son-in-law," seem mostly concerned with getting daughters to the altar, trusting in the glories of matrimony, Russian mothers often worry about what is in store after the wedding bells have ceased to sound (29). Sofia Khvoshchinskaya's *City Folk and Country Folk* (1863) describes such a mother's anxieties: "It is such a simple matter, yet at the same time so complex that loving mothers from the beginning of time have been turning it over in their heads in almost the same way, crying the same vague tears. How could she part with her? But she can't be an old maid … What kind of fellow would he turn out to be? They all seemed fine before the wedding—and so on, and so forth" (191). Russian characters' lower expectations reveal underlying reservations about the institution itself. In Vovchok's *Three Sisters*, even though Olga Voronova is marrying for love, she spends the night before her wedding in tears. "How can I not grieve and be afraid, Varya? Everything is new and unknown … Who knows what awaits me up ahead—happiness or grief?" she laments to her sister (within months, the marriage indeed turns from happiness to grief).[35] In Russian folk culture, wedding songs are amongst the saddest, and the assumption is that the bride is going to a life of suffering in her husband's family.[36] So this vision of marriage has deep traditional roots.

Adultery and Fixing a Broken Marriage: The Russians' Breach with Realism

Though Russian characters tend to fail at the courtship stage, when relations begin to founder in a marriage they prove more flexible and resilient in their ways of understanding the situation. This applies particularly to adultery. *Anna Karenina* (1875–1878)—far and away Russia's most famous adultery novel—is actually quite an outlier in the Russian tradition. The novel opens with a classic set-up of marriage and triangular love: a wife begins contented with her husband, but then falls in love with someone else who seems more suitable. The standard Russian pattern—which occurs in *Who Is to Blame?* (1845–1846), *Polinka Saks* (1847), *The Underwater Stone* (1860), *In Hope of Something Better* (1860), *What Is to Be*

[35] Vovchok, "Zhili da byli tri sestry" *Sovremennik* 90 (1861), 282.
[36] See Pushkareva, *Women in Russian History*, 95.

Done? (1863), *The Adolescent* (1875), and *Twice Married* (1875)—is for the husband to accept and forgive his adulterous wife. Karenin, however, first tries to close his eyes to the situation, then once it is thrust upon him he contemplates a divorce (Tolstoy accurately portrays all the legal difficulties). These intentions are upended when he is called to Anna's bedside as she is presumed to be dying after childbirth and he experiences a moment of genuine Christian forgiveness. But when Anna survives, she again feels trapped and ultimately leaves Karenin to become Vronsky's mistress and Karenin returns to his antagonistic stance, keeping their son and attempting to block out all memory of the mother. This behavior puts him in the distinct minority. Dolly, who remains with her philandering husband Stiva, trying not to see his infidelity and profligacy, and who works to accept a far from perfect situation, is closer to the Russian norm.

While infidelity (or even ungrounded fears of it) can bring out the worst in English husbands—Valentine murders his wife in *Like and Unlike* (1887), Mr. Carlyle mercilessly divorces Isabel in *East Lynne*, and Trevelyan goes mad and kidnaps his son in *He Knew He Was Right*—in Russian novels it usually brings out their highest nature. Instead of weak, superfluous men, we suddenly find larger than life heroes with super-human self-control. The ur-text for this heroic plotline in the Russian tradition was Alexander Druzhinin's immensely popular *Polinka Saks*, modeled on George Sand's *Jacques* (1833). Like *Jacques*, Druzhinin's novel features a wise and self-reflective hero, Saks, who has fallen in love with and married a much younger woman whom he idealizes for her youth and innocence. When Polinka falls in love with a younger man, Saks attempts to win his wife's happiness by enacting a divorce without her knowledge (asking her to sign some unspecified documents) so that she can remarry, something that would have been completely illegal under Russian law.[37] In narrative terms, removing the marriage enables a less extreme solution to the love triangle than the one found by Sand's Jacques, who commits suicide, framing it as an accident. Leaving two men in the narrative, Druzhinin allows Saks to remain a protective guardian to the weak Polinka, discretely following her and her new husband for a year to make sure that she is indeed happy.[38] Yet he does not discover her secret realization: that she truly loved Saks himself all along.[39]

---

[37] A divorce in this period was extremely difficult to attain in Russia. From 1836–1860, in the whole Russian empire there were an average of 58 divorces per year and almost 90% of them were for Siberian exile or desertion. Adultery accounted for only three per year on average, or 6%. To obtain a divorce for adultery, there needed to be eyewitnesses and the guilty party would face a punishment and then not be allowed to remarry. See Freeze, "Bringing Order to the Russian Family," 733.

[38] In English novels, such an exchange of the woman between men is often treated as a capitalist transaction. Here it is enacted unilaterally by Saks, who treats his wife as an ignorant and innocent child for whom he must make decisions. But ironically, it also shows his respect for Polinka as an independent being, rather than his property that must be guarded from "theft."

[39] She writes this to him in a letter to be delivered upon her death, and the novel closes a year later, on the evening when the letter is delivered.

Saks' saintly selflessness as he arranges to give his adored wife to her lover defies all verisimilitude, but he became a model for future Russian heroes facing the threat of adultery. Saks himself claims in his anguish that philosophy will not help him because he is a real man and not the hero of a novel, yet numerous novels copied his super-human example. Chernyshevsky's *What Is to Be Done?* involves a mismatch of temperament rather than of age, but it is resolved by a similar freeing of the wife, this time through a faked suicide (again demonstrating remarkable selflessness). Herzen's *Who Is to Blame?* was not ready to contemplate such a radical gesture, so, rather than finding resolution, the three caught in the love triangle waste away, destroyed yet not blaming each other. In Krestovsky (pseud.)'s *In Hope of Something Better*—which Dostoevsky highly regarded—Aleksinsky forgives his adored wife when she confesses her affair ("God will forgive you," 746) and then commits suicide.[40] Like Saks, all these husbands avoid blaming their wives for falling in love with another man.

These may be the most famous examples, but this plot also occurs in Mikhail Avdeev's *Underwater Stone*, where Natasha marries her older husband, Sergei Sokovlin, for love half-way through the novel, but after six years of happy marriage and the birth of a son falls for a man her own age.[41] Her husband helps make the arrangements for her to go to her lover, and when she returns, after realizing it was just a passing passion, he takes her back and the family is reunited, though with the acknowledgement that the simple happiness of former days is gone.[42] The closing lines register the characters' acceptance of their new, compromised reality. Sokovlin says to the tearful and guilt-stricken Natasha:

—Everything conventional can be forgiven and forgotten, but feeling does not forgive and forget ... What then! he said, raising his head and looking boldly at his wife:—the storm is past; why lose heart over the debris? We comported ourselves honestly, and we have nothing about which to reproach each other. Let's bear to the end, without retreating, all that life has left to us. And can it really be that fate and time have no more happy and peaceful moments for us!...

He reached out his hands to Natasha with subdued emotion and trust, and she, looking at her husband's honest and open face, fell upon his breast with a blush of shame...

And sobbing, they faced the first minutes of their happiness, [now] poisoned—poisoned by the burning pain of their shame and recollections. (79)

The couple awaits "bright and quiet moments," not a life of unending bliss.

---

[40] For Dostoevsky's comments on the novel, see 27:149.

[41] Pisemsky opened his review of the novel by citing its debt to *Polinka Saks* and *Who Is to Blame?* (9:547).

[42] One of the original critics specifically attacked this plotline for its lack of verisimilitude. See the unsigned review in *Sovremennik* 1860, №10 and 11.

Tolstoy wrote a novel with almost the same ending the previous year. Masha in *Family Happiness* (1859) only gets as far as contemplating an affair and leaving her older husband, but she and her husband move through a similar progression from love, to a state of division, to rapprochement and a new kind of "family happiness." Tolstoy's novel concludes: "From that day my romance with my husband ended; the old feeling became a precious, irretrievable memory, and a new feeling of love for my children and the father of my children laid the foundations of another, but already completely different happy life that I am still living at the present minute..." (5:143). The romance is gone, her husband's kiss is now that of "an old friend" but Masha has accepted this more prosaic reality and, consequently, she finds it happy (or claims she does). In all the novels I have just discussed, characters attempt to accept the realities of changeable feelings and to make the best of a difficult situation in the present. Many of these novels lead to relatively happy conclusions. And they present Russian men in a more favorable light than the courtship plots; in accepting their wives they demonstrate strength and self-denial, rather than the weakness of the superfluous man.

Liberal versus Conservative Marriage Scripts

While I have been arguing that it is the Russians, not the English, who wrote novels about marriages being salvaged or redeemed, there is one category of English novels that fits this mold: those with a strong Christian message. In moralizing novels, like those by Yonge, characters can be reformed and chastened. In *Heartsease, Or Brother's Wife* (1854), Arthur takes his wife Violet for granted and neglects her. "It had been grace missed and neglected, rather than willfully abused," as the narrator explains, and, in the moralizing spirit of Yonge, this grace can be restored (447). After being duped by a scoundrel, losing all his money, and falling gravely ill, Arthur truly repents and comes to appreciate his angelic wife. When his son recites to him that "there is joy among the Holy Angels in Heaven when one sinner grieves and comes back," the two agree that "the Angels must have faces like mamma" (448). This marriage ends up stronger than it began. In Yonge's *Three Brides*, Rosamond is at first too headstrong and fun-loving for a curate's wife, but she ultimately learns to defer to her husband Julius and they end with marital harmony. Harriet Martineau's *Deerbrook* (1839) is more sophisticated in its treatment of troubled marriage, with a series of misunderstandings leading Mr. Hope to marry Hester Ibbotson, while he was really in love with her sister Margaret. When the family is seriously tried, Hester learns to curb her jealousy and difficult moods and to selflessly support her husband, and, seeing her rise to the challenges, he in turn learns to truly love her. All these novels are designed to teach model behavior, so the straying and shortcomings of the characters contribute to their didactic mission. They all end with a glorification of the patriarchal norm.

While for the English happy marriage tended to be conservative (as in these moralizing, Christian models), for the Russians it was decidedly progressive. Happy outcomes for Russia's marriage plots come when the characters—both men and women—seek a liberalization of the family model that will enable peace to be maintained or restored. Fyodor Stulli's 1875 novella *Twice Married* typifies this pattern. Though it follows the more typically English model of an unhappy marriage superseded by a happy one, its narrative arc charts what I will argue is the classic Russian pattern: pushing against the traditional Russian family model to create a more progressive alternative.

The novel begins with a traditional, patriarchal model. Before Maria Ignatevna's marriage to the much older Nikolai Petrovich Voskresensky, her future husband spouts ideology to her, explaining that "The purpose of marriage is the creation of a family, and the honest upbringing of children is possible only when the husband and wife are united not only by external concerns but when they have the same goals, hopes and even convictions" (676). Clearly, these shared convictions—in his view—must be his own, which his wife should adopt. He is incapable of even conceiving of Maria as an individual who might have her own views. Voskresensky expounds on women's responsibilities, but never thinks of their rights. "It never entered his head that his wife could have views and convictions aside from his views and convictions; loyalties and connections not coinciding with his connections and loyalties (only a difference in degree was permitted); concerns, not arising more or less from his own person" (704). His views on gender roles are entirely traditional, as he explains: "the role of the man is active and creative, while the role of the woman is protective; the sphere of the man is society and the outside world, with all its tempests and troubles, while the sphere of the woman is the close circle of acquaintances, but most important are the family, home and hearth" (706).

Needless to say, with such a husband Maria is not happy in her married life. She is bored in the provincial town where they live, and their baby daughter dies, leaving her no maternal outlet for her energies. She reads novels and imagines herself as the heroine of *Onegin, On the Eve* (1860), *Noble Nest* (1859), *Vanity Fair*, and as Edith in *Dombey and Son* (683). None of her choices, it should be noted, culminate with lovers happily married (aside from Amelia and Dobbin). Maria, like Edith Dombey, comes to understand her married life as a state of slavery, but for her the confinement applies to her thoughts as well as her person:

> The trouble is powerlessness. The trouble is that I do not belong to myself, that I am not only unfree in my actions, not only a thing which, by an arbitrary decision, can be torn away from everything and taken off to distant lands,—yet I am free in my words, but not free in my thoughts. Like a dog, accustomed to its collar, like a slave who feels uncomfortable without the pillory [*bez kolodki*], even I myself

am ready to consider a thought, one that wanders unbidden into my head, to be a crime ... (723).

Recognizing her entrapment, however, Maria will break free of this stifling mold.

Following the same path as another heroine of an 1875 novel (Anna Karenina), Maria uses adultery as an escape from her stultifying life, having an affair with a man she meets at a train station. The affair leaves her with child. And here enters a new progressive script. Maria's husband agrees to acknowledge the child as his own, meaning it will not suffer the lack of rights that comes with illegitimacy. His condition is that upon his death the biological father must marry Maria. This is quite similar to yet another 1875 novel that I will discuss in the next chapter: Dostoevsky's *The Adolescent*, where Arkady's legal father, Makar Dolgoruky, asks his wife's lover and the biological father of her children to marry her upon his death (something Versilov promises to do, but does not follow through on). Such concerns were clearly in the air. In *Twice Married* it is Maria herself who insists on a delay to the wedding, using the time to educate herself through reading. She chooses to become somewhat emancipated and to learn to have her own opinions before binding herself to another man.

The novel, however, closes with a return to the traditional family: Maria marries her lover, he becomes a more upstanding person through entering this new family life, they have a second child, and family harmony reigns at the close. Stulli's resolution is both trite and paradoxical in its reliance on normative family structures while simultaneously trying to suggest that it is based on reform. Yet technically it is still a blended family, as Maria's first child is legally heir to her first husband. *Twice Married* illustrates the need for a rejection of the backward, traditional norm that Voskresensky begins with, and a loosening of conservative ideology to arrive at a new, more egalitarian model of family. In their various ways, most novels about courtship and marriage in Russia can be understood as participating in this form of critique, rather than reinforcing the status quo—though few will end as happily.

This liberalizing tendency offers a link to the English tradition in the failed-marriage plot, which Hager sees as a loosening of social restrictions. Despite the fact that women who leave their husbands, like Louisa Bounderby in *Hard Times* (1854), often end up back with a father-figure in another patriarchal structure, at least now it is one of their own choosing. Plotting the failure of wedlock, then, becomes a feminist plot, "a plot that concerns itself primarily with the matter of female agency: it tends to revolve around a wife leaving her husband, an act that was both illegal and unacceptable."[43] The censure for the English wife, however, is much greater than for the Russian one, whose husband often accepts her choice.

---

[43] Hager, *Dickens and the Rise of Divorce*, 8.

Evaluating Marriage's Component Parts: Form versus Content

Thus far, this chapter has primarily been concerned with English idealism versus Russian realism in approaching marriage. The remaining pages turn to another crucial opposition. Marriage can be thought of as two components: form and content, or what Evelyn J. Hinz calls the "social and legal institution" and the "conjugal relationship."[44] Most discussions of marriage in the novel assume that the form—the legal status of official wedlock—should be accompanied by a particular kind of content: relations between the couple characterized by some combination of emotional and physical intimacy, respect, and/or obedience. Our theories only address one special case in which form and content are not united: adultery. With adultery, the legal union and the intimate relations are actively split onto two different people. Yet even outside of this unique exception, the form and content of marriage can easily be separated. The legal status and the emotional connection fill different functions, and recognizing and isolating these can help explain how and why English and Russian novels about marriage differ. The content of marriage—the type of connection the couple shares—is always present oriented; it has no goal beyond their current state of being, but the legal form has implications for the family's past and future.

Anna Karenina clearly demonstrates the ways form and content can be split and what it means to emphasize one versus the other. While Karenin focuses on form, asking only "that the outward conventions of propriety be observed" when Anna first tells him of the affair (18:224/213), Anna is fixated on content, believing that once she has made her confession "all is over" with Karenin (18:225), as if they were not still legally bound. In her affair with Vronsky, she does *not* want to be his wife, but rather his mistress because she wants the intensity of passion in the here and now and feels that to be a wife would mean obligation (a formal structure), which is not really love.[45] As she thinks, "For me, everything is in him alone, and I demand that he give his entire self to me more and more ... If I could be anything else but a mistress who passionately loves only his caresses—but I cannot and do not want to be anything else" (19:343/763). Even Vronsky wishes for formal structures. As I discuss in Chapter 7, he sets up his estate on the English model, and, fashioning himself as the hero of an English novel, he worries about having heirs. Anna, meanwhile, takes to squinting, literally blinding herself to questions of structure and form.[46]

In the English novel, the formal institution of matrimony serves the vertical aims of the marriage plot. Legal wedlock is necessary for the production of legitimate

[44] Hinz, "Hierogamy versus Wedlock," 900.

[45] Similarly, in *The Adolescent* Liza initially refuses an offer of marriage from Prince Sokolsky, whose child she is carrying, because she wants a relationship based on love, not obligation.

[46] Dolly notices this new habit in Anna when she visits her on Vronsky's estate. "As if she narrows her eyes at her life in order not to see it all" (19:204/628).

heirs and for the transmission of name and property: it is future oriented. Mr. Sownds, the Beadle in *Dombey and Son*, alludes to this as he expounds the need for weddings: "We must marry 'em. We must have our national schools to walk at the head of, and we must have our standing armies. We must marry 'em, Ma'am ... and keep the country going" (868). Marriage, by this logic, is necessary for procreation, and England needs its next generation. The Beadle performs a patriotic act in performing marriages. Mr. Dombey is also thinking about having children when the Beadle performs his second marriage. The narrator reflects that "his dead boy was now superseded by new ties," which presumably means he expects the union will produce a new heir (547).

In the Russian novel, the legal union holds surprisingly little value in its own right. While illegitimate children had no rights under the law, Russian novels showed remarkably little concern about this. As earlier chapters have shown, the Russians were far less worried about family futurity, so in novels marriage did not carry the same weight for legitimizing future heirs. At the same time, however, marriage was often a practical necessity in the present because it was one of the only means of freeing a woman from her parental home. In such escape-oriented marriages, the goal was liberation in the here and now, not reproductive futurity.

English novelists tended to reinforce the idea that form and content would naturally come together, and clashes occur when the couple does not share the same vision of what content is required. Edith's disastrous marriage to Paul Dombey fails on exactly this point: she has only agreed to participate in the legal union and its formal trappings (accepting his name, home, and social status), while expecting the "content" of their relations to remain empty because both parties understand there is no love. He, however, expects the content of obedience and reverence for his wealth (and also to be provided with a new heir). Some scholars have approached this mismatch through the division of public versus private. As Ginsburg puts it, "Dombey sees the role of his wife in doing the honors of his house as representing him (and his other house, Dombey and Son) to the outside world rather than creating an intimate private space."[47] This limits the critique of wedlock to their individual union, as the lack of a private sphere in the family is described as unnatural, not representative of the norm.[48] Walter's loving union with Florence—while potentially the more unusual (we see few other examples of such perfection)—is treated as a more organic marriage, where natural inclinations and legal wedlock mutually reinforce each other. This is what novel readers *expect* English marriage to do.

In Russian novels it was much more typical to treat legal marriage and loving romantic unions as radically separate; given a choice, the Russians valued content over the formal structure. For example, in Druzhinin's *Polinka Saks*, Saks's

[47] Ginsburg, "House and Home," 60.
[48] The term "dysfunctional domesticity" comes from Ginsburg, "House and Home," 58.

hazily defined divorce that ignored/contradicted legal realities undermines the underlying legal structures of Russian society, as well as the Church, which treated marriage as a binding sacrament. Yet in the end it matters little to whom Polinka is actually married, because the novel values not her legal ties, but her deepest emotions, which turn out to lie with Saks all along. This values system—placing the type of connection shared above the legal status of the union—is clearly apparent in Aleeva's *Two Worlds* (1875) as well. Early in the novel, the wealthy Alexander Lopatin seduces a beautiful young seamstress, Masha. The couple shares a period of love, and then Alexander abandons Masha with his illegitimate child. Years later, after Alexander has wed a woman of his own station, he compares his life with Masha to that with his new young wife: "In Masha, without wedlock, he had *a wife*, in other words, a faithful friend and devoted woman. With his own wife, Verochka, he had only a foolish little child" (444, emphasis in original). Alexander's reflection reveals a view of the world in which the type of connection is what matters, not its legal status. Alexander shows no concern for family futurity, not even remembering the child who would have been his heir had he and Masha wed.

In many Russian novels we see a similar devaluing of the institution of marriage in its own right. One way this manifests is in heroines' indifference to becoming a "fallen woman." In the Russian novel, purity is an inner state, not dictated by the presence of a matrimonial bond. Dostoevsky reinforces these values in his interpretation of the ending of *Eugene Onegin*. Faced with the choice between Onegin—whom she never ceased to love—and her unloved husband, Tatiana decides *not* to follow her heart ("But I am now another's wife, / And I'll be faithful all my life"). Dostoevsky makes this a *Russian* choice ("She says this specifically as a Russian woman") and rejects the possibility that her motivations could have anything to do with the institution of marriage: "Oh, I shall not say a word about her religious convictions, about her view of the sacrament of marriage" (26:141/2:1287). He suggests that such thoughts would have been cowardice, while "the Russian woman is bold [...and] will boldly follow one in whom she believes" (26:141/2:1287). Such logic completely divorces moral purity from honoring legal wedlock. Instead, Dostoevsky argues that Tatiana cannot build her happiness on the suffering of her innocent husband who loves her (essentially giving her the same morality as Ivan Karamazov in his rebellion). She is moral *in her treatment of another human being*, not in her respect for the institution of marriage.

We see the Russian woman boldly ready to "follow one in whom she believes" and to disregard wedlock in Turgenev's *Rudin*. The young Natalia is inspired by Rudin's passionate speeches when he is a guest at her mother's estate, and she falls in love with him. When her mother discovers their attachment and forbids it, Natalia calls Rudin to a secret meeting, ready to follow him to the ends of the earth, even though under Russian law she would have been unable to marry him without her mother's permission. She shows not even a hint of concern about losing her honor; in the Russian novel, it would be untainted by steadfast devotion to a beloved outside of wedlock. It is Rudin's cowardice (telling her they must "submit to fate") that prevents their union. Following Dostoevsky's logic, Natalia's willingness to be a fallen woman actually contributes to her heroic strength and purity.[49] As Joe Andrew has observed, once Karamzin's Poor Liza "is 'a fallen woman,' she is nonetheless described as 'an angel.'"[50] There is little moral judgment on her "fall," instead it is tragic because it leads to the cooling of Erast's passion and her ultimate abandonment. By contrast, even when England's most innocent and virtuous maiden is seduced there may be pity, but the act of extra-marital sex is harshly condemned. For example, in Gaskell's *Ruth* (1853), readerly sympathy is staunchly behind the betrayed and defenseless heroine, but her fall is treated by both narrator and characters as a grave sin. Ruth herself is convinced that she "deserved suffering" for what she has done (104).[51] I would argue that the Russians were less conflicted about distinguishing between true moral or spiritual purity and the act of extra-marital sex than the English.

Dostoevsky was not such an outlier in his depiction of the pure prostitute in Sonya Marmeladova (*Crime and Punishment*, 1866). And the scene when Raskolnikov seats Sonya next to his sister has echoes of Russian cultural norms from the early nineteenth century. As we learn from the writings of Martha Wilmot (and English woman who visited Russian in the early nineteenth century), she was shocked to see the French mistress of General Kissiloff attending a respectable gathering at his house, and socializing in an intimate manner with his daughter and other unmarried girls. Interpreting Wilmot's response, Judith Vowles notes the English woman's shock that "these women fail to uphold the crucial distinctions separating the innocent from the fallen, the virtuous from the corrupt. Their modesty is not affronted, nor their virtue sullied."[52] This was unthinkable in England. As a worldly aunt explains to the marriageable heroine in Edgeworth's *Belinda* (1801), "Ladies of the best families, with rank and fortune, and beauty and fashion, and every thing in their favour, cannot (as yet in this country) dispense with the strictest observance of the rules of virtue and decorum" (182). Such rules of "virtue and decorum" can clearly collapse in the Russian context. We see this in the real-life case of Elizaveta Rubanovskaya (1757–1797). Not allowed to marry the widowed Alexander Radishchev because she was his sister-in-law, Rubanovskaya nonetheless chose to follow him when he was exiled to Siberia. They lived together there for six years, during which time she bore three children. Far from being

---

[49] George Sand's writings on women's rights to follow their heart no doubt were an important influence.

[50] Joe Andrew, *Women in Russian Literature, 1780–1863*, 25. Similarly, in Vsevolod Krestovsky's *Petersburg Slums* (1864–1866) the unmarried Princess Anna Chechevinskaya bears an illegitimate child in the opening chapters, but is still regarded by the narrator as a virtuous character.

[51] Boone points to *Ruth* as an exception in the English tradition, where seduction usually appears in "admonitory subplots" (like Em'ly's story in *David Copperfield*, or Hetty's in *Adam Bede*) (*Tradition Counter Tradition*, 113).

[52] Vowles, "Marriage à la russe," 63.

denigrated as a "fallen woman," Rubanovskaya was hailed for her goodness: "A skilled pen might compose a whole book about her virtues, her suffering and her constancy of spirit," according to a former schoolmate.[53] The Russian value system places inner goodness and purity above its genteel, legalistic, or institutionalized trappings.

Another indication of the devaluing of legal marriage in the Russian novel is that it can be almost irrelevant to plot. In fact, authors wrote the same plotlines for both married and unmarried characters. The previous chapter explored the common trope of a marriageable hero and heroine failing to unite in matrimony. But Russian authors wrote this same plot for characters who already were married and, therefore, where there was no possibility of a new legal union.[54] We see this clearly in Krestovsky (pseud.)'s magnum opus, *Ursa Major* (written 1865–1871, but set in the 1850s). The hero, Andrei Verkhovskoi, is a poor tutor who is coerced early in the novel into marriage to the rich Lidia Matveevna, whom he does not love and to whom he never proposed. He hopes that through the marriage he will have enough money to finally be reunited with his beloved mother who lives far away. His wife does not allow this, and thus begins a miserable marriage. While visiting Enns to buy an estate, Verkhovskoi encounters the novel's heroine, the young, idealistic, and morally pure and strong Katerina. The weak but well-meaning Verkhovskoi— who is busy trying to free peasants on the estate he is buying before his wife arrives—falls in love with Katerina. Katerina and Verkhovskoi ultimately declare their love to each other.

Of course their love is not consummated and there is no trajectory toward any end goal.[55] This cannot be a marriage plot, as Verkhovskoi *is already married*. Yet in its essence, Katerina and Verkhovskoi's romance looks just like the weak man/morally superior woman plot of *A Mistake* that was discussed in the previous chapter—the marriage to the wrong woman has just been put at the beginning, rather than the end. This, however, does not change the plot; the obstacle to Katerina and Verkhovskoi's union does not prove to be Lidia Matveevna, but Verkhovskoi's own weakness.

In the pair's final meeting, Katerina tells Verkhovskoi that she is going to live in a village, while he tries to convince her to come to Petersburg with him. She adamantly refuses, saying she loved the citizen and honest man in him, *not* saying

---

[53] Qtd. in Engel, *Women in Russia, 1700–2000*, 39. Engel's source: "Introduction," *Russia Through Women's Eyes*, 14–15; Quote from David Marshall Lang, *The First Russian Radical. Alexander Radishchev, 1749–1802*, 211.

[54] Making a similar point about Turgenev, Armstrong argues "The question of legal and non-legal unions is less interesting to Turgenev than the basic desire to avoid the whole issue of marriage as a personal confrontation between two people. [For example,] the existence of Fedya's wife in *A Nest of Gentry* [i.e. *Noble Nest*] is really only a necessary device to allow Fedya to avoid marriage with Lisa" (*The Novel of Adultery*, 93).

[55] Katerina compares her love of Verkhovskoi to his mother's love: "But his mother loved him in a different way. Not less, of course, but more happily—that was the difference. His mother could always be with him and could show her love in action" (486).

that he is married. She has become disillusioned by his failure to accomplish any-thing and explains that she does not want to go to Petersburg with him *to watch him do nothing*. Her refusal has nothing to do with whether they could marry or if she would become his mistress; she seems rather indifferent to this point (5:724). This is exactly what we saw in *Rudin*. Like Natalia, who is horrified to discover Rudin's weakness when he tells her to "submit to fate," Katerina is disillusioned by Verkhovskoi's floundering. The marital status of the characters is not what shapes the plot in either of these novels. This point is affirmed by the ending of *Ursa Major*. After Katerina rejects Verkhovskoi's offer to come hide in Petersburg and goes off to a village, the end of the novel jumps ahead three years. Verkhovskoi is now with a new but equally vapid young wife, which means there was a point when his wife died and he was single and *could* have proposed to Katerina. So clearly his initial marriage was not the obstacle to their union.

Marriage as an Escape: Form as Practical Necessity

There is a paradox in the Russian novel's relationship to marriage. While on the one hand marriage seems to have little value for its own sake, on the other hand the legal institution is often necessary as an escape from the deprivations of poverty or from the parental home.[56] For bare survival there were few options for women to support themselves in this period. A writer in *Women's Herald* (1867) complained that while in America women could work in various fields, in Russia the range was quite limited: "Not everyone can be translators and sales clerks, and the doors to other places are closed tight, with a sign that reads: 'women not allowed.' And thus, on the basis of these reasons, life goes along unhappily everywhere; a woman often hurries to forget herself in marriage with a person she does not love, and her life becomes even less bearable."[57] Exemplifying this point, Katerina Ivanovna in *Crime and Punishment* is trapped in her unequal marriage to the drunkard Marmeladov because as a young widow she had no other way to provide for her children. Marmeladov then drinks them to utter destitution.

The idea of marriage as an escape from a miserable home life was openly discussed in the periodical press at mid-century. In a piece entitled "My neigh-borhood. First sketch. The Garin family," F. Matveev described a young girl tyrannized by an older sister who was the father's favorite. She sees marriage as a way out: "It must be said that the vexations from her sister alone were enough to make her wish earnestly for a speedy departure from home."[58] This is a trope

---

[56] Catriona Kelly writes of the importance of escape—either through marriage or from marriage (*A History of Russian Women's Writing 1820–1992*, 63).

[57] *Zhenskii vestnik* №8 (1867), 49–54 (here 50).

[58] Here's how the narrator describes the situation: "In this way, Sonichka drank for her entire life the bitter cup her sister had given her. She drank it in silence, finding no protection even from her mother;

in novels as well, though usually it is the parents or guardian and not a sibling causing the suffering. In Evgenia Tur's *The Niece* (1851), the orphaned heroine, Masha, is miserable in the home of her tyrannical aunt. In a moment of anger, her aunt shouts at her "When will I get rid of you? If only you would marry!" to which Masha replies "I will marry the first who asks, without fail" (1:68). This is her only way out, as she is reminded in a later conversation, after her aunt discovers she has made a visit without permission: "You still haven't married, you still live in my house, you still eat my bread," her aunt exclaims, reasserting her authority (1:117). After living with this aunt and then a second repressive aunt, Masha expects freedom when she ultimately marries, but wedlock turns out to be little improvement.

Rather than chasing passionate romantic love, characters in the Russian novel are more often using marriage as either an escape from poverty or from an unhappy home. This occurs in Herzen's *Who Is to Blame?* and Panaeva's *Talnikov Family* (1848). Tolstoy's Marya Bolkonskaya in *War and Peace* dreams of such an escape from her loving but tyrannical father as she prepares to meet her first suitor, Anatole Kuragin: "She imagined a husband, a man, a strong, dominant and inexplicably attractive being, suddenly carrying her away to his own, completely different and happy world" (9:270). It is only chance (finding him embracing her French companion) that saves her from what would have been a disastrous marriage. In other novels, one marriage can be the only way to escape entering another.[59] In Pomialovsky's *Molotov*, Nadya's father tries to make her to accept a proposal from a wealthy, elderly general, forcing her to reflect on her trapped position: "She had long wanted to live in her own way, to see a different type of life and different faces, to be a self-sufficient woman; but it was evident to her that only a spouse could take her from home, only arm in arm with him could she leave her *terem*: it was necessary to kiss and embrace someone, and only then would she be acknowledged to be an adult with the right to answer for herself" (108). The escape from this unwanted marriage for Nadya comes through another marriage to the hero Molotov.

While Nadya ultimately marries for love—fusing the formal structure of marriage with the intended content of spousal love—another kind of marriage was specifically designed to provide only the legal structure: the "fictitious marriage." These became popular among Russian radicals in the 1860s as a way to help girls

it was these circumstances, reinforced by the thought that Silinsky intended to marry her, a girl with no wealth, education, or dowry, that made Sonichka disregard the information regarding Silinsky that reached her from the neighbors, who were likely envious and might make wrongful accusations out of envy." F. Matveev. "Moe sosedstvo. Ocherk pervyi. Semeistvo Garinykh" *Semeinyi krug* №9 (1859), 48–82 (here 56).

[59] Catriona Kelly observes a shift in this plot across time: "Though views on the appropriate means of escape diverged—later examples of the provincial tale placed an emphasis on liberation from marriage, rather than on liberation through marriage—the 'escape plot' as such, that is, a plot illustrating obstacles overcome, was standard" (*A History of Russian Women's Writing*, 63).

escape their parental home. The marriage would be left unconsummated, with the "brother" (typical code word) giving his "sister" total freedom. So fictitious marriages are an extreme instance of the legal union—the form—being fully divorced from any content. This, of course, offered a tremendous threat to the institution of marriage as a sacrament, challenging the Orthodox belief that the couple becomes "flesh of one flesh."

Novels about fictitious marriage offered a critique of Russian wedlock. The most famous example is in Chernyshevsky's *What Is to Be Done?*, where the enlightened student, Lopukhov, marries Vera Pavlovna (whose brother he tutors) to free her of her oppressive mother and an odious marriage the mother is planning for financial gain. The legal union is necessary as an escape, but is not imbued with the traditional content of spousal relations. And once Vera's escape is successful and the legal bond is no longer needed, its lack of worth is revealed in the fact that Lopukhov fakes his own death to free Vera Pavlova of the legal union they had contracted. This enables her to wed the man she has actually fallen in love with. Rather than resolving this bigamous situation through the death of the first husband, Chernyshevsky allows Lopukhov to remarry as well, again showing how little weight he accorded to the legal or religious institution.

S. Dolgina's *Fictitious Marriage* (published 1876 but set in the 1860s) offers a more sophisticated treatment of her titular theme. One of the "new people" in the novel explains fictitious marriages thus: "It's unlike our weddings of old where two unhappy victims were fettered to each other with indissoluble chains for their whole lives. Here marriage is only an empty formality, and both parties in it stay just as free as they were outside of it" (107). Many people in the novel consider such marriages: for some of the women, it is the only way to come into their inheritance and have access to money and freedom, for others it is a way out of a stifling home. The heroine, Marianna, ultimately enters a fictitious marriage with a very honorable widower, Boris Nerovin, who is trying to save her from a fictitious marriage with an untrustworthy rake. They move to Nerovin's country estate and set up life with separate rooms, but communal dining. Marianna tells Boris "I call you 'brother,' but I don't know if things would be this good for me with a brother!" (203). The irony in this novel is that the "happy couple" who are married in form but not content, then fall in love with each other. Each thinks he or she must hide these feelings from the other because it would break their promises, so the difficulty here is reintegrating the two halves of marriage—the formal structure and the inner relations between the couple. In essence, their "marriage plot" begins *after* they are legally married.[60]

---

[60] Hager mentions this type of plot occurring in Dinah Craik's *Agatha's Husband*, Trollope's Palliser series (between Glencora and Plantagenet Palliser), and in Eden's *The Semi-Attached Couple* (*Dickens and the Rise of Divorce*, 48).

I want to make the rather counter-intuitive suggestion that marriage is *not* the aim of the Russian marriage plot, or rather that while the plot may have the trappings of a courtship or marriage plot, the institution of marriage itself is often superfluous. The parallel plotlines for both married and unmarried characters, the emphasis on content—the state of connection—over legal form, and the unconcern about being a "fallen woman," all point to the fact that marriage itself is not the primary locus of value, as it is the English novel. Recognizing this can also help explain the outcome of Tur's *A Mistake* (1849) (topic of Chapter 5), where Olga releases her beloved from their engagement once she discovers he has fallen out of love with her. Olga is seeking a deep intellectual and soulful connection with Alexander, not just wedlock. Indeed, she still *could* have married him at the end, but she rejects this option because she does not want the form/structure of marriage without the content; she is not seeking future stability and an established place in society, but the merging of two loving hearts. Jehanne Gheith has argued that "The morally upright woman in Tur's universe is typically rewarded not with the happy marriage plot, as is the case in much English (or Anglo-Irish) fiction ... but with the anti-marriage plot; a sense that peace and integrity are better than marriage (and are rare within marriage)."[61] I would go further and say that the same value system holds for *most* Russian authors, not just Tur. If the thing of value for the text is at this inner, spiritual level and the point of love is to find a deep and pure resonance of souls, then marriage itself is not actually the aim.

The Goal of Russian Marriage Plots

Underlying this discussion is the deeper and more vexed question of how the Russian novel defines success—both in familial and in broader existential terms. If we were to take away the genealogical imperative of the English novel, that propulsion toward family continuity and heir, what would the objective of the marriage plot be? The Russian novel explores this alternative value system that a present-oriented marriage plot would entail, staring the question of telos straight in the face. In Goncharov's *Oblomov* (1859), Olga is deeply depressed after attaining her loving husband, estate, and precious heir. "'What is it?' she thought, horrified. 'Is there something else I need and ought to desire? Where am I to go? Nowhere. This is the end of the road ... But is it? Have I completed the circle of life? Is this all—all?' she asked herself, leaving something unsaid—and—looking around anxiously to make sure that no one had overheard this whisper of her soul" (4:456/448). Russian happiness is more than material success and involves an intangible *something* always still to be striven for. At the end of *Anna Karenina*, Levin, too, has attained his equivalent of the "English happiness" in the novel Anna reads on the train, as

---

[61] Gheith, *Finding the Middle Ground*, 147.

he is settled on his family estate of Pokrovskoe with his loving wife and baby son; yet this ending leaves Levin "several times so close to suicide that he hid a rope lest he hang himself with it, and was afraid to go about with a rifle lest he shoot himself" (19:371/789). And these are two of the most "successful" characters by any conventional standard; they have reaped all the rewards an English novel could have offered: marriage for love, estate, and heir. Yet none of this creates fulfillment.

The ultimate, intangible, un-nameable goal of the Russian novel is about spiritual development and the level of connectivity a character experiences, though—as Part III will explore—this connectivity does not need to come through traditional family relations. If what matters is the state of connection the characters share, then marriage must be rethought, as simply going through a ceremony will not achieve that desired state. Thus, the reflective Stoltz wrestles with the meaning of marriage in *Oblomov* as a problem *in the present*, even after achieving the legal union:

> He looked at marriage, at husbands, and in their attitude to their wives he always saw the riddle of the sphinx; there was something in it that was not understood, something that, somehow, remained unspoken; and yet those husbands did not puzzle their heads over complicated problems, but walked through married life with such even and deliberate steps as though they had nothing to solve and discover ... [M]ost men enter into matrimony as they buy an estate and enjoy its substantial amenities: a wife keeps the house in excellent order—she is the housekeeper, the mother, the governess; they look upon love as a practical-minded farmer looks upon the beautiful surroundings of his estate; that is, he gets used to it at once and never notices it again. (4:449/442).

Clear in Stoltz's reflection is the fact that marriage should *not* be simply "enjoy[ing] the substantial amenities" of a wife. There should be a spiritual component to the union.

In addition to the depth of connection shared between the spouses, marriage is also supposed to spur personal growth. We saw this with Maria's self-education in *Twice Married*. Only once she is an independent thinker is she able to form a harmonious family life where she will contribute to the moral and intellectual growth of her spouse and children. Marianna and Boris Nerovin (*Fictitious Marriage*) have this from the start, as it was the whole purpose of their "fictitious" marriage. This emphasis on personal growth appears even more clearly in novels that feature a bride almost immediately widowed, as in Turgenev's *On the Eve* and Aleeva's *Two Worlds*. In both these novels, a young woman is released from a stultifying home life through encountering a passionate intellectual who dies of illness shortly after their marriage. But in each case the marriage can hardly be counted as a failure, as it has left the woman intellectually alive and emancipated from her family of origin. Elena (*On the Eve*) ends up in the Balkans as a Sister of Mercy and Polina (*Two Worlds*) has formed a group of intellectual friends and become a writer. No heirs were produced (Polina's marriage was never even consummated), but this does not read as a mark of failure because the terms of success are independent of the genealogical imperative and include space for personal growth *in the present*.

***

Marriage serves the vertical aims of the English novel. As the structure that legitimates the production of heirs it is the lynchpin in family succession. And as the instantiation of the patriarchal order it reinforces gender roles and the separate spheres around which the English social system was based. All these things are only made possible and desirable by the English idealization of a secure and happy past for the family, one that must be defended and continued. Value is placed on the future that will result from the successful conclusion of the plot. With its closing resolution, its "end that is also a beginning," the English marriage plot serves a conservative function as the family literally recreates itself.[62]

Clearly in the Russian novel, where marriage plots rarely lead to a happy marriage and the birth of an heir (and when they do, Levin, for example, still contemplates suicide), this forward-looking continuity cannot be the central goal. Gogol could even be seen as mocking this genealogical imperative in *Dead Souls* (1842), as the narrator continually reminds us that "Our hero was very much concerned over his descendants," even though Chichikov has no actual progeny or real marriage prospects (5:92/84). As marriage loses its valence, what has true value in the Russian novel is the spiritual growth and state of connectedness that the characters share in the present. Institutional trappings remain only trappings, and it is better for a heroine to remain in a state of moral strength and purity yet single than to have compromised herself through marriage to an unworthy spouse. Almost never could her husband proclaim at the end of a novel: "I need not tell you how happily my [wife] and I have lived and loved together, and how blessed we still are in each other's society, and in the promising young scions that are growing up about us," as Gilbert does at the close of *The Tenant of Wildfell Hall* (488).

Yet Russian novels *can* close with happy family. As Part III will explore, the path to get there lies not through the marriage plot—where family is created vertically through creating an heir—but through intentionally *choosing* to make others kin in the present. The Russians will choose lateral expansion over vertical progression.

---

[62] *Dombey and Son*, for example, begins with two children, Paul and Florence, and ends with two grandchildren, Paul and Florence. Their grandfather considers little Paul "the object of his life" (947).

PART III
ALTERNATIVE KINSHIP

7

Alternative Family Models in Time

For since it is a law of nature, admitting only rare exceptions, that the qualities of the ancestors should be transmitted to the race—the fact seems patent enough, that even allowing equal advantages, a gentleman's son has more chances of growing up a gentleman than the son of a working man.

—Dinah Mulock Craik, *John Halifax, Gentleman*

"It is always so in England," said Lucius after pausing for a while. "Sir Peregrine is a man of family, and a baronet; of course all the world, the world of Hamworth that is, should bow down at his feet."

—Anthony Trollope, *Orley Farm*

Genealogy was her favourite insanity.

—Anthony Trollope, *Barchester Towers*

The Introduction to this book considered the historical complexity and slippery nature of the term "family," which means different things in different cultures, can evolve in meaning across time in a single culture, and can mean different things in different contexts or to different individuals even within a single time and culture. So far I have treated the "traditional" family as that supposedly normative idea of a married couple and their children, so a group bound by blood and legal ties. The 1851 census in England defined it as "the persons under one head," reinforcing a patriarchal arrangement, even though many households did not fit this model.[1] In Russia, there were a variety of ways to define family, not all of them based on blood or affinity, but instead relying on household membership or sharing a common experience.[2] So to label Part III "alternative" kinship is itself problematic, as that assumes the kinship types I will be considering are outside of the "norm," when—as I will argue—it is the idea of the norm itself that needs reconsidering.

This chapter is devoted to non-nuclear family models—extended, blended, or intentional—that have fallen outside the framework of the first two parts of the book. Specifically, I am interested in the conditions that enable and encourage such

---

[1] Chase and Levenson, *The Spectacle of Intimacy*, 4.
[2] See Tovrov, *The Russian Noble Family*, 66–67.

The Family Novel in Russia and England, 1800–1880. Anna A. Berman, Oxford University Press.
© Anna A. Berman (2022). DOI: 10.1093/oso/9780192866622.003.0008

alternative models to take a prominent place in the novel. This causes me to focus on the vertical axis of family progressing through time. The vertical family axis is a conservative force. With its legacy of ancestors and the promise held in its progeny, vertical family is built on continuity from past to future. It pushes for restrictions: family as a line of legitimate heirs who do not disperse their inheritance.[3] It is also gendered male. As John Tosh argues in his study of Victorian masculinity, "Fatherhood embodies hopes and fears about the future, in the sense that a man's place in posterity depends on leaving sons behind him who can carry forward his name."[4] Maternal care, by contrast, takes place in the present tense. Many real-life Victorian men recorded the pressure they felt to "live up to their family's name."[5] As we saw in the chapter on courtship, the vertical pushes for stability and for valuing family name and title above present desires.

The English found ways to harness alternative family constructions in service of the vertical. When such groupings appear in English novels, they are often a means of providing heirs when traditional reproduction is not an option; only in rare cases do English novels glorify the creation of lateral bonds. In Russian novels, by contrast, alternative family constructions run counter to the vertical, conservative force. They are a thing entirely of the present: active creations, not inherent to inherited structures. Their expansive potential is on the lateral axis—reaching outward to connect distant or non-legal relations as "family" in the here and now. That expansion will be the topic of Chapter 8, but before we get there, this chapter explores the preconditions that enable such lateral sprawl. Present-oriented loosenings of traditional family models tend not to form when there is a strong vertical emphasis on the family's progression across time. They spring up in defiance of patriarchy or in its absence.

A Family by Any Other Name

While the traditional family model of parents and their offspring is still central to family studies, in recent years sociologists have offered a more flexible and inclusive social constructionist definition not reliant on biology or legal state sanction: "Networks of people who share their lives over long periods of time bound by marriage, blood, or commitment, legal or otherwise, who consider themselves as family and who share a significant history and anticipated futures

---

[3] Supporting these points, Isobel Armstrong claims genealogy in the English novel "is about the law of exclusion. It is committed to hierarchy. It turns on the law," a comment that emphasizes both its restrictive function and the conservative role it plays (*Novel Politics*, 8).

[4] Tosh, *A Man's Place*, 4. See also Tosh, *Manliness and Masculinities in Nineteenth-Century Britain*, 132.

[5] Mintz provides examples from Samuel Butler, Charles Darwin, and Henry Adams (*A Prison of Expectations*, 171–172).

of functioning in a family relationship."[6] This definition takes seriously the subjects' own beliefs about whom they "consider themselves as family" with, rather than applying a rigid objective standard.[7] These definitions approach family as a social construct and set of behaviors, shifting the emphasis to the affective bonds, actions, and activities that *create* familial relationships rather than bloodline or legal unions.

While such definitions better reflect the way family is understood in some of the novels I will be discussing, there are also dangers to such a loosening of the definition. As Judith Butler cautions, "Kinship loses its specificity as an object once it becomes characterized loosely as modes of enduring relationship."[8] The boundary between "kin" and "community" threatens to become too ambiguous for family to remain a meaningful concept unless limits are drawn. I will derive these limits from the language with which the relationships are discussed in the texts. If a novel's narrator or characters are calling a relationship familial, then— I argue—it is worth taking such claims seriously. However, I will not impose a "family" label on relations that are not so-called in the texts.

Anthropology and sociology have a long tradition of studying kinship structures that fall outside of the heteronormative nuclear family, and over the last fifty years numerous terms have been applied to these structures. Originally, the standard term was *fictive kin*, but many found it to be "fraught with problems" because of its "deficit model" that placed "real" (bio-legal) kin as the standard and defined fictive kin through what they *lacked*, inherently making them lesser.[9] Kath Weston popularized the term "chosen kin" in her study of LGBT families in the 1980s in the Bay Area.[10] Others have used the terms "voluntary kin," "self-ascribed kin," or "ritual kin."[11] I will use "alternative kinship" as a blanket term to encompass all non-nuclear families, even though I am fully aware that there is nothing inherently alternative about this. Within that blanket category, "blended family" will refer to those comprised of a mixture of biological and legal kin, potentially including in-laws, step-relations, adoptees, and extended kin.[12]

I am calling kinship relations that bear no blood or legal ties "intentional family." As explained by Margaret K. Nelson, intentional kin

---

[6] Galvin, Brommel, and Bylund (2004). Qtd. in Braithwaite et al., "Constructing family: A typology of voluntary kin," 389.

[7] Judith Butler uses a similar approach when she tries to understand "kinship as a set of practices that institutes relationships of various kinds which negotiate the reproduction of life and the demands of death..." ("Is Kinship Always Already Heterosexual?" 14–15).

[8] Butler, "Is Kinship Always Already Heterosexual?" 37.

[9] Braithwaite et al., "Constructing family: A typology of voluntary kin," 390.

[10] Weston, *The Families We Choose* (1991).

[11] An overview of the terminology debate is provided by Margaret K. Nelson, "Fictive Kin, Families We Choose, and Voluntary Kin," 259–260.

[12] On the prevalence of blended family in Petrine Russia, see Engel, *Marriage, Household, and Home in Modern Russia: From Peter the Great to Putin*, 7.

refers to those relationships developed by individuals when others in their social worlds come to be regarded as being like a member of their family...The word is meant to imply that these relationships do not happen by chance or at random; the word also implies that because these relationships may persist over time, they may develop complexities so that they feel neither voluntary nor chosen at particular moments (even though individuals are clearly free to leave them); and finally, the word implies that these relationships do not merely exist (as does formal kinship) but are sustained through action.[13]

Not only does this definition map precisely onto the meaning I intend, but I also use "intentional family" as a deliberate response to Dostoevsky's "accidental family" (*sluchainoe semeistvo*). Indeed, one aim of Part III will be to situate Dostoevsky's famous and well-studied accidental families in their broader context and to show that they were not an isolated and unique creation on his part, but instead participated in a much wider trend in the Russian novel. The "alternative" was actually a Russian novelistic norm.

Dostoevsky and Russian Family Breakdown

In order to work against vertical inertia of the traditional family model, the powerful forces of the past must be weakened. New family configurations tend to take shape only when the old is either absent (as is the case of orphans with no kin) or no longer carries moral force. Many Russians in the nineteenth century believed that the Russian family was experiencing this latter kind of breakdown. As Chapter 4 explored, the rapid transformation of Russian society in the period of the Great Reforms shook every aspect of Russian life. With "public" and "private" spheres tightly interwound, the family was not buffered against the radical changes happening at the societal or state level; it was equally unmoored.[14] The gentry way of life was torn apart by the emancipation. Traditional ideas about gender roles were being challenged with the rise of the Woman Question, but new ones had yet to solidify and women still had few economic possibilities. Jurists were challenging the all-powerful status of the father, just as articles in the press used contemporary court cases about abuses to highlight the desperate need for reform. Moving away from patriarchal norms did not mean peace and tranquility for the family, however; instead it meant a loss of stability and a period of flux.

---

[13] Nelson, "Fictive Kin, Families We Choose, and Voluntary Kin," 269.
[14] William Wagner argues that in Europe public and private were usually believed to differ fundamentally (the former based on contractual or consensual foundations and the latter on natural or organic ones), but in Russia there was an "essential homogeneity between the structures of and values embodied in the family, society, and the state" ("Family Law, the Rule of Law, and Liberalism in Late Imperial Russia," 521).

Russian novels are full of broken families, yet most scholarly discussions of family breakdown single out one author: Dostoevsky. While I will devote significant attention to his novels in this chapter, I would like to situate him in the broader context of the literary tradition to which he was contributing and to acknowledge that his works were in no way unique in taking up this theme. The "conflict of generations" popularized by Turgenev's *Fathers and Children* (1862)—an important influence for Dostoevsky—put the generational rift between fathers and sons at the center of Russian consciousness. But broken family goes beyond this theme and women were also crucial to the picture of rupture. A classic example appears in Evgenia Tur's *The Niece* (1851). In part 3 of the novel, the music teacher Antonina recounts her life (a tale which was also published as its own novella, *Antonina*). Reminiscent of Jane Eyre, Antonina lost her parents at an early age, leaving her in the hands of her stepmother and the stepmother's abusive new husband (whose advances she must repulse as an adolescent). She is literally locked up by her stepparents to prevent her marriage to a worthy suitor. The vertical axis has failed her. She ultimately marries an Italian widower with a daughter, despite being unable to return his passionate feelings. The marriage is a disaster; he gambles away all their money. Traditional family has broken down, so Antonina must start again to create a new kind of kinship network.

This pattern of failures on the vertical axis repeats again and again in novels written both before and after emancipation. Avdotia Panaeva's *The Talnikov Family* (1848) features similarly abusive parents to those of Antonina, this time with their own children, not stepchildren. The first third of Herzen's *Who Is to Blame?* (1845–1846) recounts the histories of a series of broken families. The father in Sergei Durov's *Someone Else's Child* (1846) is ready to marry off his daughter to his evil creditor so that his debts will be forgiven, and, after taking pity on her, he still allows her younger sister to marry the man. Saltykov-Shchedrin's Golovlyov mother essentially allows her eldest son to starve. There is no moral authority in the generation of the parents in any of these novels. In novels about "fictitious marriages," the younger generation is deliberately rebelling against the elder, escaping its rigid constraints. Similarly, in Turgenev's *On the Eve* (1860), Elena's rebellious marriage to Insarov without parental consent (even if not technically legal) demonstrates the breakdown of vertical family structures.

So Dostoevsky was far from alone or unique in seeing the breakdown of the Russian family as a failure on the vertical axis (and this theme persisted across the period of this study). In his *Writer's Diary*, he told fathers that their children's souls "demand uninterrupted and constant contact with your parental souls; they demand that spiritually you should always be on a pedestal for them, so to say, as an object of love, of great and genuine respect and beautiful imitation" (25:189/2:1055). Yet Dostoevsky believed Russia's fathers were failing to provide this "good, conspicuous example of all the moral conclusions" their children needed (25:190/2:1056). In another entry he opined:

given our universal indifference to the higher aims of life, of course, the family in certain strata of our nation perhaps already has fallen apart. At least it is perfectly clear that our young generation is destined to seek out its ideals and the higher meaning of life for itself. But this isolation of our younger generation, this abandonment of them to their own devices is something dreadful. (24:51/1:738)

The "dreadful" consequences saturate all the novels cited above. Concerned that "[n]ever has the Russian family been more unsettled, more disintegrated, more disarranged and unformed than it is now," Dostoevsky painted a dire picture of what it had become: "The contemporary Russian family is becoming more and more an *accidental* family...It seems to have suddenly lost its old features, unexpectedly even, while the new ones...will it be capable of creating for itself new, desirable features that satisfy the Russian heart? Some even very serious people say frankly that the Russian family of today 'doesn't exist'" (25:173/2:1034–1035).

This breakdown of the family motivated Dostoevsky's quest to define a new type of Russian family—and family plot—in his novels.[15] He first used the term "accidental family" in his fiction to describe the family at the heart of his penultimate novel, *The Adolescent* (1875), where failures on the vertical axis lead to a most chaotic and a-traditional family structure. The novel is a first-person account from an illegitimate son, Arkady, who is the product of an adulterous relationship between a gentry widower and his married serf. Arkady was raised apart from his family, so at the start of the novel when he is called to St. Petersburg to join them, he comes to know his biological father, mother, and sister for the first time as well as his legal father (the former serf who is married to his mother) and also his legitimate half-siblings, who respond in different ways to their "brother" through this more dubious linkage. There are two fathers—biological and legal—but neither has been present to guide the adolescent. This is an even more unformed and amorphous family structure than that of the Karamazovs, where we have three legitimate brothers—the sons of two mothers—and one illegitimate (unacknowledged) son, mostly raised apart and also coming to know each other for the first time as young adults.

Dostoevsky presents this type of fractured family as a failure on the part of Russian society. In Dmitri's trial for parricide in *The Brothers Karamazov* (1880), both prosecution and defense raise the stakes to the national level as they discuss the Karamazov family. The prosecutor notes that "certain basic, general elements of our modern-day educated society shine through, as it were, in the picture of this nice little family" (15:125/695) and he reminds jurors that Fyodor Pavlovich "is a father, and one of our modern-day fathers" (15:126/696). In a similar vein, the

---

[15] Donald Fanger touches on this briefly in a fascinating passage where he intriguingly blames St. Petersburg for the "dissolution" of the family, claiming that it too is "accidental" (*Dostoevsky and Romantic Realism*, 202–203).

defense attorney claims to be heard by "the whole of Russia" when he cries out to fathers to "provoke not your children!" (15:169/744). In many senses, what is on trial is the modern Russian family. *The Adolescent* also closes by passing judgment on the Russian family, this time in the form of Arkady's former tutor writing a response to Arkady's manuscript (i.e. the novel).[16] Writing of Arkady's gentry father and his legal heirs, the tutor proclaims that "a multitude of such unquestionably hereditary Russian families are, with irresistible force, going over *en masse* into *accidental* families and merging with them in general disorder and chaos" (13:455/563). The emancipation of the serfs and shake-up of the Russian estate system has shaken the foundations of the family.

Part of the "disorder and chaos" comes from the failure to have any clear vertical axis at all. The novels challenge the traditional interrelationship of wedlock and procreation, the link needed to produce legitimate heirs. Indeed, almost all the babies born in Dostoevsky's novels are illegitimate, problematizing standard definitions of family that assume an overlap between legal and biological ties.[17] In *Demons* (1872), Stavrogin weds an invalid in a marriage that remains unconsummated, while he spreads his seed outside the marital bed.[18] Amongst his conquests is Shatov's wife, who returns to her husband on the night she gives birth to Stavrogin's illegitimate child. When Shatov announces the baby will not be sent to an orphanage as the midwife had assumed, she asks if Shatov is adopting him, forgetting the child is legally—though not biologically—a Shatov. Shatov's bold (and some might say generous) declaration "he is my son" [*on i est' moi syn*] (10:452) reminds us that standard alignments of consanguineal and conjugal relations do not apply. In *The Adolescent*, Arkady's unwed sister Liza is carrying Prince Sokolsky's child, and the reader learns of an incredibly convoluted back story involving their father, Versilov, caring for an infant that turns out *not* to be his own illegitimate baby but another of Prince Sokolsky's.

Dostoevsky's families also include many illegitimate older children or young adults, like Nellie (*The Insulted and Injured*, 1861), Arkady and Liza (*The Adolescent*), and Smerdyakov (*The Brothers Karamazov*), who are mature enough to wrestle with the shame of their birth and rejection—or ultimate acceptance—by their biological fathers. These children of accidental families must each determine for themselves what defines a family relationship: is bloodline enough if there has

---

[16] Kate Holland has analyzed the way the shape of the family affected the form of the novel. She astutely explores Dostoevsky's challenge to the "'noble family novel,' which he saw encapsulated in the works of Tolstoi, Turgenev, and to a lesser extent Goncharov," through looking at the formal issue of fragmentation, tracing parallels between the breakdown of the family and the disintegration of narrative form (*The Novel in the Age of Disintegration*, 103).

[17] Illegitimacy was a much greater concern in the eighteenth-century English novel than the nineteenth, and the extramarital affairs could be treated with humor, as in Fielding's *Tom Jones* (1749).

[18] Viacheslav Ivanov provides a symbolic reading of Stavrogin's marriage to Maria Shatova, seeing her as the embodiment of Russia and Stavrogin as Russia's betrayer. ("Ekskurs osnovoi mif v romane 'Besy,'" in *Sobranie sochinenii*, 4:442–443).

been no contact or acknowledgement? Nellie believes not, pridefully hiding the letter that proves Valkovsky's paternity. For the adolescent Arkady, too, the blood tie alone does not signify. When asked early in the novel if he is Versilov's son, he answers "That means nothing. However, let's suppose I am his son, though my name is Dolgoruky. I'm illegitimate. This gentleman has endless illegitimate children. When conscience and honor demand, a son can leave home. It's in the Bible" (13:131/157). Arkady's total misinterpretation of the parable of the prodigal son (Luke 15:11–32) should make us suspicious of this claim. Yet questioning the meaning of "fatherhood" in the absence of paternal care is a potent theme in Dostoevsky's novels.

The link between procreation and family is actively challenged in *The Brothers Karamazov* during Dmitri's trial. The defense attorney offers up the pro-forma answer a typical youth is given as to why he should love his father:

> "He begot you, you are of his blood, that is why you must love him." The young man involuntarily begins to think: "But did he love me when he was begetting me?" he asks, wondering more and more. "Did he beget me for my sake? He did not know me, nor even my sex at that moment, the moment of passion, probably heated up with wine, and probably all he did for me was pass on to me an inclination to drink—so much for his good deeds…Why should I love him just because he begot me and then never loved me all my life?" (15:171/745)[19]

The act of begetting a child is here separated from the creation of a family.[20] This is a direct assault on the vertical. If biologically siring a child does not make one a father, then all the parents failing to care for their progeny and to provide a moral model are *literally* leaving them fatherless.

Broken Family in England

The same breaking and remaking of kinship bonds can be found in the English novel as well. Orphans like David Copperfield, Pip, and Oliver Twist populate the

---

[19] While in *The Brothers Karamazov* this idea that love must be earned is actively challenged (the chapter containing the defense attorney's speech is titled "An Adulterer of Thought"), Fusso notes in his discussion of the Kroneberg trial, Dostoevsky "refuses to admit an *a priori* sacredness for the family" ("Dostoevskii and the family," 185). The difference, she argues, is that Dmitri's lawyer was trying to help him evade responsibility, whereas the in the Kroneberg case, Dostoevsky wanted to *make* the father responsible for torturing his daughter.

[20] In *Demons*, Stepan Trofimovich similarly claims "I find I have so little right to be called a father," after noting how long it has been since he has seen "Pétrusha" (10:75/92). In the reverse, in *Antonina* (1851), Tur "presents maternity as not mainly a matter of bearing children, but rather one of caring for them" as Antonina becomes an ideal step-mother to Lena (Gheith, "Introduction" to *Antonina*, xvi). What makes one a father is similarly challenged in Praskovia Khvoshchinskaya's "Tale of a Housekeeper" (1864), in this case by the daughter.

pages of Dickens' novels, and illegitimate children like Esther Summerson struggle with the shame of their illicit birth.[21] There were societal concerns about the family being under threat or in decline, but most novels that included broken family balanced it against more positive models, just as they balance failed marriages against successful courtships that promise connubial bliss.[22] More extreme conditions were needed in the English novel to remove the emphasis from the bloodline.

Daniel Deronda (1876) tests just how extreme those conditions need to be. The novel is a disquisition on the fragility of lineage and its ties to inheritance, but it ultimately confirms the powerful force of these vertical currents. Daniel is raised by Sir Hugo as an English gentleman, strongly suspecting that Sir Hugo may be his actual father. But his Jewish lineage finds him, first through discovering spiritual brotherhood with Mordecai, who proclaims "I will take nothing less precious from you than your soul's brotherhood" (432). And then, after having been primed by Mordecai, Daniel learns his legacy explicitly from his mother, Leonora, when she reveals herself to him. The encounter is permeated by the question of how much an individual can choose his or her place in the world. How much can anyone control what is passed on, and what withheld? By giving Daniel to Sir Hugo to be raised, and leaving him with his father's fortune, Leonora gave him entry into the world of the English gentleman—the life she would have wished for in his place. But Daniel presses her: "How could you choose my birthright for me?" (538).

Daniel's months of friendship with Mordecai had already drawn him to Judaism in a way that suggests birthright *cannot* be chosen, that one's true lineage will triumph. "How could I know that you would have the spirit of my father in you?" Leonora asks him in their meeting (538). Leonora cannot pass on what she has gained through her self-chosen artistic career: "A great singer and actress is a queen, but she gives no royalty to her son," she observes (544). Despite her choices for her own life, or the upbringing she created for Daniel, it is her father's legacy that triumphs, reasserting the dominance of the vertical axis. In words that echo the central themes of Dombey and Son (1846–1848), Leonora explains "My father had tyrannized over me—he cared more about a grandson to come than he did about me: I counted as nothing. You were to be such a Jew as he" (544). Blood is destiny; Daniel's marriage to Mirah and their departure for the East to build a nation for his people fulfills his grandfather's legacy as well as the legacy of his spiritual brother, Mordecai, who had told him "When my long-wandering soul is liberated from this weary body, it will join yours, and its work will be perfected" (461). The novel complicates the distinction between the bio-legal family and chosen kin because Daniel's chosen brother turns out to be bound to him through their shared Jewish ancestry.

---

[21] See Sadrin, *Parentage and Inheritance in the Novels of Charles Dickens*, 13–15.
[22] On decline see Hatten, *The End of Domesticity*; Kilroy, *The Nineteenth-Century English Novel*.

Orphanhood like Daniel's is a powerful starting point for creating a-traditional family models. In Dinah Craik's *John Halifax, Gentleman* (1856), the shift from blood to chosen kin is a way of filling a void. The novel is narrated by the motherless invalid Phineas Fletcher, who meets the penniless orphan John Halifax in childhood. On the day of their first encounter, after John has helped Phineas home, the lonely invalid thinks of him as a replacement for the missing family ties in his life, wishing "to keep near me this lad, whose companionship and help seemed to me, *brotherless, sisterless, and friendless as I was*, the very thing that would give me an interest in life" (12, my italics). The relationship is coded as family replacement from the start. Early in the novel, when Phineas' father commands the boys not to communicate, Phineas is impressed that John honors the injunction even more strongly than he himself does. He marvels "how it was that he who had never known his father should uphold so sternly the duty of filial obedience" (94). This leads him to reflect that "it ought to act as a solemn warning to those who exact so much from the mere fact and name of parenthood, without having in any way fulfilled its duties, that orphans from birth often revere the ideal of that bond far more than those who have known it in reality" (94). Just as in Dostoevsky's novels, blood ties alone mean little if one has not "fulfilled [the] duties" of kin. Craik returned to this idea a decade later in *A Noble Life* (1866). When the last Earl of Cairnforth must choose an heir because he cannot sire one, the family lawyer tells him "There are many instances in which blood is *not* thicker than water—and a friend, by election, is often worthier and dearer—besides begin closer—than any relative" (82).

Even in England, where there was an idea of the normative family being whole and complete unto itself, many novels looked to the exceptions where this ideal model failed to materialize. Rather than taking apart the norm and suggesting that the family had become "accidental," authors like Craik, Dickens, Gaskell, and Geraldine Jewsbury turned to cases where family ties were simply absent, as is the case for orphans like John Halifax, the Earl of Cairnforth, Oliver Twist, Gaskell's Ruth (1853), or Jewsbury's Constance (*Constance Herbert*, 1855). John Halifax and Phineas can become "brothers" because neither owes anything to past or future, nor do they have extended kin-groups in the present who would force them to maintain their class distinctions. Phineas' father (and only relation) imposes such a separation for a time, until he, like his son, comes to appreciate John's true worth and dignity. After that point, the two are at liberty to call each other "brother" as their highest—and only—kinship duties are to each other. As Phineas tells John's future wife, "John is a brother, friend, everything in the world to me" (166). We find a similar kind of "brotherly" attachment in Wilkie Collins' *Armadale* (1866) between the wealthy Allan Armadale and "Ozias Midwinter" (true name, also Allan Armadale), who was thrown out of his family of origin and raised as a vagabond. Not beholden to any other family relations, the pair end up living together, even though neither realizes they are actually second cousins. Although the orphaned Oliver Twist eventually finds his way "back" to his family, the constellation he ends with is distinctly non-traditional.[23] The link underlying this new family was Mr. Brownlow's love for Oliver's aunt, who died just before they would have wed. That affection was then transferred to her brother—Oliver's father—so there is neither a blood nor an affinal tie between the adoptive pair.

Gaskell's *Ruth* demonstrates the dangers as well as the benefits of chosen kin. The orphaned heroine is initially susceptible to Mr. Bellingham's seduction because he positions himself as family, coaxing her "Tell me everything, Ruth, as you would to a brother" (37). He then takes her to her childhood home, linking himself with all her warm memories of family life. The narrator explicitly credits the loss of Ruth's parents and her need for love with making her ready to fall (40). When Mr. Bellingham asks Ruth to go to London with him, he too reminds her "Here you are, an orphan, with only one person to love you, poor child!" (50). Of course what he is offering is not true kinship. After this false choice that provides only a passing passion, Ruth will next find herself taken into a family of the opposite make—one not based on heterosexual desire. The minister, Thurston, and his sister, Faith Benson, are already an untraditional family with a sibling bond, not a conjugal knot, as the basis (Faith turned down a suitor to remain with her brother). There is no vertical here and no possibility of reproduction. Steeped in Christian faith and broken free of the normative model of the bounded nuclear family, they offer a haven for the orphaned girl and her illegitimate son. Ironically, in the English novel it is often the most religious characters (whom one might expect to be conservative) who are also the most flexible in their family relations (as we saw as well with mending marriages in Chapter 6).

Dostoevsky and Family Freed of Futurity

Another essential condition that enables the loosening of traditional family structures and makes space for alternative kinship bonds to appear is a temporal outlook that puts weight on the present, something much more commonly encountered in Russia than England. Marriage—*the* central plot for the English family—is future-oriented, with its goal lying in a cradle that appears *after* the narrative threads have been neatly tied. Many novels end explicitly with the birth of a child on the final pages.[24] In the Russian novel, where marriage plots tend to fail and the ultimate telos is not the precious heir, the value of family exists in the present, enabling new types of families and family plots.

---

[23] As Barry McCrea notes, "it includes, after all, an adoptive father, and eventually attracts such extraneous appendages as Mr. Grimwig, the Colonel Pickering to Mr. Brownlow's Henry Higgins" (*In the Company of Strangers*, 40).

[24] Even when they do not, I concur with D. A. Miller that we can still usually assume this event to be imminent. As he notes of Austen's *Emma*, "We need not follow Emma and Mr. Knightly beyond the threshold of their 'perfect union' through visits, balls, business, lyings-in (little Henry Knightley's claim to the Donwell estate has surely gone for good)" (*Narrative and Its Discontents*, 43).

I will again use Dostoevsky to illuminate this point. A writer obsessed with the family, Dostoevsky managed to produce a whole career's worth of novels *not* structured primarily or exclusively on the marriage plot and in which *not a single legal heir was produced.* Indeed, neither marriage nor reproduction seems to be of great concern to Dostoevsky's heroes. They never fret about having progeny or about the legacy they will pass on to their heirs, aside from intangible family pride or honor.[25] This enables them to focus on questions of spiritual worth and connection that will not produce (or reproduce) anything. In *The Brothers Karamazov*, Snegiryov cares about his son's respect after Dmitri Karamazov humiliatingly pulls him by the beard, not about a legacy of family honor. As he opines to Alyosha, "this genealogical family picture [of his father being pulled by the beard] forever imprinted itself in the memory of Ilyusha's soul" (14:186/204). This event leads to Ilyusha's teasing, but rather than feeling ashamed for his father, "the one stood up for his father, alone against everyone" (14:187/205). The issue of family pride here is not about origins and lineage, but about present behavior.

The Adolescent similarly focuses attention on father-son dynamics in the present, rather than as part of a genealogical progression. After having ignored his illegitimate son, Arkady, for his whole upbringing, Versilov suddenly seeks intimacy with him "now"; literally, the word "now" (*teper'*) appears thirty-four times in the scene when father and son finally come together, and variants of "today" (*segodnia/shnee*) an additional seven. In more than just word choice, *The Adolescent* "presents an all-pervasive present" and "takes as its starting point a blank slate, the denial of memory, but gradually acknowledges that without memory form is not possible."[26] Even in this hyper-charged present, Arkady longs for a family past, puzzling out his origin story: how his father and mother first became a couple. He wishes to understand the genealogy he never had.[27] The whole project of writing his notes—i.e. the novel, which he narrates in the first person—is his way of constructing a plot for this "accidental" family that had never been the subject of a novel.[28] But in addition to looking back during his meeting with his father, the young adolescent is also looking forward, and the future proves an even more vexed topic; talk of it leads to Versilov sharing his vision of the end of the world.[29]

---

[25] This does not mean that Dostoevsky ignored genetic inheritance. The Karamazov brothers, for example, make repeated references to their shared blood, what Ivan calls "the Karamazov force" [*karamazovskaia sila*] (14:240/263).

[26] Holland, *Novel in the Age of Disintegration*, 122.

[27] I am grateful to Greta Matzner-Gore for pointing out Arkady's confusion with genealogical time when Arkady refers to Versilov as his "future father" [*budushchii otets*] (13:17).

[28] Arkady reflects on the novels that served as models for his father and mother's romance; Versilov told him he had recently read *Polinka Saks* and *Anton Goremyka* (1847) before meeting Arkady's mother. He is deliberate about fashioning his own notes as a novel, with comments like "And by the way: bringing this 'new character' on stage in my "Notes" (I'm speaking of Versilov), I'll give a brief account of his service record..." (13:64/76). He even refers to the notes as "my Petersburg novel" (13:65/77).

[29] The importance of endings is analyzed by Greta Matzner-Gore (*Dostoevsky and the Ethics of Narrative Form*, 44).

Versilov has nothing to pass on but existential questions; he has not even given Arkady a name or status in society. In this new version of the family plot, the focus is distinctly *not* on lineage (past) or inheritance (future). This present-ness is a general tendency in Dostoevsky's novels.

Dostoevsky's families exist outside the spaces of traditional family life as defined in the English novel. This realm, which Bakhtin calls "biographical time," where characters "are born, they pass through childhood and youth, they marry, give birth to children, die" Dostoevsky "leaps over."[30] His protagonists tend to appear already as young adults whose childhoods we see only in brief snatches. What do we know of the "family life" of Raskolnikov before he came to St. Petersburg? In *Demons, The Adolescent*, and *The Brothers Karamazov*, such family life never existed, as the characters spent years apart and only come together when the "children" are already young adults.[31] *Crime and Punishment, Demons, The Adolescent,* and *The Brothers Karamazov* all begin with a family reuniting after years apart.[32] And even their family life in the present tends to lack roots, as many families in Dostoevsky's novels are living in rented rooms rather than an ancestral home (*Poor Folk* [1846], *The Insulted and Injured, Crime and Punishment, The Gambler* [1866], *The Adolescent*).

Just as Dostoevsky's families have "leapt over" biographical time, they also defy the narrative propulsion toward a future.[33] Resisting the "genealogical imperative," none of them produce an heir. The death of Shatov's wife and illegitimate child right after they have been reunited in *Demons* is emblematic of this absolute negation of family continuity. Few characters seem troubled about their families' futures.[34] Fyodor Pavlovich Karamazov, for example, concerns himself with money to seduce a concubine, not with the inheritance for his sons. Dostoevskian

---

[30] Bakhtin, *Problems of Dostoevsky's Poetics*, 169. Robin Feuer Miller notes that *The Idiot* provides an exception to this general rule (*Dostoevsky and* The Idiot: *Author, Narrator, and Reader,* 97).

[31] See Fusso, "Dostoevskii and the family," 179.

[32] As Corrigan has noted, "the dramatic crises of Dostoevsky's major novels...are all, without exception, catalyzed by his characters' sudden confrontation with the distant past: Raskolnikov's discovery that his mother and sister are coming to Petersburg in *Crime and Punishment*; Myshkin's return to Russia in *The Idiot*; Stavrogin's arrival in his hometown in *Demons*; Arkady's reunion with his family in *The Adolescent*; and the brothers' homecoming in *The Brothers Karamazov*" ("Dostoevskii on Evil as Safe Haven and Anesthetic," 229). While Corrigan is interested in the characters' "reckoning with the past," these are also important moments of family reunion.

[33] Here I am disagreeing with Semenov, who argues that the conflict of fathers and children is a conflict of the present and future (Semenov, *Roman Dostoevskogo "Podrostok,"* 138).

[34] The one seeming exception is in Dostoevsky's very first novel, *Poor Folk*, where Bykov's express purpose in marrying Varenka is to produce an heir. But as Varenka reports, his true motivation—that he openly explains to her—is that "he had, as he put it, a 'no-good nephew' whom he had sworn to deprive of his inheritance, and it was for this very reason—that of acquiring some lawful inheritors—that he sought my hand" (1:100/118). He is not actually concerned with creating his own line. Varenka, in turn, departs the novel as if going to her death, her final words to Devushkin are "My tears are choking me, breaking me. Farewell. God, how sad! Remember, remember your poor Varenka!" (1:106/127). We have no indication of whether the sought-after heir ever materializes.

heroes may obsess about love and passion, but not about matrimony, which carries with it the promise of future obligation. Their failure to marry and produce heirs emphasizes kinship ties in the present, not as a means toward a (reproductive) end. Jennifer Wilson's study of the Skoptsy (a self-castrating religious sect) in Dostoevsky's novels reveals a counter-intuitive truth: while Skoptsy might be thought to be resisting futurity through castration, Dostoevsky "often connected [them] to ideas of prophecy, premature aging, accumulation of wealth (all ways of engaging the future), whereas Dostoevsky elsewhere depicts characters focused on questions of family as preoccupied with the present moment."[35] Dostoevsky contrasted the non-reproducing Skoptsy's future-oriented greed and hoarding "with the [present-oriented] generosity of those fully enmeshed in family affairs."[36]

I do not mean to suggest that Dostoevsky did not care about the future. He was deeply concerned about it, but this future was not about individual families but rather about a broader form of unity, the universal brotherhood he ecstatically preached in his "Pushkin speech" (1880). It is the children who will bring about this dreamed-of brotherhood, but it does not matter specifically *whose* children (except that they be Russian). Dostoevsky envisioned a communal future, where family unity would spread to the whole of Russia, and then the Russians could in turn bring brotherhood to Europe. In this vision, there is no significance for the future of an individual family line. Family matters are present concerns.

Tolstoy and Family in the Present

While Dostoevsky is obviously an exceptional writer and cannot be taken to represent the Russian tradition, his focus on the family's present is a widespread Russian trait. Part II explored its effect on the marriage plot, looking especially at novels by Alexander Druzhinin, Evgenia Tur, Ivan Goncharov, Nikolai Pomialovsky, and Turgenev. Even Tolstoy's marriage-centric reproductive families that lead to the nursery still retain a remarkable emphasis on living and loving in the here and now. As Tolstoy would seem to be the obvious counter-example to the point I am making, I would like to explore two of his novels to show how they actually conform to the present-emphasis more than it might at first appear.

Tolstoy's most idealized family—the Rostovs in *War and Peace* (1865–1869)—are living far beyond their means, welcoming in distant relations like Sonya (and for a time before the novel started Boris Drubetskoi), hosting lavish dinners, and

---

[35] Wilson, "Dostoevsky's Timely Castration," 567.

[36] Wilson, "Dostoevsky's Timely Castration," 567. According to Wilson, the Skoptsy "provide an example of queer time that is not belated, delayed, or without a future but one that rushes to the future, unencumbered by the quotidian demands of the present. It is precisely this overwhelming futurity that makes them antisocial to Dostoevsky" (570).

keeping their door open to all. Their estate of Otradnoe is home to more than twenty people, "almost members of the family," that includes a musician and his wife, the dancing master and his family, an old maiden lady, teachers, a former governess, and "simply people who for some reason found it better or more advantageous to live in the count's house than in their own" (10:270/515). As Caryl Emerson has noted, Tolstoy glorifies the selflessness and authenticity of the Rostovs' joyful and generous descent into impoverishment, rather than chastising them for their light-mindedness and failure to provide for the family's future.[37] The "egg teaches the hen" to give up all their possessions to make room for wounded soldiers on their flight from burning Moscow and everyone rejoices, with Tolstoy's narrator affirming the choice.

> The whole household, as if to atone for not having done it sooner, set eagerly to work at the new task of placing the wounded in the carts...Cases full of china, bronzes, pictures and mirrors, that had been so carefully packed the night before, now lay about the yard, and still they went on searching for and finding of unloading this or that and letting the wounded have another and yet another cart. (11:317/863)

This family is remarkably fecund, so I do not mean to suggest that the Rostov clan has no future, rather to emphasize the value they place on the present. This enables them to expand on the lateral axis, embracing a looser conglomeration than the traditional nuclear norm. On this issue of time perspective, Tolstoy's values are not that far removed from Dostoevsky's, though the families the two authors depict are in most other ways radically opposed.

Anna Karenina also makes family an issue of present connection, rather than futurity. More than most Russian novels, it directly addresses the issue of genealogical progression, which would seem to suggest the verticality I have been associating with the English. However, it does so within an underlying values system that emphasizes present over future.[38] In Chapter Five I discussed the English novel's emphasis on the production of an heir, citing Osborne's "honest British exultation" as he imagined his son's marriage leading to him being "the progenitor of a glorious line of baronets" (*Vanity Fair*, 250). I also pointed to Mr. Palliser's sense of "almost unconscious exaltation" on learning of his wife's pregnancy and

---

[37] This point comes from numerous conversations with Caryl, who always thought my vision of the Rostovs was too idealistic (like Tolstoi's).

[38] Catriona Kelly links this kind of family to the Slavophile outlook: "'The family' that is championed in *Anna Karenina*, as generally in Slavophile conservatism, is the extended family, *rod* (clan). One of the reasons for the success of Levin and Kitty's relationship is that the two are supported by a network of congenial and sympathetic blood relatives and family connections who mitigate the tension that (in Tolstoi's view) inevitably accompanied sexual connections. The extended family in this sense has been celebrated in Sergei Aksakov's important Slavophile text *Family Chronicle*, a memoir that was also concerned with blood ties in the broader sense of family tradition (*War and Peace* can be seen as a generic descendant of the 'family chronicle' in this respect)" (*Refining Russia*, 138).

his friend's comment that "When there's a dukedom and heaven know how many thousands a year to be disposed of, the question of their future ownership does become important" (*Can You Forgive Her?* [1864], 612, 615). Compare Trollope's and Thackeray's descriptions of filiation with the way the same theme appears in *Anna Karenina* when the narrator describes Levin and Kitty's newborn son: "like a small flame over a lamp, wavered the life of a human being who had never existed before and who, with the same right, with the same importance for itself, would live and produce its own kind [*plodit' sebe podobnykh*]" (19:294/716). Tolstoy's narrator—like Levin himself—is awed by the mystery of new life appearing and the formation of a self-conscious being. This is a spiritual concern, not a material one about lineage and title. The passage would be no different if Kitty had borne a daughter, not a son, or if this were a *second* son, because what matters is life, not line, continuing.

Dolly, too, reflects on this process of generational progression during the carriage ride on her way to visit Anna in the middle of the novel. Her emphasis, however, is on the more quotidian aspects of the children's upbringing and the hardships of mothering: "What will come of it all? That I, having not a moment's peace, now pregnant, now nursing, eternally angry, grumpy, tormented myself and tormenting others, repulsive to my husband, will live my life out and bring up unfortunate, poorly educated and destitute children. Even now, if we weren't with the Levins, I don't know how we'd live" (19:181–182/607). Even in this moment of thinking about vertical, intergenerational family bonds, Dolly still falls back on the lateral: the sister and brother-in-law who are supporting her. Of course this is a low moment for her and she later revels in motherhood, but she never thinks about a glorious future for the Oblonsky line. Notably, Stiva Oblonsky—who is impoverishing these children through his extravagant spending—does not think about filiation at all. His failures as a father merge with the failures of the gentry class to provide for its own future as he under-sells his woods, leaving even less of an inheritance to be split amongst his many children.

The one character who obsesses about heirs and inheritance is Vronsky, who tries to fashion himself as the hero of an English novel. In the second half of the book, he sets up life on his estate at Vozdvizhenskoe surrounded by English technology and fashion. Vronsky complains about family futurity to Dolly when she visits, telling her that his daughter is legally Karenin's, and that "however many children we have, there will be no connection between me and them" (19:202/627). Claiming "no connection" with potential future biological children, Vronsky completely disregards the emotional and spiritual sides of kinship—the ones that typically matter most in Russian novels. Vronsky, who "had never known family life," latches onto the formal element of family—legal inheritance of name and property—but misses all the content: the active love that Tolstoy values (Anna, by contrast sees only content—love—and tries to close her eyes to the form). Vronsky's emphasis on form over content mirrors how he functions as a son as well, polite and dutiful to his mother, filling all outward obligations, but without any love for her. And this is the same problem with his estate: the sense of heritage and tradition that makes caring for an estate a worthy task in an English novel is absent from Vozdvizhenskoe. The reader is given to understand that the "opulence and display and that new European luxury [Dolly] had only read about in English novels but had never seen in Russia" (19:191/616) lacks the moral purpose that seems ingrained in the very fiber of the English novel.

At Pokrovskoe, where Levin has deliberately attempted to recreate the family life of his childhood, that sense of heritage is present. Even when Levin is wrestling with the meaning of his existence he knows "As undoubtedly as it was necessary to pay debts, it was also necessary to maintain the family land in such a condition that when his son inherited it he would thank his father, as Levin had thanked his grandfather for everything he had built and planted" (19:372/790). But continuing this legacy does not give Levin enough reason to live, and "happy in his family life, a healthy man, Levin was several times so close to suicide that he hid a rope lest he hang himself with it, and was afraid to go about with a rifle lest he shoot himself" (19:371/789). As he struggles with existential despair, what keeps Levin going is "Farming, relations with the muzhiks and his neighbours, running the household, his sister's and brother's affairs, which were in his hands, relations with his wife and family, cares about the baby, the new interest in bees he had acquired that last spring" (19:371/789). This list expands care and concern outward in the present; Levin's duties to his wife and child are couched between the muzhiks, his siblings, and the bees in his apiary.

The lack of concern for (or de-emphasis on) family futurity takes other forms in other authors' works, but I would argue that it is a fairly consistent pattern across many Russian novels. The almost-immediately-widowed heroines, like those we find in Turgenev's *On the Eve* and Aleeva's *Two Worlds* (1875), did not have time to reproduce. Yet their marriages could hardly be called failures because in each case the heroine has become socially conscious and has broken free of a stifling home. She has set forth on a new path of intellectual and spiritual activity as a result of her relationship with her short-while husband, and this new life for her in the present is itself the fruit of their union. Similarly, "fictitious marriages" are specifically designed *not* to produce families, as they are meant to remain unconsummated. In Dolgina's *Fictitious Marriage* (1876), even though the couple in the marriage ultimately fall in love, there is no mention of children, and the final description is of their good deeds for society, with Marianna in the role of helpmate to her husband, rather than mother to his offspring. Chernyshevsky does include children in the conclusion of *What Is to Be Done?* (1863), but has virtually nothing to tell us about their upbringing. With so much narrative attention devoted to the system of sharing umbrellas and so little said about child-care duties or education, the reader could be excused for assuming that these future representatives of the Kirsanov and Beaumont families are not a central concern for the narrator...or even for their parents, whom we last see having pleasure parties without them. So while fictitious marriages might solve some of the problems of female liberation or rethinking marriage, they are not a model of family futurity.

Escaping Futurity in the English Novel

For Russian authors, emphasis on the present was part of a national values system, linked in part to the unstable social and political conditions discussed in the Introduction. Such a focus on the present can be met in the English novel as well, and there, too, it enables alternative forms of family to thrive. However, for the English, the lack of reproductive futurity is generally not a chosen state, but one imposed by some unalterable condition, like disability, fear of hereditary disease, or the early death of a beloved to whose memory a character remains faithful. For example, in Chapter 3 we encountered John Martindale, eldest brother in Yonge's *Heartsease, or Brother's Wife* (1854). After the early death of his beloved (before the novel begins), John has become weak of health, putting him almost in the category of an infirm person and making it easier for his family and the reader to accept that he has recused himself from the possibility of a future marriage plot ("I never thought he would rally again," his brother reflects, 21). Instead, the semi-invalid brother is now freed to remain connected to his younger brother Arthur's family and to take on the role of care-giver for Arthur's children. It is his removal from the possibility of reproductive futurity that enables this alternative constellation.

Craik's *John Halifax, Gentleman* foregrounds the alternative kinship bonds that can arise in the absence of concern for the future. The invalid narrator, Phineas, sees himself as cut off from genealogical futurity. On the first day of the novel, he tells his new friend John that "most likely I shan't live long," setting himself up as a character without a future (16). He believes—and everyone in the novel seems to accept—that his "character was too feeble and womanish to win any woman's reverence and love. Or, even if this had been possible, one sickly as I was, stricken with hereditary disease, ought never to seek to perpetuate it by marriage" (62). After a "brief" but "hard" struggle, Phineas overcomes his "dreams of the divinity of womanhood" and accepts that his sickly constitution removes him from the possibility of heterosexual love and procreation (62). Phineas also knows himself to be too weak to work and inherit his father's tanning business: "That I should ever be what was my poor father's one desire, his assistant and successor in his business, was, I knew, a thing totally impossible" (32). He is cut off from both the main modes of family transmission: business and blood. This both enforces and enables Phineas to focus on present attachment and to forge lateral familial bonds, making John Halifax his brother. Not carrying the weight of the future, he is free to follow his heart in the present, and he describes the passage of years with John as a perpetual present: "Neither of us counted the days, nor looked backwards or forwards" (60).

Significantly, Craik also portrays John as outside of genealogical progression.[39] Most scholars have approached his lack of origins in terms of class, rather than family, emphasizing the rise of the self-made man.[40] Karen Bourrier, for example, argues that "the novel's central claim" is that "one need not be well born to be a true gentleman."[41] John has the names of his parents and their death dates written in a Bible, which is all he know of his parentage. "He was indebted to no forefathers for a family history: the chronicle commenced with himself, and was altogether his own making. No romantic antecedents ever turned up: his lineage remained uninvestigated, and his pedigree began and ended with his own honest name— John Halifax" (14).[42] This claim by the narrator is not strictly true, however, as the family Bible lists John's father as "gentleman," so his attainments *do* align with his pedigree in terms of class. But in terms of family, he is "loosed from the moorings of the past."[43]

The reader is repeatedly reminded of John's name representing the whole of himself without antecedents. On his first entry into society when asked about his past and who his parents were, "'Madame,' he said gravely, 'I was introduced to you simply as John Halifax. It seems to me that, so long as I do no discredit to it, the name suffices to the world" (220). His engagement to Ursula March hinges on both of them lacking a family line. Making the announcement, he tells Phineas' father "We have no parents, neither she nor I. Bless her—for she has promised to be my wife" (246). Released from the constraints of a family line, John, like Phineas, is free to create a more flexible vision of family that will cross class lines and take in his chosen brother. *John Halifax, Gentleman* shares with the Russian novel a distinctive de-emphasis on family pedigree, futurity, or the inherent primacy of blood relations, making family a matter of actions and emotions as well as a bio-legal bond. This is not to say there is no future for the family—John and Ursula leave behind a thriving brood—but that value is placed on their present relations.[44]

---

[39] Both boys have also lost mothers, a point of connection (15).

[40] Bourrier notes the ways *John Halifax, Gentleman* anticipates Samuel Smile's *Self-Help* (1859) (*The Measure of Manliness*, 65–66). Gilmour goes further with the comparison, noting the contradictory messages in *John Halifax, Gentleman*, where Craik argues both that the poor man can become a gentleman and that what matters is "independence, integrity and dignity, [but] at the same time, John Halifax is only secure in social status when he has *justified* himself by acquiring the symbols of hereditary class—the large estate, the county acquaintance, an aristocratic son-in-law, a carriage that is 'tasteful...as any of the country gentry'" ("Dickens and the Self-Help Idea," 79–80).

[41] Bourrier, *The Measure of Manliness*, 52.

[42] Later, the narrator also notes of John that "The lad, like many another, owed nothing to his father but his mere existence" (38).

[43] Mascarenhas, "*John Halifax, Gentleman*: A Counter Story," 257.

[44] Similarly, in Dickens' *Our Mutual Friend* (1864-1865) it is only when Eugene Wrayburn is lying beaten to near death (and thus functionally like a disabled character) that he feels enabled to act on his love for the poor Lizzie Hexam and to actually marry her. He tells her that "I have been thinking

In the Queer and Now?

When faced with family models that do not match the standard of married parents with biological offspring, the theoretical model most often invoked recently is
queer theory. Early pioneers like Lee Edelman and Jack Halberstam defined queer
in opposition to the family, focusing on its lack of heterosexual reproduction. Their
approach assumes the primacy of the vertical family axis and consequently situates
queerness as a challenge. Edelman, for example, specifically objects to "the trope
of the child as figure for the universal value attributed to political futurity," and
the "absolute privilege of heteronormativity" that accompanies it.[45] Such theories
offer a counter to the values system illustrated so clearly in Trollope's *Barchester
Towers* (1857), where Mrs. Bold reflects on "that greatest of mortals, that important atom of humanity, that little god upon earth, Johnny Bold her baby" (28).
Taking on such a system in which the "Child remains the perpetual horizon of
every acknowledged politics" Edelman suggests that "*queerness* names the side of
those *not* 'fighting for the children,' the side outside the consensus by which all politics confirms the absolute value of reproductive futurism."[46] Or in Halberstam's
words, "Queer uses of time and space develop, at least in part, in opposition to the
institutions of family, heterosexuality, and reproduction."[47]

Being in opposition to reproductive futurity does not, however, necessarily
mean being in opposition to the family. More recent theorists have attempted
to queer the family itself.[48] The next chapter will explore the ways queer desire
can facilitate lateral family expansion. Here, I would like to acknowledge some
of the ways English authors have created queer versions of futurity. *Great Expectations* (1860-1861) hinges on producing heirs without biologically *reproducing*
them. Both the convict Magwitch and Miss Havisham create their chosen heirs
from non-biological kin. Dickens symbolically situates Magwitch's initial meeting
with Pip in the graveyard where Pip's deceased relations are interred. As McCrea
observes, "The first scene of the novel encapsulates the queer family system to
which Dickens has been tending: the biological family is in the grave; life and
meaning are generated by a connection with a queer outlaw."[49] Magwitch will
"generate" family by generating Pip. His bequest stipulates that Pip must retain
this nickname, not his true family name, thus in a sense giving Magwitch the

whether it is not the best thing I can do, to die" (754), indicating that it is the (believed) lack of futurity
that enabled this cross-class union.

[45] Edelman, "The Future is Kid Stuff," 19; *No Future*, 2.

[46] Edelman, *No Future*, 3.

[47] Halberstam, *In a Queer Time and Place*, 1. Similarly, Judith Butler's attack on the conservative
(homophobic) argument "what happens to the child, the child, the poor child, martyred figure of an
ostensibly selfish or dogged social progressivism?" reveals the assumption that queer is *against* the
family ("Is Kinship Always Already Heterosexual?" 21).

[48] Furneaux, *Queer Dickens*; Dau and Preston (eds.), *Queer Victorian Families*; McCrea, *In the
Company of Strangers*.

[49] McCrea, *In the Company of Strangers*, 55.

right to name his chosen offspring. When he reveals himself as Pip's anonymous benefactor, he exclaims "Yes, Pip, dear boy, I've made a gentleman on you! It's me wot has done it!" (365).

For Magwitch, this is a familial tie: "I'm your second father. You're my son—more to me nor any son" (365). The scene where he reveals himself is structured as a reworking of the classic literary trope of recognition between parent and child—featured in both *Bleak House* (1852-1853) and *Oliver Twist* (1837-1839)—reinforcing the family nature of the narrative.[50] Yet there is a twist; the relationship is not fully familial. Magwitch also speaks of Pip as property, calling himself the "owner" of "a brought-up London gentleman," and from Pip's side he does not feel fully like a son (367).

Miss Havisham has a similar relationship to her progeny. Estella calls Miss Havisham her "mother by adoption" and tells her "I am what you have made me. Take all the praise, take all the blame; take all the success, take all the failure; in short, take me" (349, 348). Miss Havisham seems almost in love with her creation: "She hung upon Estella's beauty, hung upon her words, hung upon her gestures, and sat mumbling her own trembling fingers while she looked at her, as though she were devouring the beautiful creature she had reared" (346). These polluted versions of kinship creation are based on selfish aims and pride and lack true family love. Yet when Pip has given up his dream of Estella and believes he will remain "an old bachelor" (550), he imagines doing something similar, and asks Biddy to "give [little] Pip to me, one of these days; or lend him, at all events" (550).[51] In English novels, alternative family constellations like these only spring up when there is some obstacle to the traditional model. Miss Havisham has rejected the world after being jilted by her suitor and has given up all hope of conceiving her own child. Magwitch is unaware of the existence of his biological daughter. Fleeing the law, he can only "create" his gentleman from afar.

In Eliot's *Silas Marner* (1861), fostering is validated over ties of blood, but without the element of a queer challenge. Silas has been thrown out of his community and rejected by his fiancée after being falsely accused of theft, so he begins the novel with the traditional path to family closed to him. He has given up on human relations when little Eppie wanders into his cottage after her mother froze to death, and he ends up raising her like a daughter. When her wealthy biological father, Godfrey Cass, ultimately confesses to his paternity and he and his wife attempt to take in the teenage Eppie, she rejects their offer and stays with Silas. While her stepmother believes that "a father by blood must have a claim above that of any foster-father," Eppie declares "I can't feel as I've got any father but one" (167).

---

[50] See McCrea, *In the Company of Strangers*, 59.
[51] McCrea calls him "a bachelor and a borrower, not a generator, of children" (*In the Company of Strangers*, 65). With the revised ending, this becomes less clear...

After traditional models have failed, family bonds are created through care, not bloodline. This is the model we find in the Russian novel as well.

Another group of English novels relies on disability as the impediment to heteronormative reproductivity that enables queer family formation. Clare Walker Gore has pointed to the "inextricabl[e] intertwin[ing]" of disability and gender in *John Halifax, Gentleman*: "Phineas's disability queers his gender identity, rendering him less than fully male in his own eyes and in those of other characters."[52] Indeed, as she shows, this pairing plays an important role in many Victorian novels, with disability enabling "the articulation of alternative forms of desire, and the formation of alternative families."[53] Rather than treating disability as a liability, Walker Gore reveals its enabling power, as it opens a space outside of the norm, a realm that includes alternative families.[54] It was, perhaps, easier for a Victorian readership to accept Phineas as a live-in uncle because he posed no threat to the reproductive pairing at the heart of the family, his masculinity in a sense being neutralized by his disability and all possibility of his own family futurity removed. As noted above, the same model appears in Charlotte Yonge's *Heartsease, or Brother's Wife*, with John Martindale's ill health easing him into the role of live-in uncle to his brother's children. Disability frees him from the pressure to procreate his own line and helps enable the extended family constellation he joins.

Craik's *A Noble Life* also features a disabled protagonist, this time the severely deformed and crippled last Earl of Cairnforth, who is left orphaned within days of his birth with only some very distant and morally suspect cousins, the Bruces, for kin. Given his deformity, the Earl can never marry and sire a child, and thus the title will die with him, as it is entailed.[55] This removes the possibility of reproductive futurity and, given the Earl's delicate health, it is questionable how much future he has. Yet despite all this, the Earl nevertheless manages to create a family. He has shared a "brother and sister relation" (134) with the minister's daughter, Helen Cardross (six years his senior), and chooses to make her his heir. Helen is then seduced by Captain Bruce, one of the distant cousins who discovers this choice and wishes to profit by it. Their disastrous marriage lasts only two years, leaving Helen widowed with an infant son. The narrator is assured that "Helen Bruce was left a mother only. It was easy to see that she would be one of those women who remain such—mothers and nothing but mothers, to the end of their

---

[52] Walker Gore, "The right and natural law of things," 117.

[53] Walker Gore, "'The right and natural law of things,'" 117–118.

[54] "While disabled characters are generally excluded from the marriage plot because of the authors' unwillingness to write disability into reproductive heterosexual unions, they are not necessarily excluded from the families which are formed over the course of these novels" (Walker Gore, "'The right and natural law of things,'" 117).

[55] Pointing out the prevalence of this pattern, Michael Ragussis reminds us that "family plots are drawn to the sole surviving carrier of the family name—Jack Durbeyfield in *Tess of the D'Urbervilles*, or Lovelace in *Clarissa*, or Roderick Usher in Poe's 'The Fall of the House of Usher,' or Maury Bascomb in *The Sound and the Fury*" (*Acts of Naming*, 59).

days" (132). Helen is reunited with the Earl, but the brief marriage has now technically made her his cousin by affinity, and her son the Earl's next of kin. Helen also wears a diamond ring given by the Earl as a "pledge of amity" next to her wedding ring, symbolically linking them in an a-sexual union (157).

The final third of the novel finds this pair coparenting Helen's child. Although she does not wish for her son or anyone else to know that he is the Earl's heir, the Earl repeatedly states his claims to the child, reminding Helen "The boy is my boy too" and "he is my son too...my adopted son" (159, 161). The young Cardross ultimately takes the Earl's name, becoming Alexander Cardross Bruce-Montgomerie. When he goes to study at St. Andrews, the Earl accompanies him and the pair live together, with many people there saying "that very few fathers were blessed with a son half so attentive and devoted as this young man was to the Earl of Cairnforth" (169). At Alexander's coming of age celebration at Cairnforth Castle, the Earl officially introduces him as his chosen heir: "Deliberately chosen, he added, "not merely as being my cousin and my nearest of kin, but because he is his mother's son, and Mr. Cardross's grandson, and worthy of them both—also, because, for his own sake, I respect him, and I love him" (174). The speech is an explicit celebration of intentional kinship. The crippled invalid literally produces an heir by forming the mind and character of the child born to his dearest friend who bears his ring of amity. Again in this novel, serious obstacles to the vertical family structure enable the formation of an alternative that is not based on heterosexual desire or the standard linkage of marriage and procreation, but instead on the "deliberate" choice of an heir.

In a final example, Jewsbury's action-packed *Constance Herbert*, which involves all kinds of love affairs, heartbreaks, bigamy, gambling, and bank robbery, is at the same time a tale of resilient women who find connection and meaning outside of the reproductive family. The plot is too complex and improbable to be worth recounting, but at the center is a family blighted with hereditary insanity. The primary reason the heroine's aunt, Margaret, ends up an old maid caring for Constance is because her beloved refused to legally marry her due to "an hereditary taint of insanity in your family." "[I]t was natural and praiseworthy that the Earl should, by every means, guard against its introduction, especially into what had become the chief male branch of his noble house," his cousin later explains (2:251). The primary concern is the future of the family line, which must be protected from Margaret's dangerous bloodline. Constance must similarly sacrifice the chance at matrimonial bliss because, as Margaret warns her, "I appeal to you whether you will transmit this terrible heritage, or whether you will endure your own lot alone, to prevent another being made as wretched as you are at this moment?" (that is, the moment when she meets her crazed and demented mother) (2:130).

Without the possibility of having children of their own, these women create an alternative, more inclusive family. They are ultimately joined by Sarah Wilmot, who was jilted by her fiancé and devoted herself to her nephew "like a mother," until his early suicide (2:15). "In Constance she had found a younger sister, who needed all the care and affection she could bestow, all the strength that may be given through example" (3:13). When Mr. Harrop, a suitor for Miss Wilmot, comes to stay with the three women, he "became quite domesticated amongst them. Constance declared he was just like a relation" (3:33). This constellation can expand to absorb more members. After Mr. Harrop and Miss Wilmot wed, Margaret, aware of her deteriorating health, asks the new Mrs. Harrop to "Be a mother to Constance when I am taken away" (3:55). "'I consider Constance like my own sister,' said Edward Harrop, 'and she shall never want a brother so long as I live'" (3:55). This is intentional family. Ultimately, Mrs. Harrop will bear a son and a daughter, and at the end of the novel "Constance adopted for her heir her young namesake and godchild, who was allowed to spend part of every year with her" (3:301). So she succeeds in creating a family and having an heir without marriage or procreation.

Conclusion

The vertical family axis is defined by legitimacy, by bloodline, and by sanctioned marriages that produce legal heirs. This axis is resistant to change. With powerful ancestors or pressing concerns about progeny, it is difficult for the family to break out of its traditional, linear mold. However, this conservative force can be neutralized if something other than lineage becomes the basis of family. Even as Dostoevsky was challenging the idea that siring a child made one a father, he was offering up a new definition of family based on the *acts* of kinship. As he claimed in his *Writer's Diary*, "The family is created by the untiring labor of love" (22:70).[56] And this "untiring labor" need not be carried out by people with blood or legal ties. When the vertical axis is weakened—when parents are absent or derelict in their duties, or when characters cannot reproduce—novels can create alternative forms of continuity through adoption or expansion on the lateral axis. Characters who are freed of duties to their ancestors and progeny can focus on kinship connection in the here and now, the "expansion in space" that I take up in Chapter 8.

[56] In her study of memory, Diane Oenning Thompson arrives at this point through its inverse: forgetting one's children as a form of form of neglect and "a critical index of morality" (The Brothers Karamazov *and the Poetics of Memory*, 165).

8

Alternative Family Models in Space

"You want to exchange crosses? Very well, Parfyon, if that's what you
want, I'll be glad to; we'll be brothers."

—Dostoevsky, *The Idiot*

The boundaries of family membership are not a given in the nineteenth-century
novel, but depend on context and motivations. When it is conducive to have
a broad range of connections—in business, or to demonstrate social status—
characters tend to spread the net wide, including distant cousins, in-laws, and
others who are *almost* like kin. However, when there are limited resources to be
shared—in questions of wills and inheritance—they tend to restrict the boundaries, becoming more scrupulous about questions of legitimacy and legal sanction.
These contrasting ways of delineating membership speak to the potential for
expansion or contraction of the family's borders on the lateral axis (in a given
moment in time, as opposed to across time).

The inclusiveness or restrictiveness of the family can be a generator of plot. At
the start of *War and Peace* (1865–1869), for example, the most diverse set of characters are suddenly drawn to the palace of the dying Count Bezukhov as "kin"
when a struggle commences for control of his property. All hinges on a letter
requesting the legitimation of his bastard son. When there are spoils to be divided,
characters become deeply concerned about issues of legitimacy/illegitimacy and
the precise nature of the family tree. A life's fortune can depend on a single line
in a marriage registry. The villain of Wilkie Collins' *The Woman in White* (1859–
1860) locks his wife away in an insane asylum under a false identity to hide the
secret of his illegitimacy (he forged his parents' wedding in the church registry),
which meant that he was not entitled to his wealth or title. By contrast, when nothing is at stake but familial love, characters tend to be much more willing to open
the gates of kinship and to disregard its legal sanction.

England's and Russia's laws and social structures that defined the boundaries of
the family were shaped by each nation's prevailing ideological concerns, and these
in turn shifted in the nineteenth century as the family evolved. Novels reflected the
tensions between conflicting ideas of who was "in" and "out" and how far family
should extend. On the whole, English novels more often advocate a model of family
closely bound by blood, while in Russian novels characters are more prepared to

The Family Novel in Russia and England, 1800–1880. Anna A. Berman, Oxford University Press.
© Anna A. Berman (2022). DOI: 10.1093/oso/9780192866622.003.0009

include family members assembled from disparate backgrounds. Yet this is not always the case. This chapter explores the ways novels approached lateral family expansion and what this demonstrates about both narrative form and national ideology.

Mechanisms of Expansion: To Say or Be Family

According to sociologists, being a family is more than a matter of blood or legal ties. Pierre Bourdieu highlights the "continuous creation of family feeling" needed for the family to turn "from a nominal fiction into a real group whose members are united by intense affective bonds."[1] Such *active* kinship is an essential feature of intentional family in the Russian novel, as described in the previous chapter. Dostoevsky used the term "active love" (*deiatel'naia liubov'*) to refer to the bonds needed in the family, highlighting—like sociologists—that true family is not a passive state.[2] As he explained in his *Writer's Diary*, "The family, after all, is also *created*, and not given already ready … The family is created by the untiring labor of love" (22:70/1:381). Yet even when the active quality of kinship is paramount, intentional family is often described or defined in opposition to the "real" family, reifying "real" kin. In this sense, intentional family serves as an indicator of "how people would like to see blood or legal families operate—as sites of affection and belonging, where people easily claim their rights from, and fulfill their obligations to, others."[3] When characters or narrators draw on kinship terminology to refer to non-biological or legal kin, they are invoking this ideal of family.

Family can be created through language, and in Russian novels we find a range of linguistic possibilities for making another character kin.[4] In *War and Peace*, although Pierre Bezukhov has no blood or legal tie to his best friend Andrei Bolkonsky, when he arrives at Andrei's home before his host he goes straight to the study and lies down on the couch "like a member of the household" [*kak domashnii chelovek*]. When Andrei's wife speaks in a flirtatious manner, the narrator comments that her tone "was so obviously unsuited to the family circle, where Pierre was like a member" (9:32/26). Hundreds of pages later, when Pierre visits Bald Hills, Andrei's sister Marya tells him "I've known you a long time and love you like a brother" (10:122/393). All these comments establish a familial bond. Many Russian characters claim siblinghood with non-bio-legal kin. The terms "brother"

[1] Bourdieu, Pierre. "On the Family as Realized Category," 22.

[2] In *The Brothers Karamazov* (1880), Zosima explains to Mme Khokhlakova that "active love is labor and perseverance, and for some people, perhaps, a whole science" (14:54/58).

[3] Nelson, "Fictive Kin, Families We Choose, and Voluntary Kin," 277–278.

[4] Examining the way "families are created via discourse," Dawn O. Braithwaite et al. claim intentional family constructions "bear a heavier legitimation burden" than those built on blood or law, and thus the act of their being "literally talked into being" takes on greater weight (Braithwaite et al., "Constructing family: A typology of voluntary kin," 392).

and "sister" fly fast and free in Dostoevsky's *The Insulted and Injured* (1861), where a whole series of characters—Natasha, Alyosha, Katya, and the narrator Vanya—all try variously to bind themselves in siblinghood. In *The Brothers Karamazov* (1880), when Grushenka treats Alyosha with compassion after Zosima's death, he tells her "I found a true sister, I found a treasure—a loving soul ..." (14:318). In Russian novels, such instances are too numerous to count.

Russian, like other Slavic languages, also has the opposition of *svoi* (one's own, native) and *chuzhoi* (other, alien) that can be applied to people to make them intimates or strangers. For example, when Levin becomes engaged to Kitty in *Anna Karenina* (1875–1878) and finds himself participating in private family discussions, the narrator notes that he is now *svoi*. And after Dolly discovers her husband's infidelity and believes they are permanently ruptured, she repeatedly calls him *chuzhoi*. Or in Goncharov's *The Precipice* (1869), when Raisky invites his friend Leonty to stay with him after Leonty has been deserted by his wife, Leonty initially resists, concerned "That I would be such a monster to bring my grief to someone else's house [*po chuzhim uglam*]!" Raisky replies to this "This isn't someone else's house, Leonty: we are brothers. Our kinship [*rodstvo*] is stronger than the kinship of blood [*rodstva krovi*] ..." (7:563).

I note all these examples to illustrate their ubiquity and because they fit with a broader pattern in Russian culture of linguistically making others kin. As noted in the Introduction, George Fedotov famously claimed "In this procedure all social life is shaped as an extension of family life and all moral relations among men are raised to the level of blood kinship. This is of tremendous importance in understanding Russian social ethics."[5] As will be explored below, this hints at the expansive nature of Russian kinship bonds and a more unbounded conception of the family, a point also reflected in the wide range of kin covered by incest laws.[6] The Russians were not as concerned with patrolling the boundaries of the family, and were more willing and eager to welcome in others as *literally* part of the family.

In the English novel, such extensive use of kinship language is a much rarer occurrence. Scholars like Barry McCrea have approached certain groupings of strangers brought together through contingency in Dickens' novels as "alternative families": Fagin and his gang in *Oliver Twist* (1837–1839), or the "ersatz-family" grouping above Krook's rag-and-bottle shop in *Bleak House* (1852–1853).[7] Yet even McCrea does not seem convinced that these alternatives are truly families,

---

[5] Fedotov, *The Russian Religious Mind: Kievan Christianity*, 16. See also Tovrov, *The Russian Noble Family*, 72.

[6] See the discussion of incest in Chapter 1, pp. 29–31.

[7] McCrea, *In the Company of Strangers*, 52, 53. James Kilroy makes a similar observation about Mr. Sleary's circus troupe in *Hard Times*, calling it "a model, if only a surrogate, family unit" (*The Nineteenth-Century Novel*, 84). Catherine Waters also refers to "Fagin's family," claiming "Fagin's den offers perhaps the most notable parody of the middle-class family in the novel" (*Dickens and the Politics of the Family*, 34).

also referring to these "extemporized affiliations that spring up around the London of [*Bleak House*]" as "antifamilies that grow like dustballs in the corners of the metropolis and its institutions."[8] While McCrea equivocates between calling one and the same grouping family and antifamily, Dickens himself never refers to these communities with familial terminology. When the term "brotherhood" appears in Dickens' novels, its use is often negative and ironic, referring to a corrupted institutional version of the ideal. The metaphor of the human family is ironically negated in *Nicholas Nickleby* (1838–1839) when the narrator reflects on the "grisly family" in a wretched London burial-ground: "all those dear departed brothers and sisters of the ruddy clergyman who did his task so speedily when they were hidden in the ground!" (750). Similarly, in *Hard Times* (1854), Slackbridge's call for "brotherhood" among the workers is really a rejection of brotherly love, as he pushes the honorable Steven Blackpool out of the fold. And in *A Tale of Two Cities* (1859), "fraternity" appears repeatedly in the French revolutionary slogan where it is defiled by blood. "Fraternal embraces" are those of murderers on a break from killing their "brothers." In the same novel, Darnay and Carton may *act* in many ways like brothers, but Dickens never uses the term "brother" to describe them, even when suggesting their physical resemblance.

Eliot, too, shies away from using kinship terminology when she writes of the connection between strangers. Where a Russian author would likely have seen "brotherhood," she sees "fellow feeling." Thus, for example, in *The Mill on the Floss* (1860) when the Tulliver children arrive at their first great period of trial and the school master's wife reaches out with kindness:

> Maggie's heart went out toward this woman whom she had never liked, and she kissed her silently. It was the first sign within the poor child of that new sense which is the gift of sorrow,—that susceptibility to the bare offices of humanity which raises them into a bond of loving fellowship, as to haggard men among the ice-bergs the mere presence of an ordinary comrade stirs the deep fountains of affection. (214)

Maggie is made aware of fellowship, but not of a human *family*.

Some English novels arrive at family-like relations through religion, but they tend to remain only metaphoric. For example, in Harriet Martineau's *Deerbrook* (1839), the devoted nurse and servant, Morris, wishing to help one of the suffering sisters in her charge, offers up a wordless prayer, which the narrator tells us would have been: "Thou hast been pleased to take to thyself the parents of these dear children; and surely thou wilt be therefore pleased to be to them as father and mother, or to raise up or spare to them such as may be so. This is what I would ask for myself, that I may be that comfort to them" (228). Even while wishing for such

---

[8] McCrea, *In the Company of Strangers*, 53.

a parental role, Morris never considers herself an actual relation, nor expects or desires the Ibbotson sisters to see her in this way. To cross such class divides—as we will see in the endings of Turgenev's *Fathers and Children* (1862) and Dostoevky's *The Adolescent* (1875)—certain conditions were needed that were more easily met in Russia than in England.

The Contracting English Ideal

From the eighteenth to the nineteenth century, there was a shift in English conceptions of the family from one emphasizing an expansive kinship network of blood relations (including uncles, aunts, and cousins) to one valorizing a nuclear core formed by a married couple and their offspring,[9] This self-contained nuclear family group would be connected to the larger family and outside society "only on the basis of economic self-interest and voluntary consent."[10] There is clear historical evidence of the new, bounded conception of family. Common law, for example, only required a man to support his wife and minor children, not other kin.[11] In linguistic norms, by the mid-nineteenth century "sister" and "brother" had ceased to be used as "umbrella terms for a range of female or male relatives, referring not only to the blood relationships of the birth family."[12] And as terms for parents and siblings became restricted to flesh and blood relations, children started calling parents "daddy" and "mommy" instead of Sir/Madame, as they did with other adults. All these things helped create the idea of a separate, special world for the family. As the Registrar General commented in the 1851 census, "the possession of an entire house is, it is true, strongly desired by every Englishman; for it throws a sharp, well-defined circle round his family and hearth—the shrine of his sorrows, joys, and meditations."[13] People wished for families to be discrete units sharing their own micro-culture.

This wish for family closure did not map comfortably onto real families. Even as family discourse shifted from the eighteenth to the nineteenth century, one family model did not immediately or completely replace the other. Indeed, the fantasy of the "walled off private haven" was *not* the reality for most Victorian families, as in 1851 only 36% of households had married parents, children, and no one

---

[9] Ruth Perry calls this a shift from "an axis of kinship based on consanguineal ties or blood lineage to an axis based on conjugal and affinal ties of the married couple" (*Novel Relations*, 2). For a concise overview of scholarship on the rise of the nuclear family in Europe, see Cohen, *Daughter's Dilemma*, 9–10.

[10] Mintz, *A Prison of Expectations*, 14.

[11] Behlmer, *Friends of the Family*, 26.

[12] Corbett, *Family Likeness*, 39. In addition to noting the linguistic patterns, Mintz also points to sociological trends like the increased time adolescents spent living in their parents' homes and the decline in households taking in apprentices, trade assistants, and clerks (*A Prison of Expectations*, 14–16).

[13] Qtd. in Chase and Levenson, *Spectacles of Intimacy*, 4. Source: *Census of Great Britain, 1851*, xxxvi.

else (the definition of the "natural family" given in the 1871 census).[14] Moreover, even as the ideal of the nuclear family—wise and benevolent father; tender, loving mother; and devoted and obedient children—was gaining strength, historical forces were putting strains on this very ideal. According to John Gillis, the Industrial Revolution increased "the importance of families of strangers and kin."[15] Gillis emphasizes economic factors that made kinship networks desirable. Banking and the stock market were still in a poor stage of development, so capital came from either inheritance, loans from kin, or marriages (and kinship networks enhanced marital prospects). In addition, both business and farming relied on cooperation amongst households for their success. Thus, extended kin had a large role to play in the economic well-being of the nuclear family.

Beyond these extended families, many people in England participated in wider forms of kinship organized around religious or social organizations. Spiritual family (Godparents/children) tended to overlap with biological or legal kin, and there was also a tendency to intermarry with members of the same faith group. Women joined mutual aid societies and mothers' unions. Many of these societies used sibling terminology, fostering a spirit of "brotherhood" or "sisterhood" among their members. So amidst the idealization of an enclosed, restricted model, family was at the same time expanding through metaphorical language and actual bonds of practical support amongst extended kin groups. There is a clear tension between the two trends just described: seeking families of strangers as the strains on the nuclear family became too great, yet still touting the increased separateness and boundedness of the Victorian family.

As would be expected, these (sometimes opposing) shifts in family structure and ideology are reflected in English novels. The novels in my study provide a testament to the continued importance of consanguineal networks of kin—especially siblings or aunts and uncles—that harkens back to the older model, but in their resolutions and the families that mark narrative closure, they tended to reflect the ideal of boundedness more than the messier reality.[16] Many English novels rely on siblings (or aunts and uncles, i.e. parents' siblings) during some phase of their heroes' marriage plot, but then these relations are left out of the final unity. For example, in Trollope's *He Knew He Was Right* (1869), Nora begins living with her elder, married sister, Emily Trevelyan, but ends in her own conjugal pair. When Emily's marriage begins to collapse, the sisters are taken in by an uncle and aunt, and it becomes the uncle's role to defend Emily and her child from her angry husband. Meanwhile, in another of the novel's multiple plots, the childless Miss

---

[14] Behlmer, *Friends of the Family*, 26.

[15] Gillis, *A World of Their Own Making: Myth, Ritual and the Quest for Family Values*, 64.

[16] Novels' reliance on avuncular bonds reflected historical realities. "Among the new middle classes, the circulation of children actually accelerated with aunts and uncles acting as surrogate parents and older siblings bringing up younger ones" (Gillis, *A World of Their Own Making: Myth, Ritual and the Quest for Family Values*, 64).

Stanbury chooses her nephew, Hugh, as her heir, then falls out with him, disinherits Hugh, and invites his sister, Dorothy to live with her. While Miss Stanbury is central to their family constellation for a time, Hugh and Dorothy ultimately form separate conjugal families at the novel's conclusion.

This coexistence in the nineteenth century of both a consanguineal kinship network and a bounded conjugal ideal reflects the tension between two models for marriage. Talia Schaffer describes an earlier "familiar marriage model" that creates a porous home "accommodating passage and space for extended family, servants, apprentices, poor relations, visitors, customers, parishioners" in competition with the new romantic marriage model glorified by traditional studies of the novel, one "stressing the specialness of the home, the sacredness of the nuclear family."[17] The chronotope of the new marriage model is thus "one of intense contraction."[18] Linking familial and narrative form, Paula Cohen makes an analogous point, arguing that the "ideology of closure ... was a driving force in the development and elaboration of the form in which families and novels defined themselves."[19] If we look at how nineteenth-century English novels resolve their family plots, the dominant tradition is definitely one of bounded family.

The moments when characters reach beyond their immediate family are highlighted by the very shock they elicit within the novels. When Colonel Brandon decides to help the disinherited Edward Ferrars at the end of *Sense and Sensibility* (1811), Edward himself asks "Can it be possible?" and John Dashwood lays bare the root of the shock when he exclaims "Really!—Well, this is very astonishing!—no relationship!—no connection between them!"[20] In an English novel, it is not done to treat someone with "no connection" (meaning consanguineal or affinal) as kin, even though in this case the two men are shortly to become brothers-in-law. As Schaffer interprets this act, it is "a sign of the future: a world where affiliations are voluntary rather than kinship based, where relations with strangers can be fruitful, where one is judged on the moral merits of one's acts instead of the inherited status of one's birth, and where good men want work rather than inherited wealth" (though the fact that the two are soon to marry a pair of sisters mitigates this claim).[21]

[17] Schaffer, *Romance's Rival*, 82, 86. I think she may go too far when she points to Georgiana Darcy and Kitty Bennet living with their married sisters as evidence that *Pride and Prejudice* does not close with closed nuclear family structures (103). Both those sisters are young and marriageable and there is every expectation that they will soon enough enter wedlock themselves, and Jane and Bingley quickly leave Netherfield because "So near a vicinity to her mother and Meryton relations was not desirable even to *his* easy temper, or *her* affectionate heart" (385).

[18] Schaffer, *Romance's Rival*, 86.

[19] Cohen, *The Daughter's Dilemma*, 4.

[20] Qtd. and discussed in Schaffer, *Romance's Rival*, 102.

[21] Schaffer, *Romance's Rival*, 102–103.

Russia's Expansive Model

Schaffer's description sounds uncannily like the nineteenth-century Russian novel. In contrast to the English ideal of every man in his castle with the family haven walled off from the rest of the world, the Russians treated family as a more porous and expansive construct (closer to the eighteenth-century English model). As Barbara Alpern Engel claims, "What is often perceived as the private domain of the family was not particularly private in Russia."[22] One could add that the Russian language lacks a word for privacy. The "expansive" Russian noble family could include numerous impoverished relatives or neighbors, wards, tutors and governesses, a family physician, and servants.[23] Tolstoy's novels tend to close with these expansive visions of family life: the Rostovs staying with the Bezukhovs, and their dear friend Denisov visiting at the close of *War and Peace*, or the Oblonskys with the Levins at the end of *Anna Karenina*. An extended Kirsanov clan sits down to the final dinner in Turgenev's *Fathers and Children*.

On the other end of the political spectrum, Chernyshevsky closes *What Is to Be Done?* (1863) with a radical re-envisioning of the family that also demonstrates expansion. After Lopukhov fakes his own death to free Vera Pavolvna from her marriage to him, she marries his friend Kirsanov. Lopukhov then returns to Russia as "the Englishman Beaumont" and marries Katya, and this bigamous Kirsanov/Beaumont quartet sets up their domestic life in connected apartments. "They see one another as kin do (*vidiatsia kak rodnye*): ten times some days, but each time only for a minute or two, on other days, for almost the whole day one half [of the connected apartments] is empty, as its inhabitants are in the other half" (458). The comfortable accommodation of bigamy shows a disregard for legal sanction that would be unthinkable in an English novel. But in the Russian context, what matters is this alternative family's happy and productive relations in the present.

The shape of the Russian family was concordant with the more communal outlook Russians considered to be a national trait. While I am certainly not suggesting Dostoevsky was correct, he voiced what many *wished* to believe when he claimed in his *Writer's Diary* (1877) "all of us in Russia, despite our many discordant voices, still agree and come to this single, definitive, common idea of the unity of all humanity" (25:20/2:830). In proof of this type of claim, intellectuals pointed to the peasant commune. The *mir* or *obshchina* was a group of village-based peasants who regulated the use of communal land, redistributing periodically based

---

[22] Engel, *Women in Russia, 1700–2000*, 37.

[23] In almost none of the novels in my study do characters refer to servants using kinship terms, but there are exceptions. The heroine of Krestovsky (pseudonym)'s *Ursa Major* (set in 1854) has a close relationship with her maid and reflects "But is Masha really a maid? She's a sister" (411).

on household size.[24] The Slavophile Aleksei Khomiakov (1804–1860) started the process of giving the term *obshchina* a revised meaning of community and religious brotherhood, and Ivan Kireevsky (1806–1856) added to his ideas.[25] They opposed this pure, communal Russian outlook to polluted western ideas of individualism.

Slavophile thinkers also used Russian Orthodoxy as evidence of a uniquely Russian communal spirit. They claimed that *sobornost'* (from the word *sobor*, meaning congregation) was the central feature of the Church. Khomiakov defined *sobornost'* as "a free, organic unity, the living source of which is the divine grace of mutual love."[26] As Vasily Zenkovsky explains, "*Sobornost* was substantially a *new* notion and for the Russian conscience it spelled the idea of the Church's *unity in grace*, with the emphasis on the grace. In other words, the congregation is united in the Church through the very essence of the Church, where all the faithful are one in Christ, and not merely united by formal, outer bonds."[27] As with *obshchina*, the term is largely a mid-nineteenth century Slavophile creation, but its lack of "authenticity" in no way diminished its force in shaping national identity.

The ideal of *sobornost'* penetrated the thought of Russia's great authors, who often used it to contrast Russia with the individualist West. Dostoevsky's characters who have absorbed European ideas struggle against these isolationist tendencies (for example, Raskolnikov and his Napoleon idea, Arkady's dream of becoming a Rothschild, or Kirillov and Stavrogin's self-will) that take them away from "the heritage of instinctive *sobornost'*."[28] Dostoevsky's contemporary readers certainly sensed this ideal of *sobornost'* in his works. One claimed that Dostoevsky "magically and sweetly expanded our hearts and thoughts [... and] penetrated our souls with loving pity, with compassion for all who suffer, so that we begin to feel cramped in our families, and all who are sick, downtrodden and humiliated became to us close and kin-like (*rodstvenno*), like our own (*svoe*)!"[29] This comment also links *sobornost'* to the family, suggesting that the expansive unity Russians felt was coded as kinship. In authors like Dostoevsky, the Orthodox underpinnings of their novelistic worlds are quite explicit, but Ivan Esaulov has

[24] For a thorough examination of the differences between these two terms (which have often been used interchangeably), see Grant, "Obshchina and Mir." Grant also traces the origins of this communal landholding and distribution.
[25] Khomiakov first used the term *obshchina* in an 1838 speech. See Grant, "Obshchina and Mir," 644.
[26] Qtd. in Esaulov, "*Sobornost'* in Nineteenth-Century Russian Literature," 29. The term, deriving from a philological mistake in translating the Greek word *katholiki*, does not exist in other Orthodox countries, which allowed Slavophile thinkers like Khomiakov to make it into a uniquely Russian trait. See Zenkovsky, "The Spirit of Russian Orthodoxy," 44.
[27] Zenkovsky, "The Spirit of Russian Orthodoxy," 44.
[28] Hudspith, *Dostoevsky and the Idea of Russianness*, 104. See also Morson, "Introductory Study: Dostoevsky's Great Experiment," 14.
[29] Timofeeva, "God raboty s znamenitym pisatelem," 2:127. I am grateful to Greta Matzner-Gore for sharing this passage with me.

argued that all Russian authors were influenced by the Orthodox project, even if unconsciously.[30]

It is worth noting that Dostoevsky offered a pointed attack on the English and their inability to enter into a spiritual unity and brotherhood as the Russians could: "look at almost any Englishman of the higher or lower variety—lord or laborer, scholar or uneducated—and you will be convinced that every Englishman tries above all to be an Englishman, to preserve his Englishness in all aspects of his life, private and public, political and cosmopolitan, and even tries to love humanity in no other manner than an English one" (25:18/2:827). Love of humanity "in an English manner" feels like a parody, placing English snobbery above universal brotherhood. I certainly do not mean to suggest, along with Dostoevsky, that Russians, *and only the Russians*, were all capable of selfless love of humanity. However, I do believe that the expansive, communal spirit of inclusion many Russian authors *believed* was inherent to Russian national character helped enable them to conceive of plots where family expanded on the lateral axis (regardless of official sanction) and alternative forms of family could thrive.

Russia's Intentional Families

Thus far I have been discussing the conditions that enable intentional family and the reasons for its frequency in Russian novels. To ground the discussion, I will now analyze how intentional family functions, using Evgenia Tur's *The Niece* (1851) as an exemplar of classic Russian patterns. Like Herzen's *Who Is to Blame?* (1845–1846) and many other novels of the period, it includes extensive family backgrounds for the characters. It thus opens with the generation of the heroine Masha's grandparents, detailing their marriage and then the fates of their two children: Masha's father Alexander, who marries for love and then squanders his fortune, and her aunt Varvara, who is left to raise Masha after her parents die. Left isolated on a country estate with a loving grandmother and a tyrannical and hostile aunt, the lonely child faces constant verbal attacks. Varvara portrays marriage as Masha's only way out from under her authority.

Not finding affection from her blood kin (and legal guardian), Masha is hungry for loving, family bonds, and creates these with intentional kin. The first—and most important—is her tutor, Nikolai Ilmenev, whom she calls "my brother and my friend, forever" (1:56). On meeting Ilmenev's tender-hearted mother, Masha tells her "I love your son, like my own [*rodnogo*] brother" (91). Even Varvara Petrovna invokes a familial relationship with Ilmenev, telling him "you lived in my home for five years not like a teacher, but like a member of my family" [*chlen sem'i moei*] (1:267). Readers may well expect this will become a version of what

---

[30] Esaulov, "*Sobornost'* in Nineteenth-Century Russian Literature," 35.

Irina Paperno calls "the tutor-scheme," where the tutor marries the daughter of the house, and when Masha's distant cousin Prince Chelsky arrives at his neighboring estate, he makes this assumption.[31] But his friend Pletneev—who had gone to school with Ilmenev—disagrees: "Can't one love a woman—especially one whom one has known as a child and raised—like a sister, like a friend, like a daughter?" (1:143). The Prince (wrongly) says no, and starts calling the couple Abelard and Heloise, revealing his failure to understand family love.

Masha will bring more people into her chosen family circle. Her initial intimacy with Prince Chelsky is based on their distant cousinship, but Masha also comes to look on Pletneev as a relation. After Masha's grandmother dies, she prepares to move to Moscow under the care of an aunt on her mother's side. Returning home the day before her departure, Masha sees through the window a "picture of peaceful family and its daily life" [kartinu mirnoi sem'i i ee byta] that is composed of Ilmenev's mother pouring tea, her aunt (who softened to her before the departure), and Pletneev—a perfect vignette of intentional family (1:350).[32]

When Varvara leaves Masha in Moscow, she bids Masha's new guardian to love her, and this second aunt promises "My niece will be for me a fourth daughter," a formulation that leaves out the word "love" (2:4). And indeed love is in short supply in this Moscow household. After the freedom of country life, Masha finds herself stifled by her aunt's rules of respectability and decorum, which make her a virtual prisoner. From her near-captivity, Masha writes to her beloved tutor, Ilmenev, calling him "my only friend, my tenderly loving brother, bound to me not by bonds of blood, but just as strong triple bonds of friendship, fellow feeling [simpatami] and past life. Is it necessary to say that in my opinion these are stronger?" (2:38). It is hard to imagine a more forceful glorification of chosen kinship ties.

While Ilmenev is powerless to help Masha, her one escape lies through marriage, and she knows little enough of the world or men to realize that she is making a false step in accepting a proposal from her cousin, Prince Chelsky. In her Moscow life, Masha has become like all the heroines we saw in Chapter 5, whose courtships happen at balls and in drawing rooms where artifice reigns. The faithful Ilmenev continues to look out for Masha, telling Chelsky that his new fiancée is a "sister" to him, but he cannot alter the Prince's character (2:237). In her joy after the engagement, Masha looks around at a lunch with friends and "saw around her a whole family of friends" [tseluiu sem'iu druzei] (2:267, my emphasis). Family for her is an expansive concept that exists where love is.

Six years later, as Masha's husband philanders with her cousin Mary and treats Masha with increasing coldness and disdain, she comes to appreciate even more deeply the importance of her chosen kin. Sensing that Prince Chelsky did not

[31] Paperno discusses the tutor scheme in *Chernyshevsky and the Age of Realism* (1988).
[32] The narrator describes the parting embrace of Ilmenev and Masha "like brother and sister" (1:356).

appreciate his presence, Ilmenev had distanced himself from Masha, but when he learns that her cousin Mary is spreading rumors that Masha is the one having an affair, he intervenes, reaching out to the Prince's curmudgeonly uncle, Ochinin. Ochinin is initially reluctant to do anything, telling Ilmenev "Father [*batushka*], it seems that in our time, kin [*rodnye*] are superfluous, and if she has no friends, she herself is to blame" (4:101). But Ochinin ultimately takes an interest in Masha and comes to treat her tenderly, like a parent.

It is in this third experience of being a niece—this time to a non-blood relation—that Masha finds true sympathy and love. When Masha's young son, Lev, becomes sick, it is Ilmenev who brings a doctor and saves the child's life. After a fight with her husband (who has run up huge debts), Masha falls dangerously ill and Ilmenev and his mother sell their house to get money for Masha. She tells him that if she dies, she leaves her son to him and Ochinin, not to her husband, which indicates where her true sense of family lies. Upon discovering that Ilmenev has given up all his savings for her, she begs forgiveness, but his mother answers "wouldn't I have paid the debt for my daughter, and he for his sister, if God had given us a daughter and sister? But he sent us one in you" (4:255). Ultimately, Masha survives, her uncle Ochinin frees her from Prince Chelsky by threatening to disinherit him, and Ochinin takes Masha and her son off to live in Crimea with him, with the understanding that Ilmenev and his mother will accompany them. Mary's husband discovers her affair and kills Chelsky in a duel at five paces. So the "family" left standing at the end of the novel is the intentional one Masha created with her son, non-blood uncle, and close friends she considers to be kin.

The Niece illustrates how the absence or failure of blood or legal relations enables intentional kin to take primacy. For if Masha's parents had not died, we have every reason to believe she would have remained happily with them and *not* forged such expansive "family circles" with chosen kin. Her orphaned status enabled her alternative family to thrive. Sofia Khvoshchinskaya's novella, "Acquaintances" (1857) also demonstrates chosen kin filling a void left by the absence of blood or legal relations. When the childless protagonist inherits a fortune, he asks a friend to take his wealth and make him a member of his family: "Take what I have, for your children; take me to live with you, like a son takes his own father, or come to live with me, like a son to his father, totally, with your children, so that we were all one, soul to soul ..."[33] It is the absence of family that enables the creation of new family. Goncharov, too, highlights the possibility of new kinship bonds forming in a void. In *The Precipice*, when the protagonist, Raisky, moves to his rural estate which is being overseen by his grandmother, the narrator comments "For the orphan, it was as if a family suddenly appeared: mother and sisters, and in Tit Nikonych, the ideal of a kind

---

[33] Sof'ia Khvoshchinskaia. "Znakomye liudi" *Otechestvennye zapiski* № 4 (1857), 125–173 (here 168).

uncle" (7:71). His grandmother and cousins are assigned closer biological roles in this assessment, and the non-blood Tit Nikonych becomes close kin. Notably, Goncharov highlights Raisky's orphaned status in making this claim.

Dmitri Begichev suggests that such intentional kin may actually be *better* than blood kin in *The Kholmsky Family* (1832). When the heroine, Sofia, and her husband arrive for a visit at Pronskaya's home, the narrator notes that

> Pronskaya respected and loved her, like a true (*rodnuiu*) mother, and she always said that she didn't know if she could have loved her own children as strongly as she loved Sofia, because if she had had a daughter, then she would have had at least some kind of anxiety and unpleasantness, either in her grown years or during her upbringing. But from Sofia, in her whole life, she had felt nothing but comfort and joy. She called her her *spiritual* daughter, and kissed her with tears in her eyes. (145–146)

This suggests that spiritual kinship can thrive even more deeply when other quotidian concerns are removed.

Intentional family need not be predicated on a lack, but can also coexist with natural family. In *The Idiot* (1869)—written before Dostoevsky's stated interest in "accidental family"—Lebedev and General Ivolgin both have biological families, and yet they also form a new kinship bond. When Lebedev tells Prince Myshkin that General Ivolgin wants to come live with him, he explains "In the first place, he wants to come and live in my house; that would be all right, sir, but he's too excitable, he wants to be one of the family right away. He and I have worked out the genealogy several times now, it turns out that we're related. You also turn out to be a distant nephew of his on your mother's side, he explained to me yesterday" (8:198/278–279).[34] Lebedev soon makes it clear that he is aware that all these supposed kinship links are pure fiction. Myshkin is surprised to hear about all the lies and asks "But you and he seem to be on very good terms?" to which Lebedev replies "On brotherly terms, and I take it all as a joke; so we're relations: what's it to me—the honour is all the greater" (8:198/279). Lebedev is a trickster who often speaks ironically, and he has a penchant for collecting noble "acquaintances," which might make this statement seem insincere. But it echoes the sentiments of one of the deepest spiritual moments in the novel: Rogozhin and Myshkin's exchange of crosses and choice to become brothers (the epigraph to this chapter). The conscious decision to create family ties permeates all levels of the novel— from comic to poignant, from the central figures to the minor characters in their shadows. Lebedev is voicing a central tenet of the novel when he claims the lack

---

[34] This example tends to be overlooked by scholars, who treat the accidental family as an invention of Dostoevsky's 1870s novels. Nedzvetskii is an exception in referring to the Ivolgins as an "accidental family" (*Istoriia russkogo romana XIX veka*, 48).

of actual blood *rodstvo* (consanguinity/relatedness) does not in any way diminish "kinship"; intentional creation of kin bestows greater honor *because* it is chosen.

In a final and less well-known example, Natalia Shalikova's *Two Sisters* (1858), intentional family supplants blood kin. The novel is structured around the fates of two half-sisters: the morally strong, soulful heroine Olga and her younger, more materialistic sister Elena. While the sisters never cease to love each other, their choices and styles of living are radically opposed, with Elena marrying for money and going off to live an empty life in St. Petersburg high society while Olga struggles to support herself as an artist and to maintain her independence and her ideals. At the end of the novel, Olga ultimately marries a man who shares her values, Aleksei Grigorevich Alimov, but the final family unity she creates is not centered on them as an isolated pair. Before agreeing to marry him, Olga has already asked her young ward, Nadia, if she would like to live with Aleksei Grigorevich and his mother, making the decision to wed a familial one. Even the scene of their engagement includes their close friend, Dr. Strelsky, who helped bring the pair together. And as soon as Olga has accepted Alimov, they quickly call in Nadia and then hurry to Alimov's mother, who is deeply devoted to Olga. By the end of the day, Alimov's cousin and her family (who helped him with his courtship), have also arrived and the narrator rejoices "What a pleasant evening they all passed in this happy family!" (2:321). Olga is visited after her marriage by her sister, Elena, and her husband, and although "Elena contended that she had never been as happy as among ... all the acquaintances and relatives of the Alimovs," she ultimately chooses to return to St. Petersburg and her empty life (2:331). So the blood sister is not part of the final intentional family.

While all the examples I have given highlight the positive nature of intentional family, conservatives saw the loosening it allowed as a potential path to the destruction of the family. Tolstoy takes up this theme in a humorous passage in *Anna Karenina* when Stiva Oblonsky compares the values system of Moscow—of which Tolstoy approved—with that of dissolute St. Petersburg. In Moscow, Stiva reaches the point "of worrying about his wife's bad moods and reproaches, his children's health and education, the petty concerns of his service"—all valid and worthy concerns for Tolstoy. Whereas, in St. Petersburg:

> immediately all these thoughts vanished and melted away like wax before the face of fire. Wife? ... Only that day he had been talking with Prince Chechensky. Prince Chechensky had a wife and family—grown-up boys serving as pages—and there was another illegitimate family, in which there were also children. Though the first family was good as well, Prince Chechensky felt happier in the second family. (19:306–307/728–729)

Tolstoy was not alone in seeing the way a more liberal conception of family could be abused toward selfish and immoral ends.

England's Queer Intentional Families

Russian characters create intentional family because the traditional model of marriage and parenthood has failed them. Since the Russian novel did not hold marriage sacrosanct and did not typically portray wedlock and procreation as a path to happy family, expanding the circle was often a way of making up for deficiencies. By contrast, the English novel had a thriving normative model of marriage and procreation, so characters almost always turned to an alternative model only when there was some reason that the traditional nuclear model would not work. One of the most common reasons was the presence of forms of desire that could not be contained by heterosexual wedlock. Given this dominant impetus for creating alternative family, I believe scholars like Holly Furneaux and Barry McCrea have been right to approach the resulting kinship constructions through the lens of queer theory.

Before discussing these queer English families, let me note why I do not think queer theory is the most appropriate theoretical framework for analyzing the Russian novels I have been discussing. Furneaux's "other forms of intimacy, affinity, and family formation" than marriage and procreation and McCrea's family plots that do not "blindly or naïvely insist upon a primacy of the biological family as the guarantor of structure and meaning in the world" might at first sound like they are good descriptors of my Russian examples.[35] But there is more at stake in labeling the family queer. I would reply to Judith Butler's famous question "Is Kinship Always Already Heterosexual?" by asking in reverse, is non-nuclear family always already queer?[36] Butler's question is based on the assumption that sexual desire is an essential basis for the family. As we saw in *The Niece*, however, family could be a non-blood uncle, mother and child, former tutor and his mother—a grouping that includes no sexual relationships. And they are not absent because the characters have rejected sexuality or found that their desires did not fit within accepted norms; erotic love is simply not what they are seeking.

There is no general agreement about how broadly queerness can extend, but I am leery of making it so general as to be synonymous with "different."[37] In order for queer to remain a meaningful category, I believe it must in some way pertain

---

[35] Furneaux, *Queer Dickens*, 10; McCrea, *In the Company of Strangers*, 7, 8.

[36] Butler, "Is Kinship Always Already Heterosexual?"

[37] This issue is addressed in the Introduction to *Queer Victorian Families*. At the extreme, the editors, Duc Dau and Shale Preston, quote David M. Halprin, who claims "Queer is by definition whatever is at odds with the normal, the legitimate, the dominant. *There is nothing in particular to which it necessarily refers*" (*Queer Victorian Families*, 7). Dau and Preston claim to treat the word as the Victorians themselves did, "to denote something unusual or strange" (7). While they "can appreciate understandings of queer that are tied, if only loosely, to sexuality," Dau and Preston "wish to expand on this" (*Queer Victorian Families*, 7). Yet they follow their discussion of the openness of the term with the disclaimer "Needless to say, of course, there is still a strong emphasis in *Queer Victorian Families* on families structured around same-sex relationships and/or gender non-conformity" (8). See also Freccero, "Queer Times," 489.

to the realm of sex, sexuality, or gender. And while these issues may certainly be present, they are not the central ones being raised or challenged in Russian novels that turn away from reproductive futurity and offer up lateral kinship expansion in the present as an alternative. The choice of the queer label also raises the issue of cultural hegemony. If "queerness" is always defined in opposition to a norm, who gets to define what the norm is?[38] Part II explored how *rare* it is for a Russian novel to have a "successful" marriage plot that culminates in the creation of family. So I would be uncomfortable labeling all the unwed Russian heroes and heroines, the "fictitious marriages" that saved women from patriarchal tyranny, the intentional families that formed around compassionate, loving bonds that do not involve wedlock, as "queer." The English novel, by contrast, does have a clear norm of heterosexual reproduction. So when characters do not fit into the mold of marrying and producing children, it is often because their desires do not align with this model.

Queer family is clearly exemplified in Dinah Mulock Craik's extremely popular *John Halifax, Gentleman* (1856), where the eponymous hero enjoys an ideal marriage yet shares an equally strong bond with his best friend and chosen brother. When the invalid Phineas meets the poor orphaned John as a child, the two boys become instantly attached, and Phineas describes John helping him "as if he had been a big elder brother, and I a little ailing child" (29). Phineas' father takes John into his tanning business and ultimately makes John his successor, since Phineas is too weak ever to take on that role. When Abel Fletcher announces that he will make John a partner and the heir to the business, he looks at his son and cautions John to "remember, thee has in some measure taken that lad's place. May God deal with thee as thou dealst with my son Phineas—my only son!" (117). John's new role cements his position as an "elder brother" who must look after Phineas. After John has married and Phineas' father has died, he and his wife take Phineas to live with them. John's wife Ursula March becomes a "sister" to Phineas.[39] After years of cohabitation, Phineas notes that "They invariably called me their brother now; and it seemed as if the name had been mine by right of blood always" (324). Their children call him "Uncle Phineas." The marriage of John and Ursula is the definition of domestic bliss—"a full and perfect whole"—yet there is still room for them to welcome their chosen "brother" who becomes an uncle to their children (262). Furneaux calls the novel "a celebration of the expandability of family beyond relations of marriage and biology."[40]

---

[38] Here I am thinking of David Halperin's argument that "queer" "acquires its meaning from its oppositional relation to the norm," and must be thought of as "a positionality vis-à-vis the normative" (*Saint Foucault*, 62).

[39] Phineas notes of Ursula that "From the very first of her betrothal there had been a thorough brother-and-sister bond established between her and me" (267).

[40] Furneaux, "Negotiating the Gentle-Man," 117. She emphasizes the importance care-taking can play in the formation of alternative family, also citing the example of Herbert and his wife Clara, with

While John and Phineas' relationship is coded as familial, at the root of the bond is an erotic component so intense that the pair cleaves to each other all their lives. From their early days together, Phineas likens his relationship with John to that of Jonathan and David in the Bible, quoting the famous line where "the soul of Jonathan was knit unto the soul of David; and Jonathan loved him as his own soul" (10).[41] Throughout their lives he frequently calls his friend David, keeping alive the allusion to this pair whose love was "passing the love of women" (Samuel 1:26). As Clare Walker Gore has noted, disability plays a crucial role in enabling their intimacy and breaking down gender norms. The first moment that cements their friendship is when John offers to carry Phineas to his door, suggesting "it would be great fun, you know," with a "tremble in his voice [that] was as tender as any woman's—tenderer than any woman's I ever was used to hear" (9). The relationship will enable John to exhibit a "tender," feminine side, to which Phineas responds.[42] Putting his arms around John's neck, he lets John carry him, after which he claims "My heart cried after him with an irrepressible cry" (9). Given John's physical strength and vigor and Phineas's slight frame, John will frequently carry him, and on one such occasion Phineas notes "I let John do as he would with me" (49). Moments like this are rife with sexual innuendo. When Phineas attempts to describe John's appearance to him before his eighteenth birthday, he is lost for words: "My heart came up into my throat and choked me" (63). He is awed by his friend's manliness and beauty.

Even when John is wrestling with his new passion for Ursula, the two men remain deeply connected. Phineas falls one night while desperately seeking John in the dark, and is caught by his friend. "His tenderness over me, even then, made me break down. I forgot my manhood, or else it slipped from me unawares. In the old Bible language, 'I fell on his neck and wept'" (193). This outburst gives John strength, as it reminded him "that it was something to have a friend and brother who loved him with a love—like Jonathan's—'passing the love of women'" (193). John tries to reassure Phineas that his new love is not a threat to their bond: "you must not think I could ever think less, or feel less, about my brother," and Phineas is comforted that "whatever new ties might gather round each, our two hearts would cleave together unto death (195, 196). Yet despite Phineas' repeated claims that he and Ursula are not rivals and that he is contented with his place in their lives, his constant observation and detailed descriptions of their intimate moments suggests a latent pain. For example, in the early days of the marriage, Phineas describes how each time John returned home Ursula "ran to open the door and I could hear his

whom Pip lives for a time in *Great Expectations* (1860–1861). Herbert had been an attentive nurse to Pip.

[41] Bourrier explores how "the biblical language gives Phineas a way to describe some of the most intensely erotic moments in the novel" (*The Measure of Manliness*, 59).

[42] Walker Gore, "'The right and natural law of things': Disability and the Form of the Family in the Fiction of Dinah Mulock Craik and Charlotte M. Yonge," 119.

low 'my darling!' and *a long, long pause* in the hall. They were very, very happy in those early days ..." (274, my italics).

Many other English novels depict similar queer desire as the basis for their alternative kinship structures. Chapter 2 explored the erotic component to close brother-brother relations. The intense bonding between the Bede brothers and the feminization of Seth enables him to be content remaining with his brother and caring for Adam and Dinah's children.[43] As he reassures Adam on learning that he has won Dinah's love, "Have I felt thy trouble so little that I shouldna feel thy joy?" (451). His happiness comes through identification with his brother. In Collins' *The Woman in White*, there is a similar triangle with Marian living with her half-sister Laura and Laura's husband, Walter. At the end of the novel, when Walter worries that they are selfishly keeping Marian, she claims "After all that we three have suffered together ... there can be no parting between us, till the last parting of all ... Wait a little till there are children's voices at your fireside ... the first lesson they say to their father and mother shall be—We can't spare our aunt!" (621). Some scholars have argued that the attachment between the two women is actually the strongest in this triangle.[44]

Collins' *Armadale* (1866) closes with a marriage, but the strongest attachment is clearly between the male friends. Early in the novel, "Ozias Midwinter" confesses his love of Allan Armadale to Allan's mentor: "I do love him! It *will* come out of me; I can't keep it back. I love the very ground he treads on! I would give my life— yes, the life that is precious to me now, because his kindness has made it a happy one—I tell you I would give my life—" at which point he breaks down and cries (104). He does ultimately offer his life in place of Allan's, and after he is saved the Epilogue finds the two men together on the night before Allan's wedding. Allan says to Midwinter "You have promised me, I know, that, if you take to literature, it shan't part us, and that, if you go on a sea-voyage, you will remember, when you come back, that my house is your home" (655). He tries to reassure his friend that they will always belong together. Midwinter, in turn, speaks of himself as "the friendless man whom you had taken as a brother to your heart" and assures Allan that "while we live, brother, your love and mine will never be divided again" (656). Although Allan has long been impatient to marry and is deeply in love, nothing is said of the bride.

While those novels still glorify wedlock, and use queer desire to accommodate a third, some authors rejected matrimony altogether. Samuel Butler's *The Way of All Flesh* (written 1873–1884) traces the maturation of Ernest Pontifex from his abusive parental home through boarding school, a failed marriage, and finally into

---

[43] On the feminization of Seth, see MacDonald, *The New Man, Masculinity, and Marriage in the Victorian Novel*; Reed, "Soldier Boy: Forming Masculinity in *Adam Bede*"; Sopher, "Gender and Sympathy in *Adam Bede*: The Case of Seth Bede."

[44] As I note in Chapter 2, Hoffer and Kersh explore the potential erotic component of the sisters' relationship ("The Victorian Family in Queer Time").

settled bachelor life. Ernest is helped in his early years by his unmarried aunt, Alethea, and then by her friend, Overton, who narrates the novel. Thus he has "two unmarried and asexual sages" for guides.[45] Overton is openly hostile to the idea of marriage, even drawing away from his protégée when Ernest ties the conjugal knot. Only after the marriage turns out to be void (the bride was already married), does their warm bond recommence.

The Way of All Flesh is consistently skeptical about the assumed joys of the genealogical family, frequently challenging its exalted status. As Ernest's father Theobald laments:

> oh, why, he was inclined to ask himself, could not children be born into the world grown-up? If Christina could have given birth to a few full-grown clergymen in priest's orders—of moderate views, but inclining rather to Evangelicalism, with comfortable livings and in all respects facsimiles of Theobald himself—why, there might have been more sense to it; or if people could buy ready-made children at the shop of whatever age and sex they liked, instead of always having to make them at home and to begin at the beginning with them—that might do better, but as it was he did not like it. (67)

Parental feeling is far from idealized. When Theobald thinks of the tenth plague in Egypt, "It seemed to him that if the little Egyptians had been anything like Ernest, the plague must have been something very like a blessing in disguise" (94). At the end of the novel, Overton is almost apologetic about his god-son/god-father like relationship with Ernest: "To myself he has been a son and more than a son; at times I am half afraid—as for example when I talk to him about his books—that I may have been to him more like a father than I ought; If I have, I trust he has forgiven me" (314).

Why this fear of being a parent? It is easy to see the threat of incest lurking in Overton's fear. Herbert Sussman calls Butler's novel "a cunning and coherent manifesto for the homoerotic as natural, healthy, and universal," and suggests that it "advocates the bachelor mode as the proper style for men of homoerotic temperament living at the boundary of the homosocial and the homosexual."[46] If we follow Sussman's lead (and Butler's autobiographical precedent) in understanding Overton and Ernest's relationship as that of "the elite Athenian adult male to the adolescent of the same class, a bond merging mentoring and sexual relations," then Overton would have every reason to fear the title of "father."[47]

Given the novel's ambivalence about the familial nature of the relations between Overton and Ernest, it is difficult to consider the two bachelors a true family at the

---

[45] Sussman, "Samuel Butler as Late Victorian Bachelor," 190. Sussman also notes the significance of Alethea's name (the Greek the word for truth) as a link to Greek life and love.

[46] Sussman, "Samuel Butler as Late Victorian Bachelor," 186.

[47] Sussman, "Samuel Butler as Late Victorian Bachelor," 190.

close of the novel, but they certainly present a model of companionship devoid of heterosexual desire. And, indeed, many Victorian novels show that bachelorhood need not be antithetical to family. Often bachelors take on a foster-father role— like Dickens' Brownlow (*Oliver Twist*), Jarndyce (*Bleak House*), and Dan Peggoty (*David Copperfield*, 1849–1850), or the eponymous hero of Eliot's *Silas Marner* (1861)—and in so doing open up an alternative family structure not reliant on heterosexual reproduction.

Queer desire can also facilitate the creation of lateral kinship through the process Furneaux calls "in-lawing": transferring affection from a same-sex friend to that friend's opposite-sex sibling. In-lawing allows the same sex couple to become affinal kin. This type of triangulated desire is fairly ubiquitous in English novels, though rarely does it actually culminate in the same-sex friend pair living together. We find an illustrative example in Trollope's *Can You Forgive Her?* (1864), where Kate Vavasar attempts to bring about a union between her beloved brother George and their cousin, Alice (Kate's best friend).[48] The three travel together on the continent in a triangle that blurs the boundaries between familial and romantic love, though in the end Alice marries someone else, so this does not actually produce a queer family construction.[49] While in-lawing is far less common in Russian novels, it occurs in *Crime and Punishment* (1866), when Razumikhin transfers his extreme devotion for Raskolnikov to the latter's sister, Dunya.[50] And in *War and Peace*, Nikolai Rostov's best friend Denisov spontaneously proposes to Nikolai's sister Natasha on a visit to the family, although the proposal leads nowhere and he does not become Nikolai's *beau frère*.

Trollope's *The Warden* (1855) and *Barchester Towers* (1857)—the first two books in the *Chronicles of Barsetshire*—push in-lawing further by removing the romantic partner and leaving the new "sisters" as their own family unit. In the first novel, John Bold's courtship of Eleanor is all mediated via his sister Mary, Eleanor's best friend. When Eleanor comes to beg Mr. Bold to drop a lawsuit against her father, he uses it as an occasion to declare his love, yet the whole scene of wooing is triangulated around Mary:

> "Surely, surely, John, you cannot refuse her," said his sister.
> "I would give her my soul," he said, "if it would serve her."
> "Oh, Mr Bold, said Eleanor, "do not speak so; I ask nothing for myself; and what I ask for my father, it cannot harm you to grant."
> "I would give her my soul, if it would serve her, said Bold, *still*

---

[48] Sharon Marcus provides a brilliant reading of these dynamics (*Between Women*, 236–237).

[49] In *The Pickwick Papers* (1836), Furneaux traces "Ben and Bob's romance, which has blossomed around the enabling figure of Ben's sister, Arabella," but this too is an example of an abortive romance that does not lead to wedlock (*Queer Dickens*, 119).

[50] See my "Incest and the Limits of Family in the Nineteenth-Century Russian Novel," 98–99.

> *addressing his sister*; "everything I have is hers, if she will accept it
> ..." (112, my italics)

Mary is advocating for Eleanor, while John speaks to her, not to his beloved. When Eleanor elicits Mr. Bold's promise of help, she blesses him "and falling on her knees with her face on Mary's lap," she wept (113). Mary then shifts to helping push her brother's suit, symbolically making room for him between herself and Eleanor on the sofa. "And then Mary would talk as though they three were joined in some close peculiar bond together; as though they were in future always to wish together, contrive together, and act together" (114). John and Eleanor wed at the end of the novel, but by the start of *Barchester Towers* Eleanor is already widowed, and the sisters-in-law are living together. Eleanor has borne a son, John (after his father), and "Mary Bold was a second worshipper at the same shrine" of the child (16). So the two women are the pair who cohabitate and raise a child together. But this configuration is time limited, as Eleanor remarries at the end of the novel. Narrative closure still comes from hetero-normative family formation.[51]

While in-lawing is a form of lateral family expansion that puts the emphasis on erotic desire that must be channelled to a more acceptable object, it can also work in reverse to create non-romantic bonds. The family Oliver Twist is ultimately (re)united with could be said to have this inverse in-lawing at its base. Mr. Brownlow was in love with Oliver's aunt who died before Brownlow could marry her, but through this loss he became attached to her brother (Oliver's father). He describes himself as Oliver's father's "oldest friend," explaining:

> the hopes and wishes of young and happy years were bound up with him, and that fair creature of his blood and kindred who rejoined her God in youth, and left me here a solitary, lonely man: it is because he knelt with me beside his only sister's death-bed when he was yet a boy, on the morning that would—but Heaven willed otherwise—have made her my young wife; it is because my seared heart clung to him, from that time forth, through all his trials and errors, till he died. (331–332)

This "old and early friend, whose strong attachment had taken root in the earth that covered one most dear to both" is moved to adopt the son who was left orphaned (334). Rather than producing his own offspring, he will raise the child who shares the blood of the beloved whom he lost.

---

[51] This fits with Valerie Sanders' observation about the similarity between Charlotte Yonge's *The Clever Woman of the Family* (1865) and Jane Austen's novels, where the configuration of two spinster sisters together is not treated as a long-term choice: "Same-sex devotion seems to be seen as an immature state, a preparation for the firmer guidance that only men can provide" ("Marriage and the antifeminist woman novelist," 29).

Liberalizing the Family

With all the forms of lateral expansion this chapter has been exploring, the ultimate result is the same: the liberalizing of the traditional family model. The English novel accomplished this through making an acceptable space for forms of desire beyond the hetero-norm. Same-sex desire can be the basis for new lateral kinship bonds, and disabled characters who cannot reproduce need not be ousted from the family, but instead can find a place in expansive family configurations. There are, however, limits. In *David Copperfield*, for example, Mr. Peggotty must go off to untamed Australia to make a place for his family group that includes his fallen daughter Em'ly, the former prostitute Martha, and the "lone lorn creetur" Mrs. Gummidge. English society held no place for a woman of tarnished virtue, but in the bush, with looser strictures, Martha is ultimately able to wed. I would argue that in the English novel, liberalizing is a by-product, a result of other forces; something first prevents a character from following the norm.

In many Russian novels, the liberalizing push arguably *was* the main point. Often it linked back to the ideal of *sobornost'* or earlier in the century (1840s), to Romantic ideas of friendship and unity.[52] As noted in Part II, many Russian novels used the marriage plot to make the family a site of liberal experimentation, rather than a bastion of conservative patriarchalism. The ending of *Fathers and Children*, for example, finds harmony reigning in the family as it expands across class lines. The double wedding of Arkady to Katya and Nikolai to his peasant mistress Fenechka provides traditional comedic closure, yet it also makes a major statement about class to have Fenechka now seated at the table as part of the family. A "nanny in a brocaded peasant headdress" takes her place in caring for baby Mitya, while Fenechka is dressed in silk with a velvet headband and gold chain, her clothing symbolizing her admittance into the gentry estate of her husband. Their illegitimate, cross-class son—of whose existence Nikolai Petrovich was at first ashamed for Arkady to even know—now also has a place at the table. Even the embodiment of aristocratic values, Pavel Petrovich, kisses little Mitya after being toasted, a fact that the narrator distinctly emphasizes ("not leaving out, of course, Mitya"). And he goes through the symbolic gesture of kissing Fenechka's hand,

---

[52] Outside of literature, and therefore not explored in this chapter, the Herzens and Herweghs had ecstatic, romantic ideals about unity in friendship and tried to unite their households (ultimately Natalia Herzen ended up in an affair with George Herwegh). They were deeply inspired by George Sand's life and writings. Their experiment in communal living provides an interesting Romantic era vision of expansive family. When the two families reunited as a single household in Nice in June 1850 (at which time Natalia Herzen's husband did not yet know that she was in a sexual relationship with George, but George's wife Emma already knew), Natalia wrote "And what if Ogarev and Natalie came here—we would form a colony! ... And after that what is the point of destroying the family! Then we would all be one family!" Qtd. in Irina Paperno, "Introduction: Intimacy and History, The Gercen Family Drama Reconsidered," 10.

another way of indicating her acceptance in this new gentry milieu (he himself encouraged his brother to marry her).

This blended family provided an important model for authors like Dostoevsky, whose *The Adolescent* was partly intended as a response to *Fathers and Children*.[53] The family structure in both novels is predicated on a loosening of the traditional family to make a place for an illegitimate, cross-class son. While Dostoevsky framed his explicit comments about the "accidental family" in distinctly negative terms—as a disintegration of the family unit and a regression from Tolstoy's idyllic jam-making gentry clans—the ending of *The Adolescent* illustrates the positive side of the new, looser kinship conglomerations that emerged.[54] From its fractious and fractured beginnings, Arkady's family stabilizes into a kind of harmony. Rifts between gentry and peasant are symbolically mended as Versilov "no longer leaves mama's side and never will again" (13:446/553). So here, too, the peasant mistress finds a secure place, even becoming "bold" with the father of her children (although the marriage Versilov promised to her does not take place).[55] Arkady reconciles himself with what Versilov is able to offer as a paternal model and declares: "I'll say directly that I've never loved him as I do now" (13:446/553). The family does not desert Arkady's sister, Liza, despite her illicit pregnancy and miscarriage. And all of them are living at the expense of Tatyana Pavlovna Prutkova, whom Arkady has called "aunt" for his whole life and who oversees Versilov's estate despite the fact that she is a landowner in her own right and only "almost" a relation of the Versilovs (*chut' li i v samom dele ne srodni*).[56] Arkady—who had been lashing out throughout the novel—learns how to belong to this "accidental" family and to accept its love.

The breakdown or "accidentalizing" of the family, which has received so much attention from scholars, is complemented in these novels by a re-conception of what family can be and a more flexible form to kinship ties. And this pattern holds across Russian literature. While Tolstoy may seem like one of the most conservative guardians of patriarchal family values, even he includes such an accidental family at the heart of *Anna Karenina*. It is easy to forget that after Anna's death, Vronsky leaves baby Annie—his biological daughter—to be raised by Karenin, her legal father. So Karenin is left parenting Seriozha and Annie, two half-siblings, one of whom shares no genetic relation to him.

---

[53] Steiner, *For Humanity's Sake: The Bildungsroman in Russian Culture*, 150.

[54] For a summary of the negative view, see Susanne Fusso, "Dostoevskii and the Family," 175–176. Robin Feuer Miller notes the more positive potentials in the "new kind of accidental family, the brotherhood, forged at the end of *The Brothers Karamazov*" ("Children," 141).

[55] See Steiner, *For Humanity's Sake* 148–150.

[56] As Arkady explains, "At that time, aunt was at the estate; that is, she was not my aunt, but a landowner herself. I do not know why, but everyone always called her Aunt, not only as if she were my aunt, but as if she were Aunt, period. It was the same in Versilov's family, to which she was almost truly related" (13:8/8–9).

While the examples just discussed used blended family or chosen kin mainly to overcome class rifts, in *Oblomov* (1859) Goncharov also bridges national divides. The titular hero takes offense when an acquaintance, Tarantev, speaks ill of his dear friend Stoltz:

—Listen, Mikhei Andreich,—said Oblomov sternly,—I asked you to be more tempered in your language, especially when speaking about a person close to me ...

—Close to you!—Tarantev retorted with hatred.—How is he any relation to you? He's a German, of course.

—He's closer than any relation [*blizhe vsiakoi rodni*]: I grew up and studied with him, and I won't allow any rudeness ... (4:51)

Their bond "closer than any relation" can unite German and Russian. While the novel seems to center on a traditional patriarchal family, with Olga ultimately married to Stoltz and producing a robust brood of children, it is in part an intentional family, as Stoltz takes in Oblomov's son to raise with his own. And this child is the product of a mixed-class marriage between Oblomov and his housekeeper. Given that intentional kin needs *no* root in blood or marriage, its expansive potential goes further than that of the blended family.

These examples of liberalizing the family had serious social and political implications. Some scholars have argued that Russia (compared to Europe) had few groups or institutions that "could propagate eccentric beliefs."[57] While the political landscape may have been inhospitable to new ideas, in Russia's novels the family becomes a site for exploring alternatives to the patriarchal tyranny of the past and envisioning a progressive future order for Russia. We see this with cross-class unions, fictitious marriages, and other conglomerations that mended societal rifts and righted historic power imbalances.

In some texts, progressive re-envisioning of the family comes close to looking like a rejection of the family. In Chapter 5 I discussed Krestovsky (pseud.)'s *The Boarding School Girl* (1861), where instead of marrying, the heroine Lolenka escapes to St. Petersburg and lives independently with an aunt, supporting herself by becoming an artist. While Anne Lounsbery is right that "the *telos* in this book is emphatically *not* family life," even as Lolenka rejects the conjugal family, it is family—in the form of a generous aunt—that enables her escape.[58] Lolenka's independent life St. Petersburg brings her into a wider kind of community than the family, with her reading initiating her into the "deep, horizontal comradeship"

[57] Ripp, "Turgenev as a Social Novelist: The Problem of the Part and the Whole," 239.
[58] Lounsbery, "Russian Families, Accidental and Other," 505.

created by print culture. The family is replaced by what Lounsbery calls "a fraternal web" of Lolenka's enlightened peers.[59]

While that example goes beyond the bounds of what could reasonably be considered "family" unity, I would argue that the Russian novel did have the capacity to conceive of the family in broader national terms than the English novel did. The English never embraced the same ecstatic potential for family expansion that came from the Russian ideas of *sobornost'* and *narodnost'* (national identity). There was something uniquely Russian in this outlook, something captured most eloquently by the final lines of Goncharov's *The Precipice*. By the end of the novel, the hero Raisky has left his country estate of Malinovka and his beloved cousins (Vera and Marfenka) and grandmother there, and from sunny Rome, where he is working on his art, he thinks back on home:

> And everywhere, amidst this impassioned artistic life, he was not unfaithful to his family, his group, did not take root in this foreign soil, and continued to feel like a guest and newcomer there. Often in his hours of rest from work, in his hours of disillusionment from the new and strong impressions made by the stimulating colors of the south, he felt drawn back home. He would have liked to gather up this eternal beauty of nature and art, become completely saturated by the spirit of legends turned to stone, and carry it all off with him there, to his Malinovka ...
>
> Behind him all the while three figures stood and called to him warmly: his Vera, his Marfenka, and his babushka. And behind them stood, drawing him to herself more strongly than they, still another figure, gigantic, another great "babushka"— Russia. (7:772)

The Russians embraced a national model of family: tsar *batushka* (father), *matushka* (mother) *Rus'*, and their children, the suffering Russian people. Such thinking underpinned Dostoevsky's concerns about "the dissociation of educated Russians from their native soil,"[60] a concern that would be unthinkable in an English novel. Perhaps this metaphoric "great family" underlying the Russian worldview facilitated envisioning expansive families on the micro-level, as all Russians by this logic were kin at some deeper level.

There was also, of course, a darker side to this nationalist vision, one that continues to haunt us in the twenty first century. The idea of laterally extended, intentional family mirrors the rhetoric of imperial expansion used at the time to talk about the *bratia menshie* (little brothers) of the surrounding minority peoples.[61] As the Russian empire expanded into Central Asia, officials sought to cast

[59] Lounsbery is drawing on Benedict Anderson for the point about print culture ("Russian Families, Accidental and Other," 507).

[60] Hudspith, *Dostoevsky and the Idea of Russianness*, 89.

[61] Alexander Rittikh (1831–1914), a Russian general staff official and a military cartographer and writer, presents Russia as a "big family, where each of the brothers does different crafts and works for

newly conquered peoples as Russia's Aryan brothers to be integrated into the big family of the State (based on a very dubious sense of racial unity).[62] Tolstoy—more concerned about the human family than the Russian one—showed skepticism at the end of *Anna Karenina* about saving "brother Slavs" in Serbia if this involved warfare and the shedding of blood. But regardless the response of any individual author, the Russian family—both national-scale and around-the-table-scale—was expanding and diversifying and Russian novelists reflected and mostly valorized this shift.

This vision of a national family would persist in twentieth-century literature, and would be used in Socialist Realist novels, where the "great family" (*bol'shaia sem'ia*) of the State was contrasted with the nuclear family (*malaia sem'ia*). Authors returned to the same questions nineteenth-century authors wrestled with about defining the family's boundaries. As Jacob Emery has argued, Andrei Bely's *Petersburg* (1916) actively challenges the meaning of bloodline and the limits of kinship. Bely introduces Apollon Apollonovich Ableukhov (whose matching first name and patronymic emphasize vertical descent) with a parody of the novelistic convention of defining characters by their genealogy. He notes that Ableukhov was of "venerable stock" and "had Adam as his ancestor."[63] Yet being "children of Adam" makes everyone a member of a single human family, undermining the relevance of individual family bloodline. Authors like Alexander Bogdanov (*Red Star*, 1908) and Yuri Olesha (*Envy*, 1927) explored technological means of constructing kinship across a broad spectrum of people through production, as opposed to reproduction. In Olesha's vision, for example, the communal kitchen would replace the maternal breast.

In the hopeful 1920s, most "great family" metaphors emphasized fraternal unity among equals, the same lateral expansion we saw in their nineteenth-century predecessors. Katerina Clark emphasizes this continuity, pointing to the "rejection of corrupt blood ties in favor of the higher-order bonds of political community" that we find in works like Chernyshevsky's *What Is to Be Done?*.[64] In the nineteenth-century novel, these bonds were less overtly political, but the principal of choosing family based on shared values remains the same. The rise of Stalinism in the 1930s brought a shift in family metaphors away from equal siblinghood to a father-son paradigm, reinstating the powerful vertical.[65] Generational metaphors were used to justify the progression of leaders, with Stalin legitimated by the legend that

the common good. Over them dominates [*glavenstvovat'*] the older brother—that is Russian people." A. Rittikh, *Materialy dlia etnografii Rossii. Kazanskaia Gubernia*, 1:3–4.

[62] See Issiyeva, *Representing Russia's Orient* (Ch. 6, specifically about the Taranchi and Uighurs). She also cites scientists who legitimized imperial expansion in Central Asia. See V.E. Paisel', *Materialy dlia antropologii Taranchei*; G.E. Grum-Grzhimailo, "Belokuraia rasa v Srednei Azii."

[63] Emery, *Alternative Kinships*, 14.

[64] Clark, *Soviet Novel*, 115.

[65] Clark, *Soviet Novel*, 118.

Lenin had blessed him as his successor.[66] Stalin became the ultimate "father" to his heroic "sons," the daring Soviet men whom he helped to gain consciousness and maturity. The master plot of the Socialist Realist novel was based on this vertical familially-coded mentorship. Many of the "sons" are literally orphans, seeking a father in their calm, wise mentor from higher up in the party. As Clark has observed, "in the great tale of Soviet society ... all are orphans until they find their identity in the 'great family.'"[67] A "son" could have many brothers and comrades, but the most powerful relationship that structured the Soviet novel was that with his father.

Conclusion

This chapter began by describing the contracting English ideal of family, and I would like to conclude by returning to the implications of that shift and by contrasting it with Russia. Eve Kosovsky Sedgwick has called this shift an "avunculosuppressive move from 'kinship' to 'family.'"[68] The term itself emphasizes the importance of extended kin, and specifically of aunts and uncles, who "carve out" a space for nonconformity; as their role is not dependent "on their own pairing or procreation," they can represent "nonconforming or nonreproductive sexualities."[69] Although Sedgwick does not pursue the ramifications of this statement for plot, her further reflections have important implications for the narrative possibilities such kin hold. "If having grandparents means perceiving your parents as somebody's children, then having aunts and uncles, even the most conventional aunts and uncles, means perceiving your parents as somebody's sibs—not, that is, as alternately abject and omnipotent links in a chain of compulsion and replication that leads inevitably to *you*; ..." If we stopped the quotation here, Sedgwick might seem to be challenging the idea of a linear family teleology and, consequently, a linear family plot. However, she continues "but rather as elements in a varied, contingent, recalcitrant but re-forming seriality, as people who demonstrably could have turned out very differently—indeed as people who, in the differing, refractive relations among their own generation, can be seen already to have done so."[70] By returning to "seriality," Sedgwick reinserts the idea of sequence, but she still gives weight to relations within a generation that are not based on romantic unions and procreation.

---

[66] This legend was discredited by Khrushchev when he published Lenin's Last Testament, contradicting it. See Clark, *Soviet Novel*, 128–129.

[67] Clark, *Soviet Novel*, 135.

[68] Sedgwick, "Tales of the Avunculate," 62.

[69] Sedgwick, "Tales of the Avunculate," 63.

[70] Sedgwick, "Tales of the Avunculate," 63.

What Sedgwick calls for to "redeem" the family actually sounds a great deal like the Russian "intentional family" I have described in this chapter. For Sedgwick it "would be advocacy of a more elastic, inclusive definition of 'family,' beginning with a relegitimation of the avunculate: an advocacy that would appeal backward to precapitalist models of kinship organization, or the supposed early-capitalist extended family, in order to project into the future a vision of 'family' elastic enough to do justice to the depth and sometimes durability of nonmarital and/or nonprocreative bonds, same-sex bonds, nondyadic bonds, nonbiological bonds across generations, etc."[71] Many Russian novels do just that.

Certainly I am far from the first to note these trends. But I hope that Part III has helped to explain the difference between alternative kinship's appearance in the Russian and English novel by contextualizing it in the two nations' conceptions of the family and the stories they were using the family to tell. On the English side, this meant focusing on a smaller number of texts because I was looking to the exceptions; the preponderance of novels close with the normative wedding bells. On the Russian side, I devoted significant attention to the works of Dostoevsky, but placed them in the context of a wide range of authors: Tur, Goncharov, Sofia Khvoshchinskaya, Shalikova, Tolstoy, Turgenev, Chernyshevsky, etc. This was by design. Dostoevsky's "accidental family" is the non-normative family model that has received by far the most attention in scholarship, but when we stay too immersed in one major author, looking at his works in isolation, it is easy to overlook the fact that Dostoevsky's accidental families were actually part of a much wider pattern in Russian literature of his time.

The Russian pattern is one of family formation that disregards legal sanction or the future wealth of a family line. Although Russian novels often deny us the satisfactory ending of Emma and Knightly's "perfect union" or the rosy-cheeked child, they are not devoid of newly formed families at their conclusions. The path to achieving such families, however, and the form they take, lies outside of reproductive futurity and the linear English model. Instead, they involve lateral expansion in the present, *choosing* to make others kin or to accept unsought, a-traditional bonds. Karenin raising baby Annie, Masha and her former tutor and non-blood uncle raising baby Lev in Crimea, Stoltz and Olga raising baby Oblomov—all these characters are participating in a new Russian kinship tradition, one that glorifies intentional family.

While both the Russian and English novel embraced kinship configurations other than the normative heterosexual married couple and their biological offspring, a more flexible and inclusive conception of the family came far more naturally to the Russian pen than the English. In Russia this loosening and liberalizing was a necessity: marriage was *not* a path to stable, happy family, so the

[71] Sedgwick, "Tales of the Avunculate," 71.

successful family could not take the form of husband, wife, and heir. By contrast, the English novel turned to alternatives only when reproductive futurity was impossible—due to disability or some other insurmountable obstacle—or when attempting to accommodate forms of desire that fell outside of the heterosexual norm, like Overton and Ernest or Phineas and John. In such cases, we see the binary oppositions between the Russian and English traditions collapse. English families based around sibling or avuncular bonds, men who call each other "brothers" and settle in one household, those who create "family" bonds with chosen kin—all these groups and characters participate in a liberalizing of the family akin to what I have been arguing is central to the Russian tradition.

Conclusion

Love, like death, is congenial to a novelist because it ends a book conve-
niently. He can make it a permanency, and his readers easily acquiesce,
because one of the illusions attached to love is that it will be permanent.
Not has been—will be.

—E. M. Forster, *Aspects of the Novel*

There is no need for any plots. Life doesn't have plots; in life, everything
is mixed together—the profound with the shallow, the great with the
trivial, the tragic with the ludicrous.

—Anton Chekhov

"Our tale is now done, and it only remains to us to collect the scattered threads
of our little story, and to tie them into a seemly knot" (207). Thus commences
the concluding chapter of Trollope's *The Warden* (1855). The conjugal knot—
tied between Eleanor and Mr. Bold—features prominently in those final pages,
as this classic English novel brings about a supreme state of narrative closure and
resolves all family plots. Although there will be five more novels to follow in the
Chronicles of Barsetshire, at this point all conflicts and imbalances have been solved
or resolved and even the newly-made brothers-in-law—who had been archrivals
throughout the text—are at peace. This is narrative closure par excellence.

   The conclusion of this book is concerned with endings and how authors tie
the seemly knot or leave the threads scattered at the end of their novels. What
marks closure for a family plot? And why does that look so different in England
and Russia?

The Goal

What will provide closure depends on the "the incitement to narrative" and the
ultimate goal it put forth for the novel.[1] Each national tradition has its own value
system that influences what would mark such an ending. For the English novel,
"the end" is both conclusion and goal.[2] If the objective of the English family is

---

[1] Miller, *Narrative and Its Discontents*, ix. See Chapter 6, p. 143 for a discussion of Miller's theory of
the "narratable."
[2] Frank, *Law, Literature, and the Transmission of Culture in England, 1837–1925*, 114.

The Family Novel in Russia and England, 1800–1880. Anna A. Berman, Oxford University Press.
© Anna A. Berman (2022). DOI: 10.1093/oso/9780192866622.003.0010

its own continuity, then ending with marriage (and a child) provides the ultimate telos. As D. A. Miller argues, "The 'perfect union' of [Austen's] Emma and Mr. Knightly virtually *must* end the novel; otherwise, it would not be a 'perfect' union. It would be brought back to the state of insufficiency and lack that has characterized the novelistic movement."[3] The novel closes when the characters have achieved "success," however that success is defined. Semyon Vengerov argues that Russian literature differs from that of the West because Russia had no dominant bourgeoisie, and "thus one of the central themes of Western fiction, the pursuit of success, occupies the most minor of places in Russian writing, Russian characters being more concerned with making a life than with making a living."[4] This point can be applied to the family as well. "Making a life" can involve learning to live with one's kin, struggling to love one's brother, trying to make sure one's children do not come out as scoundrels; it has no clear moment of attainment or arrival like marriage or the birth of an heir. This is Gary Saul Morson's "prosaics" writ large: "recogniz[ing] the importance and value of the ordinary, everyday, and undramatic" that leads to no climax.[5]

When Tolstoy wrote *Anna Karenina* (1875–1878)—which he adamantly insisted was his *first* novel (despite the fact that it came after *War and Peace* [1865–1869])—he took up the challenge of plotting "making a life." Anna's quest for passionate love ends the way many French novels do, with the death of the adulteress (scholars have argued that she is deliberately fashioning herself as a novel heroine).[6] However, this does not end *Tolstoy's* multi-plot novel. Levin, Kitty, Stiva, Dolly, and Koznyzhev are still generating narrative in Part 8. When expansive, lateral relations with siblings and extended kin gain importance, and once filiation is no longer about a family *line*, then the end goal for family—and the novel—becomes less straightforward. Both Levin and Anna raise the eternal Russian questions "Where am I? What am I doing? Why?" (Anna's formulation) or "What am I? And where am I? And why am I here?" (Levin). The English rarely ask this, perhaps because their goal is clearer.

Having mocked "English happiness" in the Victorian novel Anna reads on the train, Tolstoy does not define "Russian happiness." Wealth was, no doubt, a positive, as was social standing and perhaps a title, but these alone are far from enough. Nor is a beloved spouse and healthy child. As I discussed in Chapter 6, after setting up life on his estate with his beloved wife and son, Levin is still suicidal. In Goncharov's *Oblomov* (1859), Olga is similarly depressed after attaining her loving

---

[3] Miller, *Narrative and Its Discontents*, 5.

[4] As paraphrased by Donald Fanger in "On the Russianness of the Russian Nineteenth-Century Novel," 42. According to Vengerov, personal happiness is "either criminal, if it is achieved at the expense of others, or, in the best of situations, vulgar" ("On the Russianness of the Russian Nineteenth-Century Novel," 42).

[5] Morson, *Prosaics and Other Provocations*, 12. In Morson's words, prosaic works of literature "demand not a poetics of product but a prosaics of process" (6).

[6] See, for example, Morson, *Anna Karenina in Our Time*, 67.

husband, estate, and precious heir. The questions she asks are like Anna's and Levin's: "'What is it?' she thought, horrified. 'Is there something else I need and ought to desire? Where am I to go? Nowhere. This is the end of the road ... But is it? Have I completed the circle of life? Is this all—all?' she asked herself, leaving something unsaid—and—looking around anxiously to make sure that no one had overheard this whisper of her soul" (4:456/448). Russian happiness is more than material success and involves an intangible *something* always still to be striven for. Even the family is not enough.

Levin ends *Anna Karenina* by contemplating the reason for his existence and ultimately concluding that his soul is closed to his wife, but that he can accept that. His *hopeful* final realization that moves him beyond suicide is that "there will be the same wall between my soul's holy of holies and other people, even my wife ... but my life now, my whole life, regardless of all that may happen to me, every minute of it, is not only not meaningless, as it was before, but has the unquestion-able meaning of the good which it is in my power to put into it!" (19:399/817). That meaning is not defined by legacy and tradition, as in England. Baby Mitya is not enough to provide closure for Levin because his family concerns expand outward in the present, rather than focusing on linear descent. Levin still has his sister's affairs to manage, his half-brother's visit to navigate as he works on smooth-ing their tense relations. Dolly and her children still depend on his support. His marriage offers challenges; family life is a bundle of synchronic concerns, and thus it cannot be "solved" or resolved into the closing wedding bells of the English, just as the big existential questions of life cannot be answered once and for all by his spiritual awakening.[7] *Anna Karenina*—in typical Russian fashion—looks beyond the end of the classic novel to what happens after the wedding bells cease to sound. And what we find is the quintessentially Russian alternative to English happiness: a sense of existential striving. Every day Levin must struggle to love his half-brother Koznyzhev; every day Dolly must work to make sure her children do not come out scoundrels, and Vronsky must face the loss of his lover *and* the baby daughter he left Karenin to raise. These ongoing, quotidian, but monumental tasks are at the root of the Russian family plot.

Thus, the Russians defied linear narrative constraints. Tolstoy's aim in *War and Peace* was specifically to capture the unending interconnectedness of events and people. Family form and novel form align on this point. The Russians were not afraid of but actually embraced the messiness of interconnected stories that lacked a clear linear form. As the French literary critic E. M. De Vogüé complained in 1886:

---

[7] Miller has argued that "the assumptions under which erotic desire is locked into place—in holy matrimony and wholly in matrimony—also permit a story whose subject this is to come to a com-plete close" (*Narrative and Its Discontents*, 96). Tolstoy's novel cannot come to such a "complete close" because it demands more than romantic love.

As we enter into their works we are disoriented by the lack of composition and apparent action, and are wearied by the effort of attention and memory which they demand of us. These lazy and reflective minds delay at every step, come back in their tracks, raise up visions precise in detail and confused in the ensemble, with ill-defined contours; they create on too large a scale and bring in too extraneous material for our taste.[8]

This made their works appear as "fluid puddings" to Henry James, who applied this term to Tolstoy's and Dostoevsky's novels, considering their "lack of composition" to be a great "vice."[9] But for the Russians, this fluidity and "extraneous material" was in fact a virtue.[10] It enabled them to avoid artifice. Sensing this, Virginia Woolf praised the Russian novel for "allow[ing] human life in all its width and depth," noting that for the Russians, life was "too important to be manipulated."[11]

The type of closure—what would mark the ending of a novel—relates quite directly to the form that novel has taken and the plotline(s) that have guided it. As Frank Kermode has argued, "we use fictions to enable the end to confer organization and form on the temporal structure."[12] Using the analogy of the *tick-tock* of a clock, Kermode claims "such plotting presupposes and requires that an end will bestow upon the whole duration and meaning."[13] The form that final *tock* will take relates to the form of the family. Or to return to Miller's formulation, the "instances of disequilibrium, suspense, [or] general insufficiency" that create the "incitement to narrative" also dictate what form the resolution must take. When our single men are in want of wives, we know they will find them. D. A. Miller calls this the "the tyranny of a narrative so thoroughly predestined that it does nothing but produce spurious problems for a solution already in place."[14] The Russians would fight against this.[15] When unhappy families are unhappy in their own way, their fates are more radically open. It is not always clear where Russian novels are going, but arriving at the alter rarely resolves and removes the "incitement to narrative."

The End

For the novel, there are two classic ways to provide resolution; as E. M. Forster famously observed, "If it was not for death and marriage I do not know how the

---

[8] De Vogüé, "Preface" to *Le Roman russe* (excerpted as "On Russian and French Realism," 29).
[9] Qtd. in Miller, "Henry James: A Theory of Fiction," 347.
[10] See Morson, "Philosophy in the Nineteenth-Century Novel."
[11] Woolf, "On Rereading Meredith," 49.
[12] Kermode, *The Sense of an Ending*, 45.
[13] Kermode, *The Sense of an Ending*, 46.
[14] Miller, *Narrative and Its Discontents*, xiii.
[15] See also Morson, "Philosophy in the Nineteenth-Century Novel," 163. Morson's theory of prosaics links this rejection of predetermined plots to "works of process" that are not guided by a given outcome, but remain radically open in each moment to various possible paths (*Prosaics and Other Provocations*, Ch. 3: The Prosaics of Process).

average novelist would conclude."[16] Clearly, the Russians were not "the average novelist" Forster had in mind. Marriages in Russian novels often come toward the beginning or mid-point (if at all), as in: Herzen's *Who Is to Blame?* (1845–1846), Evgenia Tur's *The Niece* (1851), Tolstoy's *Family Happiness* (1859), Mikhail Avdeev's *Underwater Stone* (1860), Chernyshevsky's *What Is to Be Done?* (1863), Aleksei Potekhin's *Poor Gentry* (1863), Krestovsky (pseud.)'s *Ursa Major* (1871), and S. Dolgina's *Fictitious Marriage* (1876). Tolstoy played with this convention, giving us *both* the standard endings Forster mentioned at the midpoint of *Anna Karenina*, rather than at the end: Anna's dramatic (near-)death in childbirth and Kitty's wedding.[17] The fact that they do not end the narrative indicates that for-giveness and reunion with her husband (for Anna) or the ideal partner (for Kitty and Levin) are not enough to return us to Miller's "'nonnarratable' state of quies-cence assumed by a novel before its beginning and supposedly recovered by it at the end."[18]

Many scholars who do not take Russia into account have argued that open-ended narrative is a modernist invention. According to Joseph Allen Boone, "the twentieth century's 'answer' to the seemingly closed system of Victorian thought and literature, the prototypically open-ended text refuses to bring its multiple nar-rative lines together in one univocal pattern, because, as Robert Adams puts it, 'unresolvedness' is part of the meaning."[19] But this was not a "modernist break-through" as Boone claims; the Russians were already writing such endings in the nineteenth century.

With such "formless" novels, what would recovering "the 'nonnarratable' state of quiescence" look like? Or is the point for the Russians to *avoid* such closure? Per-haps a "fluid pudding" does not end; one simply stops serving more. Krestovsky (pseud.) ends *Ursa Major* with her unwed heroine looking up at the stars and hearing her former beloved call her name: "No one was visible. / It was late! And tomorrow she had a lot to do" (5:731). Similarly, Potekhin closes *Poor Gentry* with Nikanor continuing to seek in vain for noble benefactors: "And meanwhile, des-titution pressed its heavy hand upon his unhappy family ..." (5:490). Nothing has ended here, aside from the narration. Dostoevsky makes this explicit in *Crime and Punishment* (1866), where he closes with the words "But here begins a new account ... It might make the subject of a new story—but our present story is

---

[16] E. M. Forster, *Aspects of the Novel*, 128. Not all critics agree; according to Kelley Hager, it is critics, not the novels themselves, that create the pressure to see marriage as offering final closure (*Dickens and the Rise of Divorce*, 21). However, we find this same idea in the novels themselves, as in, for example, the meta-conversation about novel endings that closes Edgeworth's *Belinda* (1801). All the characters agree that the conclusion should be the happy marriages of the heroes, though they quibble about the speed with which the weddings should be brought about.

[17] Eikhenbaum cites V. Lazursky's *reminiscences*, where he quoted Tolstoy as saying "those who finish their novels with a wedding, as if that were so good that there is no reason to write any further—they all babble sheer nonsense" (Eikhenbaum, "On Tolstoy's Crises," 53).

[18] *Narrative and Its Discontent*, ix.

[19] Boone, *Tradition Counter Tradition*, 146. See also Caserio, *Plot, Story, and the Novel*.

ended" (6:422/551). The threads have not been neatly tied; there is more to be told. In that future, untold story lies the potential family plot of marriage and pro-creation, but they fall outside the novel and do not aid in its resolution. The same could be said of many Russian novels.

Trollope opens the "Conclusion" of *Barchester Towers* (1857) by claiming "The end of a novel, like the end of a children's dinner-party, must be made up of sweetmeats and sugar-plums" (421).[20] It is a truth—perhaps too uncritically—acknowledged, that Russian novels end sadly, but there is certainly much to bear it out. The cessation of struggle, the acceptance of suffering—this can provide a stopping point. In Dostoevsky's *Poor Folk* (1846), for example, Varenka marries her former seducer, Bykov, and departs the novel as if going to her death. Her final words to her friend and benefactor, Devushkin, are "My tears are choking me, breaking me. Farewell. God, how sad! Remember, remember your poor Varenka!" (1:106/127).[21] Going off to a life of suffering provides its own "'nonnarratable' state of quiescence." In the closing lines of Turgenev's *Noble Nest* (1859), Lavretsky says goodbye to his youth and strength with the words "Hello, lonely old age! Burn out, useless life!" (7:293). This line is followed by a break and then a closing para-graph, where we learn that Lavretsky visited the convent where his beloved had shut herself up as a nun and watched as she passed by him without turning her head. A contemporary review of the novel defended the unhappy ending: "It ends sadly, you may say, reader, but my God, in real life do things really end as they do in ancient fairy tales, with a feast and rejoicing? No, it is precisely because Mr. Turgenev is a great artist, because he reproduces the qualities of true and living people, precisely for this reason almost all Mr. Turgenev's novels end sadly."[22]

Nikolai Pomialovsky played on this Russian penchant for unhappy endings. *Bourgeois Happiness* (1861) ends with the hero, having rejected the woman who loved him, departing, disillusioned, from the family where he had worked as a tutor. The novel's final line is addressed to the reader: "'So where is happiness?—the reader asks. Isn't it happiness that's promised in the title?' Readers, it's yet to

[20] Sadrin has similarly noted of Dickens' novels when pointing to all the happy marriages at their conclusions, "Dickens seems unable to disappoint his heroes and, by so doing, to disappoint himself" (*Parentage and Inheritance in the Novels of Charles Dickens*, 21).

[21] We find a similarly hopeless departure ending in "Diary of a Woman," a fictional memoir pub-lished in *Women's Herald* (1867) in which the narrative arc traces the path of the memoirist's miserable life of poverty as she struggles to support herself through work, a brief period of happiness after mar-rying an employer, then more poverty, a still-birth, her husband's illness and death, and in the end she gives up and goes to live in a village wither her aunt. K. G-va. "Dnevnik zhenshchiny" *Zhenskii vest-nik* №6 (1867), 35–64. There is an explanatory note on the first page: "This notebook belonged to an already deceased friend of my childhood. Finding the life described in it a fairly faithful representation of the life of a Russian working woman, I decided to publish it. L Nechaev" (35). The closing lines are "There's nothing more for me to do! Or should I work again? Or live? There's no work for us ... I am going to my old, deaf aunt, who has been inviting me to [live with] her for a long time, and I will live out my life there ... goodbye, life! ..." (64) A textual note alerts readers that the diary was only published because its author had already passed away, so we know what awaited her in the village.

[22] Review: "Dvorianskoe gnezdo, roman I. S. Turgeneva (*Sovremennik*, 1859 g. Ianvar')" *Semeinyi krug* №5 (1859), 228–234 (here 233).

come. Happiness is always yet to come. This is a law of nature" (64). Yet Pomi-alovsky did look ahead to that happy future in the sequel, *Molotov* (1861), where the protagonist ultimately weds the virtuous heroine, causing Pomialovsky to close with the words "Here is the end of bourgeois happiness. Ah, gentlemen, it's rather depressing [*chto-to skuchno*]!" (147). A different set of aesthetic priorities guided the Russians than those that Trollope pokes fun at in *Barchester Towers*.

Barry McCrea has claimed that "The ideas of narrative and family are so closely interwoven that it is hard to separate them."[23] It has been the aim of this book to interrogate the implications of that statement by exploring the way the differ-ing forms of the family in Russia and England led to different dominant plots. Each Part has explored a type of family relationship—consanguineal, conjugal, alternative—and the related plotlines it engenders. Linear inheritance structures shape the roles available for brothers in the English novel, while in Russia the pat-tern of splitting estates leads to an opening out of concerns that do not advance a singular plot through time, but rather focus attention on the present. English mar-riage plots are designed to reinforce the existing order and produce heirs who will continue the family line, while Russian marriage plots push against a backward past and offer new visions of what the family should be. Family in the Russian novel is created laterally, through expanding the circle of kin in the present, lead-ing to a positive portrayal of alternative kinship constructions. In English novels, such constructions only occur when reproductive futurity is not an option or when there are queer forms of desire that it cannot accommodate in the standard nuclear model.

While the basic structure of the argument has been to oppose the two tradi-tions, in each chapter we also saw a point where these binaries collapsed. Among consanguineal kin, sisters or sister-brother pairs play similar roles in each other's plots in both English and Russian novels. And when English brothers can find two sources of income, they—like their Russian counterparts—can settle beside each other in harmony. In other words, when family conditions can be made to resem-ble each other, the plotlines likewise converge. Similarly, in the marriage plot, we find England's unmarrying heroines (like Ethel May in Charlotte Yonge's *Daisy Chain*, 1856) following the same values system as the Russians, placing the com-mon good and the needs of a broader kinship group above personal desires. And when English characters are blocked from marriage and reproductive futurity, they create the same forms of alternative kinship constructions as the Russians. These points of convergence give support to the basic argument that family struc-ture is a crucial determiner of narrative form. In those cases where we are able to control for variables in the conditions, we can predict the outcome. This is not an argument for a unique essence of Russianness, or "Russian soul" that creates the

[23] McCrea, *In the Company of Strangers*, 8

exceptionalism of the Russian novel. Instead it is an argument that historical conditions shape the structure of the family and in turn the plotlines each nation uses the family to tell.

Recognizing this interdependence of narrative form, family form, and historical conditions forces us to reevaluate some of our standard theories of "the novel" and to see them for what they are: theories of the English (or English and French) novel. The linear driving force of plot is a function of the progressive drive of the English family striving for vertical continuity. While scholars have noted its breakdown in the modernist period with the rise of the self-made man and the declining importance of ancestry, they have not taken the next step to acknowledge that on the other side of Europe, in a culture that already deemphasized ancestry, lateral plotting was already alive and thriving in the nineteenth century.[24] Expanding our view to include Russia, we see that there is a lateral, sprawling alternative to the progression of single sons, one that roots meaning in the present, rather than the future. The nineteenth-century family novel can be a conservative story of marriage and reproductive futurity, but it can also be a story of breaking with the past and embracing the messy and unfinalizable present. It is family form that determines which course it will take.

---

[24] Caserio provides a classic instance of such an argument about the shift to modernism, when he claims that modernist novels demonstrate "antagonism to family as a fact and ordering of life" (*Plot, Story, and the Novel*, 233). In the modernist novel he argues that "genealogical forms of narration—strictly dependent and interdependent lines of continuity—are replaced by mutuality and adjacency of parts" (235). See also Sadrin, *Parentage and Inheritance in the Novels of Charles Dickens*, 25.

List of Novels Considered in the Study

Note: authors are listed by the name by which they were most commonly known, in some cases their real name and in others their pseudonym.

Russian Novels

Aksakov, Sergei. *The Childhood Years of Bagrov's Grandson* (*Detskie gody Bagrova vnuka*, 1858)

Aksakov, Sergei. *Family Chronicle* (*Semeinaia khronika*, 1856)

Aleeva, N. *Two Worlds* (*Dva mira*, 1875), real name: Natalia Utina

Avdeev, Mikhail. *The Underwater Stone* (*Podvodnyi kamen'*, 1860)

Begichev, Dmitri. *The Kholmsky Family: Some Characteristics of the Morals and Way of Life, Familial and Single, of the Russian Gentry* (*Semeistvo Kholmskikh. Nekotorye cherty nravov i obraz zhizni, semeinoi i odinokoi, russkikh dvorian*, 1832)

Chernyshevsky, Nikolai. *What Is to Be Done?* (*Chto delat'?*, 1863)

Dolgina, S. *Fictitious Marriage* (*Fiktivnyi brak*, 1876), real name: Sofia Mundt

Dostoevsky, Fyodor. *The Adolescent* (*Podrostok*, 1875)

Dostoevsky, Fyodor. *The Brothers Karamazov* (*Brat'ia Karamazovy*, 1880)

Dostoevsky, Fyodor. *Crime and Punishment* (*Prestuplenie i nakazanie*, 1866)

Dostoevsky, Fyodor. *Demons* (*Besy*, 1871–1872)

Dostoevsky, Fyodor. *The Idiot* (*Idiot*, 1868–1869)

Dostoevsky, Fyodor. *The Insulted and Injured* (*Unizhennye i oskorblennye*, 1861)

Dostoevsky, Fyodor. *Netochka Nezvanova* (1849)

Dostoevsky, Fyodor. *Poor Folk* (*Bednye liudi*, 1846)

Druzhinin, Alexander. *Polinka Saks* (1847)

Durov, Sergei. *Someone Else's Child* (*Chuzhoe ditia*, 1846)

Goncharov, Ivan. *An Ordinary Story* (*Obyknovennaia istoriia*, 1847)

Goncharov, Ivan. *Oblomov* (1859)

Goncharov, Ivan. *The Precipice* (*Obryv*, 1869)

Grigorovich, Dmitri. *Anton Goremyka* (1847)

Herzen, Alexander. *Who Is to Blame?* (*Kto vinovat?*, 1845–1846)

Khvoshchinskaya, Sofia. *Acquaintances* (*Znakomye liudi*, 1857), pen name: Iv. Vesenev

Khvoshchinskaya, Sofia. *City Folk and Country Folk* (*Gorodskie i derevenskie*, 1863)

V. Krestovsky (pseudonym). *Anna Mikhailovna* (1849), real name: Nadezhda Khvoshchinskaya

V. Krestovsky (pseudonym). *The Boarding School Girl* (*Pansionerka*, 1861)

V. Krestovsky (pseudonym). *Brother Dear* (*Bratets*, 1858)

V. Krestovsky (pseudonym). *In Hope of Something Better* (*V ozhidanii luchshego*, 1860)

V. Krestovsky (pseudonym). *Ursa Major* (*Bol'shaia medveditsa*, 1871)

Krestovsky, Vsevolod. *Petersburg Slums* (*Peterburgskie trushchoby*, 1864–1866)

Lermontov, Mikhail. *A Hero of Our Time* (*Geroi nashego vremeni*, 1842)

Leskov, Nikolai. *A Decayed Family* (*Zakhudalyi rod*, 1874)

Panaeva, Avdotia. *The Talnikov Family* (*Semeistvo Tal'nikovykh*, 1848)

Pavlova, Karolina. *Double Life* (*Dvoinaia zhizn'*, 1848)
Pomialovsky, Nikolai. *Bourgeois Happiness* (*Meshchanskoe schast'e*, 1861)
Pomialovsky, Nikolai. *Molotov* (1861)
Potekhin, Aleksei. *Poor Gentry* (*Bednye dvoriane*, 1863)
Pushkin, Alexander. *Eugene Onegin* (*Evgenii Onegin*, 1825–1832)
Saltykov-Shchedrin, Mikhail. *The Golovlyovs* (*Gospoda Golovlevy*, 1875–1880)
Shalikova, Natalia. *Two Sisters* (*Dve sestry*, 1858), pen name: E. Narskaya
Smirnova, Sofia. *Strength of Character* (*Sila kharaktera*, 1876)
Stulli, Fyodor. *Twice Married* (*Dva raza zamuzhem*, 1875)
Tolstoy, Lev. *Anna Karenina* (1875–1878)
Tolstoy, Lev. *Family Happiness* (*Semeinoe schastie*, 1859)
Tolstoy, Lev. *War and Peace* (*Voina i mir*, 1865–1869)
Tur, Evgenia. *A Mistake* (*Oshibka*, 1849), real name: Elizaveta Vasilevna Salias De Tournemire
Tur, Evgenia. *The Niece* (*Plemiannitsa*, 1851)
Tur, Evgenia. *Two Sisters* (*Dve sestry*, 1851)
Turgenev, Ivan. *Asya* (*Asia*, 1858)
Turgenev, Ivan. *Fathers and Children* (*Ottsy i deti*, 1862)
Turgenev, Ivan. *Noble Nest* (*Dvorianskoe gnezdo* 1859)
Turgenev, Ivan. *On the Eve* (*Nakanune*, 1860)
Turgenev, Ivan. *Rudin* (1856)
Vovchok, Marko. *Three Sisters* (*Zhili da byli tri sestry*, 1861), real name: Mariya Vilinska
Zhukova, Maria. *Two Sisters* (*Dve sestry*, 1843)

English Novels

Austen, Jane. *Emma* (1815)
Austen, Jane. *Mansfield Park* (1814)
Austen, Jane. *Persuasion* (1817)
Austen, Jane. *Pride and Prejudice* (1813)
Austen, Jane. *Sense and Sensibility* (1811)
Braddon, Mary Elizabeth. *Aurora Floyd* (1862–1863)
Braddon, Mary Elizabeth. *Like and Unlike* (1887)
Brontë, Anne. *The Tenant of Wildfell Hall* (1848)
Brontë, Charlotte. *Jane Eyre* (1847)
Brontë, Charlotte. *Shirley* (1849)
Brontë, Charlotte. *Villette* (1853)
Butler, Samuel. *The Way of All Flesh* (written 1873–1884)
Collins, Wilkie. *Armadale* (1866)
Collins, Wilkie. *Poor Miss Finch* (1872)
Collins, Wilkie. *The Woman in White* (1859-1860)
Criak, Dinah. *Agatha's Husband* (1853)
Criak, Dinah. *Hannah* (1871)
Criak, Dinah. *John Halifax, Gentleman* (1856)
Criak, Dinah. *A Noble Life* (1866)
Dickens, Charles. *Bleak House* (1852–1853)
Dickens, Charles. *David Copperfield* (1849–1850)
Dickens, Charles. *Dombey and Son* (1846–1848)

Dickens, Charles. *Great Expectations* (1860-1861)
Dickens, Charles. *Hard Times* (1854)
Dickens, Charles. *The Old Curiosity Shop* (1840–1841)
Dickens, Charles. *Oliver Twist* (1837-1839)
Dickens, Charles. *Our Mutual Friend* (1864–1865)
Dickens, Charles. *Nicholas Nickleby* (1838–1839)
Dickens, Charles. *A Tale of Two Cities* (1859)
Drury, Anna Harriet. *The Brothers* (1865)
Edgeworth, Maria. *Belinda* (1801)
Eliot, George. *Adam Bede* (1859)
Eliot, George. *Daniel Deronda* (1876)
Eliot, George. *Middlemarch* (1871–1872)
Eliot, George. *The Mill on the Floss* (1860)
Eliot, George. *Silas Marner* (1861)
Gaskell, Elizabeth. *Cranford* (1853)
Gaskell, Elizabeth. *North and South* (1854–1855)
Gaskell, Elizabeth. *Ruth* (1853)
Gaskell, Elizabeth. *Wives and Daughters* (1864–1866)
Jewsbury, Geraldine Endsor. *Constance Herbert* (1855)
Kavanagh, Julia. *Daisy Burns* (1853)
Martineau, Harriet. *Deerbrook* (1839)
Oliphant, Margaret. *The Doctor's Family* (1863)
Ouida. *Under Two Flags* (1867)
Thackeray, William. *Vanity Fair* (1848)
Trollope, Anthony. *Barchester Towers* (1857)
Trollope, Anthony. *Can You Forgive Her?* (1864)
Trollope, Anthony. *An Eye for an Eye* (1879)
Trollope, Anthony. *He Knew He Was Right* (1869)
Trollope, Anthony. *Orley Farm* (1862)
Trollope, Anthony. *The Warden* (1855)
Wood, Mrs. Henry (Ellen). *East Lynne* (1860–1861)
Yonge, Charlotte. *The Daisy Chain* (1856)
Yonge, Charlotte. *Heartsease, or Brother's Wife* (1854)
Yonge, Charlotte. *Three Brides* (1876)

Works Cited

Aleeva, N. *Dva mira.* Sankt-Peterburg, 1875.

Andrew, Joe. *Women in Russian Literature, 1780–1863.* Basingstoke, Hampshire: Palgrave Macmillan, 1988.

Antonova, Katherine Pickering. *An Ordinary Marriage: The World of a Gentry Family in Provincial Russia.* New York: Oxford University Press, 2013.

Armstrong, Isobel. *Novel Politics: Democratic Imaginations in Nineteenth-Century Fiction.* Oxford: Oxford University Press, 2016.

Armstrong, Judith. *The Novel of Adultery.* New York: Barnes & Noble, 1976.

Armstrong, Nancy. *Desire and Domestic Fiction: A Political History of the Novel.* New York: Oxford University Press, 1987.

Atteberry, Phillip D. "Regenerative and Degenerative Forces in Turgenev's 'Fathers and Sons,'" *South Central Review,* vol. 5, no. 1 (1988), 48–60.

Austen, Jane. *Emma.* Oxford: Oxford University Press, 1988.

Austen, Jane. *Mansfield Park.* Oxford: Oxford University Press, 1988.

Austen, Jane. *Pride and Prejudice.* Oxford: Oxford University Press, 1988.

Austen, Jane. *Sense and Sensibility.* Oxford: Oxford University Press, 1988.

Avastsaturova, V. V. "Ch. Dikkens v tvorcheskom soznanii L. Tolstogo." Dissertation, Leningrad, 1990.

Avdeev, M. V. *Podvodnyi kamen'* in *Sochineniia M. V. Avdeeva,* tom 1. Sankt-Peterburg: Izd. F. Stellovskago, 1868.

Bailey, Victor and Sheila Blackburn, "The Punishment of Incest Act 1908: A Case Study of Law Creation," *Criminal Law Review,* (1979), 708–718.

Bakhtin, M. M. "Author and Hero in Aesthetic Activity," in Holquist, Michael, and Vadim Liapunov (eds.), *Art and Answerability: Early Philosophical Essays by M. M. Bakhtin.* Translated by Vadim Liapunov, 4–256. Austin: University of Texas Press, 1990.

Bakhtin, M. M. "Forms of Time and of the Chronotope in the Novel," in Holquist, Michael (ed.), *The Dialogic Imagination.* Translated by Caryl Emerson and Michael Holquist, 84–258. Austin: University of Texas Press, 1981.

Bakhtin, M. M. *Problems of Dostoevsky's Poetics.* Translated by Caryl Emerson. Minneapolis: University of Minnesota Press, 1984.

Barthes, Roland. *The Pleasure of the Text.* Translated by Richard Miller. New York: Hill and Wang, 1975.

Beer, Gillian. *Darwin's Plots: Evolutionary Narrative in Darwin, George Eliot, and Nineteenth-Century Fiction.* Cambridge: Cambridge University Press, 2009.

Begichev, Dmitrii Nikitich. *Semeistvo Kholmskikh. Nekotoryia cherty nravov i obraza zhizni, semeinoi i odinokoi, russkikh dvorian.* Moskva: Tipografiia A. Semena, 1832.

Behlmer, George K. *Friends of the Family: The English Home and Its Guardians, 1850–1940.* Stanford: Stanford University Press, 1998.

Beizer, Janet L. *Family Plots: Balzac's Narrative Generations.* New Haven: Yale University Press, 1986.

Belinskii, Vissarion. *Polnoe sobranie sochinenii.* Moskva: Izdatel'stvo Akademii Nauk SSSR, 1953–1959.

Belknap, Robert L. *Plots.* New York: Columbia University Press, 2016.

Bell, Susan G. and Karen M. Offen (eds.) *Women, the Family, and Freedom: The Debate in Documents*. Stanford: Stanford University Press, 1983.

Bem, A. L. *U istokov tvorchestva Dostoevskogo*. Berlin: Petropolis, 1936.

Berman, Anna A. "Dostoevsky and the (Missing) Marriage Plot," in Bowers, Katherine and Kate Holand (eds.) *Dostoevsky at 200*, 41–60. Toronto: University of Toronto Press, 2021.

Berman, Anna A. "The Family Novel (and Its Curious Disappearance)," *Comparative Literature*, vol. 72, no. 1 (2020), 1–18.

Berman, Anna A. "Incest and the Limits of Family in the Nineteenth-Century Russian Novel," *Russian Review*, vol. 78, no. 1 (2019), 82–101.

Berman, Anna A. *Siblings in Tolstoy and Dostoevsky: The Path to Universal Brotherhood*. Evanston: Northwestern University Press, 2015.

Bessmertnyi, Iu. L. *Chelovek v krugu sem'i: ocherki po istorii chastnoi zhizni v Evrope do nachala novogo vremeni*. Moskva: Izdatel'skii tsentr RGGU, 1996.

Bisha, Robin, (ed.) *Russian Women, 1698–1917: Experience and Expression, an Anthology of Sources*. Bloomington: Indiana University Press, 2002.

Bloom, Harold. *The Anxiety of Influence: A Theory of Poetry*. New York: Oxford University Press, 1997.

Blum, Jerome. *Lord and Peasant in Russia: From the Ninth to the Nineteenth Century*. Princeton: Princeton University Press, 1972.

Boone, Joseph Allen. *Tradition Counter Tradition: Love and the Form of Fiction*. Chicago: University of Chicago Press, 1987.

Bourdieu, Pierre. "On the Family as Realized Category," *Theory, Culture & Society*, vol. 13, no. 3 (1996), 19–26.

Bourrier, Karen. *The Measure of Manliness: Disability and Masculinity in the Mid-Victorian Novel*. Ann Arbor: University of Michigan Press, 2015.

Braddon, Mary Elizabeth. *Aurora Floyd*. Oxford: Oxford World's Classics, 2008.

Braddon, Mary Elizabeth. *Like and Unlike*. London: Spencer Blackett, 1887.

Braithwaite et al., "Constructing Family: A Typology of Voluntary Kin," *Journal of Social and Personal Relationships*, vol. 27, no. 3 (2010), 388–407.

Brontë, Anne. *The Tenant of Wildfell Hall*. London: Penguin Books, 1996.

Brontë, Charlotte. *Shirley*. Oxford: Oxford World's Classics, 2008.

Brontë, Charlotte. *Villette*. London: Penguin English Library, 2012.

Brooks, Peter. *Reading for the Plot: Design and Intention in Narrative*. New York: Alfred A. Knopf, 1984.

Broughton, Trev Lynn, and Helen Rogers, "Introduction: The Empire of the Father," in Broughton, Trev Lynn and Helen Rogers (eds.) *Gender and Fatherhood in the Nineteenth Century*, 1–28. Houndmills: Palgrave Macmillan, 2007.

Brown, Edward J. "Pisarev and the Transformation of Two Russian Novels," in Todd, William Mills (ed.). *Literature and Society in Imperial Russia 1800–1914*, 151–172. Stanford: Stanford University Press, 1978.

Brown, Sarah Annes. *Devoted Sisters: Representations of the Sister Relationship in Nineteenth-Century British and American Literature*. Aldershot: Ashgate, 2003.

Buckler, Julie. "Victorian Literature and Russian Culture: Translation, Reception, Influence, Affinity," in Rodensky, Lisa (ed.), *The Oxford Handbook of the Victorian Novel*, 206–226. Oxford: Oxford University Press, 2013.

Bueler, Lois E. *The Tested Woman Plot: Women's Choices, Men's Judgments, and the Shaping of Stories*. Columbus: Ohio State University Press, 2001.

Burke, Edmond. *Reflections on the Revolution in France*. Harmondsworth: Penguin Books, 1983.

Butler, Judith. "Is Kinship Always Already Heterosexual?" *differences: A Journal of Feminist Cultural Studies*, vol. 13, no. 1 (2002), 14–44.

Butler, Samuel. *The Way of All Flesh*. Mineola: Dover Publications, Inc., 2004.

Calder, Jenni. *Women and Marriage in Victorian Fiction*. New York: Oxford University Press, 1976.

Casanova, Pascale. *The World Republic of Letters*. Translated by M. B. DeBevoise. Cambridge: Harvard University Press, 2004.

Caserio, Robert L. *Plot, Story, and the Novel: From Dickens and Poe to the Modern Period*. Princeton: Princeton University Press, 1979.

Cassedy, Steven. *Dostoevsky's Religion*. Stanford: Stanford University Press, 2005.

Castle, Terry. "Sylvia Townsend Warner and Lesbian Fiction," in Bristow, Joseph (ed.), *Sexual Sameness: Textual Differences in Lesbian and Gay Writing*, 128–147. London: Routledge, 1992.

Cecil, Evelyn. *Primogeniture: A Short History of Its Development in Various Countries and Its Practical Effects*. London: John Murray, 1895.

Chambers, Diane M. "Triangular Desire and the Sororal Bond: The 'Deceased Wife's Sister Bill,'" *Mosaic*, vol. 29 (1996), 19–36.

Chase, Karen, and Michael H. Levenson. *The Spectacle of Intimacy: A Public Life for the Victorian Family*. Princeton and Oxford: Princeton University Press, 2000.

Chernyshevskii, N. G. *Chto delat'? Raskazy o novykh liudiakh*. Leipzig: E.L. Kasrovich, 1864.

Chernyshevsky, N. G. "The Russian at the Rendez-vous," in Matlaw, Ralph E. (ed.) *Belinsky, Chernyshevsky, and Dobrolyubov: Selected Criticism*, 108 –129. New York: E. P. Dutton & Co., Inc., 1962.

Chukovskii, K. "O 'Semeistve Tal'nikovykh.'" Introductory essay to Panaeva, Avdot'ia. *Semeistvo Tal'nikovykh*, 97–101. Leningrad: Akademiia, 1928.

Clark, Katerina. *The Soviet Novel: History as Ritual*. Bloomington and Indianapolis: Indiana University Press, 2000.

Clark, Lorna J. "The Family in the Novels of Sarah Harriet Burney," *Lumen*, vol. 20 (2001), 71–81.

Cohen, Michael. *Sisters: Relation and Rescue in Nineteenth-Century British Novels and Paintings*. Cranbury: Fairleigh Dickinson University Press, 1995.

Cohen, Paula Marantz. *The Daughter's Dilemma: Family Process and the Nineteenth-Century Domestic Novel*. Ann Arbor: University of Michigan Press, 1991.

Collins, Wilkie. *Armadale*. New York: Harper & Brothers, 1873.

Collins, Wilkie. *Poor Miss Finch*. Oxford: Oxford University Press, 2008.

Collins, Wilkie. *The Woman in White*. London: Penguin Books, 2008.

Corbett, Mary Jean. *Family Likeness: Sex, Marriage, and Incest from Jane Austen to Virginia Woolf*. Ithaca: Cornell University Press, 2008.

Corrigan, Yuri. "Dostoevskii on Evil as Safe Haven and Anesthetic," *Slavic and East European Journal*, vol. 63, no. 2 (2019), 226–243.

Corrigan, Yuri. *Dostoevsky and the Riddle of the Self*. Evanston: Northwestern University Press, 2017.

Counter, Andrew J. *Inheritance in Nineteenth-Century French Culture: Wealth, Knowledge and the Family*. London: Legenda, 2010.

Craik, Dinah Mulock. *John Halifax, Gentleman*. New York: HarperCollins, 2014. [published under Dinah Maria Mulock]

Craik, Dinah Mulock. *A Noble Life*. Brighton: Victorian Secrets, 2016.

Cross, Wilbur L. *The Development of the English Novel*. New York, 1957.

Cruise, Edwina. "Tracking the English novel in Anna Karenina: who wrote the English novel that Anna reads?" in Orwin, Donna (ed.), *Anniversary Essays on Tolstoy*, 159–182. New York: Cambridge University Press, 2010.

D'Albertis, Deirdre. *Dissembling Fictions: Elizabeth Gaskell and the Victorian Social Text*. New York: St. Martin's Press, 1997.

Dau, Duc and Shale Preston (eds.). *Queer Victorian Families: Curious Relations in Literature*. London and New York: Taylor & Francis Group, 2015.

Davidoff, Leonore. *The Best Circles: Society, Etiquette and the Season.* London: Croom Helm, 1973.

Davidoff, Leonore. *Thicker Than Water: Siblings and Their Relations, 1780–1920.* Oxford: Oxford University Press, 2012.

Davidoff, Leonore and Catherine Hall. *Family Fortunes. Revised Edition.* London and New York: Routledge, 2002.

De Vogüé, E.-M. "On Russian and French Realism," in Becker, George Joseph (ed.), *Documents of Modern Literary Realism*, 310–343. Princeton: Princeton University Press, 2015.

Debrabant, Mary. "Birds, Bees and Darwinian Survival Strategies in 'Wives and Daughters,'" *The Gaskell Society Journal*, vol. 16 (2002), 14–29.

Demidova, O. R. "The Reception of Charlotte Brontë's Work in Nineteenth-Century Russia," *The Modern Language Review*, vol. 89, no. 3 (1994), 689–696.

Dickens, Charles. *David Copperfield.* London: Penguin Books, 2004.

Dickens, Charles. *Dombey and Son.* London: Penguin Books, 2002.

Dickens, Charles. *Great Expectations.* London: Penguin English Library, 2012.

Dickens, Charles. *Nicholas Nickleby.* London: Penguin Books, 2003.

Dickens, Charles. *Oliver Twist.* Oxford: Oxford University Press, 1966.

Dickens, Charles. *Our Mutual Friend.* Oxford: Oxford University Press, 2008.

Dickens, Charles. *A Tale of Two Cities.* London: Penguin English Library, 2012.

Doak, Connor. "Myshkin's Queer Failure: (Mis)reading Masculinity in Dostoevskii's *The Idiot*," *Slavic and East European Journal*, vol. 63, no. 1 (2019), 1–27.

Dobroliubov, N. A. *Sobranie sochinenii. Pod obshchei redaktsiei B.I. Bursova i dr.* Leningrad: Gosudarstvennoe izdatel'stvo khudozhestvennoi literatury [Leningradskoe otdelenie], 1961.

Dodd, William. *Sermons to Young Men, Vol. III.* London: Printed for T. Caldwell and T. Vernor, 1792.

Dolgina, S. *Fiktivnyi brak: original'nyi roman.* S.-Peterburg: Izdanie redaktsii zhurnal russkikh i perevodnykh romanov i puteshestvii, 1876.

Dostoevskii, Fedor. *Polnoe sobranie sochinenii v tridtsati tomakh.* Leningrad: Izdatel'stvo "Nauka," 1972–1990.

Dostoevsky, Fyodor. *The Adolescent.* Translated by Richard Pevear, and Larissa Volokhonsky. New York: Alfred A. Knopf, 2003.

Dostoevsky, Fyodor. *The Brothers Karamazov.* Translated by Richard Pevear and Larissa Volokhonsky. London: Vintage Books, 2004.

Dostoevsky, Fyodor. *Crime and Punishment.* Translated by Richard Pevear and Larissa Volokhonsky. London: Vintage Books, 2007.

Dostoevsky, Fyodor. *Demons.* Translated by Richard Pevear and Larissa Volokhonsky. London: Vintage Books, 2006.

Dostoevsky, Fyodor. *The Idiot.* Translated by David McDuff. London: Penguin Books, 2004.

Dostoevsky, Fyodor. *Poor Folk and Other Stories.* Translated by David McDuff. London: Penguin Books, 1988.

Dostoevsky, Fyodor. *A Writer's Diary: Volume 1, 1873–1876.* Translated by Kenneth Lantz. Evanston: Northwestern University Press, 1994.

Dostoevsky, Fyodor. *A Writer's Diary: Volume 2, 1877–1881.* Translated by Kenneth Lantz. Evanston: Northwestern University Press, 1994.

Drury, Anna Harriet. *The Brothers: A Novel.* London: Chapman and Hall, 1865.

Duthie, Enid Lowry. *The Themes of Elizabeth Gaskell.* Totowa: Rowman and Littlefield, 1980.

Edelman, Lee. "The Future is Kid Stuff: Queer Theory, Disidentification, and the Death Drive," *NARRATIVE*, vol. 6, no. 1 (1998), 18–30.

Edelman, Lee. *No Future: Queer Theory and the Death Drive.* Durham: Duke University Press, 2004.

Edgeworth, Maria. *Belinda.* Oxford: Oxford University Press, 2020.

Ehre, Milton. "A Classic of Russian Realism: Form and Meaning in 'The Golovlyovs,'" *Studies in the Novel*, vol. 9, no. 1 (1977), 3–16.

Eikhenbaum, Boris. "On Tolstoy's Crises," in Matlaw, Ralph E. (ed.), *Tolstoy: A Collection of Critical Essays*, 52–55. Englewood Cliffs: Prentice-Hall, Inc., 1967.

Eikhenbaum, Boris. *Tolstoy in the Seventies*. Translated by Albert Kaspin. Ann Arbor: Ardis, 1982.

Eliot, George. *Adam Bede*. Oxford: Oxford World's Classics, 2008.

Eliot, George. *Daniel Deronda*. Oxford; New York: Oxford University Press, 2009.

Eliot, George. *Middlemarch*. London: Penguin Books, 2011.

Eliot, George. *The Mill on the Floss*. London: Penguin English Library, 2012.

Eliot, George. *Silas Marner*. Oxford: Oxford University Press, 2008.

Ellingson, Laura L., and Patricia J. Sotirin. *Aunting: Cultural Practices that Sustain Family and Community Life*. Waco: Baylor University Press, 2010.

Elnett, Elaine. *Historic Origin and Social Development of Family Life in Russia*. New York: Columbia University Press, 1927.

Emerson, Caryl. "Polyphony and its Discontents," in Bury, Alexander and Michael Katz (eds.), *Approaches to Teaching World Literature: Dostoevsky's* Crime and Punishment, 51–57. New York: Modern Language Association of America, 2022.

Emerson, Caryl. "Pretenders to History: Four Plays for Undoing Pushkin's Boris Godunov," *Slavic Review*, vol. 44, no. 2 (1985), 257–279.

Emery, Jacob. *Alternative Kinships: Economy and Family in Russian Modernism*. DeKalb: Northern Illinois University Press, 2017.

Engel, Barbara Alpern. *Between the Fields and the City: Women, Work, and Family in Russia, 1861–1914*. Cambridge and New York: Cambridge University Press, 1994.

Engel, Barbara Alpern. *Breaking the Ties That Bound: The Politics of Marital Strife in Late Imperial Russia*. Ithaca: Cornell University Press, 2011.

Engel, Barbara Alpern. *Marriage, Household, and Home in Modern Russia: From Peter the Great to Putin*. London: Bloomsbury Academic, 2022.

Engel, Barbara Alpern. *Mothers and Daughters: Women of the Intelligentsia in Nineteenth-Century Russia*. Cambridge: Cambridge University Press, 1983.

Engel, Barbara Alpern. *Women in Russia, 1700–2000*. Cambridge: Cambridge University Press, 2004.

Esaulov, Ivan. "*Sobornost'* in Nineteenth-Century Russian Literature," in Børtnes, Jostein and Ingunn Lunde (eds.), *Cultural Discontinuity and Reconstruction: the Byzanto-Slav Heritage and the Creation of a Russian National Literature in the Nineteenth Century*, 29–45. Oslo: Solum Forlag, 1987.

Fanger, Donald. *Dostoevsky and Romantic Realism: A Study of Dostoevsky in Relation to Balzac, Dickens, and Gogol*. Chicago: University of Chicago Press, 1965.

Fanger, Donald. "On the Russianness of the Russian Nineteenth-Century Novel," in Stavrou, Theofanis George (ed.), *Art and Culture in Nineteenth-Century Russia*, 40–56. Bloomington: Indiana University Press, 1983.

Farrow, Lee A. *Between Clan and Crown: The Struggle to Define Noble Property Rights in Imperial Russia*. Newark: University of Delaware Press, 2004.

Fedotov, George P. *The Russian Religious Mind: Kievan Christianity from the Tenth to the Thirteenth Centuries*. New York: Harper and Brothers, 1960.

Filaret. *Slovo i rechi, Tom IV, 1836–1848*. Moskva: Tipografiia A. I. Mamontova, 1882.

Flandrin, Jean-Louis. *Families in Former Times: Kinship, Household, and Sexuality in Early Modern France*. Translated by Richard Southern. Cambridge and New York: Cambridge University Press, 1979.

Foote, I. P. *Saltykov-Shchedrin's* The Golovlyovs: *A Critical Companion*. Evanston: Northwestern University Press, 1997.

Forster, E. M. *Aspects of the Novel*. London: Penguin, 1963.

Foster, John Burt. *Transnational Tolstoy: Between the West and the World*. New York: Bloomsbury Academic, 2013.

Frank, Catherine O. *Law, Literature, and the Transmission of Culture in England, 1837–1925*. Farnham, Surrey and Burlington: Ashgate, 2010.

Franklin, Simon. "Russia in Time," in Franklin, Simon and Emma Widdis (eds.), *National Identity in Russian Culture: An Introduction*, 11–29. Cambridge, Cambridge University Press, 2004.

Frawley, Maria. "The Victorian Age, 1832–1901," in, Poplawski, Paul (ed.) *English Literature in Context*, 364–469. Cambridge: Cambridge University Press, 2017.

Freccero, Carla. "Queer Times," *South Atlantic Quarterly*, vol. 106, no. 3 (2007), 485–494.

Freeborn, Richard. *Turgenev: The Novelist's Novelist: A Study*. Oxford: Oxford University Press, 1960.

Freedgood, Elaine. *Worlds Enough: The Invention of Realism in the Victorian Novel*. Princeton: Princeton University Press, 2019.

Freeze, Gregory L. "Bringing Order to the Russian Family: Marriage and Divorce in Imperial Russia, 1760–1860," *The Journal of Modern History*, vol. 62, no. 4 (1990), 709–746.

Frew, Charlotte. "The Marriage to a Deceased Wife's Sister Narrative: A Comparison of Novels," *Law & Literature*, vol. 24, no. 2 (2012), 265–291.

Frey, Emily. "Boris Godunov and the Terrorist," *Journal of the American Musicological Society*, vol. 70, no. 1 (2017), 129–169.

Friedman, Rebecca. *Modernity, Domesticity and Temporality in Russia: Time at Home*. London: Bloomsbury Academic, 2020.

Friedrich, Paul. "Semantic Structure and Social Structure: An Instance for Russian," in Goodenough, Ward H. (ed.), *Explorations in Cultural Anthropology: Essays in Honor of George Peter Murdock*, 131–166. New York: McGraw-Hill Book Co., 1964.

Furneaux, Holly, "Negotiating the Gentle-Man: Male Nursing and Class Conflict in the 'High' Victorian Period," in Birch, D. et al. (eds.), *Conflict and Difference in Nineteenth-Century Literature*, 109–125. Houndmills, Basingstoke and New York: Palgrave MacMillan, 2010.

Furneaux, Holly. *Queer Dickens: Erotics, Families, Masculinities*. Oxford; New York: Oxford University Press, 2009.

Fusso, Susanne. "Dostoevskii and the Family," in Leatherbarrow, William J. (ed.), *The Cambridge Companion to Dostoevskii*, 175–190. Cambridge: Cambridge University Press, 2002.

Fyodorov, Nicholas. "The Question of Brotherhood or Relatedness, and of the Reasons for the Unbrotherly, Dis-related, or Unpeaceful State of the World, and of the Means for the Restoration of Relatedness," in Edie, James M., James P. Scanlan, Mary-Barbard Zelin, and George L. Kline (eds.), *Russian Philosophy Volume III: Pre-Revolutionary Philosophy and Theology, Philosophers in Exile, Marxists and Communists*, 16–54. Chicago: Quadrangle Books, 1969.

Gardner, Julia. "'Neither Monsters Nor Temptresses Nor Terrors': Representing Desire in Charlotte Brontë's *Shirley*," *Victorian Literature and Culture*, vol. 26, no. 2 (1998), 409–420.

Garrett, Peter K. *The Victorian Multiplot Novel: Studies in Dialogic Form*. New Haven: Yale University Press, 1980.

Gaskell, Elizabeth. *Cranford*. Oxford: Oxford University Press, 2011.

Gaskell, Elizabeth. *Ruth*. London: Penguin Books, 2004.

Gaskell, Elizabeth. *Wives and Daughters*. London: Penguin English Library, 2012.

Gerschenkron, Alexander. "Time Horizon in Russian Literature," *Slavic Review*, vol. 34, no. 4 (1975), 692–715.

Gheith, Jehanne M. *Finding the Middle Ground: Krestovskii, Tur, and the Power of Ambivalence in Nineteenth-Century Russian Women's Prose*. Evanston: Northwestern University Press, 2004.

Gheith, Jehanne M. "Introduction," to *Antonina*, by Tur, Evgeniya, vii–xxxvi. Evanston: Northwestern University Press, 1996.

Gheith, Jehanne M. "Women of the 1830s and 1850s," in Barker, Adele Marie and Jehanne M. Gheith (eds.), *A History of Women's Writing in Russia*, 85–100. Cambridge and New York: Cambridge University Press, 2002.

Gillis, John R. *A World of Their Own Making: Myth, Ritual, and the Quest for Family Values.* Cambridge: Harvard University Press, 1997.

Gilmartin, Sophie. *Ancestry and Narrative in Nineteenth-Century British Literature: Blood Relations from Edgeworth to Hardy.* Cambridge: Cambridge University Press, 1998.

Gilmour, Robin. "Dickens and the Self-Help Idea," in Butt J. and I. F. Clarke (eds.), *The Victorians and Social Protest: A Symposium*, 71–101. Newton Abbot, David and Charles; Hamden: Archon Books, 1973.

Gilmour, Robin. *The Novel in the Victorian Age: A Modern Introduction.* London: Edward Arnold, 1986.

Ginsborg, Paul. *Family Politics: Domestic Life, Devastation and Survival, 1900–1950.* New Haven: Yale University Press, 2014.

Ginsburg, Michal Peled. "House and Home in 'Dombey and Son,'" *Dickens Studies Annual*, vol. 36 (2005), 57–73.

Girard, René. *Deceit, Desire, and the Novel: Self and Other in Literary Structure.* Translated by Yvonne Freccero. Baltimore: Johns Hopkins Press, 1965.

Gogol', Nikolai. *Sobranie sochinenii v shesti tomakh.* Moskva: Gosudarstvennoe izdatel'stvo khudozhestvennoi literatury, 1953.

Gogol, Nikolai. *Dead Souls.* Translated by Bernard Guilbert Guerney. Revised Susanne Fusso. New Haven: Yale University Press, 1996.

Gogol, Nikolai. *Selected Passages from Correspondence with Friends.* Translated by Jesse Zeldin. Nashville: Vanderbilt University Press, 1969.

Goldman, Wendy Z. *Women, the State, and Revolution: Soviet Family Policy and Social Life, 1917–1936.* Cambridge; New York: Cambridge University Press, 1993.

Goldsmith, Oliver. *The Vicar of Wakefield.* Oxford: Oxford University Press, 2008.

Goldstein, Melvyn C. "Stratification, Polyandry, and Family Structure in Central Tibet," *Southwestern Journal of Anthropology*, vol. 27, no. 1 (Spring, 1971), 64–74.

Goncharov, I. A. *Polnoe sobranie sochinenii i pisem v dvadtsati tomakh.* Sankt-Peterburg: Nauka, 1997.

Goncharov, I. A. *Oblomov.* Translated by David Magarshack. London: Penguin, 2005.

Goody, Jack. "Introduction," in Goody, Jack, Joan Thirsk, and E. P. Thompson (eds.), *Family and Inheritance: Rural Society in Western Europe 1200–1800*, 1–10. Cambridge: Cambridge University Press, 1976.

Gorsky, Susan Rubinow. *Femininity to Feminism: Women and Literature in the Nineteenth Century.* New York: Twayne Publishers, 1992.

Goubert, Denis. "Did Tolstoy Read 'East Lynne'?" *The Slavonic and East European Review*, vol. 58, no. 1 (1980), 22–39.

Grant, Steven A. "Obshchina and Mir," *Slavic Review*, vol. 35, no. 4 (1976), 636–651.

Greene, Diana. "Gender and Genre in Pavlova's a Double Life," *Slavic Review,* vol. 54, no. 3 (1995), 563–577.

Greene, Diana. "Mid-Nineteenth-Century Domestic Ideology in Russia," in Marsh, Rosalind J. (ed.), *Women and Russian Culture: Projections and Self-Perceptions*, 78–97. New York: Berghahn Books, 1998.

Greenwood, Frederick. "Concluding Remarks," in Gaskell, Elizabeth, *Wives and Daughters.* gutenberg.org/files/4274/4274-h/4274-h.htm#c61 (Accessed July 7, 2020).

Grigoryan, Bella. *Noble Subjects: The Russian Novel and the Gentry, 1762–1861.* DeKalb: Northern Illinois University Press, 2018.

Grum-Grzhimailo, G.E. "Belokuraia rasa v Srednei Azii," *ZIRGOOE*, vol. 34 (1909), 163–88.

Gruner, Elisabeth Rose. "'Loving Difference': Sisters and Brothers from Frances Burney to Emily Brontë," in Mink, JoAnna Stephens, and Janet Doubler Ward (eds.), *The Significance of Sibling Relationships in Literature*, 32–46. Bowling Green: Bowling Green State University Popular Press, 1993.

Hager, Kelly. *Dickens and the Rise of Divorce: The Failed-Marriage Plot and the Novel Tradition.* Farnham, England; Burlington: Ashgate, 2010.

Hager, Kelly. "Estranging *David Copperfield*: Reading the Novel of Divorce," *ELH,* vol. 63, no. 4 (1996), 989–1019.

Halberstam, Judith. *In a Queer Time and Place: Transgender Bodies, Subcultural Lives.* New York: New York University Press, 2005.

Halperin, David. *Saint Foucault: Towards a Gay Hagiography.* New York: Oxford University Press, 1995.

Hardy, Thomas. *Tess of the D'Urbervilles.* London: Penguin Classics, 2008.

Hatten, Charles. *The End of Domesticity: Alienation from the Family in Dickens, Eliot, and James.* Newark: University of Delaware Press, 2010.

Heilbrun, Carolyn G. "Marriage and Contemporary Fiction," *Critical Inquiry,* vol. 5, no. 2 (1978), 309–322.

Heilbrun, Carolyn G. "Marriage Perceived: English Literature, 1873–1941," in Springer, Marlene (ed.), *What Manner of Woman: Essays on English and American Life and Literature,* 160–183. Oxford: Basil Blackwell, 1978.

Heldt, Barbara. *Terrible Perfection: Women and Russian Literature.* Bloomington and Indianapolis: Indiana University Press, 1987.

Henrich, Joseph. *The WEIRDest People in the World: How the West Became Psychologically Peculiar and Particularly Prosperous.* New York: Farrar, Straus and Giroux, 2020.

Henson, Louise. "History, Science and Social Change: Elizabeth Gaskell's 'Evolutionary' Narratives," *The Gaskell Society Journal,* vol. 17 (2003), 12–33.

Herbert, Christopher. "He Knew He Was Right, Mrs. Lynn Linton, and the Duplicities of Victorian Marriage," *Texas Studies in Literature and Language,* vol. 25, no. 3 (1983), 448–469.

Herzen, Aleksandr. *Sobranie sochinenii v tridtsati tomakh.* Moskva: Izdatel'stvo akademii nauk SSSR, 1955.

Herzen, Aleksandr. *Who Is to Blame?: A Novel in Two Parts.* Translated by Michael R. Katz. Ithaca: Cornell University Press, 1984.

Hindus, Milton. "The Duels in Mann and Turgenev," *Comparative Literature,* vol. 11, no. 4 (1959), 308–312.

Hinz, Evelyn J. "Hierogamy Versus Wedlock: Types of Marriage Plots and Their Relationship to Genres of Prose Fiction," *PMLA,* vol. 91, no. 5 (1976), 900–913.

Hoffer, Lauren N. and Sarah E. Kersh. "The Victorian Family in Queer Time: Secrets, Sisters, and Lovers in *The Woman in White* and *Fingersmith*," in Dau, Duc and Shale Preston (eds.), *Queer Victorian Families: Curious Relations in Literature,* 195–210. London and New York: Taylor & Francis Group, 2015.

Holland, Kate. *The Novel in the Age of Disintegration: Dostoevsky and the Problem of Genre in the 1870s.* Evanston: Northwestern University Press, 2013.

Holland, Kate. "The Russian Rougon-Macquart: Degeneration and Biological Determinism in *The Golovlev Family*," in Bowers, Katherine and Ani Kokobobo (eds.), *Russian Writers and the Fin-de-Siècle: The Twilight of Realism,* 15–32. Cambridge: Cambridge University Press, 2015.

Hudson, Glenda A. *Sibling Love and Incest in Jane Austen's Fiction.* Houndmills: Macmillan, 1992.

Hudspith, Sarah. *Dostoevsky and the Idea of Russianness: A New Perspective on Unity and Brotherhood.* London: RoutledgeCurzon, 2004.

Hughes, Linda K. "*Cousin Phillis, Wives and Daughters,* and Modernity," in Matus, Jill L. (ed.), *The Cambridge Companion to Elizabeth Gaskell,* 90–107. Cambridge: Cambridge University Press, 2007.

Hunt, Lynn. *The Family Romance of the French Revolution*. Berkeley: University of California Press, 1992.

Issiyeva, Adalyat. *Representing Russia's Orient: From Ethnography to Art Song*. Oxford: Oxford University Press, 2020.

Ivanov, Viachislav I. "Ekskurs osnovoi mif v romane 'Besy'" in *Sobranie sochinenii*, Tom 4. Brussels: Foyer Oriental Chrétien, 1987.

James, Henry. *Roderick Hudson*. New York: Charles Scribner's Sons, 1935.

James, Henry. *The Tragic Muse*. In Two Volumes. London: MacMillan and Co., Limited, 1921.

Jameson, Fredric. "The Experiment of Time: Providence and Realism," in Moretti, Franco (ed.), *The Novel, Volume 2: Forms and Themes*, 95–127. Princeton and Oxford: Princeton University Press, 2006.

Jameson, Fredric. "Third-World Literature in the Era of Multinational Capitalism," *Social Text*, vol. 15 (1986), 65–88.

Jamoussi, Zouheir. *Primogeniture and Entail in England: A Survey of Their History and Representation in Literature*. Tunis: Cambridge Scholars Publishing, 1999.

Jewsbury, Geraldine E. *Constance Herbert*. London: Hurst and Blackett, Publishers, Successors to Henry Colburn, 1855.

Johnson, Claudia. *Jane Austen: Women, Politics, and the Novel*. Chicago: University of Chicago Press, 1988.

Jones, Gareth W. "George Eliot's 'Adam Bede' and Tolstoy's Conception of 'Anna Karenina,'" *The Modern Language Review*, vol. 100 (2005), 191–199.

Kahn, Andrew. "Rise of the Russian Novel and the Problem of Romance," in Mandler, Jenny (ed.), *Remapping the Rise of the European Novel*, 185–198. Oxford: Voltaire Foundation, 2007.

Kahan, Arcadius. "The Costs of 'Westernization' in Russia: The Gentry and the Economy in the Eighteenth Century," *Slavic Review*, vol. 25, no. 1 (1966), 40–66.

Kaminer, Jenny. *Women with a Thirst for Destruction: The Bad Mother in Russian Culture*. Evanston: Northwestern University Press, 2014.

Keen, Suzanne. "Narrative Annexes in Charlotte Brontë's *Shirley*," *The Journal of Narrative Technique*, vol. 20, no. 2 (1990), 107–119.

Kelly, Catriona. *A History of Russian Women's Writing 1820–1992*. Oxford: Clarendon Press, 1994.

Kelly, Catriona. *Refining Russia: Advice Literature, Polite Culture, and Gender from Catherine to Yeltsin*. Oxford: Oxford University Press, 2001.

Kermode, Frank. *The Sense of an Ending: Studies in the Theory of Fiction*. Oxford: Oxford University Press, 2000.

Khvoshchinskaya, Nadezhda. *The Boarding School Girl*, trans. Karen Rosneck. Evanston: Northwestern University Press, 2000.

Khvoshchinskaia, Sof'ia. "Znakomye liudi" *Otechestvennye zapiski*, vol. 4 (1857), 125–173.

Khvoshchinskaya, Sofia. *City Folk and Country Folk*. Translated by Nora Favorov. New York: Columbia University Press, 2017.

Kiely, Richard. *Beyond Egotism: The Fiction of James Joyce, Virginia Woolf, and D.H. Lawrence*. Cambridge, MA: Harvard University Press, 1980.

Kilroy, James F. *The Nineteenth-Century English Novel: Family Ideology and Narrative Form*. Palgrave MacMillan: New York, 2007.

Kliger, Ilya. "Russia (18th–19th Century)," in Logan, Peter Melville (ed.), *The Encyclopedia of the Novel*. Blackwell Publishing, 2011. Blackwell Reference Online. (Referenced October 20, 2015).

Knapp, Liza. *Anna Karenina and Others: Tolstoy's Labyrinth of Plots*. Madison: University of Wisconsin Press, 2016.

Knapp, Liza. "Tolstoy's Unorthodox Catechesis: English Novels," in Cicovacki, Predrag (ed.), *Tolstoy and Spirituality*, 53–76. Boston: Academic Studies Press, 2018.

Krasnozhen, M. *Tserkovnoe pravo*. Iur'ev: Tipografii K. Mattisena, 1906.

Krestovskii, V. (pseudonym). *Polnoe sobranie sochinenii*. S. Peterburg: A. A. Kaspari, 1913.

Krestovskii, Vsevolod. *Sobranie sochinenii Vsevoloda Vladimirovicha Krestovskago*. Sankt-Peterburg: Izdanie tovarishchestva "Obshchestvennaia pol'za," 1899.

Lanser, Susan Sniader. "No Connections Subsequent: Jane Austen's World of Sisterhood," in McNaron, Toni A. H. (ed.), *The Sister Bond: A Feminist View of a Timeless Connection*, 53–67. New York: Pergamon Press, 1985.

Lary, N. M. *Dostoevsky and Dickens: A Study of Literary Influence*. London and Boston: Routledge and Kegan Paul, 1973.

Leatherbarrow, W. J. *Dostoevskii and Britain*. Oxford: Berg, 1995.

Ledger, Sally. *The New Woman: Fiction and Feminism at the Fin de Siècle*. Manchester, UK: Manchester University Press, distributed in the USA by St. Martin's Press, 1997.

Leskov, N. S. *Sobranie sochinenii v odinadtsati tomakh*. Moskva: Gosudarstvennoe izdatel'stvo khudozhestvennoi literatury, 1958.

Levin, Amy K. *The Suppressed Sister: A Relationship in Novels by Nineteenth- and Twentieth-Century British Women*. Lewisburg; London: Bucknell University Press, 1992.

Levin, Yuri. "English Literature in Eighteenth-Century Russia," *The Modern Language Review*, vol. 89, no. 4 (1994), xxv–xxxix.

Lieber, Emma. "Investigations into the Unpoliced Novel: *Moll Flanders* and the *Comely Cook*," *Slavic Review*, vol. 74, no. 3 (2015), 575–596.

Lieber, Emma. "On the Distinctiveness of the Russian Novel: *The Brothers Karamazov* and the English Tradition." Ph.D. Dissertation, Columbia University, 2011.

Lieber, Emma. "Smerdyakov and Parricide," *Dostoevsky Studies*, vol. 19 (2015), 29–32.

Liegle, Ludwig. *The Family's Role in Soviet Education*. New York: Springer Pub. Co., 1975.

Lieven, Dominic. "The Elites," in Lieven, Dominic (ed.), *Cambridge History of Russia, Vol. 2: Imperial Russia 1689-1917*, 227–244. Cambridge: Cambridge University Press, 2006.

Livingston, Sally A. *Marriage, Property, and Women's Narratives*. New York: Palgrave Macmillan, 2012.

Lounsbery, Anne. "Russian Families, Accidental and Other," in Göttsche, Dirk, Rosa Mucignat, and Robert Weninger (eds.), *Landscapes of Realism: Rethinking Literary Realism in Comparative Perspectives, Volume 1: Mapping Realism*, 503–513. Amsterdam and Philadelphia: John Benjamins Publishing Company, 2021.

Lucey, Colleen. "'Fallen but Charming Creatures': The Demimondaine in Russian Literature and Visual Culture of the 1860s," *The Russian Review*, vol. 78, no. 1 (2019), 103–121.

Lucey, Colleen. *Love for Sale: Representing Prostitution in Imperial Russia*. Ithaca: Cornell University Press, NIU Series in Slavic Studies, 2021.

Luhmann, Niklas. *Love as Passion: The Codification of Intimacy*. Translated by Jeremy Gaines and Doris L. Jones. Cambridge: Polity Press, 1986.

Lukacs, John. *The Future of History*. New Haven: Yale University Press, 2011.

MacDonald, Tara. *The New Man, Masculinity, and Marriage in the Victorian Novel*. London: Pickering & Chatto, 2015.

Mace, D. R, and Vera Mace. *The Soviet Family*. Garden City, NY: Doubleday, 1964.

MacPike, Loralee. *Dostoevsky's Dickens: A Study of Literary Influence*. Totowa: Barnes & Noble Books, 1981.

Mandelker, Amy. *Framing Anna Karenina: Tolstoy, the Woman Question, and the Victorian Novel*. Columbus: Ohio State University Press, 1993.

Marcus, Sharon. *Between Women: Friendship, Desire, and Marriage in Victorian England*. Princeton: Princeton University Press, 2007.

Marrese, Michelle Lamarche. "Gender and the Legal Order in Imperial Russia," in Lieven, Dominic (ed.), *The Cambridge History of Russia, Volume II, Imperial Russia, 1689–1917*, 326–343. Cambridge: Cambridge University Press, 2006.

Marrese, Michelle Lamarche. *A Woman's Kingdom: Noblewomen and the Control of Property in Russia 1700–1861*. Ithaca: Cornell University Press, 2002.

Marsh, Rosalind. "An Image of Their Own?: Feminism, Revisionism and Russian Culture," in *Women and Russian Culture: Projections and Self-Perceptions*, Marsh, Rosalind (ed.), 2-41. New York: Berghahn Books, 1998.

Marsh, Rosalind. "Introduction" to *Women and Russian Culture: Projections and Self-Perceptions*, Marsh, Rosalind (ed.), ix-xix. New York: Berghahn Books, 1998.

Martin, Alexander M. "The Family Model of Society and Russian National Identity in Sergei N. Glinka's Russian Messenger (1808–1812)," *Slavic Review*, vol. 57, no. 1 (1998), 28–49.

Martineau, Harriet. *Deerbrook*. London: Virago Press, 1983.

Martinsen, Deborah. *Surprised by Shame: Dostoevsky's Liars and Narrative Exposure*. Columbus: Ohio State University Press, 2003.

Mascarenhas, Kiran. "*John Halifax, Gentleman*: A Counter Story," in Wagner, Tamara S. (ed.), *Antifeminism and the Victorian Novel: Rereading Nineteenth-Century Women Writers*, 255–270. Amherst: Cambria Press, 2009.

Matzner-Gore, Greta. *Dostoevsky and the Ethics of Narrative Form*. Evanston: Northwestern University Press, 2020.

Matzner-Gore, Greta. "Kicking Maksimov out of the Carriage: Minor Characters, Exclusion, and *The Brothers Karamazov*," *Slavic and East European Journal*, vol. 58, no. 3 (2014), 419–436.

May, Leila Silvana. *Disorderly Sisters: Sibling Relations and Sororal Resistance in Nineteenth-Century British Literature*. Lewisberg; London: Bucknell University Press, 2001.

McAleavey, Maia. *The Bigamy Plot: Sensation and Convention in the Victorian Novel*. New York: Cambridge University Press, 2015.

McCrea, Barry. *In the Company of Strangers: Family and Narrative in Dickens, Conan Doyle, Joyce, and Proust*. New York: Columbia University Press, 2011.

McKeon, Michael. "Generic Transformation and Social Change: Rethinking The Rise of the Novel," in McKeon, Michael (ed.), *Theory of the Novel: A Historical Approach*, 382–399. Baltimore and London: Johns Hopkins University Press, 2000.

McKeon, Michael. *The Secret History of Domesticity: Public, Private, and the Division of Knowledge*. Baltimore: Johns Hopkins University Press, 2005.

Meerson, Olga. *Dostoevsky's Taboos*. Dresden: Dresden University Press, 1998.

Meyer, Priscilla. *How the Russians Read the French: Lermontov, Dostoevsky, Tolstoy*. Madison: The University of Wisconsin Press, 2008.

Michie, Elsie B. "Excluding Heiresses," *Victorian Review*, vol. 39, no. 2 (2013), 50–53.

Michie, Elsie B. "Rich Woman, Poor Woman: Toward an Anthropology of the Nineteenth-Century Marriage Plot," *PMLA*, vol. 124, no. 2 (2009), 421–436.

Mikhailov, M. L. "Zhenshchiny, ikh vospitanie i znachenie v sem'e i obshchestve." Sankt-Peterburg: Izdanie P. A. Katkova, 1903.

Mill, John Stuart. "The Subjection of Women," in *Three Essays: On Liberty, Representative Government, The Subjection of Women*. London, New York, Toronto: Oxford University Press, 1975.

Miller, D. A. *Narrative and Its Discontents: Problems of Closure in the Traditional Novel*. Princeton: Princeton University Press, 1981.

Miller, James E. "Henry James: A Theory of Fiction," *Prairie Schooner*, vol. 45, no. 4 (Winter 1971/72), 330–356.

Miller, Robin Feuer. "Children," in Martinsen, Deborah and Olga Maiorova (eds.), *Dostoevsky in Context*, 139–147. Cambridge: Cambridge University Press, 2015.

Miller, Robin Feuer. *Dostoevsky and* The Idiot: *Author, Narrator, and Reader.* Cambridge: Harvard University Press, 1981.

Mintz, Steven. *The Prime of Life: A History of Modern Adulthood.* Cambridge: Harvard University Press, 2015.

Mintz, Steven. *A Prison of Expectations: The Family in Victorian Culture.* New York: New York University Press, 1983.

Mitchell, Juliet. *Siblings: Sex and Violence.* Cambridge: Polity Press, 2003.

Morson, Gary Saul. Anna Karenina *in Our Time: Seeing More Wisely.* New Haven and London: Yale University Press, 2007.

Morson, Gary Saul. "Genre and Hero," *Stanford Slavic Studies,* vol. 4, no. 1 (1991), 367–379.

Morson, Gary Saul. "Introductory Study: Dostoevsky's Great Experiment," in Dostoevsky's *A Writer's Diary, Volume 1. 1873–1876.* Translated and edited by Kenneth Lantz, 1 –117. Evanston: Northwestern University Press, 1994.

Morson, Gary Saul. "Philosophy in the Nineteenth-Century Novel," in Jones, Malcolm and Robin Feuer Miller (eds.), *Cambridge Companion to the Classic Russian Novel,* 150–168. Cambridge: Cambridge University Press, 1998.

Morson, Gary Saul. *Prosaics and Other Provocations: Empathy, Open Time, and the Novel.* Brighton: Academic Studies Press, 2013.

Morson, Gary Saul. "Verbal Pollution in *The Brothers Karamazov,*" in Miller, Robin Feuer (ed.), *Critical Essays on Dostoevsky,* 234–242. Boston: G.K. Hall & Co., 1986.

Narskaia, E. *Dve sestri.* Moskva: V tipografii Katkova, 1858.

Nedzvetskii, V. A. *Istoriia russkogo romana XIX veka: Neklassicheskie formy. Kurs lektsii.* Moskva: Izdatel'stvo Moskovskogo Universiteta, 2011.

Nelson, Claudia. *Family Ties in Victorian England.* Westport: Praeger Publishers, 2007.

Nelson, Margaret K. "Fictive Kin, Families We Choose, and Voluntary Kin: What Does the Discourse Tell Us?" *Journal of Family Theory & Review,* vol. 5 (2013), 259–281.

Nunokawa, Jeff. *The Afterlife of Property: Domestic Security and the Victorian Novel.* Princeton: Princeton University Press, 1994.

Oliphant, Margaret. *Chronicles of Carlingford.* The Rector and The Doctor's Family. London: Virago Press, 1986.

Ostrovskii, A. N. *Polnoe sobranie sochinenii.* Moskva: Gosudarstvennoe izdatel'stvo khudozhestvennoi literatury, 1949–1958.

Paisel', V.E. *Materialy dlia antropologii Taranchei.* Sankt-Peterburg: tip. Otdeleniia Korn. Zhandrm., 1897.

Panaeva, Avdot'ia. *Semeistvo Tal'nikovykh.* Leningrad: Academiia, 1928.

Paperno, Irina. *Chernyshevsky and the Age of Realism: A Study in the Semiotics of Behavior.* Stanford: Stanford University Press, 1988.

Paperno, Irina. "Introduction: Intimacy and History. The Gerzen Family Drama Reconsidered," *Russian Literature,* vol. 61 (2007), 1–65.

Perry, Ruth. *Novel Relations: The Transformation of Kinship in English Literature and Culture. 1748–1818.* Cambridge: Cambridge University Press, 2004.

Peterson, Jeanne M. *Family, Love, and Work in the Lives of Victorian Gentlewomen.* Bloomington: Indiana University Press, 1989.

Pisemskii, A. F. *Sobranie sochinenii v deviati tomakh.* Moskva: Izdatel'stvo Pravda, 1959.

Pollak, Ellen. *Incest and the English Novel, 1684–1814.* Baltimore: Johns Hopkins University Press, 2003.

Polonsky, Rachel. *English Literature and the Russian Aesthetic Renaissance.* New York: Cambridge University Press, 1998.

Pomialovskii, N. G. *Polnoe sobranie sochinenii.* Tret'e izdanie. S.-Peterburg: Knigoizdatel'skoe T-Vo "Prosveshchenie," 1913.

Poovey, Mary. *Uneven Developments: The Ideological Work of Gender in Mid-Victorian England.* Chicago: University of Chicago Press, 1988.

Potekhin, Aleksei. *Sochineniia Alekseia Potekhina.* S.-Peterburg: Izdanie knigoprodavtsa K. N. Plotnikova, 1873.

Pouncy, Carolyn (ed.). *The Domostroi: Rules for Russian Households in the Time of Ivan the Terrible.* Ithaca: Cornell University Press, 1994.

Proskurina, Tat'iana Dmitrievna. *Russkie pisateli XIX veka o sem'e.* Belgorod: Belgorodskii gosudarstvennyi universitet, 2012.

Psomiades, Kathy Alexis. "The Marriage Plot in Theory," *NOVEL: A Forum on Fiction,* vol. 43, no. 1 (2010), 53–59.

Pushkareva, Natalia. *Women in Russian History: From the Tenth to the Twentieth Century,* Translated by Eve Levin. Armonk: M. E. Sharpe, 1997.

Pushkareva, Natalia and Maria Zolotukhina. "Women's and Gender Studies of the Russian Past: two contemporary trends," *Women's History Review,* vol. 27, no. 1 (2018), 71–87.

Pushkin, Alexander. *Eugene Onegin,* Translated by James E. Falen. New York: Oxford University Press, 1998.

Ragussis, Michael. *Acts of Naming: The Family Plot in Fiction.* New York: Oxford University Press, 1986.

Randolph, John. *The House in the Garden: The Bakunin Family and the Romance of Russian Idealism.* Ithaca: Cornell University Press, 2007.

Randolph, John. "The Old Mansion: Revisiting the History of the Russian Country Estate," *Kritika: Explorations in Russian and Eurasian History,* vol. 1, no. 4 (2000), 729–749.

Ransel, David L. (ed.). *The Family in Imperial Russia: New Lines of Historical Research.* Urbana; London: University of Illinois Press, 1978.

Reed, John R. "Soldier Boy: Forming Masculinity in *Adam Bede,*" *Studies in the Novel,* vol. 33, no. 3 (2001), 268–284.

Retford, Kate. *The Art of Domestic Life: Family Portraiture in Eighteenth-century England.* New Haven: The Paul Mellon Centre for Studies in British Art, Yale University Press, 2006.

Ripp, Victor. "Turgenev as a Social Novelist: The Problem of the Part and the Whole," in Todd, William Mills (ed.), *Literature and Society in Imperial Russia,* 237–258. Stanford: Stanford University Press, 1978.

Rittikh, A. *Materialy dlia etnografii Rossii. Kazanskaia Guberniia.* Kazan: tip. Imperatorskogo kazanskogo universiteta, 1870.

Rubin, Gayle. "The Traffic in Women: Notes Toward a Political Economy of Sex," in Reiter, Rayna (ed.), *Toward an Anthropology of Women,* 157–210. New York: Monthly Review Press, 1975.

Ruskin, John. *Sesame and Lilies.* New York: Barnes & Noble, 2011.

Saarilouma, Liisa. "Virginia Woolf's The Years: Identity and Time in an Anti-Family Novel," *Orbis Litterarum,* vol. 54 (1999), 276–300.

Sadrin, Anny. *Parentage and Inheritance in the Novels of Charles Dickens.* Cambridge: Cambridge University Press, 1994.

Said, Edward W. *Beginnings: Intention and Method.* New York: Basic Books, 1975.

Saltykov-Shchedrin, M. E. *Sobranie Sochinenii.* Moskva: Izdatel'stvo Khudozhestvennaia literatura, 1965–1977.

Sanders, Valerie. *The Brother-Sister Culture in Nineteenth-Century Literature: From Austen to Woolf.* Houndmills: Palgrave, 2002.

Sanders, Valerie. "Marriage and the antifeminist woman novelist," in Thompson, Nicola Diane (ed.), *Victorian Women Writers and the Woman Question,* 24–41. Cambridge and New York: Cambridge University Press, 1999.

Schaffer, Talia. *Romance's Rival: Familiar Marriage in Victorian Fiction.* New York: Oxford University Press, 2016.

Schlesinger, Rudolf. *Changing Attitudes in Soviet Russia: Documents and Readings.* London: Routledge & Paul, 1949.

Schor, Hilary Margo. *Dickens and the Daughter of the House*. Cambridge: Cambridge University Press, 1999.

Scramm, Jan-Melissa. *Atonement and Self-Sacrifice in Nineteenth-Century Narrative*. New York: Cambridge University Press, 2012.

Scramm, Jan-Melissa. *Testimony and Advocacy in Victorian Law, Literature, and Theology*. Cambridge and New York: Cambridge University Press, 2000.

Sedgwick, Eve Kosofsky. *Between Men: English Literature and Male Homosocial Desire*. New York: Columbia University Press, 1985.

Sedgwick, Eve Kosofsky. "Tales of the Avunculate: Queer Tutelage in *The Importance of Being Earnest*," in *Tendencies*, 52 –72. Durham: Duke University Press, 1993.

Semenov, E. I. *Roman Dostoevskogo "Podrostok": (problematika i zhanr)*. Leningrad: Nauka, 1979.

Shaffer, Julie. "Familial Love, Incest, and Female Desire in Late Eighteenth- and Early Nineteenth-Century Women's Novels," *Criticism*, vol. 41, no. 1 (1999), 67–99.

Shideler, Ross. *Questioning the Father: From Darwin to Zola, Ibsen, Strindberg, and Hardy*. Stanford: Stanford University Press, 1999.

Shoemaker, Robert B. *Gender in English Society 1650–1850: The Emergence of Separate Spheres?* London and New York: Longman, 1998.

Sibthorpe, F. M. *Home is Home: A Domestic Tale*. London: William Pickering, 1851.

Simmons, Ernest J. *English Literature and Culture in Russia (1553–1840)*. Cambridge: Harvard University Press, 1935.

Sipovskii, V. V. *Ocherki iz istorii russkago romana*. Sankt-Peterburg: Tip. Sankt-Peterburgskogo t-va pech. i izd. dela "Trud," 1910.

Smirnova, S. *Sila kharaktera*. Sankt-Peterburg: Tipo-litografiia kn. V. Obolenskago, 1876.

Smith, Alison. *For the Common Good and Their Own Well-Being: Social Estates in Imperial Russia*. New York: Oxford University Press, 2015.

Somoff, Victoria. *The Imperative of Reliability: Russian Prose on the Eve of the Novel, 1820s–1850s*. Evanston: Northwestern University Press, 2015.

Sopher, R. E. "Gender and Sympathy in *Adam Bede*: The Case of Seth Bede," *George Eliot – George Henry Lewes Studies*, vol. 62/63 (2012), 1–15.

Sparks, Tabitha. *The Doctor in the Victorian Novel: Family Practices*. Farnham, England; Burlington: Ashgate, 2009.

Spencer, Jane. *Literary Relations: Kinship and the Canon 1600–1830*. Oxford: Oxford University Press, 2005.

Springer, Marlene. "Angels and Other Women in Victorian Literature," in Springer, Marlene (ed.), *What Manner of Woman: Essays on English and American Life and Literature*, 124–159. New York: New York University Press, 1977.

St. Clair, William. "Introduction" to Trelawny, Edward John (ed.) *Adventures of a Younger Son*, vii–xv. London: Oxford University Press, 1974.

Steiner, Lina. *For Humanity's Sake: The Bildungsroman in Russian Culture*. Toronto: University of Toronto Press, 2011.

Strakhov, N. N. "Zhenskii Vopros," *Zhenskii Vopros: Razbor Sochineniia Dzhona Stiuarta Millia "O Podchinenii Zhenshchiny"*, 107–149. Sankt-Peterburg: Tipografiia Maikova, 1871.

Stulli, F. S. "*Dva raza zamuzhem*," *Vestnik Evropy*, vol. 4 (1875), 670–749.

Sussman, Herbert. "Samuel Butler as Late Victorian Bachelor: Regulating and Representing the Homoerotic," in Paradis, James G. (ed.), *Samuel Butler, Victorian Against the Grain*, 170–194. Toronto: University of Toronto Press, 2007.

Syskina, A. A. "Perevody XIX veka romana 'Dzhen Eir' Sharlotty Bronte: Peredacha kharaktera i vzgliadov geroini v perevode 1849 goda Irinarkha Vvedenskogo," *Vestnik TGPU*, vol. 3, 118 (2012), 177–182.

Tadmor, Naomi. "The Concept of the Household-Family in Eighteenth-Century England," *Past and Present*, vol. 151 (1995), 111–140.

Tanner, Tony. *Adultery in the Novel: Contract and Transgression*. Baltimore: Johns Hopkins University Press, 1979.

Tanner, Tony. *Jane Austen*. London: MacMillan, 1986.

Tat'ianina, Anna Grigor'evna. *Proza molodogo L. N. Tolstogo i problema semeinogo romana*. Dissertation. Moskva: 2001.

Taylor, Helen. "Class and Gender in Charlotte Brontë's 'Shirley,'" *Feminist Review*, vol. 1 (1979), 83–93.

Thackeray, William Makepeace. *Vanity Fair*. London: Penguin Books, 2012.

Thody, P. M. W. "The Influence of Genre on Ideology: The Case of the Family Novel," in Bevan, H., M. King and A. Stephens (eds.), *Proceedings and Papers of the Sixteenth Congress of the Australasian Universities Language and Literature Association Held 21–27 August 1974 at the University of Adelaide, South Australia*, 58–70. Adelaide: A.U.L.L.A., 1974.

Thody, Philip. "The Politics of the Family Novel: Is Conservatism Inevitable?" *Mosaic*, vol. 3, no. 1 (1969), 87–101.

Thompson, Diane Oenning. The Brothers Karamazov *and the Poetics of Memory*. Cambridge: Cambridge University Press, 1991.

Thompson, E. P. *Whigs and Hunters: The Origin of the Black Act*. London: Allen Lane, 1975.

Thorlby, Anthony. *Leo Tolstoy: Anna Karenina*. Cambridge: Cambridge University Press, 1987.

Tikhonova, D. N. "Mariia Nikolaevna Volkonskaia (Tolstaia) '...Chto ia znaiu o nei......,' ili dvesti let spustia," *Russkaia Pamela, ili net pravila bez iskliucheniia*, 173–233. Tula: Iasnaia Poliana, 2009.

Timofeeva, V.V. "God raboty s znamenitym pisatelem," in Grigorenko, V. V. et al. (eds.) *F.M. Dostoevskii v vospominaniiakh sovremennikakh*, t. 2. Moskva: Khudozhestvennaia literatura, 1964.

Tobin, Patricia Drechsel. *Time and the Novel: The Genealogical Imperative*. Princeton: Princeton University Press, 1978.

Todd, William Mills. *Literature and Society in Imperial Russia 1800–1914*. Stanford: Stanford University Press, 1978.

Todd, William Mills. "The Ruse of the Russian Novel," in Moretti, Franco (ed.), *The Novel*, 401–23. Princeton: Princeton University Press, 2006.

Tolstoi, Lev. *Polnoe sobranie sochinenii (iubileinoe izdanie) v 90 tomakh*. Moskva: Gosudarstvennoe izdatel'stvo khudozhestvennoi literatury, 1928–1959.

Tolstoy, Lev. *Anna Karenina*. Translated by Richard Pevear and Larissa Volokhonsky. New York: Penguin Books, 2000.

Tolstoy, Lev. "Drafts for an Introduction to *War and Peace*," in *War and Peace*. Translated and edited by George Gibian, 1087 –1089. New York: Norton and Company, 1996.

Tolstoy, Lev. *War and Peace*. Translated by Richard Pevear and Larissa Volokhonsky. New York: Alfred A. Knopf, 2007.

Tosh, John. *A Man's Place: Masculinity and the Middle-Class Home in Victorian England*. New Haven: Yale University Press, 1999.

Tosh, John. *Manliness and Masculinity in Nineteenth-Century Britain: Essays on Gender, Family, and Empire*. London: Routledge, 2016.

Tovrov, Jessica. *The Russian Noble Family: Structure and Change*. New York: Garland, 1987.

Trelawny, Edward John. *Adventures of a Younger Son*. London: Oxford University Press, 1974.

Trollope, Anthony. *Barchester Towers*. Oxford: Oxford World's Classics, 1996.

Trollope, Anthony. *Can You Forgive Her?* Oxford: Oxford World's Classics, 2012.

Trollope, Anthony. *An Eye for an Eye*. London: Ward, Lock and Co., 1881.

Trollope, Anthony. *He Knew He Was Right*. Oxford: Oxford World's Classics, 2008.

Trollope, Anthony. *The Warden*. London: Penguin English Library, 2012.

Trumbach, Randolph. *The Rise of the Egalitarian Family: Aristocratic Kinship and Domestic Relations in Eighteenth-Century England*. New York: Academic Press, 1978.

Tur, Evgeniia. *Oshibka*, in *Povesti i razskazy*, tom 2. Moskva, 1859.

Tur, Evgeniia. *Plemiannitsa*. Moskva: V Universitetskoi tipografii, 1851.

Turgenev, Ivan. *Polnoe sobranie sochinenii i pisem v dvadtsati vos'mi tomakh*. Moskva-Leningrad: Izdatel'stvo Akademii Nauka, 1960–1968.

Turgenev, Ivan. *Fathers and Children*. Translated by Michael Katz. New York: W. W. Norton & Company, 2009.

Vishnevskii, A. G. *Evolutsiia sem'i i semeinaia politika v SSSR*. Moskva: Nauka, 1992.

Vovchok, Marko. "Zhili da byli tri sestry" *Sovremennik* № 9, 11 (1861).

Vowles, Judith. "Marriage à la Russe," in Costlow, Jane T., Stephanie Sandler, and Judith Vowles (eds.), *Sexuality and the Body in Russian Culture*, 53–72. Stanford: Stanford University Press, 1993.

Wachtel, Andrew. *The Battle for Childhood: Creation of a Russian Myth*. Stanford: Stanford University Press, 1990.

Wagner, Tamara S. "Marriage Plots and 'Matters of More Importance': Sensationalising Self-Sacrifice in Victorian Domestic Fiction," in Wagner, Tamara S. (ed.), *Antifeminism and the Victorian Novel: Reread Nineteenth-Century Women Writers*, 137–157. Amherst: Cambria Press, 2009.

Wagner, William G. "Family Law, the Rule of Law, and Liberalism in Late Imperial Russia," *Jahrbücher für Feschichte Osteuropas*, vol. 43, no. 4 (1995), 519–535.

Wagner, William G. *Marriage, Property, and Law in Late Imperial Russia*. Oxford; New York: Clarendon Press; Oxford University Press, 1994.

Wagner, William G. "'Orthodox Domesticity': Creating a Social Role for Women in Sacred Stories," in Steinberg, Mark D., and Heather J. Coleman (eds.), *Sacred Stories: Religion and Spirituality in Modern Russia*, 119–145. Bloomington Indiana: Indiana University Press, 2007.

Walker Gore, Clare. "The Right and Natural Law of Things: Disability and the Form of the Family in the Fiction of Dinah Mulock Craik and Charlotte M. Yonge," in Dau, Duc and Shale Preston (eds.), *Queer Victorian Families: Curious Relations in Literature*, 116–133. London; New York: Routledge, Taylor & Francis Group, 2015.

Wasiolek, Edward. Fathers and Sons: *Russia at the Cross-Roads*. New York: Twayne Publishers, 1993.

Waters, Catherine. *Dickens and the Politics of the Family*. Cambridge: Cambridge University Press, 1997.

Watt, Ian P. *The Rise of the Novel: Studies in Defoe, Richardson, and Fielding*. Berkeley and Los Angeles: University of California Press, 1957.

Weston, Kath. *The Families We Choose*. New York: Columbia University Press, 1991.

Wilson, Jennifer. "Dostoevsky's Timely Castration," *Transgender Studies Quarterly*, vol. 4, no. 5 (2018), 565–573.

Wirtschafter, Elise Kimerling. *Social Identity in Imperial Russia*. DeKalb: Northern Illinois University Press, 1997.

Wohl, Anthony S. *The Victorian Family: Structure and Stresses*. London: Croom Helm, 1978.

Wolff, Michael. "*Adam Bede*'s Families: At Home in Hayslope and Nuneaton," *George Eliot – George Henry Lewes Studies*, vol. 32/33 (1997), 58–69.

Wolfram, Sybil. *In-Laws and Outlaws: Kinship and Marriage in England*. London: Croom Helm, 1987.

Woloch, Alex. *The One vs. the Many: Minor Characters and the Space of the Protagonist in the Novel*. Princeton: Princeton University Press, 2003.

Wood, Ellen. *East Lynne*. Oxford: Oxford University Press, 2008.

Woolf, Virginia. "On Rereading Meredith," in *Granite and Rainbow: Essays by Virginia Woolf*, 48–52. London: Hogarth Press, 1958.

Worobec, Christine D. *Peasant Russia: Family and Community in the Post-Emancipation Period.* Princeton: Princeton University Press, 1991.

Wortman, Richard. *Scenarios of Power: Myth and Ceremony in Russian Monarchy, Volume 1.* Princeton: Princeton University Press, 1995.

Yeazell, Ruth Bernard. *Fictions of Modesty: Women and Courtship in the English Novel.* Chicago and London: University of Chicago Press, 1991.

Yonge, Charlotte Mary. *The Daisy Chain.* Cambridge: Chadwyck-Healey Ltd, 2000.

Yonge, Charlotte Mary. *Heartsease, or Brother's Wife.* Middletown: The Perfect Library, 2015.

Yonge, Charlotte Mary. *Three Brides.* Middletown: Bibliobazaar, 2016.

Zenkovsky, Vasily V. "The Spirit of Russian Orthodoxy," *The Russian Review,* vol. 22, no. 1 (1963), 38–55.

Zhirmunskii, V. M. *Bairon i Pushkin: Pushkin i zapadnye literatury.* Leningrad: Nauka, 1978.

Index

David Copperfield 3, 39, 123 n.27, 147, 149, 152 n.31, 163 n.51, 180, 216, 218
Dombey and Son 23, 48 n.5, 94, 121 n.20, 123, 128, 146, 148–9, 158, 161, 170 n.62, 181
Great Expectations 192, 212 n.40
Hard Times 58, 159, 199 n.7, 200
Household Words 106
Martin Chuzzlewit 54
Nicholas Nickleby 57 n.41, 59, 70, 78, 123 n.27, 200
Oliver Twist 180, 182, 193, 199, 216–17
Our Mutual Friend 123 n.27, 191 n.44
The Pickwick Papers 216 n.49
A Tale of Two Cities 71, 123 n.27, 200
divorce 7, 8 n.23, 11, 59 n.49, 107–8, 147, 155, 162, 167
Doak, Connor 129
Dobroliubov, Nikolai 10, 102 n.44, 104
"The Kingdom of Darkness" 10
"A Ray of Light in the Kingdom of Darkness" 10
Dodd, William
Sermon to Young Men 65
Dolgina, S. (Sof'ia Mundt)
Fictitious Marriage (Fiktivnyi brak) 16, 22, 167, 169, 189, 230
domestic(ity) 12, 13 n.47, 15, 18, 20, 21, 32 n.24, 48, 58, 66, 83, 91–2, 93 n.4, 98, 106–7, 109–111, 114, 147–9, 204
fiction/novels 62, 144, 149, 151
happiness/ideal 1, 23, 83, 91, 108, 109, 125, 144, 145, 150, 212
ideology 1, 106, 109–10
journals 8
manuals 28, 98
Domostroi 28, 98–9, 101–2
Dostoevsky, Fyodor 1, 5–6, 18–19, 23, 44, 51–2, 102 n.42, 103, 126, 139, 151, 156, 162, 176, 182–3, 185, 187, 205–6, 221, 224, 229
The Adolescent (Podrostok) 24, 42, 84 n.52, 98, 155, 159, 160 n.45, 177–9, 184–5, 201, 219
The Brothers Karamazov (Bratia Karama-zovy) 21, 72, 79, 84–7, 98, 116, 178–80, 184–5, 198 n.2, 199, 219 n.54
Crime and Punishment (Prestuplenie i nakazanie) 10 n.32, 58–9, 116, 124, 163, 165, 185, 216, 230
Demons (Besy) 38, 116, 179, 180 n.20, 185
The Gambler 185
The Idiot (Idiot) 16–17, 22, 58, 127–8, 130, 138, 185 n.30, 197, 209

The Insulted and Injured (Unizhennye i oskorblennye) 97 n.23, 98, 179, 185, 199
Netochka Nezvanova 98
Poor Folk (Bednye liudi) 97 n.23, 137, 185, 231
"Pushkin Speech" 79, 126 n.34, 142, 186
A Writer's Diary 79 n.41, 84 n.50, 104, 177, 196, 198, 204
dramas 1, 3, 10, 49, 56, 64, 84, 150, 185 n.32, 230
Drury, Anna 65
The Brothers 21, 70–2, 123 n.27
Druzhinin, Alexander 186
Polinka Saks 154–6, 161, 184 n.28
Durov, Sergei 21
Someone Else's Child (Chuzhoe ditia) 177

economics 8, 18, 31, 32, 35, 42 n.76, 56, 63, 75–6, 103, 106 n.56, 108–9, 119–20, 136–7, 153, 176, 201–2
Edelman, Lee 192
Edgeworth, Maria 18
Belinda 163, 230 n.16
Ehre, Milton 50, 81 n.44
Eikhenbaum, Boris 125 n.33, 230 n.17
Eliot, George 10, 15 n.60, 18, 51, 151
Adam Bede 17, 21, 65–70, 75, 85, 96, 123 n.27, 152 n.31, 163 n.51, 214
Daniel Deronda 23, 52 n.22, 57, 123, 146, 149, 181
Middlemarch 6, 50, 54, 96, 123 n.27, 142–3, 154
The Mill on the Floss 57, 200
Silas Marner 39, 193, 216
Ellingson, Laura L. 67 n.12
Ellis, Sarah S. 107
Elnett, Elaine 8 n.24, 101 n.37–9
Emerson, Caryl 44, 87 n.64, 187
Emery, Jacob 222
Enclosure Acts 105
Engel, Barbara A. 8 n.25, 13 n.45, 97 n.24, 102–3, 109, 111 n.83, 129 n.42, 175 n.12, 204
estates 3, 8, 18–21, 31–4, 35 n.47, 36–8, 41–2, 60–1, 63, 66, 71–2, 76, 78, 80–2, 86 n.58, 98, 100, 107 n.62, 108, 111, 125, 136, 139, 160, 162, 164, 167, 168, 169, 179, 183 n.24, 187, 188, 189, 191 n.40, 206, 207, 208, 218, 219, 221, 227, 228, 232
Europe(an) 4, 14, 31 n.21, 36 n.51, 37 n.57, 41, 45, 79, 85, 101, 108, 111, 114, 130, 176 n.15, 186, 189, 201 n.9, 205, 220, 233
literature 6, 18, 109, 125, 152